India Studies in Business and Economics

The Indian economy is considered to be one of the fastest growing economies of the world with India amongst the most important G-20 economies. Ever since the Indian economy made its presence felt on the global platform, the research community is now even more interested in studying and analyzing what India has to offer. This series aims to bring forth the latest studies and research about India from the areas of economics, business, and management science. The titles featured in this series will present rigorous empirical research, often accompanied by policy recommendations, evoke and evaluate various aspects of the economy and the business and management landscape in India, with a special focus on India's relationship with the world in terms of business and trade.

More information about this series at http://www.springer.com/series/11234

Swapnendu Banerjee • Vivekananda Mukherjee
Sushil Kumar Haldar
Editors

Understanding Development

An Indian Perspective on Legal and Economic Policy

Springer

Editors
Swapnendu Banerjee
Department of Economics
Jadavpur University
Kolkata
India

Sushil Kumar Haldar
Department of Economics
Jadavpur University
Kolkata
India

Vivekananda Mukherjee
Department of Economics
Jadavpur University
Kolkata
India

ISSN 2198-0012 ISSN 2198-0020 (electronic)
India Studies in Business and Economics
ISBN 978-81-322-2454-9 ISBN 978-81-322-2455-6 (eBook)
DOI 10.1007/978-81-322-2455-6

Library of Congress Control Number: 2015940321

Springer New Delhi Heidelberg New York Dordrecht London

Printed on acid-free paper

Springer (India) Pvt. Ltd. is part of Springer Science+Business Media (www.springer.com)

Foreword

The present volume is a collection of articles on various facets of economic development, written by a select group of researchers who have specialised in respective fields. The planning of this volume was mooted in a meeting of advisory committee of the Centre for Advanced Studies (CAS) of the Department of Economics, Jadavpur University. Since CAS has sponsored a variety of workshops and seminars and hosted visiting fellows, the external experts of the CAS, Professor Dilip Nachane (former director, Indira Gandhi Institute of Development Research) and Professor Ramprasad Sengupta (formerly of Jawaharlal Nehru University) suggested that we collate important papers in two volumes to be contributed by the visitors as well as Jadavpur's own faculty. The reason for planning two volumes is to accommodate the five thrust areas we have in the CAS, namely, International Trade, Finance, Resource and Environment, West Bengal Economy and Public Policy related to Social Sector. The idea is to produce a monograph which will help the readers with some survey papers along with some state-of-the-art research in relevant fields. The present volume *Understanding Development: An Indian Perspective on Legal and Economic Policy* edited by my three young but very energetic colleagues, Swapnendu Banerjee, Vivekananda Mukherjee and Sushil Halder, has a fine balance of topics covered under the last three thrust areas mentioned above. In addition, the chapters will satisfy the needs of various strata of readers—for example the survey on sharecropping would greatly help the graduate level students and researchers, while the chapters in the section of social sector will be of immense help for the policy planners as well as researchers. Similarly, the section on law and economics would acquaint the business practitioners along with government policymakers with some recent developments in this field. I must thank the efforts of the editors who spared their valuable time to make the volume useful and interesting. I have faith that the purpose of publishing this volume will be totally fulfilled and we will have increasing returns to knowledge after reading the volume.

Professor and Coordinator
Centre for Advanced Studies, Department of Economics
Jadavpur University, Kolkata 700032

Ajitava Raychaudhuri

Contents

Contributors

Swapnendu Banerjee Department of Economics, Jadavpur University, Kolkata, India

Tanmoyee Banerjee (Chaterjee) Department of Economics, Jadavpur University, Kolkata, India

Bidisha Chakraborty Department of Economics, Jadavpur University, Kolkata, India

Rahul Chakraborty Centre for Economic Studies and Planning, Jawaharlal Nehru University, New Delhi, India

Simonti Chakraborty Centre for Economic Studies and Planning, Jawaharlal Nehru University, New Delhi, India

Indrani Roy Chowdhury Department of Economics, Jamia Millia Islamia, New Delhi, India

Prabal Roy Chowdhury Economic and Planning Unit, Indian Statistical Institute, Delhi Centre, New Delhi, India

Vikas Dixit Department of Economics, Jadavpur University, Kolkata, India

Arpita Ghose Department of Economics, Jadavpur University, Kolkata, India

Jayanti Ghosh Sushmita Foundation, Kolkata, India

Sushil Kumar Haldar Department of Economics, Jadavpur University, Kolkata, India

Mausumi Kar Women's Christian College, Kolkata, India

Saibal Kar Centre for Studies in Social Sciences, Kolkata, India

Amit Kundu Department of Economics, Jadavpur University, Kolkata, India

Rajendra P. Kundu Centre for Economic Studies and Planning, Jawaharlal Nehru University, New Delhi, India

Soma Mandal Department of Economics, Jadavpur University, Kolkata, India

Sugata Marjit Centre for Studies in Social Sciences, Kolkata, India

Siddhartha Mitra Department of Economics, Jadavpur University, Kolkata, India

Vivekananda Mukherjee Department of Economics, Jadavpur University, Kolkata, India

Tushar K. Nandi CTRPFP, Centre for Studies in Social Sciences (CSSS), Kolkata, India

Amrita Pramanick Department of Economics, Jadavpur University, Kolkata, India

Ajitava Raychaudhuri Department of Economics, Jadavpur University, Kolkata, India

Poulomi Roy Department of Economics, Jadavpur University, Kolkata, India

Prabirjit Sarkar Economics Department, Jadavpur University, Kolkata, India

Rahuldeb Sarkar Sushmita Foundation, Kolkata, India

Medway Maritime Hospital, Gillingham, Kent, UK

Debapriya Sen Department of Economics, Ryerson University, Toronto, Canada

Sanjib Talukdar Sree Chaitanya Mahavidyalaya, Habra, India

Chapter 1
Editors' Note

Swapnendu Banerjee, Vivekananda Mukherjee and Sushil Kumar Haldar

Economic development is a dynamic concept. This book offers an Indian perspective on the dynamics of economic development and the impact of legal and public policies in India. The objective of economic development is increasing efficiency of an economy along with ensuring equity and social justice and the consequent creation of institutions so as to build capacity for meeting human needs at all levels, especially for the most vulnerable. While it solves some old problems, newer issues come to the fore. The emergence of these issues is unique to the development experience of an economy. The current volume presents some recent contributions addressing development-related issues from an Indian perspective. The volume contains 16 chapters divided into four sections: law and contract, trade and foreign aid, issues in public economics, social sector and poverty alleviation. The chapters reflect on a number of development issues, which were of concern in the recent past in India and are going to be important in India's future course of development like land acquisition, agricultural productivity, employment, institutional and contractual imperfections, protection of intellectual property rights, corruption related to aid/grants, public–private partnership (PPP), regional development, poverty alleviations programs like NREGA, microfinance and training of self-help group members and last but not least, health and education of women.

In Part I, there are four chapters that deal with the emerging issues related to law, economics of contracts and economic development. In *Does an Employment Protection Law Matter? A Panel Data Analysis of Selected OECD Countries, 1985–2012*, the second chapter of this volume, Prabirjit Sarkar examines the impact of employment protection law (EPL) between 1985 and 2012 in 26 OECD countries

V. Mukherjee (✉) · S. Banerjee · S. K. Haldar
Department of Economics, Jadavpur University, Kolkata, India
e-mail: mukherjeevivek@hotmail.com

S. Banerjee
e-mail: swapnendu@hotmail.Com

S. K. Haldar
e-mail: sushilhaldar@gmail.com

S. Banerjee et al. (eds.), *Understanding Development,* India Studies in Business and Economics, DOI 10.1007/978-81-322-2455-6_1

through dynamic panel data models and vector error correction (VEC) causality tests. Traditionally, it is perceived that EPL has a negative impact on employment rate, and economic reforms call for its relaxation. However, Sarkar shows that EPL has significant impact neither on unemployment rate nor on labour share and union penetration. Therefore, he questions the effectiveness of policies, which call for relaxation of EPL.

Chapter 3, *Network of Legal Citations: An Analysis of Some Supreme Court Decisions on Land Acquisition in India* by Rahul Chakraborty, Simonti Chakraborty and Rajendra P. Kundu, presents the citation network of land acquisition cases from the Supreme Court of India and tries to analyse the citation behaviour of the apex court in terms of the network structure. The structure of the network displays the small world phenomenon and the degree distribution of the nodes follows the *power law*. The analysis also suggests, as the network grows, the rich get richer.

Chapter 4, *Surrogacy Contracting and Intermediation,* in this section examines the issue pertaining to monitoring of surrogate's effort (care) in the market for commercial surrogacy, which is one of the emerging markets in recent times in India. Due to the presence of hidden action, surrogates have an incentive to provide suboptimal care for the would-be baby. One way to circumvent this problem is to engage an infertility clinic to monitor the effort (care) of the surrogate. In their chapter, *Surrogacy Contracting and Intermediation,* Amrita Pramanick and Swapnendu Banerjee address the issue of monitoring a surrogate and develop a model of commercial gestational surrogacy, in which a childless couple approaches an infertility clinic for selection of a prospective surrogate, and for monitoring her further during the period of gestation. The chapter points to the fact that the intermediate agency is also subject to moral hazard and therefore having a monitoring agency is neither sufficient nor necessary to wipe off the sub-optimal care problem.

Sharecropping has remained a dominant agrarian institution around the world. In its basic form, sharecropping entails sharing of the produce between a landowner and a cultivator in a land tenancy market. There is a large and growing literature that has studied this institution from both theoretical and empirical points of view. Economic theories of sharecropping have looked at aspects such as efficiency, incentives, risk and informational asymmetry. In *Sharecropping in Theory and Practice: A Selective Review* (Chap. 5), Debapriya Sen presents a review of the literature on sharecropping. Complementing with the earlier reviews of the literature, Sen's approach is purposely selective; in that he focuses on discussing the new insights given in the more recent literature. To drive his point, Sen employs the novel approach of constructing illustrative contract theoretic models and also comments on some policy implications specific to agrarian economies in transition.

Part II is on trade and foreign aid, and there we have three important contributions. In *Trade in Intermediate Goods, Endogenous Growth and Intellectual Property Rights* (Chap. 6), Bidisha Chakraborty talks about a product cycle model of North–South trade. In her chapter, the North innovates the variety of an intermediate good and the South imitates it. Final goods are not traded while variety of capital-intensive intermediate goods is traded. In this structure, she examines the effect of intellectual property rights on economic growth and shows that depending on the human capital endowment of both the countries, there may exist a unique steady state balanced growth equilibrium or multiple steady state equilibria where tighter intellectual property rights may lead to both higher and lower steady state balanced growth rate.

The international trade in goods and services is dominated by multi-market firms. A firm's decision to sell in the domestic market vis-à-vis the foreign market depends on a number of factors including transport costs, price uncertainties and the barriers to trade. In *Multi-market Firms and Export Quota: Effects of Withdrawal of the Multi-fiber Arrangement* (Chap. 7), Saibal Kar and Mausumi Kar construct a theoretical model of international trade in goods and services to study the effect of reduction in indirect trade barriers or quotas on the decision of firms to allocate output between the domestic and foreign markets. They find that the withdrawal of the quota may lead to greater focus on the domestic market at the cost of exports for firms originating in countries that were less competitive to begin with. For firms in developing countries, the removal of quota may create two opposing effects. First, the firms may become more concentrated in the domestic market; second, the domestic-to-international allocation decision may change for a range of firms. They also find that the theoretical conjecture gets valid support from the evolving pattern of exports by a large number of textile and apparel manufacturing firms originating in India. It seems that the withdrawal of the quota since 2005 has led to a greater focus on the domestic market for Indian firms, and within the country there has also been an increased concentration of firms.

In *Does Foreign Aid Corrupt? A Theoretical Note* (Chap. 8), Sugata Marjit and Vivekananda Mukherjee theoretically explore an answer to the question of whether foreign aid corrupts an economy or not. This is an important question because most of the countries that receive foreign aid are perceived to be persistently corrupt. If the foreign aid corrupts them further, the efficacy of the foreign aid policies is in doubt. The empirical answer to this question, however, is ambiguous. The chapter attempts to develop a theory, which can explain the observed ambiguity. Based on a model in which redistributive politics determines the allocation of foreign aid in different heads of expenditure and the extent of corruption, the chapter shows under certain conditions that the result that more foreign aid raises the extent of corruption in a poorer country and promotes honesty in a richer country as derived earlier is robust also for economies where the corruption proceeds leak out of the country. The result also helps us to understand the pattern of corruption and income divergence that emerges among different states in a federal democracy like India, where the states receive untied grants from the central government and fight elections at the state level.

The three contributions in Part III focus on issues in public economics. In *Public-Private Partnerships and Governance* (Chap. 9), Prabal and Indrani Roy Chowdhury examine the formation of PPPs, one of the most important organizational forms to evolve over the last few decades, and increasingly being adopted in developing countries for provision of public goods and services. Given that PPPs seem to have been incubated by the developed world (in particular the UK), with their relatively stronger governance structures, they examine whether there is any fundamental reason why countries with stronger governance levels are more likely to opt for PPPs. They construct a theoretical model and show that PPPs are more likely to be formed in case governance is strong. Otherwise, PPPs are unlikely to form and will be susceptible to contract renegotiation in case they do form.

In *Principles of Allocating Development Grant at the Sub-national Level in India: A Suggested Methodology* (Chap. 10), Sushil K. Haldar and Ajitava Raychaudhuri have developed a theoretical model on the principles of allocating development grants at subnational level. They have criticized the existing allocation rule on various grounds like arbitrary selection of indicators, equal weights assigned to the indicators, unclear objectives of the planner, among others. Keeping in mind that regional backwardness is multidimensional in nature, they propose a methodology to derive a rational allocation rule, which is based on the principal component technique. This principle can be applied at the disaggregate level if the disaggregate data on different dimensions of development vis-à-vis deprivations are available. This allocation principle simultaneously addresses two issues: amount of funds to be released to each geographical unit as well as necessity of including each development parameter considered so far in the above-mentioned devolution methodology. The proposed methodology tries to capture inclusiveness, and it is expected to be helpful to development practitioners at both policy level and academics.

Vikas Dixit in his chapter, which appears as *Fiscal Rule and Social Sector Spending: A Study of North-East India* (Chap. 11) of this volume, explores why the management of public finances continues to be a challenging task not only for the central government but also for the state governments, since the initiation of rule-based fiscal consolidation in India. According to him, the states have been facing severe fiscal constraints particularly in sharing own funds for capital formation. The problem sounds acute when it comes to the northeastern region of India, which is faced by several economic and social challenges including financial constraints, poor infrastructure and, of course, the unfriendly attitude of the neighbouring states. His chapter, therefore, makes an attempt to analyse the impact of fiscal rule on social sector spending of northeastern states of India.

Part IV on social sector and poverty alleviation has six contributions. In *An Analysis on the Impact of Employment Generation Policies on Rural Women in West Bengal, India* (Chap. 12), Tanmoyee Banerjee (Chatterjee) tries to evaluate the impacts of two poverty alleviation schemes, Sawarnajayanti Gram Swarojgar Yojana (SGSY) and Mahatma Gandhi National Rural Employment Guarantee Scheme (MGNREGS) on the employment status of rural women and income level of the corresponding households. She uses a primary survey carried out in North 24 Parganas district of West Bengal, India in 2009 for her purpose. Applying the propensity score matching method, she finds that participation in the two different schemes does not generate similar impact: while the SGSY participation has a positive significant impact on the employment status of rural women, household income, monthly savings and consumption expenditure including family food expenditure, MGNREGS participation does not have any such impact.

Siddhartha Mitra, in *Poverty in West Bengal: A Review of Recent Performance and Programmes* (Chap. 13), substantiates with data that since the 1970s, the poverty situation in West Bengal has improved relative to other states. There has also been very little urban bias in regard to poverty incidence. Poverty alleviation has however slackened in the post-liberalization period. According to Mitra, the incidence of poverty across districts in the southeastern zone exhibits low to moderate rural as well as urban poverty, whereas those in the southwestern zone exhibit moderate to high poverty; the northern districts show large variations from low to moderate to high poverty. He also observes that in regard to the performance of MGNREGS, West Bengal does very well in terms of percentage of rural households getting employment and ranks among the top 5–7 major states in this regard. However, the relative performance of districts leaves a lot to be desired; it is observed that the high poverty districts often exhibit lower impact of the programme (in terms of percentage of rural population registered and works completed per 1000 persons) when these districts should be exhibiting a higher impact.

Amit Kundu and Sanjib Talukdar, in *The Impact of MGNREGS on Rural Households: Evidence from a Quasi-Experiment* (Chap. 14), have undertaken a quasi-experimental investigation to get an impression of the impact of the implementation of MGNREGS on the average monthly income and monthly per capita consumption expenditure (MPCE) of the rural households in West Bengal. Their study is based on the primary data collected from four gram panchayats of two randomly selected blocks of Birbhum district of West Bengal considering 2012–2013 as the reference period. Kundu and Talukder observe *panchayat*-specific heterogeneity in seeking employment through MGNREGS, and thus argue that the performance of the implementation of MGNREGS depends both qualitatively and quantitatively to a large extent on the efficacy of the panchayat. However, the result of the analysis shows that getting employment through MGNREGS helps the rural households to improve their livelihood.

Female child health has been an area of concern in Indian and its development process for a long time. This is precisely what Soma Mondal and Arpita Ghose address in Chap. 15, titled *Does Parental Education Have Any Role to Play on Female Child Disadvantage*. They have addressed the issue of gender discrimination against the female child in respect to anthropometric measures of health. Using a household survey of selected villages of Nadia district in West Bengal, they observe that the incidence of underweight children in the 0–6 age group is higher among females compared to males, and this gender gap in health reduces significantly as the parents' educational level rises and the incidence of dowry falls. Therefore, as policy prescriptions, they suggest enhancing the education level of the parents and undertaking different measures for eradicating the dowry system as a necessary step for reducing the prevalence of female child disadvantage.

The employment and education of youth in India during a period of rapid economic growth after liberalization is an area of great interest for policy-making in India. The chapter by Tushar K. Nandi in Chap. 16 uses data from three successive rounds of the National Sample Survey (NSS) data on employment and unemployment, 55–66th, to study the social division in schooling and employment of young Indians (15–24 years old) during the period 1999–2009. Descriptive and econometric results show that difference in schooling and employment across caste and religious groups has declined for males. There is an indication of convergence in schooling among males. The female difference, along caste and religious lines, in schooling and employment has declined. The difference in employment shows slower signs of convergence across religions.

In *Adverse Effect of Biomass Fuel Use on Pregnancy Outcome in Rural India* (Chap. 17), Poulomi Roy, Jayanti Ghosh and Rahuldeb Sarkar have found that the effect of biomass fuel on low birth weight is more profound in relatively wealthier populations. They argue that in poorer families, the variability of the amount of cooking is wider and the families that utilize more biomass fuel (BMF) obviously cook more and in turn consume more calories, precluding adverse effects of BMF smoke on low birth weight (LBW). In wealthier families, however, they find that the amount of cooking and the duration is more homogenous, and the adverse effects of BMF get better reflected in this group.

Part I
Law and Contracts

Chapter 2
Does an Employment Protection Law Matter? A Panel Data Analysis of Selected OECD Countries, 1985–2012

Prabirjit Sarkar

2.1 Introduction

The debate centering on labor market regulation erupted with the rise of the neoliberal school of thought in the mid-1970s. In the early post-Second World War period, Keynesianism and social democratic policies dominated the developed capitalist world. The basic purpose of the labor law was to be "a means to ensure a just share of the fruits of progress to all," as the International Labour Organization's (ILO) Philadelphia Declaration put it in 1944 (Supiot 2012). The neoliberal critique of this standpoint can be summed up in the words of the World Bank (World Bank 2007, p. 19): "laws created to protect workers often hurt them." Their argument is based on the assumption that "the labor market is in a unique equilibrium prior to the law's 'intervention,' which must therefore be understood as upsetting the competitive process and distorting market outcomes" (Deakin et al. 2014, p. 3).

The contribution of this chapter to this debate is an empirical one. It uses the Organisation for Economic Co-operation and Development (OECD) indicators of employment protection law (EPL) which measure the procedures and costs involved in dismissing workers and the procedures involved in hiring workers on fixed-term or temporary work agency contracts. It analyzes the impact of labor law on the labor market using dynamic panel data techniques which can distinguish between short-run and long-run effects of legal change and take into account dynamic interactions between legal and economic variables. These techniques mark an advance on the more static cross-sectional and time invariant analyses which have mostly been used to analyze the effects of labor laws.

To supplement this dynamic panel data analysis, it uses panel causality tests. It shows that EPL for regular and temporary employment has no clear long-term or short-term effects on unemployment. Then it looks at the impact of EPL on union density and labor's share in national income and finds no impact on these variables.

P. Sarkar (✉)
Economics Department, Jadavpur University, Kolkata, India
e-mail: prabirjit@gmail.com

S. Banerjee et al. (eds.), *Understanding Development,* India Studies in Business and Economics, DOI 10.1007/978-81-322-2455-6_2

Section 2.2 below briefly overviews the existing literature. Section 2.3 presents the results of the econometric analysis and Sect. 2.4 concludes.

2.2 Debate on the Impact of Labor Regulation: A Brief Overview

There is an increasing interest among social scientists and policy makers regarding the effects of labor law on unemployment and distribution. There remains, however, a lack of a clear consensus on the effects of labor laws.

During the heydays of Keynesianism in the 1950s and 1960s, the policy of social democracy and welfare states dominated in many industrialized countries. State interventions in the labor market were thought to facilitate better or fairer income distribution and improve the quality of life of the working class. It was expected that better income distribution in favor of the working class would increase effective demand and profitability of production, thereby promoting investment, growth, and employment.

In the face of the oil price hike in the mid-1970s, the industrialized countries faced the problem of stagflation; continuation of Keynesian fiscal stimulus policy aggravated the problem of inflation without making any dent on the problem of unemployment and recession. This marked the demise of Keynesianism in favor of a "neoliberal" era of Reaganomics/Thatcherism that found its place in the subsequent IMF/World Bank policy prescriptions, known as the Washington Consensus (Sarkar 2013).

In essence, the policies shifted towards deregulation of markets (including labor markets) to pave the way for free market forces. In the 1990s, the OECD's Jobs Study (Organisation for Economic Cooperation and Development 1994) made the argument for liberalizing labor laws as part of a strategy for enhancing labor market flexibility and thereby boosting job creation. During the 2000s, similar arguments have been made by the World Bank through its Doing Business initiatives (see, e.g., World Bank 2007).

It is argued that firms would respond to stringent labor regulation by substituting capital for labor; there would be even a shift in production from the formal sector to unregulated areas of the economy and/or flight of capital and relocation of production in a country with more market-friendly labor regulation (Fallon and Lucas 1993; Heckman and Pagés 2004; Botero et al. 2004). In the words of Besley and Burgess (2004, p. 101), "labor regulation will typically create adjustment costs in hiring and firing labor."

The strong case in favor of labor regulations comes from the perspective of fair income distribution, social justice, social security, etc. These are often brushed aside by the proponents of economics as "science" that precludes value judgment and interpersonal utility comparisons (Sarkar 2013). From the "structuralist"/neo-Kaleckian macroeconomic model one can get a "positive" argument in favor of labor regulations promoting fair income distribution and higher rate of profit and growth (see, e.g., Dutt 1984 and for a critique of this "structuralist" model see Bhaduri and Margin 1990; Sarkar 1992, 1993).

There are some other arguments:

- The laws setting basic labor standards in the areas of pay and working time and providing employees with protection against arbitrary discipline or dismissal may encourage firms and workers to coinvest in firm-specific skills and complementary productive assets (Sengenberger and Campbell 1994).
- Legislation mandating collective employee representation in the workplace can help raise worker commitment and morale (Rogers and Streeck 1995).
- For other arguments and references, see Deakin and Sarkar (2008, 2011).

There are different studies to examine the economic consequences of labor regulation. One influential work was conducted by Botero et al. (2004), partly funded by the World Bank. Botero et al. (2004) based their analysis on an index of labor regulation consisting of around 60 individual indicators, covering a full range of labor law rules, including laws on the employment relationship, collective labor relations, and social security. Their index covered 85 countries and coded for their laws as they stood in the late 1990s. The econometric analysis carried out by Botero et al. (2004) found that higher scores on the labor index were correlated with lower male employment, higher youth unemployment, and a larger informal sector.

On the contrary, a number of studies suggest that the supposed negative effects of labor laws may be either very small or simply nonexistent (Baker et al. 2004, 2005), and that such laws could, in fact, have beneficial effects on productivity and innovation (Acharya et al. 2012).

In light of this evidence, some scholars have called for a reappraisal of the assumptions underlying equilibrium-based models of the labor market (Freeman 1992, 2005).

In this perspective, a team of legal scholars at Centre for Business Research (CBR), University of Cambridge, UK, generated a detailed dataset for six OECD countries (UK, USA, France, Germany, Sweden, and Japan) over a long time span (see Deakin et al. 2007). Using this dataset, Deakin et al. (2014) showed that worker-protective labor laws in general have no consistent relationship to unemployment but are positively correlated with equality. Laws relating to working time and employee representation are found to have beneficial impacts on both efficiency and distribution.

The present study seeks to carry these analyses further. Since the CBR data cover only six OECD countries, the present study uses the OECD indicators of EPL available for the OECD countries over the time span, 1985–2013. There are various limitations of these data as pointed out by various scholars (see, e.g., Heckman and Pages 2004; Deakin and Sarkar 2008). For details of index construction and OECD response to the various criticisms, see Venn (2009). It is beyond the scope of the present chapter to go into the details of leximetrics. The study will take the OECD EPL indicators at their face values (in the absence of better data available for a large number of countries over a long time span) and examine the unemployment consequences of strictness of regular and temporary labor employment protection through dynamic panel data modeling. This will be supplemented by the panel causality tests.

2.3 The Present Study

The following two OECD series on EPL are considered in this chapter:

(i) Strictness of employment protection—individual and collective dismissals (regular contracts), REGEPL
(ii) Strictness of employment protection—temporary contracts, TEMPOEPL

There is another series: strictness of employment protection—individual dismissals (regular contracts); it was used in an earlier study (Sarkar 2013).

For unemployment rate, this chapter uses three alternative series available in the OECD iLibrary:

(i) Unemployment as percentage of civilian labor force (TOTALU)
(ii) Long-term (1 year and above) unemployment as percentage of total labor force (LONGU)
(iii) Long-term (1 year and above) youth unemployment as percentage of total labor force in the age group 15–24 (LONGYU)

For measuring distributional consequence of EPL, the chapter uses OECD iLibrary data on labor share, LABSHRE. The annual labor income share is calculated for this database as total labor costs (labor income adjusted for the self-employed) divided by nominal output.

Finally, to examine the impact of EPL on trade union penetration, it uses the variable, trade union density (UNION). Trade union density corresponds to the ratio of wage and salary earners that are trade union members, divided by the total number of wage and salary earners (OECD Labor Force Statistics).

The objective is to examine the effect of the employment protection index on unemployment, income distribution, and union density. To control for the level of economic activity of a country, the (log of) gross domestic product (GDP) in purchasing power parity dollars (LPPPY) is used.[1] This is expected to net out the country-specific effects of time-trend and cyclical fluctuations in the level of economic activities. The period of this study is 1985–2012. It covers 26 OECD countries[2] for which the relevant data are available. Due to lack of data, the study cannot be based on a perfectly balanced panel: for countries such as the Czech Republic and the Slovak Republic, the starting year is 1993; for Hungary, New Zealand, Poland, and Turkey, the starting year is 1990. For the study on labor share, a shorter time span (1985–2010) is used due to nonavailable data; here also the coverage of time span is not uniform across the countries.

This chapter uses the dynamic panel data methodology recommended by Pesaran et al. (1999) for panels with a sizable time dimension. This methodology takes

[1] GDP figures are very high; so log-scale is needed to bring parity with other variables.

[2] The countries covered in these studies are: Australia, Austria, Belgium, Canada, Czech Republic, Denmark, Finland, France, Germany, Greece, Hungary, Ireland, Italy, Japan, Netherland, Norway, Poland, Portugal, Slovak Republic, Spain, Sweden, Switzerland, Turkey, UK, and USA.

into account a short-term relationship and a time path leading to a long-term relationship. This helps us to ascertain whether there exists a short-term impact of EPL and whether there exists a stable adjustment path leading to a long-term effect. The conventional regression study assumes that the relationship between the dependent and independent variables is instantaneous. To get a meaningful long-run relationship, one should analyze a short-term relationship (if any) and examine whether there exist a stable adjustment process leading to the long-run relationship (if any). A panel regression based on a short-term time series has the constraint of studying only the instantaneous relationship, which may not be meaningful; rather it may be spurious. The present study covers a sufficiently long (1985–2010/2012) panel data for 26 countries to remove this lacuna of the existing literature.

Start by postulating a long-run relationship involving the dependent or outcome variable X (the unemployment rate, labor share, or union density), the control variable Y (GDP in natural log), and the independent or causal variable Z (labor regulation as measured by the OECD EPL indicators) as follows:

$$X_{it} = \psi_i Y_{it} + \pi_i Z_{it} + \eta_{it}, \qquad (2.1)$$

where i (=1, 2, 3,.. 26) stands for countries, t (=1, 2,…) stands for time periods (years), ψ_i and π_i are the long-run parameters, and η_{it} is the error term.

The questions are: whether there are long-term and short-term effects of Z (employment protection) along with Y (GDP measuring economic activities) on X (unemployment rate, labor share, or union density) and whether there is a stable adjustment path from the short-term relationship (if any) to the long-run relationship (if any).

Following Pesaran et al. (1999), this panel data analysis is based on the following error correction representation:

$$X_{it} = \theta_i(\eta_{it-1}) + \sum_{j=1}^{p-1} \lambda_{ij}\Delta X_{i,t-j} + \sum_{k=0}^{q-1} \psi_{ik}\Delta Y_{i,t-k} + \sum_{l=0}^{r-1} \pi_{il}\Delta Z_{i,t-l} + \mu_i + \phi_{it}, \qquad (2.2)$$

where Δ is the difference operator, θ_i is the country-specific error-correcting speed of adjustment term, λ_{ij}, ψ_{ik}, and π_{il} are the coefficients of the lagged variables, μ_i is the country-specific effect, and ϕ_{it} is the disturbance term. The existence of a meaningful long-run relationship with a stable adjustment dynamics requires $\theta_i < 0$.

Within this general structure, three alternative models can be postulated:

(i) Dynamic fixed effect (DFE) model where intercepts are assumed to vary across the countries but all other parameters and error variances are constrained to be the same.
(ii) Mean group (MG) model, where separate equation is estimated for each country and the mean of the estimates is calculated to get a glimpse of the overall picture.

(iii) Pooled mean group (PMG) estimator is the intermediate alternative suggested by Pesaran et al. (1999). This model assumes that intercepts, short-run coefficients, and error variances are different across the countries, but the long run coefficients are the same.

Using the STATA-based software developed by Blackburne and Frank (2007), this study estimates each of the three alternative models, MG, PMG, and DFE. The Lag Exclusion Wald Test is used for each variable separately to determine the lag structure of the regression. The Hausman test is used to select the appropriate model, comparing two at a time (PMG vs. MG, MG vs. DFE, and so on). This test is based on the null hypothesis: the difference between the estimated coefficients is not systematic. If the null hypothesis is accepted, implying no systematic difference between the two estimates, the choice of the appropriate model is based on the efficiency property of the estimated coefficients. If the null hypothesis is rejected, implying systematic difference between the two estimates, the choice of the appropriate model is based on the consistency property of the estimated coefficients. All the estimates are reported in Table 2.1.

To supplement the analysis of dynamic panel data models, the vector error correction (VEC) Granger causality/block exogeneity Wald tests (based on DFE model) are used to ascertain the direction of causality.[3] These are reported in Table 2.2.

On the basis of the estimates of Tables 2.1 and 2.2, the following observations can be made:

1. In none of the three dynamic panel data models (MG, PMG, and DFE), the legal variable REGEPL (strictness of employment protection—individual and collective dismissals in regular contracts) has a long-term or short-term rising effect on unemployment as measured by TOTALU, LONGU, and LONGYU. For LONGU and LONGYU, however, PMG model finds a negative (!) long-term relationship with REGEPL. The causality test finds no causal relationship and the Hausman test supports the DFE model. So the conclusion that can be derived here is that REGEPL has no unemployment consequence, irrespective of whether one considers total, long-term total, or long-term youth unemployment.[4]
2. In the PMG model, TEMPOEPL has long-term rising relationships with two measures of unemployment: TOTALU and LONGU. The DFE model supports the same type of relationship between TEMPOEPL and LONGYU. The causality tests, however, find no causal relationship between TEMPOEPL and various measures of unemployment. So the unemployment consequence of TEMPOEPL cannot be ascertained.

[3] For these tests we have used the Eviews 6 program.

[4] We find a causal influence of REGEPL on TOTALU, but none of the dynamic panel data models ascertain a relationship that is worth reporting.

Table 2.1 Short-run and long-run impact of the employment protection law on unemployment, labor share, and union density, 1985–2012: dynamic panel data models

Part no		PMG	MG[a]	DFE
	I. Impact of strictness of employment protection-regular employment, REGEPL (*Z*)			
	On			
I.A	Rate of unemployment (as percentage of civilian labor force), TOTALU (*X*)			
	Long-term relationship			
	Y (LPPPY)	−9.057**	−14.304**	−6.806**
	Z (REGEPL)	1.812	−17.951	−1.276
	Short-term relationship			
	θ	−0.126**	−0.204**	−0.115**
	ΔX_t^{-1}	0.242**	0.218**	0.387**
	ΔY_t	−27.018**	−26.601**	−25.704**
	ΔY_t^{-1}	−8.581**	−11.105**	−2.979
	ΔZ_t	−0.798	0.356	−0.154
	μ	24.273**	32.162**	17.526**
	Chosen model[b]			DFE
I.B	Long-term (1 year and above) unemployment as percentage of total labor force, LONGU (*X*)			
	Long-term Relationship			
	Y (LPPPCY)	−28.45**	−35.239	−17.437**
	Z (TEMPOEPL)	−13.077**	−40.426	−2.451
	Short-term relationship			
	θ	−0.302**	−0.444**	−0.17**
	ΔX_t^{-2}	0.053	0.08*	0.0817
	ΔY_t	62.892**	73.639**	40.093**
	ΔY_t^{-1}	−68.26**	−53.435**	−75.019**
	ΔZ_t	1.022	1.676	−0.997
	μ	187.494**	197.86**	67.235**
	Chosen model[b]			DFE
I.C	Long-term (1 year and above) youth unemployment as percentage of total labor force in the age group 15–24, LONGYU (*X*)			
	Long-term relationship			
	Y (LPPPY)	−24.437**	−28.609**	−17.706**
	Z (REGEPL)	−12.31**	1.359	3.407
	Short-term relationship			
	θ	−0.272**	−0.404**	−0.179**
	ΔY_t	16.1	22.511*	12.538*
	ΔY_t^{-1}	−61.5**	−53.078**	−59.801**
	ΔZ_t	0.849	0.494	−1.412

Table 2.1 (continued)

Part no		PMG	MG[a]	DFE
	μ	144.16**	234.34**	67.6**
	Chosen model[b]			DFE
I.D	Labor share, LABSHRE (*X*)			
	Y (LPPPY)	−0.214**	−0.132*	−0.163**
	Z (REGEPL)	0.021	0.033	0.027
	Short-term relationship			
	θ	−0.22**	−0.461**	−0.219**
	ΔY_t	−0.408**	−0.419**	−0.304**
	ΔY_t^{-1}	0.304**	0.181	0.286**
	ΔZ_t	0.019	0.018	0.017
	μ	1.074**	1.563**	0.819**
	Chosen model[b]			DFE
I.E	Union density, UNION (*X*)			
	Long-term relationship			
	Y (LPPPY)	−2.474*	−19.43**	−17.052**
	Z (REGEPL)	0.073	−7.94	0.223
	Short-term relationship			
	θ	−0.119**	−0.319**	−0.188**
	ΔX_t^{-2}	−0.001	0.021	0.152**
	ΔY_t	−8.458*	−4.277	−6.019**
	ΔZ_t	−0.044	1.06	0.587
	μ	7.942**	121.519**	70.276**
	Chosen model[b]			DFE
	II. Impact of strictness of employment protection-temporary employment, TEMPOEPL (*Z*)			
	On			
II.A	Rate of unemployment (as percentage of civilian labor force), TOTALU (*X*)			
	Long-term relationship			
	Y (LPPPCY)	−8.844**	−9.076*	−7.402**
	Z (TEMPOEPL)	0.933**	−0.201	0.072
	Short-term relationship			
	θ	−0.157**	−0.211**	−0.122**
	ΔX_t^{-1}	0.259**	0.204**	0.402**
	ΔX_t^{-2}	−0.007	0.002	−0.012
	ΔY_t	−26.292**	−25.839**	−25.655**
	ΔY_t^{-1}	−9.941**	−13.682**	−3.924*
	ΔZ_t	−0.062	0.033	−0.17
	μ	29.657**	41.317**	19.712**
	Chosen model[2]			DFE

Table 2.1 (continued)

Part no		PMG	MG[a]	DFE
II.B	Long-term unemployment (more than 1 year) as percentage of total unemployment, LONGU (*X*)			
	Long-term relationship			
	Y (LPPPCY)	−22.798**	−23.152**	−17.259**
	Z (TEMPOEPL)	2.684**	1.662	−0.321
	Short-term relationship			
	θ	−0.317**	−0.502**	−0.169**
	ΔX^{t-2}	0.069	0.098*	0.083*
	ΔY_t	63.133**	73.392**	39.735**
	ΔY_t^{-2}	−71.664	−56.837**	−75.265**
	ΔZ_t	−1.998	−1.772	−0.656
	μ	152.002	204.683	65.439**
	Chosen model[b]			DFE
II.C	Long-run (1 year and above) youth unemployment as percentage of total labor force in the age group 15–24, LONGYU (*X*)			
	Long-term relationship			
	Y (LPPPCY)	−12.371**	−10.809	−16.213**
	Z (TEMPOEPL)	0.84	−11.577	2.753*
	Short-term relationship			
	θ	−0.257**	−0.408**	−0.184**
	ΔY_t	17.43	21.024*	12.417*
	ΔY_t^{-1}	−64.129**	−59.103**	−60.098**
	ΔZ_t	−0.198	−0.99	−0.723
	μ	68.351**	173.247**	64.314**
	Chosen model[2]	PMG		
II.D	Labor share, LABSHRE (*X*)			
	Long-term relationship			
	Y (LPPPY)	−0.211**	−0.096	−0.163**
	Z (TEMPOEPL)	0.001	−0.019	0.006
	Short-term relationship			
	θ	−0.238**	−0.486**	−0.222**
	ΔY_t	−0.418**	−0.416**	−0.303**
	ΔY_t^{-1}	0.314**	0.217*	0.284**
	ΔZ_t	0.01	0.011	0.003
	μ	1.134**	1.6**	0.845**
	Chosen model[b]			DFE
II.E	Union density, UNION (*X*)			
	Long-term relationship			
	Y (LPPPY)	−2.188	−11.774	−16.383**
	Z (TEMPOEPL)	−0.163	−2.073	0.856

Table 2.1 (continued)

Part no		PMG	MG[a]	DFE
	Short-term relationship			
	θ	−0.117*	−0.311*	−0.189**
	ΔX_t^{-2}	−0.007	0.001	0.144**
	ΔY_t	−8.346*	−4.969	−6.068**
	ΔZ_t	0.101	0.214	−0.06
	μ	7.017*	114.429**	67.874**
	Chosen model[b]			DFE

*Significant at 5 % level; **Significant at 1 % level.

[a] The regressors are estimated from the following long-term relationship and its error correction form

Long-run Relationship:

$X_{it} = \psi_i Y_{it} + \pi_i Z_{it} + \eta_{it}$,

where i (=1,2,3,..26) represents countries, t (=1,2,… T) represents periods (years), ψ_i and π_i are the long-run parameters and η_{it} is the error term

Its Error Correction Form:

$$\Delta X_{it} = \theta_i\left(\eta_{it-1}\right) + \sum_{j=1}^{p-1} \lambda_{ij}\Delta X_{i,t-j} + \sum_{k=0}^{q-1} \psi_{ik}\Delta Y_{i,t-k} + \sum_{l=0}^{r-1} \pi_{il}\Delta z_{i,t-1} + \mu_i + \phi_{it},$$

where Δ is the difference operator, θ_i is the group-specific error-correcting speed of adjustment term, λ_{ij}, ψ_{ik} and π_{il} are the coefficients of the lagged variables, μ_i is the country fixed effect and ϕ_{it} is the disturbance term. The existence of a meaningful long-run relationship with a stable adjustment dynamics requires $\theta_i<0$

[b] An appropriate model is chosen on the basis of a series of Hausman tests

Data Source: OECD iLibrary

Table 2.2 Causal relationship among labor regulation, unemployment, union density, labor share, and GDP in 26 OECD countries, 1985–2012: VEC causality analysis[a]

Part no	Dependent variable	Excluded independent variable	Chi-square	Degree of freedom	Probability
I.A					
	TOTALU				
		LPPPY	31.96594**	5	0.0000
		REGEPL	13.38359*	5	0.0200
	LPPPY				
		TOTALU	2.851068	5	0.7229
		REGEPL	7.660077	5	0.1760
	REGEPL				
		TOTALU	7.748744	5	0.1706
		LPPPY	5.499612	5	0.3580
I.B					
	LONGU				
		LPPPY	145.8818**	5	0.0000
		REGEPL	4.205010	5	0.5203
	LPPPY				
		LONGU	7.914072	5	0.1610

Table 2.2 (continued)

Part no	Dependent variable	Excluded independent variable	Chi-square	Degree of freedom	Probability
		REGEPL	5.429275	5	0.3658
	REGEPL				
		LONGU	4.626289	5	0.4632
		LPPPY	3.198563	5	0.6694
I.C					
	LONGYU				
		LPPPY	112.6116**	5	0.0000
		REGEPL	2.180372	5	0.8237
	LPPPY				
		LONGYU	7.671710	5	0.1753
		REGEPL	5.453938	5	0.3630
	REGEPL				
		YOUTHU	8.251051	5	0.1429
		LPPPY	2.359214	5	0.7975
I.D					
	LABSHRE				
		LPPPY	34.65645**	5	0.0000
		REGEPL	3.008481	5	0.6987
	LPPPY				
		LABSHRE	3.792734	5	0.5796
		REGEPL	5.173480	5	0.3951
	REGEPL				
		LABSHRE	3.934059	5	0.5589
		LPPPY	3.548479	5	0.6161
I.E					
	UNION				
		LPPPY	27.36609**	5	0.0000
		REGEPL	0.789289	5	0.9777
	LPPPY				
		UNION	9.264335	5	0.0990
		REGEPL	4.303547	5	0.5066
	REGEPL				
		UNION	6.384829	5	0.2706
		LPPPY	3.367354	5	0.6435
II.A					
	TOTALU				
		LPPPY	35.58698**	5	0.0000
		TEMPOEPL	2.879326	5	0.7186
	LPPPY				
		TOTALU	4.101937	5	0.5348
		TEMPOEPL	2.646240	5	0.7543
	TEMPOEPL				
		TOTALU	3.372555	5	0.6428
		LPPPY	4.528936	5	0.4760

Table 2.2 (continued)

Part no	Dependent variable	Excluded independent variable	Chi-square	Degree of freedom	Probability
II.B					
	LONGU				
		LPPPY	146.1188**	5	0.0000
		TEMPOEPL	13.12589*	5	0.0222
	LPPPY				
		LONGU	7.691030	5	0.1741
		TEMPOEPL	2.005974	5	0.8483
	TEMPOEPL				
		LONGU	7.613358	5	0.1789
		LPPPY	9.336499	5	0.0964
II.C					
	LONGYU				
		LPPPY	114.1623**	5	0.0000
		TEMPOEPL	10.75108	5	0.0565
	LPPPY				
		LONGYU	7.068281	5	0.2156
		TEMPOEPL	1.894003	5	0.8636
	TEMPOEPL				
		LONGYU	7.597198	5	0.1799
		LPPPY	9.848095	5	0.0797
II.D					
	LABSHRE				
		LPPPY	31.12399**	5	0.0000
		TEMPOEPL	2.576900	5	0.7649
	LPPPY				
		LABSHRE	4.369873	5	0.4975
		TEMPOEPL	1.852827	5	0.8691
	TEMPOEPL				
		LABSHRE	3.267367	5	0.6588
		LPPPY	9.673042	5	0.0850
II.E					
	UNION				
		LPPPY	27.71600**	5	0.0000
		TEMPOEPL	9.462346	5	0.0920
	LPPPY				
		UNION	6.834127	5	0.2333
		TEMPOEPL	3.106407	5	0.6836
	TEMPOEPL				
		UNION	5.827595	5	0.3234
		LPPPY	6.661555	5	0.2471

*Significant at 5% level: The null hypothesis of no causality is rejected; **Significant at 1% level: The null hypothesis of no causality is rejected

[a] The VEC Granger panel causality tests are done with the aid of the Eviews 6 statistical program. Data Source: OECD iLibrary

3. None of the models show a short-term or long-term impact of REGEPL and TEMPOEPL on labor share (LABSHRE) and union density (UNION).
4. In almost all the cases one can observe one expected relationship: the higher the GDP, the lower is the unemployment (TOTALU, LONGU, and LONGYU). The causality tests ascertain the direction of causality from GDP to unemployment.
5. There is no sign of endogeneity in the EPL: the higher or lower unemployment or GDP has no causal effect on EPL (REGEPL or TEMPOEPL). Similarly the trade union penetration (union density) does not have a causal influence on EPL. This implies that governments do not relax (tighten) EPL in response to the unemployment scenario. Nor do they relax or tighten EPL because of trade union penetration.
6. In almost all the cases, the Hausman test supports DFE models. The implication is that the 26 OECD countries considered in the sample differ only in their (time-invariant) initial conditions (history). This also supports the appropriateness of the causality test which is based on the assumptions of the DFE model.

2.4 Summary and Conclusion

This study examines the economic effects of EPL between 1985 and 2012 in 26 OECD countries through a dynamic panel data analysis. It uses three alternative dynamic panel data models—DFE, MG, and PMG models—and examines the short-term as well as long-term effects of employment protection on various measures of unemployment rate—overall unemployment rate, long-term total unemployment rate, and long-term youth unemployment rate. Apart from the effect on the unemployment rate, it also considers the impact on union density and labor share. To supplement the dynamic panel data modeling, it also uses VEC Granger causality tests.

This study shows that EPL does not increase long-term unemployment rate irrespective of whether one considers total or youth working population. Nor there is any impact on labor share. A more disaggregative study of the impact of labor regulation for 6 OECD countries (Deakin et al. 2014) finds its favorable effect on wage share: certain components of labor regulation (such as working time and employee representation) are driving this result. None of these components are covered in the OECD EPL indicators as these deal with the issues of dismissal.

The causal impact of EPL on trade union penetration (as measured by union density) is also insignificant. There is no reverse causality. The implication is: EPL is independent of union penetration—they are not related in a bond of mutual causation. Furthermore, the unemployment scenario does not lead to relaxation of EPL and vice versa.

To sum up, the state of unemployment, union penetration, and wage share do not follow from labor regulations; they depend on more complex factors which determine the level of economic activities and growth. So the neoliberal policy prescription of flexible labor market ("hire and fire") for the countries facing the unemployment problem is unwarranted. What is needed is the state intervention to change the macro-fundamentals in favor of pro-employment growth and development.

References

Acharya V, Baghai RP, Subramanian KV (2012) Labor laws and innovation NBER Working Paper No. 16484

Baker D, Glyn A, Howell D, Schmitt J (2004) Unemployment and labour market Institutions: the Failure of the Empirical Case for Deregulation, ILO Working Paper No. 43

Baker D, Glyn A, Howell D, Schmitt J (2005) Labour market institutions and unemployment: assessment of the cross-country evidence. In: Howell D (ed) Fighting unemployment: the limits of free market orthodoxy. Oxford University Press, New York, pp 72–118

Besley T, Burgess R (2004) Can labour regulation hinder economic performance? Evidence from India. Quart J Econ 199:91–134

Bhaduri A, Marglin S (1990) Real wages and unemployment: the economic basis for contesting political ideologies. Cambridge J Econ 14:375–393

Blackburne EF III, Frank MW (2007) Estimation of non-stationary heterogeneous panels. Stata J 7:197–208

Botero JC, Djankov S, La Porta R, Lopez-de-Silanes F, Shleifer A (2004) The regulation of labor. Q J Econ 119(4):1339–1382

Deakin S, Sarkar P (2008) Assessing the long-run economic impact of labour law systems: a theoretical reappraisal and analysis of new time series data Industrial. Relat J 39:453–487

Deakin S, Sarkar P (2011) Indian labour law and its impact on unemployment, 1970–2006: a leximetric study. Indian J Labour Econ 54(4):607–629

Deakin S, Lele P, Siems M (2007) The evolution of labour law: calibrating and comparing regulatory regimes. Int Lab Rev 146:133–162

Deakin S, Malmberg J, Sarkar P (2014) Do labour laws increase equality at the expense of higher unemployment? The experience of six OECD countries, 1970–2010. Int Lab Rev 153(1):1–27

Dutt AK (1984) Stagnation, income distribution and 'monopoly power. Camb J Econ 8:25–40

Fallon P, Lucas R (1993) The impact of changes in job security legislation in India and Zimbabwe. World Bank Econ Rev 5:395–413

Freeman RB (1992) Labour market institutions and policies: help or hindrance to economic development? Proceedings of the World Bank Annual Conference on Development Economics 117–144

Freeman RB (2005) Labour market institutions without blinders: the debate over flexibility and labour market performance. Int Econ J 19:129–145

Heckman J, Pagés C (2004) Introduction. In: Heckman J, Pagés C (eds) Law and employment: lessons from Latin America and the Caribbean. University of Chicago Press, Chicago, pp 1–108

Organisation for Economic Cooperation and Development (1994) OECD jobs study, evidence and explanations, Part I: labor market trends and underlying forces of change, Organization for Economic Cooperation and Development, Paris

Pesaran MH, Shin Y, Smith RP (1999) Pooled mean group estimation of dynamic heterogeneous panels. J Amer Stat Assoc 94:621–634

Rogers J, Streeck W (1995) Works councils: consultation, representation and cooperation in industrial relations. University of Chicago, Chicago

Sarkar P (1992) Industrial growth and income inequality: an examination of 'Stagnationism' with special reference to India. J Quant Econ 8:125–138

Sarkar P (1993) Distribution and growth: a critical note on 'stagnationism'. Rev Radic Politic Econ 25:62–70

Sarkar P (2013) Does an employment protection law lead to unemployment? A panel data analysis of OECD countries, 1990–2008. Camb J Econ 37(4):1335–1348
Sengenberger W, Campbell D (1994) Creating Opportunities: role of labour standards in industrial restructuring. International Institute for Labour Studies, Geneva
Supiot A (2012) The spirit of Philadelphia: social justice vs. The Total Market. Verso, London
Venn D (2009) Legislation, collective bargaining and enforcement: updating the OECD employment protection indicators, OECD Social, Employment and Migration Working Paper
World Bank (2007) Doing Business 2008: Comparing Regulation in 178 Economies. International Bank for Reconstruction and Development, Washington, DC

Chapter 3
Network of Legal Citations: An Analysis of Some Supreme Court Decisions on Land Acquisition in India

Rahul Chakraborty, Simonti Chakraborty, and Rajendra P. Kundu

3.1 Introduction

The Indian legal system is characterised by complex dynamics of lawmaking. In this system, law is primarily judge-made and precedents play a very significant role in the lawmaking process. According to Landes and Posner (1976), 'A precedent is something done in the past that is appealed to as a reason for doing the same thing again'. Once a judgement is passed by the court it can serve as a precedent by providing a benchmark for deciding later cases of similar type in a similar manner and a series of related precedents may elucidate a norm as powerful as any statutory rule. Legal precedents, therefore, become inputs in the production of judge-made rules of law.[1] Thus, in legal parlance, it can be said that *stare decisis* occupies the centre stage of the legal system in India.

While writing an opinion, justices often cite earlier judgements as precedents to support their arguments. The citations made by justices are very important determinants of salience of judgements. Thus, the selection of judgements made by the justices and the reasons behind their choices play a very significant role in the

[1] There exists a rich literature on the role of precedents in determining and shaping court judgements. Eskridge (1991) and Knight and Epstein (1996) discuss the possible ways in which precedents can affect decisions. The conventional approach is to view precedents as a conspicuous explanation for judicial decisions. The second mechanism, as explained by the above set of papers, by which precedents enter into the decision-making process of judges, is by constraining judges from implementing their preferences. Justices have personal preferences regarding which particular rules they would like to be established in a case under consideration. However, they might have to modify their position to take into account a constraint of having to position themselves close to the established precedents. Legal scholars, however, are divided in their opinion regarding the actual strength of a norm which respects precedents and thereby aligns decisions in accordance to what the precedents demand (Landes and Posner 1976; Segal and Spaeth 1996).

R. P. Kundu (✉) · S. Chakraborty · R. Chakraborty
Centre for Economic Studies and Planning, Jawaharlal Nehru University,
New Delhi 110067, India
e-mail: rajendra.kundu@gmail.com

S. Banerjee et al. (eds.), *Understanding Development,* India Studies in Business and Economics, DOI 10.1007/978-81-322-2455-6_3

development of law. Therefore, an understanding of the citation behaviour of courts is crucial for any analysis of law and its evolution.

This paper is an attempt to understand the citation behaviour of the Supreme Court of India with specific reference to its land acquisition decisions over the period 1960–2014.[2] We construct the citation network of the above-mentioned judgements and try to analyse the behaviour of the apex court in terms of the network structure.[3] Our analysis indicates that the network displays the characteristics of a 'small world' and the degree distribution reveals that while most judgements in the network are never/very rarely cited, there are some which are cited very often. We also find that there is significant overlap between the benches of the most prominent judgements in the network.

The paper is organised as follows. In Sect. 3.2, we present the framework of analysis. Section 3.3 presents the citation network of land acquisition decisions from the Supreme Court of India and discusses the important properties of the network. In Sect. 3.4, we take a closer look at the most important judgements in the network. Section 3.5 concludes the chapter.

3.2 Framework

Let $N = \{1, 2, \ldots, n\}$ be a set of judgements and let $E \subseteq N^2$ be defined as $E = \{(i, j) \in N^2 \mid i \text{ cites } j\}$. The pair (N, E) is a citation network of judgements. We denote (N, E) by G. If i cites j then j cannot cite i. Therefore, the relation is inherently asymmetric and G is a directed network. The network G can be represented as a diagram in which every judgement (node) is represented by a circle and a citation from node i to node j is indicated by an arrow (directed edge) from circle i to circle j.

[2] The issue of land acquisition has become highly contentious in the last decade with the outbreak of several mass movements and protests against government acquisition of land and eviction of peasants from their properties in many parts of the country (Sarkar 2007). The resistance at Singur and Nandigram in West Bengal, those at POSCO in Orissa or the long drawn Narmada Bachao Andolan has left scholars and activists debating and writing on this issue extensively. The complex yet significant role that a limited resource like land plays in the Indian context makes it a potential area of legal conflicts. In fact, a close scrutiny into the case laws on land acquisition reveals a huge volume of litigation fought with reference to the Land Acquisition Act of 1894. In India, private land is acquired for public purpose by involving the principle of eminent domain which affirms that private property can only be taken for public use by compensating the land losers. Essentially it is these two aspects of the law—compensation and public purpose—which have witnessed repeated challenges in court. This has been coupled with the less than assiduous implementation of the law by the government officials—thus adding to legal contests (Banerjee et al. 2007; Desai 2011; Ghatak and Ghosh 2011).

[3] Fowler and Jeon (2008) have attempted to analyse the citation behaviour of the US Supreme Court by using the tools of network analysis. Their work clearly reveals that *stare decisis* played a crucial role in the decision-making process of the US Supreme Court and in fact, has gradually strengthened its influence. Further, the use of quantitative techniques has helped them to identify important precedents in the history of the apex court of the USA.

We define sets N_i^I, N_i^O and N_i as follows: $N_i^I = \{j \in N \mid (j,i) \in E\}$, $N_i^O = \{j \in N \mid (i,j) \in E\}$ and $N_i = N_i^I \cup N_i^O$. N_i^I is the set of all judgements which cite i and N_i^O is the set of all judgements which are cited by i. N_i is the set of all judgements which have either cited i or has been cited by i. Let $\# N_i^I = n_i^I, \# N_i^O = n_i^I$ and $\# N_i = n_i$. n_i^I is called the indegree of i and n_i^O is called the outdegree of i. Thus, for any judgement, the indegree is the number of citations received and the outdegree is the number of citations made by the judgement. The degree (indegree/outdegree) of a judgement relative to the maximum possible degree in the network $(n-1)$ gives us a measure of the importance of the judgement in the network. A judgement with high indegree is important because it acts as an authority. A judgement with high outdegree is central in the network because of its role as a hub. We call a judgement i an isolate iff $n_i = 0$. In other words, an isolate is a judgement which has no inward and no outward citation.

The distribution of indegree in G is the vector p where p_d is the relative frequency of judgements with indegree d; with $p_d \geq 0$ for all $0 \leq d \leq n-1$ and $\sum_d p(d) = 1$. The distribution of outdegree in G is the vector q where q_d is the relative frequency of judgements with outdegree d; with $q_d \geq 0$ for all $0 \leq d \leq n-1$ and $\sum_d q(d) = 1$. The average indegree in G is $n^I = \sum_d dp(d) = \frac{\sum_i n_i^I}{n}$. The average outdegree in G is $n^O = \sum_d dp(d) = \frac{\sum_i n_i^O}{n}$. It has to be noted that in any network the average indegree is always equal to the average outdegree. The average indegrees in real-world networks are very small compared to the number of nodes and there is lot of variation. Degree distributions of real-world networks often reveal that most of the nodes have very low degrees while there are some nodes with very high degrees.

A path is a sequence of judgements $i_1, i_2, \ldots, i_k$ such that $(i_j, i_{j+1}) \in E$ for all $1 \leq j \leq k-1$. If $i_1, i_2, \ldots, i_k$ is a path, then we say that there is a path from judgement i_1 to i_k. A cycle is a sequence of nodes $i_1, i_2, \ldots, i_{k+1}$ such that $i_1 = i_{k+1}$; $i_1, i_2, \ldots, i_k$ is a path, and $(i_k, i_{k+1}) \in E$. A network is acyclic iff it does not contain any cycle. The citation network G evolves with time and a judgement can only cite the existing ones. The asymmetry in the relation and the nature of the evolution makes G an acyclic network.

G is weakly connected iff for all $i, j \in N$ there is a path from i to j or there is a path from j to i. Let $\phi \neq N' \subseteq N$ and $E' \subseteq E$. (N', E') is a weakly connected component of G iff (i) (N', E') is weakly connected and (ii) $i \in N'$ and $(i, j) \in E$ implies $j \in N'$ and $(i, j) \in E'$. A network has a giant component iff the largest component covers a very large share of the nodes in the network and all other components are small.

The length of a path is the number of edges in the path. If there is a path from i to j then the geodesic (shortest path) from i to j is a path from i to j that has the minimum length among all such paths. The distance from i to j, denoted by $s(i, j)$, is the length of the geodesic from i to j. If there is no path from i to j then the distance is ∞. If G is weakly connected then the average distance between nodes in G, denoted by $s(G)$, is defined as $s(G) = \frac{\sum_i \sum_j s(i, j)}{n(n-1)}$. If G is not weakly connected then the average distance of the largest component is taken as proxy for the average distance in G.

Let $N' = \{i \in N \mid \# N_i \geq 2\}$. The clustering coefficient of $i \in N'$ is defined as $C_i = \frac{\#\{\{j,k\} \mid j,k \in N_i \text{ and } [(j,k) \in E \text{ or } (k,j) \in E]\}}{n_i(n_i - 1)}$. The clustering coefficient measures the extent of overlap between edges in the neighbourhood of a node. In the context of the citation network G, a high clustering coefficient of a judgement i implies that if we consider any two judgements, each of which has either cited i or has been cited by i, then it is very likely that one of these would cite the other. The average clustering coefficient of network G is defined as $C(G) = \frac{\sum_{i \in N'} C_i}{n}$.

A network is said to be a small-world network iff it satisfies the following properties: (1) the average degree in the network is very small relative to the number of nodes in the network, (2) the network has a giant component consisting of a significantly large proportion of nodes in the network, (3) the average distance between nodes in the network is small ($s(G)$ is of order $\ln(n)$), and (4) the clustering coefficient is high in comparison to the average clustering coefficient of a network generated by a random process.[4] Many real-world networks including citation networks display properties of the small world.

3.3 The Citation Network of Land Acquisition Judgements from the Supreme Court of India

In this section, we present the citation network of land acquisition judgements from the Supreme Court of India and draw some inferences about the pattern of citations. Our sample consists of 226 judgements decided between 1960 and 2014. The data have been obtained from Manupatra, an online legal search engine subscribed by Jawaharlal Nehru University. The judgements in our sample were listed in Manupatra under the subject head 'land acquisition'.[5] An overwhelming proportion of the judgements in our sample has been of a recent time frame, more specifically after 2000. In fact, the judgements which came in 2010 or later constitute 77% of our sample.

The graph in Fig. 3.1 presents a visualisation of the citation network of the judgements in our data set. The graph has 226 circles and 87 directed edges. Each circle represents a judgement with a larger size of a circle indicating a higher indegree, and circles of the same colour representing judgements of the same outdegree. An edge from circle i to circle j indicates a citation from i to j. It is evident from the diagram that there is a wide variation in the indegree of nodes in the network. The same holds true about the outdegree of nodes. Table 3.1 gives the distribution of indegree and Table 3.2 gives the distribution of outdegree in the network.

[4] For more on small-world network, see Watts (1999) and Goyal et al. (2006).

[5] The data were last updated from www.manupatra.com on July 10, 2014.

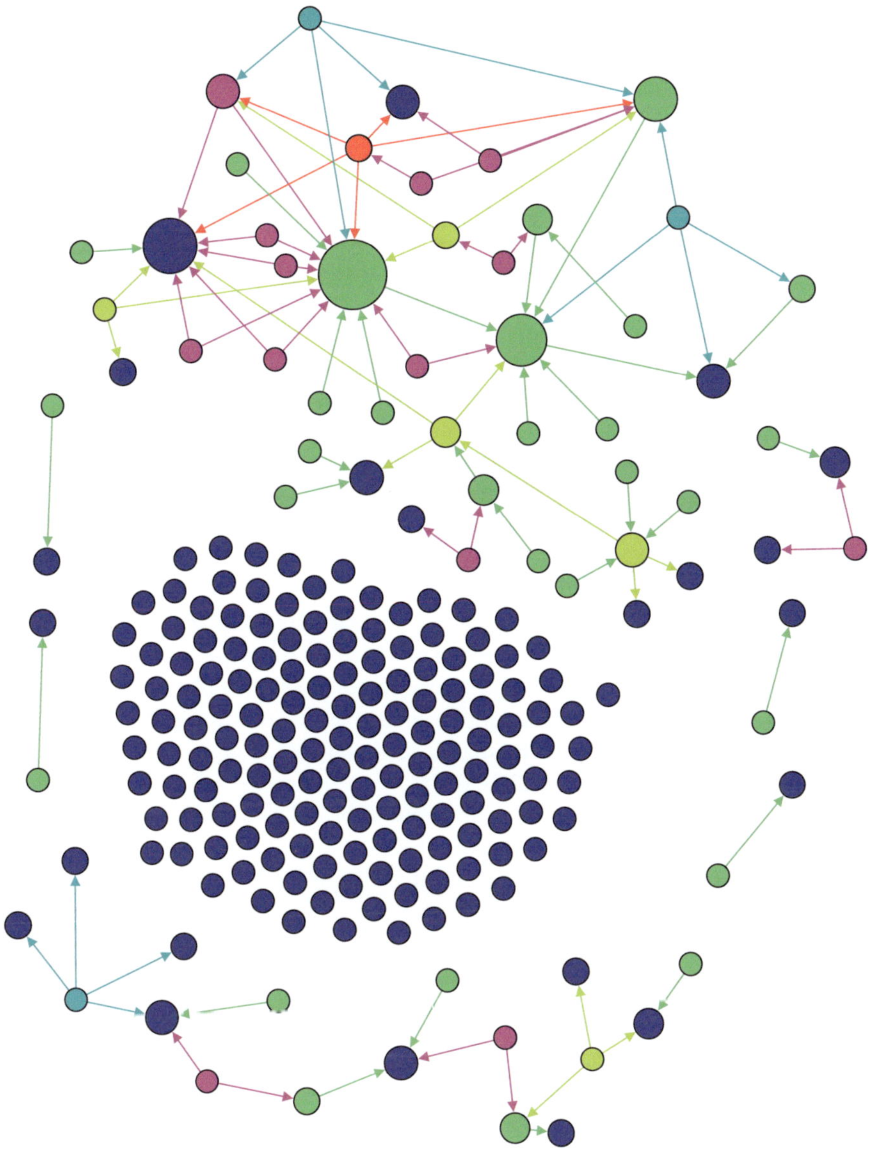

Fig. 3.1 The citation network of land acquisition decisions from the Supreme Court of India over the period 1960–2014

Table 3.1 Indegree distribution

Indegree	0	1	2	3	4	5	6	7	8	9	10	11	12	13
Relative frequency	$\frac{191}{226}$	$\frac{18}{226}$	$\frac{6}{226}$	$\frac{7}{226}$	0	0	$\frac{1}{226}$	0	$\frac{1}{226}$	$\frac{1}{226}$	0	0	0	$\frac{1}{226}$

Table 3.2 Outdegree distribution

Outdegree	0	1	2	3	4	5
Relative frequency	$\frac{175}{226}$	$\frac{29}{226}$	$\frac{13}{226}$	$\frac{5}{226}$	$\frac{3}{226}$	$\frac{1}{226}$

The two tables, along with Fig. 3.1, allow us to make the following observations about the network:

(i) There are 153 isolates in the network. This means that about 67 % of the judgements have neither cited any judgement nor have received any citation from other judgements in the network.[6]
(ii) Most judgements in the network have very few (less than or equal to 3) citations. There are only four judgement which have six or more citations.
(iii) Most judgements in the network have made very few (less than or equal to 3) citations. There are only four judgements which have cited four or five other judgements.
(iv) The average indegree in the network is 0.385. Thus, the average number of citations per judgement is very small compared to the number of judgements in the network.
(v) The existence of a giant component is evident from the graph in Fig. 3.1. The largest component has 44 judgements which accounts for about 19 % of the judgements in the network. The second largest component has only 7 % of the judgements. The size of the largest component increases significantly as we extend the network by including all land acquisition cases which appear as outward citations of these 226 cases.
(vi) The average distance in the giant component is 1.868 which is less than the log value of the number of nodes.
(vii) The average clustering coefficient of the network is 0.012, which is about 5 times the clustering coefficient of a network generated by a random process. For the extended network, which also includes all land acquisition cases that appear as outward citations of the judgements in our sample, the average clustering coefficient is about 20 times that of the clustering coefficient of a comparable random network.

From the observations (i)–(iii), it is clear that the network presented here has very few judgements which have significant citations, and it also has very few judgements which cite a sizable number of other cases. From observations (iv)–(vi), it is clear that the network satisfies properties 1, 2, and 3 of the small world. The clustering coefficient is modest but it increases significantly if we include all land acquisition cases which appear as outward citations of the judgements in our sample. Thus, we can conclude that the citation network of land acquisition judgements from the Supreme Court of India is a small world with very few judgements having significant citations.

[6] These judgements might have cited or received citations from judgements not in this network.

3.4 Some Important Cases in the Network

One of the objectives of our analysis is to identify and study some of the more prominent judgements in the network. Prominence or salience of a judgement is most commonly measured by the number of inward or outward citations that it is associated with. Tables 3.3 and 3.4 list, respectively, some of the most cited judgements (judgements having inward citations greater than or equal to three), and some of the judgements having the highest outward citations (judgements having at least three outward citations) ranked in order.

In Table 3.3, there are eleven judgements, each of which has received three or more citations with Radhy Shyam vs. State of U.P. having a maximum of thirteen inward citations. In Table 3.4, there are nine judgements which have cited three or more judgements with Women Education Trust vs. State of Haryana having a maximum of five outward citations. The two lists have only one judgement, V. Chandrasekaran vs. the Administrative Officer, in common. All judgements in the two lists taken together came in 2010 or later. A closer look into the judgements given in Table 3.4 reveals that the judgements having high outward citations tend to cite recent judgements. For instance, all five citations made by Women Education Trust vs. State of Haryana are cases decided in 2011. A similar picture emerges if the other judgements with high outdegree are looked into.

Table 3.3 Judgments with indegree greater than or equal to three

Judgement	Indegree	Year	Bench	LAA Clauses
Radhy Shyam vs. State of U.P.	13	2011	G. S. Singhvi, A. K. Ganguly	4, 5, 17
Dev Sharan vs. State of U.P.	9	2011	G. S. Singhvi, A. K. Ganguly	4, 5, 6, 17
Banda Dev. Authority vs. Agarwal	8	2011	G. S. Singhvi, A. K. Ganguly	4, 6, 11, 17
Raghbir Singh Sehrawat vs. State of Haryana	6	2011	G. S. Singhvi, S. J. Mukhopadhayay	5, 16
Kamal Trading vs. State of West Bengal	3	2011	G. S. Singhvi, R. P. Desai	4, 5, 6, 17
Offshore Holdings vs. Bangalore Dev. Authority	3	2011	S. H. Kapadia, M. Sharma, K. S. P. Radhakrishnan, S. Kumar, A. R. Dave	11
Valliyammal vs. Spl. Tehsildar	3	2011	G. S. Singhvi, H. L. Dattu	4, 18, 23, 24, 54
Anjani Molu Dessai vs. State of Goa	3	2010	R. V. Raveendran, A. K. Patnaik	23
Surinder Singh Brar vs. Union of India	3	2012	G. S. Singhvi, S. J. Mukhopadhayay	5, 6, 7
V. Chandrasekaran vs. the Administrative Officer	3	2012	B. S. Chauhan, J. S. Khehar	4, 5, 6, 18
Brij Pal Bhargava vs. State of U.P.	3	2011	V. S. Sirpurka, A. R. Dave	4, 5, 6

Table 3.4 Judgments with outdegree greater than or equal to 3

Judgement	Outdegree	Year	Bench	LAA Clauses
Women Education Trust vs. State of Haryana	5	2013	G. S. Singhvi, S. A. Bobde	48, 5
Patasi Devi vs. State of Haryana	4	2012	G. S. Singhvi, S. J. Mukhopadhyay	4, 6
Gojer Brothers vs. State of West Bengal	4	2013	G. S. Singhvi, C. Nagappan	5
Haryana Industrial Dev. Corp. vs. Udal	4	2013	G. S. Singhvi, S. J. Mukhopadhyay	28, 54
Darshan Lal Nagpal vs. Govt. of NCT of Delhi	3	2012	G. S. Singhvi, S. J. Mukhopadhyay	17
V. Chandrasekaran vs. the Administrative Officer	3	2012	B. S. Chauhan, J. S. Khehar	4, 6, 17
Delhi Airtech Services vs. State of U.P.	3	2011	A. K.Ganguly, S. Kumar	11, 17
Usha Stud vs. State of Haryana	3	2013	G. S. Singhvi, R. P. Desai, K. Joseph	5, 6
Bhule Ram vs. Union of India	3	2014	B. S. Chauhan, J. Chelameswar	23

The clauses of the Land Acquisition Act which have been discussed in each of these 19 cases are also shown in the above tables. A look into these clauses gives us an idea about the questions which have been repeatedly raised and debated in land acquisition cases. It appears from the tables that one of the most commonly litigated issues in the Land Acquisition Act, 1894 is related to the use of the Urgency Clause[7] and around 36.8 % of the listed cases have raised concerns over the application of such a strong condemnation clause. Again, a large proportion (47.37 %) of the cases have dealt with the issue of improper or unlawful notification for acquisition and the complications arising from it. More specifically, Section 4 has found its way repeatedly in the litigation process of these cases[8]. Finally, matters related to the question of public purpose[9] have come up for litigation very often. About 54.5 % of judgements with high inward citations and 33.33 % of the judgements with high outward

[7] Section 17, LAA: Special powers in case of urgency. In cases of urgency whenever the [appropriate Government], so directs, the Collector, though no such award has been made, may, on the expiration of 15 days from the publication of the notice mentioned in section 9, sub-section 1 [take possession of any land needed for a public purpose]. Such land shall thereupon [vest absolutely in the [Government], free from all encumbrances.

[8] Section 4, LAA: Publication of preliminary notification and power of officers thereupon.—(1) Whenever it appears to the [appropriate Government] the land in any locality [is needed or] is likely to be needed for any public purpose [or for a company], a notification to that effect shall be published in the Official Gazette [and in two daily newspapers circulating in that locality of which at least one shall be in the regional language], and the Collector shall cause public notice of the substance of such notification to be given at convenient places in the said locality [(the last of the dates of such publication and the giving of such public notice, being hereinafter referred to as the date of the publication of the notification)].

[9] Section 6, LAA: Declaration that land is required for a public purpose.

citations have discussed the Public Purpose Clause. Surprisingly, demands for enhancement of compensation[10] have come up in a very small number of these cases.

When we consider the composition of the benches of these judgements, what strikes us most is the overwhelming presence of a single judge, G. S. Singhvi. Seven out of eleven judgements in Table 3.3 and six out of nine judgements in Table 3.4 have been presided over by Justice Singhvi. About 27.27 % of the most cited judgements have a single and identical bench consisting of G. S.Singhvi and A. K. Ganguly whereas 33.33 % of the judgements which cite other judgements highly have been made by a bench consisting of G. S. Singhvi and Sudhansu J. Mukhopadhyay. It is also interesting to point out that the bench of almost every (all but one) judgement that has been cited by one of the six G. S. Singhvi-headed benches in Table 3.4 is also headed by G. S. Singhvi. Thus, we can say that the network displays significant overlap between the benches of important cases and the repeated presence of a few judges in a large number of these cases.

The graph in Fig. 3.2 represents the network of the top nineteen judgements discussed above. It is clear from the graph that fifteen of these judgements are densely connected and there is a large number of citations among them. Two cases out of these nineteen do not possess links with the rest and hence remain isolated while two others have a single link between them. Not surprisingly, the judgements constituting the bigger component in this network structure are cases decided and cited

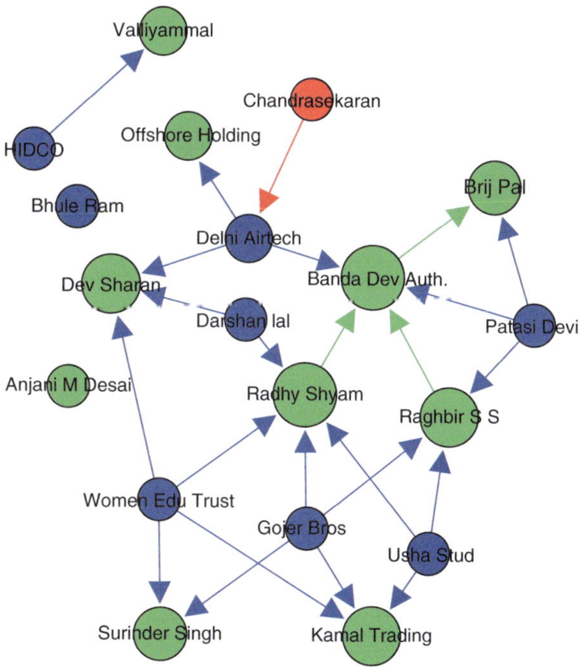

Fig. 3.2 The citation network of some of the top cited and top citing land acquisition decisions from the Supreme Court of India

[10] Section 23, LAA: Matters to be considered on determining compensation.

by benches most of which have Justice Singhvi present in them. The two isolates, on the other hand, are cases decided by benches completely different from the ones in the bigger component.

3.5 Conclusion

In this chapter, we use the tools of network analysis to study the citation behaviour of the Supreme Court of India with reference to its judgements on land acquisition. The empirical observations drawn from our analysis leads us to the following conclusions: (a) the world of land acquisition judgements of the Supreme Court of India is a small one, (b) there are very few judgements which have a significant number of citations and (c) there is substantial overlap between benches of the prominent judgements in the network. Our conclusions, though limited in scope due to the size of our dataset, are rather striking and encourage us to continue further with our exploration.[11]

References

Banerjee AV, Bardhan P, Basu K, Chaudhury MD, Ghatak M, Guha AS, Majumdar M, Mookerjee D, Ray D (2007) Beyond nandigram: industrialisation in West Bengal. Econ Polit Wkly 42(17):1487–1489

Desai M (2011) Land acquisition law and the proposed changes. Econ Polit Wkly 46(26and27): 95–100

Eskridge W (1991) Overriding supreme court statutory interpretation decisions. Yale Law J 101(2):331–455

Fowler JH, Jeon S (2008) The authority of supreme court precedent. Social Networks 30(1):16–30

Ghatak M, Ghosh P (2011) The land acquisition bill: a critique and a proposal. Econ Polit Wkly 46(41):65–72

Goyal S, Leij MJ van der, MoragaGonzalez JL (April 2006) Economics: an emerging small world. J Polit Econ 114(2):403–412

Knight J, Epstein L (1996) The norm of stare decisis. Am J Polit Sci 40(4):1018–1035

Landes WM, Posner RA (1976) Legal precedent: a theoretical and empirical analysis. J Law Econ 19(2):249–307

Sarkar A (2007) Development and displacement: land acquisition in West Bengal. Econ Polit Wkly 42(16):1435–1442

Segal JA, Spaeth HJ (1996) The influence of stare decisis on the votes of united states supreme court justices. Am J Polit Sci 40(4):971–1003

Watts DJ (1999) Small worlds: the dynamics of networks between order and randomness. Princeton university press, UK.

[11] The paper is a small part of an ongoing research on citation behaviour of Indian courts. Currently we are working on the construction of the entire network of judgements from the Supreme Court of India. Our objective is to test the robustness of the empirical results presented in this chapter and come up with a theoretical explanation of the pattern of judicial citations.

List of Important Judgements

Radhy Shyam vs. State of U.P., 2011, *MANU/SC/0429/2011*.
Dev Sharan vs. State of U.P., 2011, *MANU/SC/0178/2011*.
Banda Dev. Authority vs. Agarwal, *2011, MANU/SC/0515/2011*.
Raghbir Singh Sehrawat vs. State of Haryana, 2011, *MANU/SC/1429/2011*. Kamal Trading vs. State of West Bengal, 2011,*MANU/SC/1492/2011*.
Offshore Holdings vs. Bangalore Dev. Authority, 2011, *MANU/SC/0060/2011*.
Valliyammal vs. Spl. Tehsildar, 2011, *MANU/SC/0877/2011*.
Anjani Molu Dessai vs. State of Goa, 2010, *MANU/SC/1156/2010*.
Surinder Singh Brar vs. Union of India, 2012, *MANU/SC/0849/2012*.
V. Chandrasekaran vs. the Administrative Officer, 2012, *MANU/SC/0751/2012*.
Women Education Trust vs. State of Haryana, 2013, *MANU/SC/0504/2013*.
Patasi Devi vs. State of Haryana, 2012, *MANU/SC/0706/2012*.
Gojer Brothers vs. State of West Bengal, 2013, *MANU/SC/1279/2013*.
Haryana Industrial Dev. Corp. vs. Udal, 2013, *MANU/SC/0637/2013*.
Darshan Lal Nagpal vs. Govt. of NCT of Delhi, 2012, *MANU/SC/0008/2012*.
Delhi Airtech Services vs. State of U.P., 2011, *MANU/SC/0956/2011*.
Usha Stud vs. State of Haryana, 2013, *MANU/SC/0286/2013*.
Bhule Ram vs. Union of India, 2014, *MANU/SC/0249/2014*.
Brij Pal Bhargava vs. State of U.P., 2011, *MANU/SC/0149/2011*.

Chapter 4
Surrogacy Contracting and Intermediation

Amrita Pramanick and Swapnendu Banerjee

4.1 Introduction

> "We have helped over 8000 couples to achieve their dreams of having a baby,
> 999 successful pregnancies out of 1876 in 2012…….
> Success rates: 45–48 % IVF, 55 % Egg donation, 65 % for embryo donation, 50 % for IVF with surrogacy…….
> We have state of the art infrastructure to deliver technologically advanced and reliable services,
> Fully equipped operation theatres"…………………………
>
> An Advertisement of an Indian Infertility Clinic[1]

An online search for an infertility clinic in India would pop up several advertisements similar to the above quoted one. This is the booming infertility tourism industry of today's India, providing the world with a low-cost assisted reproductive technology (ART), promising infertile couples a haven where "prayers meet destiny" or where you will be assured to "come as couple…………leave as family." This is the world of the modern infertility business. One may criticize it, or may endorse it as a boon to childless couples, yet there is no denying the increasing importance of these intermediate agencies in today's surrogacy business.

We are thankful for the valuable comments received at the national and international conferences at Burdwan University and Rabindra Bharati University, and all the internal presentations at Jadavpur University. We are responsible for all remaining errors, if any.

[1] Dr. Rama's Institute for Fertility. Available at www.fertilityindia.com.

A. Pramanick (✉) · S. Banerjee
Department of Economics, Jadavpur University, Kolkata 700032, India
e-mail: amrita.anamika8@gmail.com

S. Banerjee
e-mail: swapnendu@hotmail.com

S. Banerjee et al. (eds.), *Understanding Development*, India Studies in Business and Economics, DOI 10.1007/978-81-322-2455-6_4

What is surrogate motherhood? According to the Merriam-Webster online dictionary, a surrogate mother is defined as "a woman who becomes pregnant usually by artificial insemination or surgical implantation of a fertilized egg for the purpose of carrying the fetus to term for another woman, who is medically incapable of doing so." Therefore, a surrogate mother is the one who carries a baby and gives birth for another woman who cannot conceive and/or carry a baby successfully. The couple who hires a surrogate is known as the intended parents (IP) or the commissioning couple (ACOG 2004). There are two kinds of surrogacy: (i) straight (natural/traditional) and (ii) gestational (or host).

To explain briefly, in straight surrogacy, the sperm of the intended father is used to inseminate the surrogate and therefore, the surrogate becomes both the genetic and gestational mother. While the intended father is also the genetic father, the intended mother is only a rearing mother (ACOG 2004)[2]. In gestational surrogacy, the egg and sperm of the IPs are fertilized externally and the embryo transferred to the uterus of the surrogate. This process is known as in-vitro-fertilization and embryo-transfer (IVF-ET). Here, the surrogate is only a gestational carrier and the IPs are the biological (or genetic) parents[3,4]. From a legal standpoint, surrogacy contracts can be of two broad types—"altruistic," where no money is paid to the surrogates for her "services" (mainly in excess of necessary medical expenses), and "commercial" where money (or incentives) is paid to the surrogates for her "services" (in excess of medical expenses).

Another important feature of the institution of surrogacy is the existence of the intermediate agencies like infertility clinics. These clinics generally match commissioning couples with prospective surrogates. They also provide various other services, ranging from finding and screening prospective surrogates, providing medical assistance, and in some cases, monitoring the surrogate throughout the entire duration of the pregnancy. Anand, a small town in Gujarat has umpteen infertility clinics and there are many more in other big cities in India.[5]

There are a large number of issues regarding the institution of surrogacy that can be addressed: Whether the institution is a "godsend" for childless couples or a threat to the very fabric of society? Does it allow fertile women to fulfill a social responsibility, or does it lead to commoditization of women? Issues like whether or not such markets should be prohibited outright or regulated[6], should the payment to

---

[2] For more details, see ICMR 2004.

[3] For more details, see ICMR 2004.

[4] We ignore the case where the donor's sperm is combined with the donor's or surrogate's eggs because the child is not genetically related to the IPs.

[5] There are almost 1000 registered and unregistered fertility centers across India, the major concentration being found in Delhi, Mumbai, Gujarat, and Kolkata. Mumbai alone has been reported to have only 20 registered ART clinics, whereas at least a 100 of them can be found operating within the city. For more detailed report visit http://www.telegraphindia.com/1131201/jsp/7days/17630848.jsp or http://www.telegraphindia.com/1030520/asp/calcutta/story_1983916.asp.

[6] For regulation and ethical guidelines in Australia, refer to the report 'Ethical Guidelines on the Use of Assisted Reproductive Technology in Clinical Practice and Research' by The National Health and Medical Research Council, Government of Australia (2007). Available at https://www.nhmrc.gov.au.

a surrogate be banned[7] so that the service remains altruistic, what the "sacredness" of human life means in an economic context, can be discussed at large. But in this chapter, we abstain from such issues.[8]

In this chapter, we model the role of intermediate agencies and try to characterize optimal surrogacy contracts in the presence of an intermediate agency which provides monitoring and other services to the IPs. No paper has attempted to model the behavior of intermediate agencies or infertility clinics till date. Therefore, this chapter makes an attempt to fill this gap, and in this regard, it is the first to do so. Specifically, with the help of a moral hazard framework with limited liability. We show that there exists moral hazard incentives for the surrogacy agency and under non-verifiability, the intermediate agency will be found to put in suboptimal monitoring effort. Interestingly, for the lower outside option of the surrogate, the agency's optimal monitoring increases with the altruism of the surrogate whereas for the higher outside option, optimal monitoring depends solely on the surrogate's outside option and is independent of the surrogate's altruism. In addition, we completely characterize the contract between the IPs and the intermediate agency. We show that it is optimum for the IPs to pay only an incentive payment to the agency, and therefore, the optimal fixed payment to the agency is zero. Note that in this chapter, without loss of generality, we focus on commercial gestational surrogacy contracts only[9] where it is assumed that money can be paid to the surrogate for her "services" either legally (or illegally) and the legality aspect is not the focus of this chapter.

Our chapter is related to the contract-theoretic literature on the "womb market" (Banerjee 2013; Banerjee and Basu 2009)[10]. Banerjee (2013) addressed the debate on whether a surrogacy institution should be "commercial or altruistic." Using the classic moral hazard framework with limited liability, he analyzed conditions under which a surrogacy contract should be commercial or altruistic. Also, Banerjee and Basu (2009), in an incomplete contracting framework, showed that if child-specific care is noncontractible then surrogates optimally invest less (take less care) than the first-best. Couples are also more likely to choose low-type surrogates, who need less compensation for foregoing cheaper outside options. Hence the popular practice of making surrogacy contracts unenforceable might be counterproductive and puts the unborn child at risk. Interestingly, both papers assume away the role of intermediate agencies, viz., infertility clinics and focus on optimal bilateral contracts between the IPs and the surrogate. In this chapter, we specifically model the behavior of intermediate agencies and characterize optimal surrogacy contracts, and this constitutes a crucial departure of this chapter with Banerjee (2013)[11].

---

[7] For example, in the UK, payments in excess of medical expenses, that is, incentive payments are strictly prohibited (For legal guidelines on surrogacy practices and legislation in UK, visit http://www.legislation.gov.uk/ukpga/2008/22/pdfs/ukpga_20080022_en.pdf).

[8] For more on ethical discussions on surrogacy markets, see Ergas (2004), Posner (1989).

[9] Other forms of surrogacy can also be analyzed under this structure with slight modification.

[10] See Hatzis (2003) for a general equilibrium approach on surrogacy.

[11] Also Banerjee and Basu (2013) to some extent.

4.1.1 Intermediate Agencies and the Indian Surrogacy Market: Recent Trends

Each year, millions of frozen embryo packages are flown into India from all over the world. Baby Daniela was one of them. She was a 5-day-old embryo in 2007 when she was first put on a plane, alone. She hopped continents, starting her journey at New York, before landing in New Delhi, and then was transferred to her destination at a Mumbai-based surrogacy clinic. Born in a Mumbai hospital through a surrogate, in association with Surrogacy India (an infertility clinic) in January 2010, Baby Daniela was a bundle of joy to her American parents Ilona and Stan Slezinger, whose hopes were repeatedly thwarted by the expenditure estimates in the USA[12] (Deshpande, *The Times Of India*, 2010[13]).

Infertility clinics and/or surrogacy agencies have become a vital component of the outsourced surrogacy industry in India.[14] These are clinics that provide medical facilities and services. The intermediate agency navigates the market and is responsible for the matching and appointment of the surrogates for each pair of intended parents that approach her. In any case, the surrogate is not directly recruited by the intended parent. After IVF-ET and successful initiation of the pregnancy, the clinic is also responsible for providing shelter and taking care of the surrogate. So, that the Clinic is in a position to monitor the surrogate throughout the pregnancy.[15]

The mediation provided by these groups has become more important against the recent splurge in international demand for surrogates in India. Information gaps, differences in language, and ethnic and cultural differences make direct communication between foreign IPs and an Indian surrogate difficult. These intermediate surrogacy agencies often help smoothening these cross-cultural frictions and hence contribute to the growth of this market to a large extent. Moreover, easy availability of low-cost surrogates coupled with quality medical facilities has made India one of the most desirable destinations for infertility tourism.

Unlike in the USA and some of the developed countries, in India the absence of legal representation for either the surrogate or the IPs has rendered the situation precarious for both parties. Problems due to asymmetry of information, incompetence of the intermediate agency and/or faulty screening of a surrogate often put the surrogate's health as well as the commissioning couples' rights at stake. The recent case of an Australian couple stands testimony to this concern: An Australian woman[16]

---

[12] The usual costs of a complete surrogacy arrangement in the USA is anything between $ 1,50,000 and $ 2,50,000, making it accessible only to a limited category of financially well-off infertility patients.

[13] Available at http://articles.timesofindia.indiatimes.com/2010-02-02/mumbai/28125556_1_ilona-surrogacy-ivf.

[14] See Krawiec (2009).

[15] This is distinct from the trend practiced in the USA. The surrogate's pregnancy is directly monitored by the IP or is periodically monitored by the agency. Constant vigilance is not the norm in the USA.

[16] Identity not revealed in the report, on request of the IPs.

had accused an Indian surrogacy agency of delivering a baby who was not genetically related to the woman and her husband (i.e., the commissioning couple). The agency initially denied all charges but the repeated DNA tests did prove the couple's allegation. In spite of this, the agency did nothing to compensate the IPs for their financial (and emotional) loss but only offered another surrogacy procedure free of charge.[17] This is a classic case of moral hazard on the part of the intermediate agencies and a blatant breach of contract as the agency had failed to deliver the couple with a biological child. The couple did not receive any proper legal support either. The intermediate agencies are supposed to monitor the surrogates, but the question remains, "Who is going to monitor the 'monitor'?"

While in India surrogacy is not illegally practiced, there is still no legislation that dictates a code of conduct for infertility clinics. India has decent guidelines in ART (ICMR 2004), but the industry for infertility treatment lacks proper legal structure and legal clarity regarding the transfer of parental rights and entitlement of nationality, among others.[18]

The structure of the chapter is as follows. In Sect. 4.2, we present the basic model of bilateral contracting between a set of intended parents and the intermediate agency. Section 4.3 will discuss ideas for further extensions. And Sect. 4.4 will conclude this chapter.

4.2 The Baseline Model

Following Banerjee (2013), we explore an interaction between a set of (IPs) and a surrogate mother (gestational carrier) who will be willing to bear their child through IVF-ET. However, we assume that the IPs can only get in touch with a surrogate through an intermediate agency (viz., an infertility clinic), and this is the crucial difference of this chapter with Banerjee (2013).[19] All parties are assumed to be risk neutral. We assume that the IP is otherwise medically capable in the sense that the husband has normal sperm count and the wife is capable of producing normal ovum, but because of certain medical problems,[20] the wife is incapable of carrying a baby till term and therefore needs a surrogate to have a biological baby. After in vitro fertilization, the embryo is transferred to the gestational surrogate and the

[17] Available at http://www.eggdonor.com/blog/2013/03/22/surrogacy-horror-stories-india.

[18] For more, see Smerdon (2008).

[19] This assumption of a mediated interaction between the IPs and the surrogate validates the market structure where there are huge search costs in finding an appropriate match as per the specific requirements of the intended parents. In addition, there is certain technical knowledge that is required to make the match. Often these intermediating agencies (infertility clinics) have the technical knowhow to make such matches. These clinics also offer services ranging from legal assistance to medical provisions and taking care of the surrogate through pregnancy. http://timesofindia.indiatimes.com/india/Meeting-the-cost-of-conceiving/articleshow/45747254.cms.

[20] Problems like (i) hysterectomy, (ii) absence or malformation of uterus since birth, (iii) diabetes, multiple sclerosis, heart and kidney diseases, and (iv) repeated miscarriages. See Sect. 1 of Banerjee and Basu (2009) for details. Also see Banerjee (2013)

surrogate starts taking care of the unborn child. Delivery takes place after the biological gestation period is over. Therefore, similar to Banerjee (2013), the the IP provides the genetic material of the baby and the surrogate is only a gestational carrier.[21] We assume that the property right of the baby remains with the IPs and the surrogate is supposed to hand over the baby to the IPs after everything is successfully completed.[22] Alternatively, the IPs can choose to adopt, if they do not want to remain childless. To focus sharply on surrogacy, we make a simplifying assumption that the IP prefers a genetic child to an adopted one. This does not affect the qualitative aspect of our chapter.

The structure of the game is as follows: The IPs approach an intermediate agency (or an infertility clinic) for a prospective surrogate. The IPs do not enter into a contract with the surrogate directly; instead, after the surrogate is selected by the intermediate agency, the IPs and the intermediate agency enter into a contract. The IP is assumed to offer the intermediate agency a fixed pay F and a fraction of the utility gain from a successful project (money equivalent, that is, an incentive bonus in case of successful delivery of a healthy child. The intermediate agency, on the other hand, contracts with the surrogate directly and in turn pays a fixed fee B to the surrogate, irrespective of whether the process succeeds or not. This assumption can be justified on the ground of limited liability, and the surrogate is assumed to have no wealth such that she cannot be punished for a bad outcome[23]. The intermediate agency (or the infertility clinic) monitors the effort of the surrogate, that is, whether or not the surrogate is putting in a requisite amount of effort (child-specific care)[24]; the infertility clinic provides unobservable and hence noncontractible monitoring effort denoted by m, which also affects the *effective* probability of success of the project, the implication of which will be made clear soon. This monitoring is costly to the agency and the cost is given as $\frac{m^2}{2}$. To fix ideas, we assume that the infertility clinic can monitor the surrogate's effort perfectly, but the question is whether it will do it properly. Therefore, in this chapter, we abstain from the surrogate's moral hazard[25]. Rather, we focus on moral hazard on the part of the intermediate agency or the infertility clinics. The outside option of the infertility clinic is normalized to zero for simplicity.

The outcome of the surrogacy process can be high, which is the birth of a normal child and we denote it by $q_H = 1$. The outcome might also be low, which can be interpreted as failure of the surrogacy process (might lead to a birth of a defective baby or a still baby or otherwise) that can be denoted by $q_L = 0$.[26] The process can succeed with an idiosyncratic probability $p \varepsilon (0,1)$, if the surrogate puts in positive

[21] Therefore without loss of generality, we focus on gestational surrogacy and other forms of surrogacy that can be easily accommodated in our model with slight modifications.

[22] ICMR guidelines in India support this assumption.

[23] Recent surrogacy contracts in India follow this pattern.

[24] Maintaining a medically restrained lifestyle, not indulging in any addiction, not undertaking any strenuous jobs, etc.

[25] This has been dealt in Banerjee (2013).

[26] Therefore without loss of generality we focus on a 0–1 outcome.

effort, but certainly fails if the surrogate puts in zero effort. This assumption can be justified on the grounds that many serious complications might arise post IVF-ET, which are beyond the control of the surrogate even if she takes proper care while gestating.[27] Therefore, with monitoring, the *effective* probability of success of the process is *mp*. This implies that the project fails certainly if the infertility clinic does not monitor at all (i.e., when $m = 0$).[28] Once again we emphasize that we do not model the effort of the surrogate, which has already been done in Banerjee (2013).

In case of success, the IPs get a fixed utility $V > 0$ for having a biological baby and 0 if the process fails. We assume that the surrogate is altruistic and receives a nonpecuniary benefit (warm-glow) of $\lambda \cdot V$ for successfully helping out the IPs where $\lambda > 0$. If $\lambda > 1$, then the surrogate is very altruistic and derives more pleasure than the IPs. Also, we assume for simplicity that, in case of a failure, the surrogate does not receive any altruistic pleasure. The surrogate is assumed to have an outside option denoted by $\overline{U} > 0$. We summarize the timeline of the game below.

4.2.1 The Timeline

1. The The IP approaches the infertility clinic and offers an outcome contingent contract $\{F, F + \alpha V\}$ to the infertility clinic where a fixed sum F is paid to the clinic in case of failure and $F + \alpha V$ is paid when the project succeeds. α is the share of satisfaction (money equivalent) that the IP pays the infertility clinic in case of success.
2. The infertility clinic then searches for a surrogate and enters in to a contract with the surrogate. The clinic offers a fixed fee B to the surrogate irrespective of whether the project succeeds or not. If any one party disagrees, the game ends.
3. After all parties agree, IVF-ET takes place and the surrogate starts taking care (surrogate's effort) of the unborn child. The clinic can monitor the surrogate's effort perfectly.
4. The infertility clinic chooses monitoring effort m.
5. Delivery takes place and payments are settled depending on the outcome.

Given the above structure, the IP's surplus function is given by

$$\pi_{IP} = m \cdot p(V - \alpha V) - F. \tag{4.1}$$

The intermediate agency's expected payoff can be written as

---

[27] Surrogates can face health risks like ectopic (outside uterus) pregnancy, multiple pregnancies, and ovarian hyperstimulation. These might lead to problems like diabetes, miscarriage, hemorrhage, kidney damage, and high blood pressure. These risks pose a threat to the unborn child as well. With ectopic pregnancy or ovarian hyperstimulation, the fetus might die or pregnancy might be terminated. In multiple pregnancies, there is a higher risk of preterm delivery, low birth weight, stillbirth, neonatal death, and subsequent problems like cerebral palsy (www.ivf-infertility.com, ICMR 2004).

[28] An alternative intuition might be that if the infertility clinic does not monitor, then the surrogate puts in zero effort and therefore the project fails with certainty.

$$\pi_{IA} = F + m{\cdot}p{\cdot}\alpha{\cdot}V - m^2/2 - B. \tag{4.2}$$

And the surrogate's expected payoff will be

$$\pi_S = m\ (B + p{\cdot}\lambda{\cdot}V) + (1-m){\cdot}B,$$

which can be simplified as

$$B + m{\cdot}p{\cdot}\lambda{\cdot}V. \tag{4.3}$$

4.2.2 The Optimal Contracting Problem

First, we examine the situation when the monitoring effort of the intermediate agency is contractible. Optimal monitoring effort in the absence of any informational asymmetry will be chosen so as to maximize the expected joint surplus of the IPs, the intermediate agency, and the surrogate. However, the contract offered to the surrogate will have no allocative role in this situation. Therefore, under the first-best, the optimization problem becomes

$$\max_{m\in[0,1]} S = m{\cdot}p{\cdot}(1+\lambda)V - \frac{m^2}{2}. \tag{4.4}$$

The optimal first-best monitoring effort will be $m^* = (1+\lambda){\cdot}p{\cdot}V$. The maximized first-best joint surplus will therefore be $S^* = \frac{(1+\lambda)^2{\cdot}p^2{\cdot}V^2}{2}$. The first-best monitoring effort and the optimal first-best joint surplus increases with the altruism of the surrogate and the idiosyncratic success probability of the process.

Now we examine the situation where the monitoring effort of the intermediate agency is unobservable and hence noncontractible. Therefore, the optimal contracting problem of the IPs can be represented as the following maximization problem:

$$\max_{\{F,\alpha\}} m{\cdot}p{\cdot}(1-\alpha){\cdot}V - F. \tag{4.5}$$

Subject to the following constraints:

1. The participation constraint of the intermediate agency (PCIA) stating that it must receive at least its outside option

$$F + m{\cdot}p{\cdot}\alpha{\cdot}V - \frac{m^2}{2} - B \geqq 0 \tag{PCIA}$$

2. The incentive compatibility constraint of the intermediate agency (ICIA) stating that it chooses the monitoring level that maximizes its expected payoff

$$m = arg\max_{\widehat{m}} \left\{ F + \widehat{m}.p.\alpha.V - \frac{\widehat{m}^2}{2} - B \right\} \qquad \text{(ICIA)}$$

3. The participation constraint of the surrogate (PCS) stating that she must at least be given her outside option:

$$B + m \cdot p \cdot \lambda \cdot V \geqq \bar{U} \qquad (PCS)$$

4. The limited liability constraints of both the intermediate agency and the surrogate

$$F \geqq 0, B \geqq 0 \qquad (LL)$$

The solution concept can be visualized as a multistage process. The intermediate agency, while offering the contract to the surrogate, will internalize the fact that the surrogate will have to be offered a "*B*" such that the PCS of the surrogate holds and assuming that the agency has all the bargaining power and will offer a B such that PCS holds with equality, that is, $B = \bar{U} - m \cdot p \cdot \lambda \cdot V$. The intermediate agency will internalize this into its payoff function and will choose its optimal monitoring effort, and this gives us the incentive compatibility of the intermediate agency which can be written as

$$m = arg\max_{\hat{m}} \left\{ F + \hat{m} \cdot p \cdot \alpha \cdot V - \frac{\hat{m}^2}{2} - \bar{U} + \hat{m} \cdot p \cdot \lambda \cdot V \right\} = (\alpha + \lambda) \cdot p \cdot V \; \ldots\ldots\ldots \; (ICIA)$$

Incorporating the above incentive compatibility constraint and the optimal *B*, the resulting optimal contracting of the IPs can be represented as the following maximization problem:

$$\max_{\{F, \alpha\}} m \cdot p \cdot (1 - \alpha) \cdot V - F$$

subject to

$$F + \frac{p^2 \cdot (\alpha + \lambda)^2 \cdot V^2}{2} - \bar{U} \geqq 0 \qquad (PCIA)$$

$$m^* = (\alpha + \lambda) \cdot p \cdot V \qquad (ICIA)$$

The limited liability constraint of the intermediate agency

$$F \geqq 0 \qquad (LLIA)$$

The above representation makes it clear that the contract between the intermediate agency and the surrogate is already assumed to be settled before the agency may decide whether to accept or reject the contract offered by the IPs. The intermediate agency's (PCIA) has now been modified to incorporate his liability to pay the surrogate at least her reservation payoff $\bar{U}$. Thus, now this model will be solved as a simple bilateral contract between the IPs and the infertility clinic. The (LLS) will always bind at the optimum whereas (PCIA) may or may not bind depending on the outside option of the surrogate.

We must understand that the principal never offers a contract that will drag his profits below zero. Let U' be the surrogate's reservation utility corresponding to which the intermediate agency receives zero expected payoff. Further, let U^0 present the value of the surrogate's reservation utility such that for all $\bar{U} > U^0$ the intermediate agency's participation constraint binds. Thus, for complete characterization of optimal contracts, we focus on two particularly relevant ranges of $\bar{U}$, (i) $\bar{U} \in [0, U^0]$ where the intermediate agency's (PCIA) does not bind and (ii) $\bar{U} \in [U^0, U']$ where the (PCIA) binds. Thus, we now attempt to specify the exact levels of $\bar{U}$ and the corresponding optimal contracts under the two above stated situations.

Case1: PCIA Does Not Bind This is the situation when PCIA does not bind, and this arises when the value of $\bar{U}$ is not very high and $\bar{U} \in [\frac{\lambda(1+\lambda)}{2} p^2V^2, \frac{1}{2}\left(\frac{1+\lambda}{2}\right)^2 p^2V^2]$ holds. The lower limit of $\bar{U}$ ensures that B is nonnegative. In addition to this, for tractability of solutions, we assume that the following holds:

Assumption

1. $\lambda \leq \frac{1}{3}$.

Assumption 1 ensures that the above range of $\bar{U}$ exists. Since F doesn't affect the intermediate agency's choice of m at the optimum, it is optimal for the IP to set $F^* = 0$, implying that at the optimum, the LLIA will bind. Internalizing ICIA and $F^* = 0$ into the IP's payoff function, we get that the IP will optimally choose α so as to $\max_{\alpha} \pi_{IP} = p^2 \cdot (\alpha + \lambda) \cdot (1 - \alpha) \cdot V^2$ and we get the following result:

Proposition 1 Suppose assumption 1 holds and

$$\bar{U} \in [\frac{\lambda(1+\lambda)}{2} p^2V^2, \frac{1}{2}\left(\frac{1+\lambda}{2}\right)^2 p^2V^2]$$

a. The IP will offer $\alpha^* = \frac{1-\lambda}{2}$ fraction of their satisfaction (money equivalent) to the intermediate agency as incentive bonus in case of success. The optimal incentive bonus decreases with the altruism of the surrogate.
b. The optimal fixed fee offered by the IP will be $F^* = 0$.
c. The optimum monitoring effort by the intermediate agency will be $m^* = \frac{(1+\lambda)}{2} p \cdot V$ which is less than the first-best effort. The optimal monitoring effort increases with the surrogates' altruism and the idiosyncratic probability of success.
d. The optimal payment offered by the intermediate agency to the surrogate is given by $B^* = \bar{U} - \frac{\lambda.(1+\lambda)}{2} p^2 \cdot V^2$. The more altruistic the surrogate is, the lower the compensation she receives for her efforts.

The proof of the above result is straightforward and follows from the above discussion. The only thing to check is the optimality of the contract for all parties. For $B^* > 0$ we need $\bar{U} > \frac{\lambda(1+\lambda)}{2} p^2V^2$. Again, putting optimal α^*, F^*, B^* and m^* in the intermediate agency's payoff function, we get $\pi_{IA}^* = \frac{1}{2}\left(\frac{1+\lambda}{2}\right)^2 p^2V^2 - \bar{U}$. For $\pi_{IA}^* > 0$ we need $\bar{U} < \frac{1}{2}\left(\frac{1+\lambda}{2}\right)^2 p^2V^2$. Given assumption 1 holds, the surrogate and the intermediate agency get at least their respective outside options. The IPs' optimal payoff is $\pi_{IP}^* = \left(\frac{1+\lambda}{2}\right)^2 p^2V^2$ which is again greater than their outside option, which is zero. Thus the solution is optimal.

The intuition of the above results is not difficult to explain. The more altruistic a surrogate, the lesser the payment needed to make her accept the contract. The impact of the surrogate's altruism on the optimal monitoring effort is a bit non-trivial. Conventional wisdom suggests that a more altruistic surrogate need not be monitored that much. But in this model, we assume that monitoring is perfect in the following sense: if monitoring is zero, the surrogate will shirk and the process is sure to fail. But if monitoring is *m*, then the effective probability of success is $m \cdot p$ (which includes the idiosyncratic success probability *p*) and this increases with *m*. Therefore, the effective probability of success depends on m perfectly and the intermediate agency can perfectly control the effective probability of success through m. Now we explain the effect of the surrogate's altruism on the optimal monitoring effort. If λ increases, *B* falls. This fall in *B* increases with an increase in *m*. Therefore, from the point of view of the intermediate agency, the gain from monitoring is higher in case of a more altruistic surrogate, and therefore optimal monitoring increases the more altruistic the surrogate is. Finally, it is optimal for the IPs to pay a lower *F* since *F* does not affect *m*. But optimal α falls with λ. This is due to the fact that *m* increases with λ so the IPs need not incentivize the intermediate agency that much the more altruistic the surrogate is.

Case 2: PCIA Binds In this situation $\bar{U}$ is sufficiently high such that PCIA binds. Specifically, we will concentrate on the value of $\bar{U}$ such that $\bar{U} \in \left[\frac{1}{2}\left(\frac{1+\lambda}{2}\right)^2 p^2V^2, \frac{p^2V^2(1+\lambda)^2}{2}\right]$ holds. The lower limit of $\bar{U}$ ensures that PCIA binds and the upper limit, as we will see, ensures that the optimal $\alpha^* < 1$. Therefore, in this case, the solution will be determined both by the binding limited liability and the PCS of the intermediate agency. Thus, the solution to the optimal contract in this situation is as follows:

Proposition 2 Suppose assumption 1 and $\bar{U} \in \left[\frac{1}{2}\left(\frac{1+\lambda}{2}\right)^2 p^2V^2, \frac{p^2V^2(1+\lambda)^2}{2}\right]$ holds. Then the optimal contract is characterized as follows:

a. The IPs will offer the intermediate agency $\alpha^* = \frac{\sqrt{2 \cdot \bar{U}}}{p \cdot V} - \lambda$ of their satisfaction (money equivalent). The optimal incentive bonus offered by the IP rises at a decreasing rate, with the surrogate's outside option $\bar{U}$. Also, for the more altruistic surrogate, the incentive bonus paid to the intermediate agency is lower.

b. The optimal fixed fee offered to the intermediate agency is $F^{*}=0$.
c. The intermediate agency's optimal monitoring effort is given by $m^{*}=\sqrt{2\bar{U}}$ and it is less than the first-best. Optimal monitoring increases with the surrogate's outside option, but is independent of the level of the surrogate's altruism.
d. The surrogate's optimal payment is given by $B^{*}=\bar{U}-\sqrt{2\bar{U}}\cdot p\cdot\lambda\cdot V\geq 0$.

The intuition of the above proposition is as follows:

As $\bar{U}$ increases, the intermediate agency has to pay the surrogate more to compensate her outside option since $\frac{dB}{d\bar{U}}=\left(1-\frac{\lambda\cdot p\cdot V}{\sqrt{2\bar{U}}}\right)\geq 0 \; for\, \bar{U}\geq\frac{\lambda^{2}\cdot p^{2}\cdot V^{2}}{2}$ which is automatically satisfied in the range of $\bar{U}$ we are considering. Therefore, an increase in $\bar{U}$ of the surrogate becomes a cost to the intermediate agency, and for sufficiently high $\bar{U}$ the agencies' PCS binds. Therefore, the IPs need to pay the agency such that it gets its outside option and therefore optimal α^{*} now increases with $\bar{U}$. Again, since F does not affect the optimal choice of monitoring effort m, the IPs will optimally pay $F^{*}=0$. Interesting to note is that the intermediate agency's optimal monitoring increases with $\bar{U}$. This is due to the fact that as $\bar{U}$ increases, the cost of hiring a surrogate increases. Therefore, it is optimal for the agency to increase its monitoring effort and hence increase the effective probability of success to break even[29].

The optimality of the above contract is easy to check. At the optimum, both the surrogate and the agency get their outside option, that is, $\pi_{S}^{*}=\bar{U}\; and\; \pi_{I.A}^{*}=0$. The IPs' optimal payoff is $\pi_{I.P}^{*}=\sqrt{2\bar{U}}\cdot[(1+\lambda)\cdot p\cdot V-\sqrt{2\bar{U}}]$ which is greater than zero, given our assumption on $\bar{U}$. Thus the above contract is optimal.

4.3 Extensions

One can extend the previous analysis by assuming that the surrogate feels a loss of utility, a pain (money equivalent) when she hands the child over to the biological parents. Thus far, our model had overlooked this possibility and had considered that the surrogate obliges to the terms of the contract without feeling any attachment to the baby she bears. Now we assume that the surrogate values having a child in the same way as the IPs. We denote the surrogate's loss of pain through a loss of utility V (money equivalent), the same as the utility that the IP receives for having a biological baby. The underlying assumption is that individuals who are either biologically or physically related to the baby, are assumed to feel identically (emotionally) attached to the baby. Given this structure, we characterize the optimal contract when the surrogate is offered a fixed fee B, just sufficient to compensate for her

[29] Technically, in this case is an increasing function of which makes optimal monitoring depending positively on

lost opportunity and the net loss in utility. Given this changed specification, the surrogate's surplus function becomes $\pi_S = m\cdot[B + p\cdot(\lambda\cdot V - V)] + (1-m)\cdot B.$ The fixed fee B offered to the surrogate must now be higher in order to compensate her for the loss in utility due to the pain that she suffers while having to give up the child. This extra cost needs to be borne by the intermediate agency which in turn affects its optimal monitoring decision. The surrogate is therefore paid $B = \bar{U} + m\cdot p\cdot(1-\lambda)\cdot V$ and internalizing this, the incentive compatibility constraint of the intermediate agency now can be written as $m = (\alpha + \lambda - 1)\cdot p\cdot V.$ The rest of the analysis qualitatively remains the same. The optimal contract under this changed specification can be summarized as follows:

Proposition 3

a. For $\bar{U} \epsilon \left[0, \frac{(\lambda\cdot p\cdot U)^2}{8}\right]$ the optimal incentive offered to the intermediating agency is $\alpha^{**} = \left(1 - \frac{\lambda}{2}\right)$ and for $\bar{U} \in \left[\frac{(\lambda^2\cdot p^2\cdot U^2)}{8}, \frac{(\lambda^2\cdot p^2\cdot U^2)}{4}\right], \alpha^{**} = \left(1 + \frac{\sqrt{2\bar{U}}}{p\cdot V} - \lambda\right).$

b. The optimal fixed fee offered by the IPs is $F^{**} = 0$ irrespective of the value of $\bar{U}$.

c. The optimal effort decision of the intermediate agency is

$$m^{**} = \frac{\lambda\cdot p\cdot V}{2} \text{ for } \bar{U} \epsilon \left[0, \frac{(\lambda\cdot p\cdot U)^2}{8}\right] \text{ and } m^{**} = \sqrt{2\bar{U}} \; for\; \bar{U} \in \left[\frac{(\lambda^2\cdot p^2\cdot U^2)}{8}, \frac{(\lambda^2\cdot p^2\cdot U^2)}{4}\right].$$

d. The optimal fixed bonus incentive paid to the surrogate is positive for all levels of $\bar{U}$. $B^{**} = \bar{U} + \frac{\lambda\cdot(1-\lambda)}{2}\cdot p^2\cdot V^2$ for low level of $\bar{U}$ whereas $B^{**} = \bar{U} + \sqrt{2\bar{U}}\cdot(1-\lambda)\cdot p\cdot V$ for higher $\bar{U}$.

The intuition of the above results is as follows. Here, we notice slight differences in results as compared to the earlier model. However, this was anticipated, considering our assumption that the surrogate feels a loss of utility in giving up the child. It would now be rational for the intermediate agency to pay a higher fixed bonus B to convince her to participate in the project understanding that she must give up all parental rights to the child after delivery. But then the intermediate agency, to just break even and accept the contract, must be offered a higher incentive in the form of a higher reward for success. As confirmed through our results, both B^{**} and α^{**} are higher as compared to the previous model. Also, the effort of the intermediate agency now seems to have fallen further. This implies that the intermediate agency has the least incentive to work with surrogates who feel emotionally attached to the baby. This is simple to understand as there are costs to convince the surrogate to give up the child when she feels attached to the baby rather than when she realizes that she must give up the child.

4.4 Conclusion

There has been a continuing debate regarding the role of the intermediaries[30] in the expanding reproductive tourism industry in India. Given the dramatic expansion of this industry, which is worth hundreds of millions of dollars and the legal, ethical, commercial, and technological challenges[31] that such expansion has created, a bill has been drafted[32] to help regulate that country's heavily market-driven fertility sector. Till date, there happens to be no enforceable legislation that could impose a code of conduct on the IPs, surrogates, the infertility clinics, and/or intermediate surrogacy agencies. Questions such as whether one should allow intermediate surrogacy agencies or infertility clinics to play an active role in promoting commercial surrogacy are yet to be settled. If it is allowed, then what must be the role and responsibilities of these agencies? One school of thought is that bringing in another player who acts as an "intermediary" in facilitating a contract is more likely to add to the degree of informational asymmetry among participants that is inherent in such markets, instead of reducing it.[33]

In this chapter, we analyze the nature of the optimal contract in the presence of an intermediate agency in surrogacy markets, using the classic moral hazard framework. It is assumed that the commissioning couple can only "hire" a surrogate through an intermediate surrogacy agency which in turn deals with the surrogate and monitors her throughout the process. We show that informational problems might exist even in the presence of the surrogacy agency and even worse, the agency's behavior is subject to moral hazard. Put differently, our model shows the possibility of moral hazard incentives among agencies called in to select and monitor a surrogate, and under nonverifiability the surrogacy agencies will be inclined to put in suboptimal effort in monitoring the surrogates. We, however, refrain from the surrogate's moral hazard problem.

An important issue open to further research is to incorporate the moral hazard incentives of the surrogate in addition to the moral hazard incentive of the intermediate surrogacy agency. Thus far, we have only focused our attention on the intermediate agency's moral hazard and abstained from the surrogate's moral hazard. Therefore, one can have a two-level moral hazard model where both the intermediate agency and the surrogate's actions are subject to moral hazard. This will be a very interesting case indeed, as no such moral hazard model has yet been applied as far as our knowledge goes. Lastly, one can consider the discrete effort case and check whether our results go through in that structure also.

---

30 For a detailed discussion, see Spar (2006).

31 See Grayson (1998).

32 See the ICMR Guidelines for ART clinics in India (2004) and ART (Regulation) Bill-2010, Ministry of Health and Family Welfare, GOI.

33 For more details refer to Galbraith et al. (2005).

References

ACOG (2004) Surrogate motherhood. Ethics in obstetrics and gynecology (2nd ed). The American college of obstetricians and gynecologists (ACOG) committee opinion. p 397
Banerjee S (2013) Gestational surrogacy contracts: altruistic or commercial? A contract theoretic approach. Manch Sch 81(3):438–460
Banerjee S, Basu S (2009) Rent a womb: surrogate selection, investment incentives and contracting. J Econ Behav Organ 69:260–273
Ergas Y (2004) Babies without borders: human rights, human dignity and the regulation of international commercial surrogacy. Emory Int Law Rev 27(1):117–188
Galbraith M, McLachlan HV, Swales JK (2005) Commercial agencies and surrogate motherhood: a transaction cost approach. Health Care Anal 13(1):11–31
Grayson DR (1998) Mediating intimacy: black surrogate mothers and the law. The Chicago University Press, Chicago. Accessed: 06/09/2013 07: 53
Hatzis AN (2003) Just the oven: a law and economics approach to gestational surrogacy contracts. In: Boele-Woelki K (ed) Perspective for the Unification or harmonization of Family Law in Europe. Intersentia, Antwerp
Indian Council of Medical Research (2004) National guidelines for accreditation, supervision and regulation of ART clinics in India
Krawiec KD (2009) Altruism and intermediation in the market for babies. Wash and Lee Law Rev 66(1):203–257
Posner R (1989) The ethics and economics of enforcing contracts of surrogate motherhood. J Contemp Health Law Policy 5(21):21–31
Smerdon UR (2008) Crossing bodies crossing borders: international surrogacy between the United States and India. Cumberland Law Rev 39(1):15–85
Spar DL (2006) The baby business: how money, science, and politics drive the commerce of conception. Harvard Business School Press, Boston
The National Health and Research Council, Government of Australia (2007) Ethical guidelines on the use of assisted reproductive technology in clinical practice and research, June 2007
The Telegraph. Available at www.telegraphindia.com, various issues
The Times of India (2015) Meeting the cost of conceiving, Jan 4. Available at www.timesofindia.com

Websites

http://www.fertilityindia.com
http://www.legislation.gov.uk.
http://www.eggdonor.com/blog/2013/03/22/surrogacy-horror-stories-india.
https://www.nhmrc.gov.au.

Chapter 5
Sharecropping in Theory and Practice: A Selective Review

Debapriya Sen

5.1 Introduction

Sharecropping has remained a dominant agrarian institution around the world. In its basic form, sharecropping entails sharing of the agricultural produce between a landowner and a tenant-cultivator in a land tenancy market. It is an ancient institution. The literature on sharecropping is large. The formal analysis of this institution can be traced back to Alfred Marshall (1920), who argued that it is an inefficient system of cultivation. Under a share contract, a tenant-cultivator pays a landlord a specific proportion of the output. As the tenant keeps only a fraction of the marginal product, his incentive is distorted. Even though there are gains in surplus from employing additional inputs, it does not pay the tenant to do so. Consequently, sharecropping leads to suboptimal application of inputs. By contrast, a fixed rental contract gives the tenant incentive to maximize the surplus as he gets to keep the entire output and makes only a lump-sum rental transfer to the landlord.

In spite of its apparent inefficiency, sharecropping has prevailed over the years. Several economic theories have been put forward to explain its existence. It has been argued that sharecropping can be explained as a compromise between risk sharing and provision of incentives (Stiglitz 1974; Newbery 1977; Newbery and Stiglitz 1979). Other explanations are based on factors such as limited liability (Basu 1992; Sengupta 1997) or screening (Hallagan 1978; Allen 1982; Muthoo 1998).[1] The empirical literature of share tenancy includes Rao (1971), Bell (1977),

[1] In the screening models, the tenant's skill is his private information and he signals his skill to the landlord through his choice of contracts. These models predict a separating contractual structure:

This article is dedicated to the memory of my father Biswadeb Sen, who remains a source of inspiration.

D. Sen (✉)
Department of Economics, Ryerson University, Toronto, Canada
e-mail: dprsen@gmail.com

S. Banerjee et al. (eds.), *Understanding Development,* India Studies in Business and Economics, DOI 10.1007/978-81-322-2455-6_5

Shaban (1987), Allen and Lueck (1992), Laffont and Matoussi (1995), and Ackerberg and Botticini (2002).[2]

This chapter presents a review of the literature on sharecropping. This literature is large and growing, and we do not attempt an exhaustive review. Complementing previous reviews (e.g., Quibria and Rashid 1984; Otsuka and Hayami 1988; Singh 1989), our approach is purposely selective. First, we discuss certain theories related to risk-based explanations of sharecropping. Following that we discuss two new models from the more recent literature that provide alternative explanations other than risk. Although the review primarily focuses on a microeconomic analysis of sharecropping, we discuss some relevant empirical papers and case studies as well. In view of the renewed interest on the role of institutions in economic development (see, e.g., Bardhan 2005b, 2013; Acemoglu and Robinson 2012), a better understanding of the micro-foundations of this ancient institution can give us insights to broader issues of development.

This chapter is organized as follows. In Sect. 2, we present the basic model of tenancy contracts. This model is followed throughout. Section 3 discusses risk-based explanations of share tenancy. Section 4 reviews two papers from the recent literature that offer alternative explanations of sharecropping. Section 5 concludes the chapter.

5.2 The Basic Model of Land Tenancy

Consider a contractual setting with one landlord and one tenant.[3] The landlord owns a piece of land, but he is not present in the land. He is an absentee landlord who is not in a position to cultivate the land[4] or to supervise day-to-day activities of

low-skilled tenants choose fixed wages, high-skilled ones choose fixed rentals and tenants with intermediate skills choose share contracts. However, Bardhan and Udry (1999, p. 63) cast some doubt on the plausibility of screening models in a close-knit village: "It is doubtful how important this role of tenancy contract as a screening device is in the small closed world of a traditional village, where the landlord usually has a fairly good idea of the ability of the different members of the village work force."

[2] For theoretical and empirical aspects of sharecropping and related issues in an agrarian economy, see also Johnson (1950), Cheung (1969), Bardhan and Srinivasan (1971), Bliss and Stern (1982), Byres (1983), Bardhan (1984, 1989, 2005a), Binswanger and Rosenzweig (1984), Otsuka et al. (1992), Hayami and Otsuka (1993), Sharma and Drèze (1996), Bhaduri (1999), and Dutta (2000).

[3] Throughout this review we consider a single landlord–tenant interaction. Models with multiple landlords and tenants have been studied in the literature to look at aspects such as strategic delegation (Ray 1999) and endogenous matching (Ackerberg and Botticini 2002; Serfes 2005).

[4] A strategic comparison of self-cultivation and share tenancy for a landlord is considered in Das (2009). His model has multiple landlords and peasant families in which any landlord can either self-cultivate or lease his land using share tenancy. It is shown that all landlords opting for share tenancy can be an equilibrium outcome when there is disguised unemployment in labor market. However, the share of the tenant is exogenously given in this model.

farming. He leases his land to a tenant to carry out production. The landlord may have chosen to be an absentee due to a higher opportunity cost from an alternative activity (e.g., running a business in town). It is a situation of land tenure where, in the words of Marshall (1920, p. 530), the landlord is the "sleeping partner" and the tenant is the "working partner."

The land lease is executed through *linear tenancy contracts*.[5] A typical contract is a pair (α, β), where $\alpha \in [0,1]$ is the share of the output of the tenant and $\beta \in \mathrm{R}$ is the fixed rental transfer from the tenant to the landlord. Suppose the tenant works under the contract (α, β) and the output is Q. Then (i) the tenant keeps αQ and leaves the rest $(1-\alpha)Q$ with the landlord and (ii) makes the rental transfer β to the landlord. These contracts can be classified into different types.

A contract (α, β) is a *sharecropping contract* (or a *share contract*) if the landlord and the tenant share the output, that is, if $0 < \alpha < 1$. Note that a share contract may potentially include a side payment from one party to another, that is, we can have either $\beta > 0$ or $\beta < 0$ in a share contract. If a share contract has no side payment (i.e., $\beta = 0$), it is a *pure share* contract. Thus, pure share contracts are of the form $(\alpha, 0)$, where $0 < \alpha < 1$.

A contract (α, β) is a *fixed rental* contract if the tenant keeps the entire output (i.e., $\alpha = 1$) and pays a rent $\beta > 0$ to the landlord. Thus, fixed rental contracts are of the form $(1, \beta)$, where $\beta > 0$.

Remark 1 We can also define a *fixed wage* contract in the set of linear contracts. A contract (α, β) is a fixed wage contract if the landlord keeps the entire output and pays a positive wage w to the tenant, that is, if $\alpha = 0$ and $w = -\beta > 0$. However, if production depends on the employment of costly labor inputs, under this contract the tenant has no incentive to incur these costs. To implement a fixed wage contract the landlord has either to supervise farming or to put more structure into the contract (e.g., specify the amount of inputs or outputs). For these reasons such contracts do not fit readily in the framework of simple linear contracts and need a separate treatment (see, e.g., Roy and Serfes 2001). Generally speaking, fixed wage contracts require more involvement of the landlord. As we focus on absentee landlords, for most of the reviews we will only consider fixed rental and share contracts.

[5] The literature has mostly considered linear contracts on the ground that contracts observed in practice are usually linear. Stiglitz (1989, p. 23) provides a justification as follows: "In general, nonlinear contracts will do better...Yet most contracts seem to be of remarkably simple form...The best we can say at this juncture is that perhaps the gains from nonlinearities are not very great...and that, if it becomes conventional to employ linear contracts, suspicions will be raised about those who deviate from the norm."

5.3 Uncertainty, Risk, and Sharecropping

Agricultural production is uncertain in nature. A good monsoon brings good harvest. Drought or excess rainfall ruins crops. Contracts based on lump-sum transfers, such as fixed rent or fixed wage, puts the entire risk of production on one of the contracting parties. A bad harvest does not affect the agent who obtains the lump-sum transfer. Thus, the tenant bears the risk of production under a fixed rental contract, while the risk falls on the landlord under a fixed wage contract. As a share contract entails sharing of the produce between two parties, it facilitates risk sharing between them. Agents concerned about risk may thus prefer sharecropping over other contracts. This rationale of sharecropping is fairly intuitive. However, as shown by Stiglitz (1974), establishing the superiority of sharecropping requires a more involved reasoning. It depends on aspects such as the type of risk (e.g., whether the risk is multiplicative or additive) and the trade-off between risk sharing and provision of incentives. It has been also argued that with only one source of uncertainty, a mixture of fixed wage and fixed rent (wage contracts in some plots and rental contracts in other plots) may do as well as sharecropping. Multiple sources of uncertainty, such as in production and in factor markets, are needed to explain sharecropping (Newbery 1977).

5.3.1 A Model of Risk Sharing

Different aspects of risk-sharing theories of sharecropping have been extensively discussed (see, e.g., Bardhan 1984; Quibria and Rashid 1984; Otsuka and Hayami 1988; Otsuka et al. 1992; Singh 1989; Basu 1998; Ray 1998; Bardhan and Udry 1999). Here we present a model of risk sharing given in Chap. 12 of Ray (1998). This is a simple, two-outcome model that brings out the risk-sharing rationale of sharecropping with particular clarity.

Consider a landlord who leases his land to a tenant. The agricultural output of the land depends on the realization of an uncertain outcome such as weather. The outcome can be either good or bad. For example, these outcomes may correspond to adequate or inadequate rainfall. The good outcome occurs with probability λ and the bad outcome occurs with probability $1-\lambda$, where $0<\lambda<1$. The output is G under the good outcome and B under the bad outcome, where $G>B\geq 0$. Therefore, the expected value of the output is $E=\lambda G+(1-\lambda)B$.

Regarding the risk attitudes of the agents, assume that the landlord is *risk neutral* and the tenant is *risk averse*. A risk-neutral agent is indifferent between two contracts that give him the same expected income. On the other hand, for two contracts that give the same expected income, a risk-averse agent prefers the one that has lower variance. It is often the case that the tenant is a poor farmer and the tenurial income is his primary source of livelihood. By contrast, the landlord has enough buffer wealth and the potentially alternative sources of income. Thus, a bad harvest hurts the tenant more than the landlord. This is why the tenant is assumed to be more sensitive towards risk.

First, consider a fixed rental contract $(1,\beta)$ with fixed rent $\beta > 0$. Under this contract, the tenant keeps the entire output and makes the lump-sum transfer β to the landlord. The expected income of the tenant under this contract is $\lambda(G-\beta)+(1-\lambda)(B-\beta)=E-\beta$ and the (fixed) income of the landlord is β. It is reasonable to assume that the tenant will not accept a contract that does not give him a positive income on average. So for a fixed rental contract to be acceptable to the tenant, we must have $\beta < E$.

Now consider a pure share contract $(\alpha,0)$ where $0<\alpha<1$. Under this contract, the tenant keeps the fraction α of the output and leaves the remaining fraction $1-\alpha$ with the landlord. Therefore, the expected income of the tenant is $\lambda\alpha G+(1-\lambda)\alpha B=\alpha E$ and the expected income of the landlord is $\lambda(1-\alpha)G+(1-\lambda)(1-\alpha)B=(1-\alpha)E$.

Choose the share α in such a way that it makes the expected income of the landlord the same from the two contracts, that is, $\beta=(1-\alpha)E$. Then $\alpha=\alpha^* \equiv (E-\beta)/E$ (note that $0<\alpha^*<1$). As the landlord is risk-neutral, he is indifferent between the fixed rental contract $(1,\beta)$ and the pure share contract $(\alpha^*,0)$.

Next, observe that since $\alpha^* E = E-\beta$, the expected income of the tenant is also the same under the two contracts. Under the contract $(1,\beta)$, the tenant obtains $G-\beta$ when the outcome is good and $B-\beta$ when it is bad. So the difference in incomes from good and bad outcomes is $G-B$. On the other hand, under the contract $(\alpha^*,0)$, the tenant obtains $\alpha^* H$ when the outcome is good and $\alpha^* L$ when it is bad, so the difference in incomes is $\alpha^*(G-B)<G-B$. Thus, both contracts give the same expected income to the tenant, but the variance of his income is lower under the share contract. The risk-averse tenant therefore prefers the share contract. These conclusions are summarized in the following proposition.

Proposition 1 Consider any fixed rental contract $(1,\beta)$ where $0<\beta<E$ and let $\alpha^* \equiv (E-\beta)/\beta$. The risk-averse tenant prefers the pure share contract $(\alpha^*,0)$ over the fixed rental contract $(1,\beta)$ and the risk-neutral landlord is indifferent between the two. Consequently, the pure share contract $(\alpha^*,0)$ Pareto dominates the fixed rental contract $(1,\beta)$.

Unlike a fixed rental contract, the burden of risk resulting from production uncertainty is shared by the two parties in a share contract. This establishes the superiority of sharecropping in this model with a risk-averse tenant and a risk-neutral landlord.

5.3.2 Choice of Techniques and Limited Liability

Production uncertainty was completely exogenous in the last model. The tenant had no role there in the realization of the output. If in addition to exogenous uncertainty, output also depends on the choices of the tenant, then production risk manifests differently to give a different risk-based explanation of sharecropping. This is discussed in the following model.

Basu (1992) provides an explanation of sharecropping based on limited liability.[6] His model is motivated by the observation that tenancy contracts in practice often involve a limited liability clause. This clause serves as a safety net that saves the tenant from going bankrupt. Specifically, the limited liability clause restricts the terms of a contract to ensure that the tenant's income must never fall below a certain minimum level. To assure this, the landlord foregoes his claim on the payments from the contract in the event of a bad contingency. As argued by Stiglitz and Weiss (1981) in the context of credit markets, a limited liability clause gives incentives to agents to undertake risky projects. Basu (1992) follows the same line of reasoning to show that in the presence of limited liability, the landlord may find it optimal to choose a share contract to discourage the tenant from choosing risky techniques of production. Here we present a simplified, two-outcome version of Basu's model.

As before, consider a contractual setting where a landlord leases his land to a tenant. In this model, we assume both parties to be risk neutral, so for any contract both care only about the expected income from that contract. This is assumed to make clear how the limited liability clause induces a risk-neutral agent to adopt more risky choices.

The tenant can choose one of the two techniques of production which correspond to two projects: $1, 2$. Outcome is uncertain under each project and as before it can be either good or bad. Assume that in both projects, there is zero output under bad outcome ($B = 0$), but under good outcome, the output is G_1 in project 1 and G_2 in project 2 where $G_2 > G_1 > 0$. That is, project 2 has a higher value of the output under good outcome.

For $i \in \{1, 2\}$, let $0 < \lambda_i < 1$ be the probability of good outcome in project i (so that $1 - \lambda_i$ is the probability of bad outcome). It is assumed that both projects have the same expected return E. Specifically, $\lambda_1 G_1 = \lambda_2 G_2 = E$. Observe that this implies $\lambda_1 > \lambda_2$ (since $G_2 > G_1$). Thus, it is less likely that project 2 will give good outcome but in the event of good outcome, it gives higher return.

Observe that the difference in returns from good and bad outcomes is higher in project 2 (since $G_2 > G_1$). This implies that although both projects have the same expected return, the variance is higher[7] in project 2, so it is a more risky project compared to project 1.

Under any contract, the tenant chooses one of the two projects. The landlord does not observe the tenant's choice of projets, only the realized output can be observed. Basu (1992) refers to this as *technique moral hazard*.[8] The riskier project 2 is more costly for the tenant. Specifically, assume that the tenant incurs no cost for project 1, but cost $c > 0$ for project 2.

---

[6] The role of limited liability has been studied earlier by Shetty (1988) who looks at rental contracts to determine contractual structure when there is wealth asymmetry among tenants.

[7] To see this formally, let V_i denote the variance from project i. Note that $V_i = \lambda_i G_i^2 - E^2 = EG_i - E^2$. Hence $V_2 - V_1 = (G_2 - G_1)E > 0$.

[8] Sengupta (1997) considers a model of sharecropping where in addition to exogenous uncertainty, the output under any project depends on the tenant's effort level. It is argued there that technique moral hazard alone is not sufficient to explain sharecropping. See also Ghatak and Pandey (2000), Ray and Singh (2001), and Dam and Ruiz-Pérez (2012).

There is a limited liability clause in tenancy contracts which in this simple model works as follows. The tenant does not have to make any payment to the landlord when the outcome is bad (i.e., when the output takes zero value). This ensures that the tenant's income does not fall below zero. The threshold of zero income is taken for analytic convenience. In more general settings, this threshold may be a specific positive level of income. In such a case, the limited liability clause ensures that the tenant's income never falls below this specific positive level.

First, consider a pure share contract $(\alpha, 0)$ where $0 < \alpha < 1$. Under this contract, when the outcome is good the tenant keeps fraction α of the output and leaves the remaining fraction $1-\alpha$ with the landlord. Due to limited liability, the tenant does not make any payment when the outcome is bad.[9] The expected income of the tenant under this contract from project 1 is $\alpha\lambda_1 G_1 = \alpha E$. Since project 2 has cost $c > 0$, his expected income from project 2 is $\alpha\lambda_2 G_2 - c = \alpha E - c < \alpha E$. Hence, under a pure share contract $(\alpha, 0)$, it is always optimal for the tenant to choose project 1. The tenant obtains expected income $\phi_S(\alpha) = \alpha E$ and the landlord obtains expected income $\pi_S(\alpha) = (1-\alpha)\lambda_1 G_1 = (1-\alpha)E$.

Next, consider a fixed rental contract $(1, \beta)$ with rent $\beta > 0$. Under this contract, the tenant makes the lump-sum transfer β to the landlord when the outcome is good. Due to limited liability, the tenant does not make any payment when the outcome is bad. Since project 1 has no cost, the expected income of the tenant from project 1 under the fixed rental contract is $\phi_F^1(\beta) = \lambda_1(G_1 - \beta) = E - \lambda_1\beta$. Since project 2 has cost $c > 0$, the expected income of the tenant from project 2 is $\phi_F^2(\beta) = \lambda_2(G_2 - \beta) - c = E - \lambda_2\beta - c$.

We assume that the tenant will not accept any contract that does not give him positive expected income. To ensure that a fixed rental contract $(1, \beta)$ is acceptable to the tenant, assume β is such that

$$\max\{\phi_F^1(\beta), \phi_F^2(\beta)\} > 0 \tag{5.1}$$

If the tenant chooses project $i \in \{1, 2\}$, the landlord's expected income is $\pi_F^i(\beta) = \lambda_i\beta$. Since $\lambda_1 > \lambda_2$, we have $\pi_F^1(\beta) > \pi_F^2(\beta)$, that is, under a fixed rental contract the landlord prefers project 1 (the less risky project). The tenant will choose the project that maximizes his own expected income. Denoting $k \equiv c/(\lambda_1 - \lambda_2)$, we observe that the tenant chooses project 2 if $\beta > k$ and project 1 if $\beta < k$.

For a fixed rental contract $(1, \beta)$ with $\beta > k$, there is a conflict between the interests of the two parties. The landlord prefers the less risky project 1 but the tenant prefers the more risky project 2. We show that there are pure share contracts that can improve the incomes of both parties in this case. To see this, note that if a pure share contract $(\alpha, 0)$ improves the incomes of both parties, then

$$\phi_S(\alpha) = \alpha E \geq \phi_F^2(\beta) = E - \lambda_2\beta - c \text{ and } \pi_S(\alpha) = (1-\alpha)E \geq \pi_F^2(\beta) = \lambda_2\beta \tag{5.2}$$

[9] In this simple model the minimum income below which limited liability takes effect is zero. The value of output under bad outcome is also zero. For this reason limited liability does not affect the payments of a pure share contract (since the payment in the event of bad outcome will be zero in any case). However, if the output under bad outcome is positive but lower than the minimum income level, then limited liability will make a difference in the payments for pure share contracts.

Let $\underline{\alpha} \equiv (E - \lambda_2\beta - c)/E$ and $\bar{\alpha} \equiv (E - \lambda_2\beta)/E$. Using (5.1), for this case $0 < \underline{\alpha} < \bar{\alpha} < 1$. The inequalities in (5.2) hold if and only if $\underline{\alpha} \le \alpha \le \bar{\alpha}$. In particular, any pure share contract $(\alpha, 0)$ with $\underline{\alpha} < \alpha < \bar{\alpha}$ strictly improves the incomes of both parties compared to the fixed rental contract $(1, \beta)$ if $\beta > k$. With the limited liability clause in place, the tenant may have incentive to choose more risky projects that are detrimental for the landlord. A share contract shifts the tenant's incentive back to less risky projects, which in turn benefits both parties.

To complete the analysis, now consider a fixed rental contract with $\beta < k$. In this case, both parties prefer the less risky project 1. A pure share contract $(\alpha, 0)$ can improve the incomes of both parties if

$$\phi_S(\alpha) = \alpha E \ge \phi_F^1(\beta) = E - \lambda_1\beta \text{ and } \pi_S(\alpha) = (1-\alpha)E \ge \pi_F^1(\beta) = \lambda_1\beta$$

The unique solution to the above inequalities is $\alpha = \hat{\alpha} \equiv (E - \lambda_1\beta)/E$ (note from (5.1) that for this case $0 < \hat{\alpha} < 1$) and both inequalities hold with equality. So for each of the two parties, the pure share contract $(\hat{\alpha}, 0)$ gives the same income as the fixed rental contract $(1, \beta)$. The conclusions are summarized in the following proposition.

Proposition 2

(i) For any $\beta > k$, there is $0 < \underline{\alpha} < \bar{\alpha} < 1$ such that for any $\underline{\alpha} < \alpha < \bar{\alpha}$, the pure share contract $(\alpha, 0)$ strictly Pareto dominates the fixed rental contract $(1, \beta)$, that is, both the landlord and the tenant obtain strictly higher income at $(\alpha, 0)$ compared to $(1, \beta)$.

(ii) For any $\beta < k$, there is $0 < \hat{\alpha} < 1$ such that both the landlord and the tenant are indifferent between the pure share contract $(\hat{\alpha}, 0)$ and the fixed rental contract $(1, \beta)$.

If there is a moral hazard in the choice of techniques of production, the presence of limited liability clause induces the tenant to choose more risky projects under certain fixed rental contracts. Share tenancy gives incentive to choose less risky projects and there always exist Pareto improving share contracts. For cases where a fixed rental contract also results in less risky projects, there exists a share contract which does well for both parties. Thus, share tenancy is always as good as fixed rentals and does strictly better in certain cases.

5.3.3 *Risk and Share Tenancy: Theory Versus Practice*

To conclude this section, let us briefly discuss some empirical aspects of risk-based theories of sharecropping. Earlier empirical works on share contracts (e.g., Rao 1971; Allen and Lueck 1992; Laffont and Matoussi 1995) did not find conclusive support for risk-sharing theory. Factors such as transaction costs and capital constraints were found to be important for contract choices. However, risk-sharing theory has been supported in some recent empirical papers. Constructing endogenous matchings of landlords and tenants as functions of their characteristics, Ackerberg and Botticini (2002) find strong evidence of risk sharing in the historical data of early Renaissance Tuscany, Italy. Brancaccio (2003) also find support for risk sharing in tenancy contracts obtained from villages in India covered by the International Crops Research Institute for the Semi-Arid Tropics (ICRISAT) for the period 1975–1984.[10]

One implication of the risk-based theory is that the specific shares in a share contract must depend on individual characteristics (e.g., wealth level and degree of risk aversion) of the contracting parties. Unless individual landlords and tenants are fairly homogeneous in a given region, the terms of share contracts should show a high degree of variation. However, it is usually observed that crop-sharing patterns do not show much variation within a region. For example, Rudra and Bardhan (1983, p. 38) find that most villages in their survey had one or two sharing patterns. In this regard, Stiglitz (1989, p. 22) writes:

> "...[T]he range of contract forms seems far more restricted than theory would suggest: most contracts have, for instance, shares of one-half, one-third, or two-thirds. Although there have been several attempts to explain this uniformity, none has gained general acceptance."

In similar vein, Bardhan and Udry (1999) also point out the inadequacy of the existing theories to explain the observed uniformity of crop-sharing patterns.

5.4 Alternative Theories of Sharecropping

Risk is the key determining factor in both models discussed before. Moving away from risk-based explanations, some recent papers have looked for alternative avenues that lead to sharecropping in a village economy. We discuss two of these papers of the recent literature. Before we discuss these papers, we depart from the two-outcome setting and introduce a production process with continuous production and cost functions.

5.4.1 The Benchmark Model

Consider as before a landlord who leases out his land to a tenant. As we will look at alternative explanations of sharecropping not based on risk, both contracting parties are taken to be risk neutral. Labor (ℓ) is the only one input of production. In the land leased out by the landlord, the production function is $f(\ell)$, where $f(0) = 0$. The

[10] For a discussion of India-specific empirical studies on tenancy contracts, see Dutta (2003). See Serfes (2005) for a theoretical explanation of ambiguous empirical evidence in favor of risk sharing.

function[11] f is twice continuously differentiable with $f'(\ell) > 0$ and $f''(\ell) < 0$ for $\ell > 0$, that is, f is strictly increasing and strictly concave. Moreover, $\lim_{\ell \to 0} f'(\ell) = \infty$ and $\lim_{\ell \to \infty} f'(\ell) = 0$. The cost of ℓ units of labor is $w(\ell)$, where $w(0) = 0$. It is assumed that w is twice continuously differentiable, strictly increasing, and convex, that is, $w'(\ell) > 0$ and $w''(\ell) \geq 0$ for $\ell > 0$.

The landlord leases his land to the tenant using linear tenancy contracts of the form (α, β), where $\alpha \in [0,1]$ and $\beta \in \mathrm{R}$. The tenant employs labor to carry out production. If the tenant works under the contract (α, β) and the output is Q, then (i) he keeps the share αQ and leaves the remaining share $(1-\alpha)Q$ with the landlord and (ii) makes the rental transfer β to the landlord. In that case, the tenant's income is $\alpha Q - \beta$ and the landlord's income is $(1-\alpha)Q + \beta$.

Recall that (α, β) is a share contract if $0 < \alpha < 1$ (the two parties share the output). Such a contract may possibly include a side payment $\beta \neq 0$. A share contract with $\beta = 0$ is a pure share contract. A contract (α, β) is a fixed rental contract if $\alpha = 1$ (the tenant keeps the entire output) and $\beta > 0$ (there is a positive rent from the tenant to the landlord).

5.4.2 *The Tenant's Problem*

Consider the tenant's problem under any contract (α, β). If he employs ℓ units of labor, the output is $f(\ell)$ and he incurs cost[12] $w(\ell)$. The tenant keeps the share $\alpha f(\ell)$, so his revenue is $\alpha f(\ell) - w(\ell)$. In addition, he has to make the rental transfer β to the landlord. So under (α, β), the tenant's income is $\alpha f(\ell) - w(\ell) - \beta$. As β is a constant, the tenant's problem under the contract (α, β) is to choose $\ell \geq 0$ to maximize

$$\phi^{\alpha}(\ell) := \alpha f(\ell) - w(\ell). \tag{5.3}$$

Since $f'' < 0$ and $w'' \geq 0$, by (5.3), $\phi^{\alpha}(\ell)$ is strictly concave in ℓ for $\alpha > 0$. For $\alpha \geq 0$, let $\ell(\alpha)$ be the unique maximizer of $\phi^{\alpha}(\ell)$. Clearly $\ell(0) = 0$. For $\alpha > 0$, $\ell(\alpha)$ is obtained from the first-order condition $\alpha f'(\ell) = w'(\ell)$. Hence,

---

[11] Production uncertainty can be incorporated in this model by taking the production function to be $Xf(\ell)$ where X is a random variable with $E(X) = 1$. As both contracting parties are risk neutral, they only care about the expected value of the output at any ℓ which is given by $E(X)f(\ell) = f(\ell)$

[12] Note that in this model the cost of production is borne by the tenant. However, the rental transfer β can be used to facilitate cost sharing. For example, consider a contract with $\beta = -50$ ₹ that is implemented as follows. The landlord pays the tenant 100 ₹ before production and the tenant pays back 50 ₹ after output is realized. Here the landlord effectively shares a lump-sum cost of production. For models of tenancy contracts where there is cost sharing *at the margin,* see, e.g., Braverman and Stiglitz (1982), Bardhan (1984), and Bardhan and Singh (1987). A tenancy contract may be also interlinked with a credit contract (see, e.g., Bhaduri 1973; Rudra and Bardhan 1983; Bardhan and Udry 1999; Dutta 2003; Kundu 2009).

$$\ell(0) = 0 \text{ and } \alpha f'(\ell(\alpha)) = w'(\ell(\alpha)) \text{ for } \alpha > 0. \tag{5.4}$$

Now define the composite functions $F, \Phi : \mathrm{R}_+ \to \mathrm{R}$ as

$$F(\alpha) := f(\ell(\alpha)) \text{ and } \Phi(\alpha) := \phi^{\alpha}(\ell(\alpha)) = \alpha F(\alpha) - w(\ell(\alpha)). \tag{5.5}$$

The following lemma, which characterizes the solution to the tenant's problem under different classes of contracts, follows from (5.3)–(5.5) and by the envelope theorem.

Lemma 1 The following hold under any linear contract (α, β), where $\alpha \in [0,1]$ and $\beta \in R$.

(i) The tenant chooses labor input $\ell(\alpha)$, the output produced is $F(\alpha)$ and the tenant obtains $\Phi(\alpha) - \beta$.

(ii) $\ell(0) = 0$, $F(0) = 0$ and $\Phi(0) = 0$.

(iii) $\ell'(\alpha) > 0$, $F'(\alpha) > 0$ and $\Phi'(\alpha) = F(\alpha) > 0$ for $\alpha > 0$.

5.4.3 *The Marshallian Inefficiency Argument*

To see the Marshallian inefficiency argument against sharecropping, we will determine the *total surplus* (the sum of incomes of two parties) under any contract (α, β). As β is a lump-sum transfer from one party to another, it will have no effect on the total surplus.

Note from Lemma 1 that when the tenant makes labor choices optimally, under the contract (α, β) the output is $F(\alpha)$. The landlord obtains share $(1-\alpha)F(\alpha)$. In addition, he obtains the rental transfer β. So the landlord's income is $(1-\alpha)F(\alpha) + \beta$. As the tenant's income is $\Phi(\alpha) - \beta$ (Lemma 1), the total surplus under (α, β) is $s(\alpha) = (1-\alpha)F(\alpha) + \Phi(\alpha) = F(\alpha) - w(\ell(\alpha))$. Using the definitions from (5.5) and (5.3), we have

$$s(\alpha) = f(\ell(\alpha)) - w(\ell(\alpha)) = \phi^1(\ell(\alpha)) \tag{5.6}$$

In other words, $s(\alpha)$ is the net production profit (output net of the cost of labor) when $\ell(\alpha)$ units of labor are employed. Since $\ell(1)$ is the unique maximizer of $\phi^1(\ell)$ and $\ell(\alpha) < \ell(1)$ for any $0 < \alpha < 1$ (Lemma 1), from (5.6), we conclude that

$$s(\alpha) = \phi^1(\ell(\alpha)) < \phi^1(\ell(1)) = s(1) \text{ for any } 0 < \alpha < 1 \tag{5.7}$$

The above inequality is a formal presentation of the Marshallian inefficiency argument against sharecropping. It shows that the total surplus $s(\alpha)$ under any share contract $(0 < \alpha < 1)$ is lower than the total surplus $s(1)$ obtained under a fixed rental contract $(\alpha = 1)$. A fixed rental contract gives the tenant incentive to employ labor $\ell(1)$ that maximizes the net production profit $\phi^1(\ell) = f(\ell) - w(\ell)$. A share contract, where the tenant keeps only a fraction of the marginal product, distorts his incentive. This leads to suboptimal application of labor $(\ell(\alpha) < \ell(1))$ and lower surplus.

If the landlord has the bargaining power in his negotiations with the tenant,[13] then by appropriately choosing the rent β, the landlord can extract all gains in surplus. A fixed rental contract, which maximizes the total surplus, then seems optimal from the viewpoint of the landlord. Why would then a landlord opt for sharecropping in a situation where he could determine the terms of the tenancy contracts? The papers we discuss now seek to answer this question by appealing to different aspects of a rural economy.

5.4.4 Soil Quality and Sharecropping

Consider a tenancy setting where opportunities to make productive investment in the land are limited. This could be either due to scarcity of funds or due to a lack of interest on part of an absentee landlord who invests elsewhere (e.g., a small business in the town). In this situation, application of more and more labor deteriorates the soil quality and makes the land less productive over time.[14] Roy and Serfes (2001) argue that sharecropping can be explained by a landlord's concerns to maintain the productivity of his land. A fixed rental contract gives the tenant incentive to employ a high level of labor input which generates a large surplus for the present. But at the same time it reduces soil quality, which is detrimental for the landlord's future income from the land. The landlord takes this into consideration while offering a tenancy contract. In a two-period model with asymmetric discount factors for the two contracting parties, Roy and Serfes (2001) show that sharecropping may emerge as the optimal tenancy contract since it induces the tenant to employ less labor which in turn ensures that soil quality does not fall too much. We present a simplified version of their model that captures the essence of their reasoning.

As before, consider a landlord who leases his land to a tenant using linear tenancy contracts of the form (α, β) where $\alpha \in [0,1]$ and $\beta \in \mathrm{R}$. There is only one input of production: labor. The tenant employs labor to carry out production. The production process and the tenant's income are the same as described in the benchmark model of Sect. 4.1. So for any contract (α, β), the tenant solves his problem

[13] This is what is often assumed in the literature and we will make this assumption in the subsequent analysis. While this seems a reasonable assumption in an agrarian economy with a large number of potential tenants, there is empirical evidence to the contrary. For instance, in his study of mid-nineteenth century tenancy contracts in South India, Reddy (1996) finds evidence where tenants had relatively high bargaining power compared to absentee landlords.

[14] In this context, the threat of eviction may either discourage or encourage the tenant to make productive investment in the land. See, e.g., Bardhan (1984), Bardhan and Udry (1999), and Banerjee et al. (2002).

as in Sect. 4.2. His optimal choices of labor and their implications are summarized in Lemma 1.

The key distinction with the benchmark model is that in addition to his present income from tenancy, the landlord also considers his future income from land. This future income depends on the post-production soil quality, which in turn depends on the amount of labor employed by the tenant in the present. Employment of higher amount of labor today makes the land less productive and hurts the landlord's income tomorrow. Specifically if ℓ units of labor are employed at present, the landlord's future discounted income from land is given by a continuous function[15] $g(\ell)$. Assume there is $\underline{\ell} > 0$ such that $g(\ell) = g(0) > 0$ for $0 \le \ell \le \underline{\ell}$ and $g(\ell)$ is differentiable and decreasing for $\ell > \underline{\ell}$. This implies that labor employment is not detrimental to future income as long as it does not exceed the threshold $\underline{\ell}$. However, beyond the threshold $\underline{\ell}$, employment of more labor decreases future income.

The landlord's income is the sum of his present and future incomes. Under the contract (α, β), the tenant chooses $\ell = \ell(\alpha)$ and the output is $F(\alpha)$ (Lemma 1). As the landlord's present income is $(1-\alpha)F(\alpha) + \beta$ and future income is $g(\ell(\alpha))$, his total income is

$$(1-\alpha)F(\alpha) + \beta + g(\ell(\alpha)). \tag{5.8}$$

Let $\underline{\Phi} > 0$ be the reservation income of the tenant. By Lemma 1, the tenant obtains $\Phi(\alpha) - \beta$ under a contract (α, β). Since the tenant will not accept any contract where he obtains less than his reservation income, this contract will be accepted by the tenant if and only if $\Phi(\alpha) - \beta \ge \underline{\Phi}$. This is the tenant's participation constraint. By (5.8), the landlord's income is increasing in β. So for any $\alpha \in [0,1]$, the optimal β for the landlord is $\overline{\beta}(\alpha) = \Phi(\alpha) - \underline{\Phi}$ that binds the tenant's participation constraint. Replacing $\beta = \overline{\beta}(\alpha)$ in (5.8), the landlord's income can be written as a function of α as follows:

$$\pi(\alpha) = (1-\alpha)F(\alpha) + \Phi(\alpha) - \underline{\Phi} + g(\ell(\alpha)). \tag{5.9}$$

Recall from Lemma 1 that $\ell(1)$ is the optimal labor employed by the tenant under a fixed rental contract. The following proposition shows that if the threshold $\underline{\ell}$ does not exceed $\ell(1)$, then[16] it is optimal for the landlord to offer a share contract.

Proposition 3 Suppose $\underline{\ell} < \ell(1)$. Then any optimal contract (α, β) for the landlord is a share contract $(0 < \alpha < 1)$ with rent $\beta = \overline{\beta}(\alpha)$ that binds the tenant's participation constraint.

---

[15] Roy and Serfes (2001) explicitly model land productivity as function of labor choices. We take a reduced form approach for ease of presentation.

[16] Note from Lemma 1 that the labor employed under any tenancy contract is bounded above by $\ell(1)$. If $\underline{\ell} \ge \ell(1)$, then labor employed will never exceed $\underline{\ell}$, so no contract will adversely affect the landlord's future income. All that will matter is the present income and the Marshallian reasoning in favor of fixed rental contracts will prevail.

Proof As $\pi(\alpha)$ in (5.9) is a continuous function for $\alpha \in [0,1]$, it attains a maximum in this interval. Since $\Phi'(\alpha) = F(\alpha)$ (Lemma 1), we have $\pi'(\alpha) = (1-\alpha)F'(\alpha) + g'(\ell(\alpha))\ell'(\alpha)$. Since $\ell(0) = 0$ and $g'(0) = 0$, we have $\pi'(0) = F'(0) + g'(0)\ell'(0) = F'(0) > 0$. As $\underline{\ell} < \ell(1)$, we have $g'(\ell(1)) < 0$, implying that $\pi'(1) = g'(\ell(1))\ell'(1) < 0$ (since $\ell'(1) > 0$ by Lemma 1). This shows that $\pi(\alpha)$ is increasing at $\alpha = 0$ and decreasing at $\alpha = 1$. So any maximum of $\pi(\alpha)$ is attained at $0 < \alpha < 1$. This completes the proof. □

In an environment where employment of more labor today hurts the landlord's income tomorrow by adversely affecting the soil quality, it is optimal for the landlord to offer a share contract. A share contract, by restricting the use of labor, helps to maintain the quality of the soil. Thus, the Roy–Serfes model puts forward a positive role of sharecropping towards land productivity. At this point it will be useful to briefly discuss the empirical literature that studies the relation between sharecropping and productivity.

5.4.5 Empirical Tests of Sharecropping and Productivity

There is a large empirical literature that studies the question of whether sharecropping leads to lower productivity (see, e.g., Bell 1977; Shaban 1987; Banerjee et al. 2002). Studies of Bell (1977), Shaban (1987), and Banerjee et al. (2002) are all based on different states of India. Bell's study area is Purnea district in the state of Bihar. Shaban's study covers selected districts in the states of Andhra Pradesh, Maharashtra, and Gujarat. To clearly distinguish potential losses in productivity driven by sharecropping, both of these papers consider households who cultivate their own lands as well as work as sharecroppers. Both Bell (1977) and Shaban (1987) find support for the Marshallian inefficiency thesis, that is, share contracts do involve lower productivity. By contrast, in their study of tenancy reform in the state of West Bengal, Banerjee et al. (2002) find evidence that security of tenure to sharecroppers has led to increased productivity in agriculture.

More recently, Arcand et al. (2007) study tenancy contracts of the village of El Oulja, Tunisia and presents a methodological critique of earlier empirical tests of Marshallian inefficiency. In their study of share tenancy in rural Pakistan, Jacoby and Mansuri (2009) conclude that supervision is important to ensure high productivity under share contracts.

5.4.6 Price Variation and Sharecropping

Price in agriculture often shows variation across seasons. The seasonal variation has a cyclical pattern. Price is the lowest immediately after the harvest. Then it rises, reaches its peak right before the next harvest and falls again in the immediate post harvest period. A rich landlord has access to storage facilities that enable him to take advantage of such variations. He can hoard the produce for a few months to sell it later when the price is high. On the other hand, a poor tenant has to sell the output at low price immediately after the harvest due to various factors such as his urgency to buy essential consumption goods or paying back his debt or simply the lack of storage facilities.

Sen (2011) argues that price variation and the resultant difference in selling behavior of the two parties can provide an explanation of sharecropping. The tenant keeps the entire output under a fixed rental contract. As the tenant receives a low price for the output, the landlord collects a low rental revenue from such a contract. The landlord may prefer a share contract since he can keep a proportion of output in this contract, which enables him to take advantage of price variation.

Formally, consider a landlord who leases his land to a tenant.[17] There are two seasons 1 and 2. Season 1 is the immediate post harvest period and season 2 corresponds to a future period. Price is low in season 1 and high in season 2. Normalize the price of season 1 to be $p_1 = 1$ and let the price of season 2 be $p_2 = p > 1$. The tenant sells any output at his disposal in season 1 at low price 1. The landlord can store output across seasons and sell his output in season 2 at price $p > 1$.

The land lease is executed through tenancy contracts of the form (α, β) where $\alpha \in [0,1]$ is the tenant's share of output and $\beta \in R$ is *rental transfer in cash*[18] from the tenant to the landlord. The tenant employs labor to carry out production. If the output is Q, the tenant keeps αQ and leaves $(1-\alpha)Q$ to the landlord. The tenant sells his output in season 1 at price 1 to receive revenue αQ. The landlord sells his output in season 2 at price $p > 1$ and obtains $p(1-\alpha)Q$. Taking the cash transfer β into account, the tenant's income is $\alpha Q - \beta$ while the landlord's income is $p(1-\alpha)Q + \beta$.

The production process is the same as described in the benchmark model of Sect. 4.1. Since the tenant receives price 1 for his output, his problem stays the same as in Sect. 4.2. Under a contract (α, β) the tenant chooses $\ell = \ell(\alpha)$, the output is $F(\alpha)$ and he obtains $\Phi(\alpha) - \beta$ (see Lemma 1). Taking $Q = F(\alpha)$ in the last paragraph, the landlord's income under (α, β) is

$$p(1-\alpha)F(\alpha) + \beta \tag{5.10}$$

As in the model of Sect. 4.4, let $\underline{\Phi} > 0$ be the reservation income of the tenant. The tenant's participation constraint is $\Phi(\alpha) - \beta \geq \underline{\Phi}$. As the landlord's income is increasing in β, for any $\alpha \in [0,1]$, the optimal β for the landlord is $\overline{\beta}(\alpha) = \Phi(\alpha) - \underline{\Phi}$

[17] This section draws from Sen (2005), an earlier working paper version of Sen (2011).

[18] Note that unlike the previous models, the two contracting parties receive different prices for their output. For this reason, whether the rental transfer is collected in cash or kind does make a difference to the incomes of the agents. Sen (2011) consider both modes of transfer. Rental transfers in practice may sometimes be more varied. In his study of tenancy contracts in Nellore district of South India between 1850 and 1930, Reddy (1996, p. 81) find items of rent that are neither in cash, nor in kind:"...hunting and game, honey and oil, or medicines and *harikathas* (story-telling)..."

that binds the tenant's participation constraint. Replacing $\beta = \bar{\beta}(\alpha)$ in (5.10), the landlord's income can be written as a function of α as follows:

$$\pi(\alpha) = p(1-\alpha)F(\alpha) + \Phi(\alpha) - \underline{\Phi} \tag{5.11}$$

As $\pi(\alpha)$ in (5.11) is a continuous function for $\alpha \in [0,1]$, it attains a maximum in this interval. Since $\Phi'(\alpha) = F(\alpha)$ (Lemma 1), we have $\pi'(\alpha) = p(1-\alpha)F'(\alpha) - (p-1)F(\alpha)$. Since $F(0) = 0$ we have $\pi'(0) = pF'(0) > 0$. As $p > 1$ and $F(1) > 0$, we have $\pi'(1) = -(p-1)F(1) < 0$. This shows that $\pi(\alpha)$ is increasing at $\alpha = 0$ and decreasing at $\alpha = 1$. So any maximum of $\pi(\alpha)$ is attained at $0 < \alpha < 1$. This establishes the following proposition.

Proposition 4 Suppose there is seasonal variation of price and compared to the landlord, the tenant sells his output at a lower price. Then any optimal contract (α, β) for the landlord is a share contract $(0 < \alpha < 1)$ with rent $\beta = \bar{\beta}(\alpha)$ that binds the tenant's participation constraint.

Proposition 4 shows the optimality of sharecropping in a model of price variation in which the two contracting parties receive different prices for the output.[19] In both Propositions 3 and 4, an optimal share contract may potentially include a side payment. There is empirical support for this, as we briefly discuss now.

5.4.7 *Side Payments in Share Contracts*

There is evidence that share contracts observed in practice may include side payments. For example, Forster (1957, p. 236) find that *mètayage* (sharecropping) contracts of eighteenth century Toulose in France included substantial side payments:

> "The sharecropper had to pay for the use of the farm animals as well as for the use of the land. In 1728 François Caseneuve, a tenant of Astre de Blagnac, was obligated under his contract for half the harvest, twenty four pairs of fowl, all the cartage necessary to carry the farm produce to the Toulose market, and a *prélèvement* (supplementary rent) of eighty *setiers* of wheat."

In his study of post-bellum sharecropping contracts in early twentieth century South Carolina, USA, Taylor (1943, p. 126) find that the contract signed between J. S. Hill [the landlord] and Milton T. Chaney [the tenant] of Laurnes County in 1907 had the following terms:

> "The said party of the first part [the landlord] furnishes to the Said party of the Second part [the tenant], one mule and all necessarily tools and impliments to be used by Said party of the Second part in making and Gathering his crop. And also agrees to furnish him Six dollars per month untill the crop is laid by Augt 9 to be paid in the following payments Six

[19] Note that multiple optimal share contracts are possible in both Propositions 3 and 4. Uniqueness of optimal contract can be obtained by imposing more structure to the model.

(6) dollars to be paid on the first-lst of every month untill all is paid—and the Said party of the Second part agrees to Give to the party of the first part A first Lien on his entire crop to Secure the Same. And the party of the Second part agrees to pay as rent to the party of the first part one half $\left(\frac{1}{2}\right)$ of his entire crop That is made on the place and he is to pay all debts to the first party out of the first proceeds—The mule and all the farming Tools are to be returned to the party of the first part after the Crop is made and Gathered in good Condition—"

This passage illustrates that it may sometimes be the case that a landlord provides a tenant with production capital or equipment. Such transactions effectively play the role of a side payment to the tenant. However, there is also evidence, such as in nineteenth century North China (Myers 1984, p. 93) and Bolivia in the 1920s (Jackson 1994, p. 163), where there is no significant side payment and the landlords are primarily interested in collecting the share of the produce.[20]

5.5 Concluding Remarks

The last two models of sharecropping has some interesting implications specific to agrarian economies in transition. If capital investment in land can improve its productivity, then deteriorating soil quality will no longer be a concern for the landlord. Similarly, if there are entities (e.g., big firms or the government) that can assure a high price to the tenant, then the price differential between the contracting parties will disappear. In both of these models, sharecropping is driven by a missing market or the lack of access to market for the contracting parties. This rationale of sharecropping will no longer hold ground if agents obtain access to relevant markets. Thus, both models suggest that as the agrarian economy goes through a phase of transition, the contract forms are likely to evolve.

This chapter has provided a selective review of the ancient institution of sharecropping. Using a basic model of landlord–tenant interaction where land leases are executed through linear tenancy contracts, the chapter has looked at different aspects of a village economy that can influence the nature of these contracts. Based on these aspects, we have presented alternative microeconomic theories of sharecropping from the literature. In this regard the remarks of Bardhan (1999) (Bardhan (2005a) p. 267) on microeconomic analysis of institutions are worth mentioning:

"...careless interpretations of the theory...can blur the thin line between *understanding* an institutional arrangement and *justifying* it...Share cropping, for example, may be a mutually beneficial compromise arrangement between a landlord and a tenant...but this does not mean that a transfer of ownership to the tenant could not be even better. This type of carelessness is only matched by the frequent tendency of the radical reformer on the opposite side to rush in to abolish a pre-existing institution without understanding the micro-economic rationale of its formation...thereby ending up in a situation which may not necessarily improve the conditions of the intended beneficiaries of the abolition programme."

[20] Parts of this section are from Sen (2009), which is a working paper version of Sen (2011). For the contract cited from Taylor (1943), original spelling and sentence structures are retained.

In conclusion, to design effective policies of development it is important to pay attention to the micro-foundations of institutional arrangements. At the same time there is a need to be careful in interpreting the underlying economic theories.

Acknowledgments This chapter was written when I was visiting the Department of Economics, Jadavpur University, whose warm hospitality and research support are gratefully acknowledged.

References

Acemoglu D, Robinson J (2012) Why nations fail: the origins of power, prosperity and poverty. Crown Business, New York
Ackerberg DA, Botticini M (2002) Endogenous matching and the empirical determinants of contract form. J Polit Econ 110:564–591
Arcand J, Ai C, Ethier F (2007) Moral hazard and Marshallian inefficiency: evidence from Tunisia. J Dev Econ 83:411–445
Allen F (1982) On share contracts and screening. Bell J Econ 13:541–547
Allen DW, Lueck D (1992) Contract choice in modern agriculture: cash rent versus cropshare. J Law Econ 35:397–426
Banerjee A, Gertler P, Ghatak M (2002) Empowerment and efficiency: tenancy reform in West Bengal. J Polit Econ 110:239–280
Bardhan P (1984) Land, labor, and rural poverty: essays in development economics. Oxford University Press, Oxford
Bardhan P (ed) (1989) The economic theory of Agrarian Institutions. Clarendon Press, Oxford
Bardhan P (1999)[2005] The economist's approach to agrarian structure. In: Guha R, Parry JP (eds) Institutions and inequalities: essays in honor of Andre Beteille. Oxford University Press, Oxford (Reprinted in: Bardhan (2005a), 262–274)
Bardhan P (2005a) Poverty, agrarian structure, and political economy in India: selected essays. Oxford University Press, Oxford
Bardhan P (2005b) Institutions matter, but which ones? Econ Transit 13:499–532
Bardhan P (20 May 2013) Little, big: two ideas about fighting global poverty. Boston Review
Bardhan P, Singh N (1987) On moral hazard and cost sharing under sharecropping. Am J Agric Econ 69:382–383
Bardhan P, Srinivasan TN (1971) Cropsharing tenancy in agriculture: a theoretical and empirical analysis. Am Econ Rev 61:48–64
Bardhan P, Udry C (1999) Development microeconomics. Oxford University Press, Oxford
Basu K (1992) Limited liability and the existence of share tenancy. J Dev Econ 38:203–220
Basu K (1998) Analytical development economics: the less developed economy revisited. Oxford University Press, Oxford
Bell C (1977) Alternative theories of sharecropping: some tests using evidence from north-east India. J Dev Stud 13:317–346
Bhaduri A (1973) A study in agricultural backwardness under semi-feudalism. Econ J 83:120–137
Bhaduri A (1999) On the border of economic theory and history. Oxford University Press, Oxford
Binswanger HP, Rosenzweig MR (eds) (1984) Contractual arrangements, employ-ment, and wages in rural labor markets in Asia. Yale University Press, New Haven
Bliss C, Stern N (1982) Palanpur: studies in the economy of an Indian village. Oxford University Press, Oxford
Brancaccio T (2003) Land contracts as a two-sided occupational choice: new evidence of risk sharing in India. Working Paper, University College Dublin

Braverman A, Stiglitz JE (1982) Cost-sharing arrangements under sharecropping: moral hazard, incentive flexibility, and risk. Am J Agric Econ 68:642–652
Byres TJ (ed) (1983) Sharecropping and sharecroppers. Routledge (Reprint edition 2005)
Cheung SNS (1969) The theory of share tenancy. University of Chicago Press, Chicago
Clark RJ (1968) Land reform and peasant market participation on the north highlands of Bolivia. Land Econ 44:153–172
Dam K, Ruiz-Pérez D (2012) On the existence of share contracts under limited liability. Econ Lett 117:552–555
Das D (2009) An explanation of share tenancy in terms of unemployment, social norms and power. J Int Trade Econ Dev 18:527–540
Dutta BK (2000) An alternative theory of sharecropping: with evidence from Karimganj District of Assam (India). Indian J Econ 80:395–412
Dutta BK (2003) Theories of share cropping: evidence from north-east India. Mittal Publications, New Delhi
Forster R (1957) The noble as landlord in the region of Toulouse at the end of the old regime. J Econ Hist 17:224–244
Ghatak M, Pandey P (2000) Contract choice in agriculture with joint moral hazard in effort and risk. J Dev Econ 63:303–326
Hallagan W (1978) Self-selection by contractual choice and the theory of sharecropping. Bell J Econ 9:344–354
Hayami Y, Otsuka K (1993) The economics of contract choice: an agrarian perspective. Clarendon Press, Oxford
Jackson RH (1994) Regional markets and agrarian transformation in Bolivia: Cochabamba, 1539–1960. University of New Mexico Press, Albuquerque
Jacoby HG, Mansuri G (2009) Incentives, supervision, and sharecropper productivity. J Dev Econ 88:232–241
Johnson DG (1950) Resource allocation under share contracts. J Polit Econ 58:111–123
Kundu A (2009) Causes and consequences of tenancy-labor interlinked contract in the agricultural labor market of West Bengal. ICFAI J Agric Econ VI:70–82
Laffont JJ, Matoussi MS (1995) Moral hazard, financial constraints and sharecropping in El Oulja. Rev Econ Stud 62:381–399
Marshall A (1920) Principles of economics. Macmillan & Co., Limited (Reprint Edition: 1961)
Muthoo A (1998) Renegotiation-proof tenurial contracts as screening mechanisms. J Dev Econ 56:1–26
Myers RH (1984) The Chinese peasant economy: agricultural development in Hopei and Shantung, 1890–1949. Harvard University Press, Cambridge
Newbery DMG (1977) Risk sharing, sharecropping and uncertain labour markets. Rev Econ Stud 44:585–594
Newbery DMG, Stiglitz JE (1979) Sharecropping, risk-sharing, and the importance of imperfect information. In: Roumasset JA, Boussard JM, Singh I (eds) Risk, uncertainty, and agricultural development. Agricultural Development Council, New York
Otsuka K, Hayami Y (1988) Theories of share tenancy: a critical survey. Econ Dev Cult Change 37:31–68
Otsuka K, Chuma H, Hayami Y (1992) Land and labor contracts in agrarian economies: theories and facts. J Econ Lit 30:1965–2018
Quibria MG, Rashid S (1984) The puzzle of sharecropping: a survey of theories. World Dev 12:103–114
Rao CHH (1971) Uncertainty, entrepreneurship, and sharecropping in India. J Polit Econ 79:578–595
Ray D (1998) Development economics. Princeton University Press, Princeton
Ray T (1999) Share tenancy as strategic delegation. J Dev Econ 58:45–60
Ray T, Singh N (2001) Limited liability, contractual choice, and the tenancy ladder. J Dev Econ 66:289–303

Reddy MA (1996) Lands and tenants in South India: a study of Nellore District 1850–1990. Oxford University Press, Oxford
Roy J, Serfes K (2001) Intertemporal discounting and tenurial contracts. J Dev Econ 64:417–436
Rudra A, Bardhan P (1983) Agrarian relations in West Bengal: results of two surveys. Somaiya Publications Private Limited, New Delhi
Sen D (2005) Sharecropping, interlinkage and price variation. Stony Brook University Department of Economics, Working Paper No. 05–10
Sen D (2009) A theory of sharecropping: the role of price behavior and imperfect competition. MPRA Paper No. 14898
Sen D (2011) A theory of sharecropping: the role of price behavior and imperfect competition. J Econ Behav Organ 80:181–199
Sengupta K (1997) Limited liability, moral hazard and share tenancy. J Dev Econ 52:393–407
Serfes K (2005) Risk sharing vs. incentives: contract design under two-sided heterogeneity. Econ Lett 3:343–349
Shaban RA (1987) Testing between competing models of sharecropping. J Polit Econ 95:893–920
Sharma N, Drèze J (1996) Sharecropping in a north Indian village. J Dev Stud 33:1–39
Shetty S (1988) Limited liability, wealth differences, and the tenancy ladder in agrarian economies. J Dev Econ 29:1–22
Singh N (1989) Theories of sharecropping. In: Bardhan P (ed) The economic theory of agrarian institutions. Oxford University Press, Oxford
Stiglitz JE (1974) Incentives and risk sharing in sharecropping. Rev Econ Stud 95:219–255
Stiglitz JE (1989) Rational peasants, efficient institutions, and a theory of rural organization: methodological remarks for development economics. In: Bardhan P (ed) The economic theory of agrarian institutions. Clarendon Press, Oxford
Stiglitz JE, Weiss A (1981) Credit rationing in markets with imperfect information. Am Econ Rev 71:393–410
Taylor RH (1943) Post-bellum southern rental contracts. Agric Hist 17:121–128

Part II
Trade and Foreign Aid

Chapter 6
Trade in Intermediate Goods, Endogenous Growth and Intellectual Property Rights

Bidisha Chakraborty

6.1 Introduction

Technological progress is one of the key components of economic growth, and intellectual property rights (IPRs) play an important role in determining technological progress. The agreement on Trade Related Intellectual Property issues (TRIPS) have been put on the agenda of the Uruguay round of trade negotiations under the General Agreement on Tariffs and Trade (GATT) 1994. This agreement requires that both developed and developing countries should mutually agree to strengthen their IPRs.

The effect of IPRs on growth rate has been a subject of debate for a long time. There is a substantial theoretical and empirical literature on international trade dealing with the issue of effect of IPRs on technological progress and growth[1]. Helpman (1993) shows that in the long run, rate of growth of technology (rate of innovation) is decreased in response to tighter IPRs. Mondal and Gupta (2008a) show that even in the presence of unemployment and the efficiency wage hypothesis, the Helpman (1993) result holds. According to Lai (1998), the Helpman (1993) result holds if imitation is the channel of production transfer, and the opposite happens if multinationalization is the channel of production transfer. Akiyama and Furukawa (2009) show that there is an inverted U-shaped relationship between IPRs and rate of innovation incorporating the concept of appropriability of innovation. When technologies are masked, strengthening IPRs encourages innovation, and when technologies are not masked, the opposite happens. Mondal and Gupta (2008b) show that strengthening

[1] See, for example, Helpman (1993); Grossman and Helpman (1991a); Lai (1998); Akiyama and Furukawa (2009); Mondal and Gupta (2008a, b); Eicher and Penalosa (2008); Schneider (2005); Falvey et al. (2004); Gould and Gruben (1996), etc.

B. Chakraborty (✉)
Department of Economics, Jadavpur University, Kolkata, India
e-mail: bidisha.chakraborty@gmail.com

S. Banerjee et al. (eds.), *Understanding Development,* India Studies in Business and Economics, DOI 10.1007/978-81-322-2455-6_6

IPRs may have a positive effect on the rate of innovation in the presence of international labour mobility in the Helpman (1993) model.

This chapter integrates the Romer (1990) model and Helpman (1993) model and considers the possibility of trade in intermediate goods. The chapter is new to the literature considering intellectual property protection in a trade model that allows capital good trade rather than trade in consumption goods. North innovates the variety of intermediate goods, and South imitates it. Like Ventura (1997), this chapter assumes that final goods are not traded, while capital-intensive intermediate goods are traded. The effect of IPRs on economic growth is studied. We show that a unique steady-state balanced growth equilibrium may exist, or there may be multiple steady-state equilibria and tighter IPRs lead to both a higher and a lower steady-state balanced growth rate depending on the human capital endowment. This contradicts the result obtained by Helpman (1993).

The rest of the chapter is organized as follows. Section 6.2 presents the basic model, Sect. 6.3 presents the market equilibrium of the model, Sect. 6.4 contains the analysis of the steady-state balanced growth equilibrium, Sect. 6.5 presents numerical results. This section gives examples of steady-state balanced growth equilibrium and also studies the effect of change in IPRs on growth rate numerically. Concluding remarks are made in Sect. 6.6.

6.2 The Model

In this chapter, an R&D-based endogenous growth model has been developed. It is assumed that there are two countries—developed North and developing South. North is developed in the sense that it is richer in human capital endowment. The skilled labour force in North knows how to innovate the design of a new intermediate good. North and South produce Y_n and Y_s final goods, respectively. These goods are used for final consumption and are not traded. They are produced with the help of human capital and intermediate input. North and South are linked by free trade in differentiated inputs which are invented in North and imitated by South. It is assumed that human capital as well as physical capital is internationally immobile. Only knowledge capital and intermediate inputs are mobile across nations. It is also assumed that the final goods and R&D sectors are perfectly competitive in North, but North has monopoly over each variety of intermediate goods innovated, whereas the final goods and intermediate goods sectors are perfectly competitive in South. We assume the total human capital stock of North and South are constant. All individuals of each country are assumed to be identical. The population size of North and South is normalized to unity.

The specification of production technology of the final goods sector and intermediate goods sector are the same as in Romer (1990). The production function of the jth country is given by

$$Y_j = T_j (H_j^Y)^\alpha \left[\int_0^A x_j(i)^{1-\alpha} di \right], \tag{6.1}$$

where $x_j(i)$ denotes the quantity of the ith variety intermediate input used by the jth country, A denotes the number of intermediate goods the society knows how to produce (measure of technical knowhow), and (H_j^Y) denotes human capital of jth country employed in the final goods sector with $0 < \alpha < 1$; T_j is the production technology parameter of jth country and $j = n$ for North and $j = s$ for South.

In North, there is a distinct firm i for each intermediate good i. In South, there is one industry i for each intermediate good i. It is assumed that there is a number of varieties of intermediate goods used by North and South. Both countries, North and South, use all these varieties of intermediate goods no matter where they are produced. The total quantity of ith intermediate good produced in jth country is given by

$$x^j(i) = x_n^j(i) + x_s^j(i), \tag{6.2}$$

where $x_n^j(i)$ is the quantity of ith intermediate good produced in jth country and sold to North, and $x_s^j(i)$ is the quantity of ith intermediate good produced in jth country and sold to South.

An intermediate good firm in North must purchase a design or blueprint for good i from an R&D firm before commencing production. Once the firm owns the design, it has the monopoly power to produce the designed intermediate good. On the other hand, in South there is no R&D firm. An intermediate good firm can convert one unit of physical capital into one unit of intermediate goods in both North and South. So, the total capital employed in the intermediate goods sector in South and North are given by

$$K_s = \int_0^{A_s} x^s(i) di \tag{6.3}$$

$$K_n = \int_{A_s}^{A} x^n(i) di. \tag{6.4}$$

The production technology of the R&D sector of North and South are the same as Helpman (1993). Here, the total number of varieties of intermediate goods is given by

$$A = A_n + A_s,$$

where A_n denotes the number of varieties that the South has not yet imitated and hence produced in North, and A_s denotes the number of varieties produced in South. North is the innovator and South is the imitator country. South imitates at exogenous rate m. It is assumed that in South, technology transfer (imitation) takes place exogenously and does not involve any cost. In South, the R&D sector and intermediate goods sector are vertically integrated, while in North, the R&D firm is a separate firm, and designs are transferred from the R&D firm to the intermediate good firm at an explicit price. It is assumed that human capital and existing knowledge are the only inputs that influence the output of designs in North, while in South no input is employed to produce designs by transferring technology. The production function of the R&D sector of North and South are given by

$$\dot{A} = \delta_n H_n^A A \tag{6.5}$$

and

$$\dot{A}_s = mA_n. \tag{6.6}$$

Let the fraction of goods that have not yet been imitated be $\xi = \dfrac{A_n}{A}$.

The total human capital stock of South is employed in the final goods production sector. So the total human capital stock of South is given by

$$\bar{H}_s = H_s^Y.$$

The total human capital stock of North is allocated between the final goods production sector and the R&D sector. Hence, the total human capital stock of North is given by

$$\bar{H}_n = H_n^Y + H_n^A.$$

Individuals of North and South derive utility from the consumption of final goods. The utility function of the representative individual is given by

$$U(C_j) = \frac{(C_j)^{1-\sigma} - 1}{(1-\sigma)},$$

where C_j is the consumption of final goods in jth country. The dynamic budget constraint of South is given by

$$\dot{K}_s = Y_s - C_s. \tag{6.7}$$

The dynamic budget constraint of North is given by

$$\dot{K}_n = Y_n - C_n. \tag{6.8}$$

We assume that trade is always balanced. The trade balance equation implies that the value of import of each country is equal to the value of export of each country and is given by

$$p_s^n x_s^n A_N = p_n^s x_n^s A_s, \tag{6.9}$$

where $p_j^{j'}(i)$ denotes the price charged by ith firm of j' country from *j*th country.

In the next section, we discuss the market equilibrium of the model.

6.3 Market Equilibrium

Suppose P_j is the price of the final good produced in jth country, and w_j is the wage given to the skilled labour of *j*th country.

Given values of H_j^Y, aggregate demand for the *i*th intermediate good by *j*th country is derived by maximizing

$$\Pi_j^Y = P_j T_j (H_j^Y)^{\alpha} \left[\int_0^{A_s} x_j^s(i)^{1-\alpha} di + \int_{A_s}^{A} x_j^N(i)^{1-\alpha} di \right] - \int_0^{A_s} p_j^s(i) x_j^s(i) - \int_{A_s}^{A} p_j^n(i) x_j^n(i) di - w_j H_j^Y,$$

with respect to $x_j^s(i)$, $x_j^n(i)$ and H_j^Y. The demand functions of $x_j^s(i)$ and $x_j^n(i)$ are given by

$$p_j^s(i) = (1-\alpha) P_j T_j (H_j^Y)^{\alpha} (x_j^s(i))^{-\alpha}, \tag{6.10}$$

$$p_j^n(i) = (1-\alpha) P_j T_j (H_j^Y)^{\alpha} (x_j^n(i))^{-\alpha} \tag{6.11}$$

and

$$w_j = \alpha P_j T_j (H_j^Y)^{\alpha-1} \left[\int_0^{A_s} x_j^s(i)^{1-\alpha} di + \int_{A_s}^{A} x_j^N(i)^{1-\alpha} di \right].$$

6.3.1 *Intermediate Goods Sector of North*

North has monopoly over each variety of intermediate goods. Faced with the given values of H_j^Y and r_n, a Northern intermediate good firm that has already incurred the fixed cost investment in a design will choose a level of output x^n to maximize revenue minus variable cost on every date. r_j is the rate of interest of *j*th country. The objective of *i*th Northern intermediate good firm is to maximize its profit

$$\pi_x^n = (1-\alpha)P_n T_n (H_n^Y)^\alpha (x_n^n(i))^{1-\alpha} + (1-\alpha)P_s T_s (H_s^Y)^\alpha (x_s^n(i))^{1-\alpha} - r_n (x_n^n(i) + x_s^n(i)) \quad (6.12)$$

with respect to $x_n^n(i)$ and $x_s^n(i)$.

In equilibrium, the outputs sold to North and South by the ith intermediate good firm of North are given by

$$x_s^n(i) = \left[\frac{r_n}{(1-\alpha)^2 P_s T_s}\right]^{-\frac{1}{\alpha}} H_s^Y \quad (6.13)$$

and

$$x_n^n(i) = \left[\frac{r_n}{(1-\alpha)^2 P_n T_n}\right]^{-\frac{1}{\alpha}} H_n^Y. \quad (6.14)$$

$\forall i$ and all Northern intermediate good firms will charge the same price to South and North and that price is

$$p_n^n(i) = p_s^n(i) = \frac{r_n}{(1-\alpha)} = p^n. \quad (6.15)$$

Hence, the monopoly profit of any Northern intermediate good firm is given by $\alpha p^n x^n$.

6.3.2 *Intermediate Goods Sector of South*

Intermediate good firms of South are perfectly competitive. In equilibrium, they must earn equal marginal revenue from North and South, and in the long run the profit of each firm must be zero. Faced with the given values of H_j^Y and r_s, a Southern intermediate good firm will choose a level of output x^s, for which the marginal revenue earned from both countries is the same and the profit is zero. The profit function of ith Southern intermediate good industry is given by

$$\pi_x^s = (1-\alpha)P_n T_n (H_n^Y)^\alpha (x_n^s(i))^{1-\alpha} + (1-\alpha)P_s T_s (H_s^Y)^\alpha (x_s^s(i))^{1-\alpha} - r_s (x_n^s(i) + x_s^s(i)). \quad (6.16)$$

As this market is perfectly competitive, in equilibrium, $\pi_x^s = 0$. Since there is free and costless trade, the marginal revenue earned from North and South is the same.

$$x_s^s(i) = \left[\frac{r_s}{(1-\alpha)P_s T_s}\right]^{-\frac{1}{\alpha}} H_s^Y \tag{6.17}$$

and

$$x_n^s(i) = \left[\frac{r_s}{(1-\alpha)P_n T_n}\right]^{-\frac{1}{\alpha}} H_n^Y \tag{6.18}$$

$\forall i$. The price charged by each Southern intermediate good industry to North as well as to South are the same, and it is

$$p_s^s(i) = p_n^s(i) = r_s = p^s. \tag{6.19}$$

6.3.3 Equilibrium Wage Determination

The profit of a research firm in North is given by

$$\pi_r^n = P_A^n \dot{A} - w^n H_n^A.$$

Since the R&D sector in North is competitive, the wage of skilled labour employed in the R&D firm of North is obtained by maximizing π_r^n with respect to H_n^A, and it is given by

$$w_A^n = P_A^n \delta_n A. \tag{6.20}$$

A Northern research firm produces a design of an intermediate good once for all and sells the design to an intermediate good firm of North. A Northern intermediate good firm which manufactures a new product at time t faces a positive probability that its product will be imitated by a Southern research firm. Once the product is imitated by South, the Northern intermediate good firm stops producing it. If the product is imitated at time T, the Northern intermediate good firm's stream of profit ends. In that event, the Northern intermediate good firm earns, in total, a sum whose present discounted value at t is

$$\Pi(t,T)_x^N = \int_t^T e^{-[R(\tau)-R(t)]}\pi_x^n(\tau)d\tau,$$

where $R(t)$ is the cumulative interest factor of North from time 0 to time t. In a time interval of length $d\tau$, the Southern intermediate good firm imitates a proportion $md\tau$ of the Northern product. Then, every Northern product that has not been imitated faces the probability $md\tau$ of being imitated in the time interval of length $d\tau$. The date T, on which imitation takes place, is a random variable. Letting $F(t,T)$

denote the cumulative distribution function for T for a product developed at t, the expected present value of profits of the Northern intermediate good firm for a time t is

$$V(t) = \int_t^{\infty} \Pi_x^N(t,T) F_T(t,T) dT. \tag{6.21}$$

Since Southern intermediate good firms choose their target products at random, each existing Northern intermediate good firm faces the same chance of being imitated. So, the hazard rate of $F(t,T)$, which is given by $\frac{F_T'}{(1-F)}$, is equal to the instantaneous rate of imitation m. This in turn implies[2]

$$F(t,T) = 1 - e^{-\int_t^T} m(\tau) d\tau.$$

Differentiating Eq. (6.21) with respect to t

$$\dot{V} = -\pi_x^n + (\dot{R} + m)V. \tag{6.22}$$

The decision by the Northern firm to produce a new intermediate input depends on a comparison of the expected present value of its profit $V(t)$ with the cost of the design P_A. Since the Northern research firm is competitive, the price of the design (P_A) is constant in equilibrium, and this price will be bid up until it is equal to the expected present value of the net revenue that a monopolist can extract. If P_A is greater than V, some firms will enter the research industry of North, and if P_A is less than V, some firms will leave the R&D sector of North. So, in equilibrium, $P_A = V$, and this is constant. Hence, $\dot{V} = 0$. Since $\dot{R} = r^n$, from Eq. (6.22) we have[3]

$$\frac{\pi_x^n}{P_A^n} = r^n + m. \tag{6.23}$$

Using Eqs. 6.12–6.15, 6.20 and 6.23 we have[4]

$$w_A^n = \frac{\alpha(1-\alpha) P_n T_n \delta_n A}{(r^n + m)} (H_n^Y)^{\alpha} (x_n^n(i))^{-\alpha} (x_s^n + x_n^n). \tag{6.24}$$

Since each intermediate good industry of South sells exactly the same quantity of output to North (x_n^s is same for all i) and each Northern firm sells exactly the same quantity of output to its own country (x_n^n is same for all i), the total output of the final goods sector in North is given by

---

[2] See Grossman and Helpman (1991b)

[3] In Romer's (1990) model . Hence, in Romer's (1990) model. Note that since the R&D sector is perfectly competitive, the profit of the R&D firm.

[4] A detailed derivation is given in the Appendix.

$$Y_n = T_n (H_n^Y)^{\alpha} [A_s (x_n^s(i))^{1-\alpha} + A_n (x_n^n(i))^{1-\alpha}]$$

Wage given to skilled labour employed in the final goods production sector of North is given by

$$w_Y^n = \alpha P_n T_n (H_n^Y)^{\alpha-1} (x_n^n(i))^{-\alpha} \left[A_s \left(\frac{x_n^s}{x_n^n} \right)^{-\alpha} x_n^s + A_n x_n^n \right]. \tag{6.25}$$

No arbitrage condition of skilled labour market implies that $w_A^n = w_Y^n = w_H^n$. Using Eqs. (6.14), (6.18), (6.24) and (6.25) implies that human capital employed in the final goods sector in North is obtained, and it is given by

$$H_n^Y = \frac{(r_n + m)}{(1-\alpha)\delta_n} \left[(1-\xi) \left\{ \frac{r_s(1-\alpha)}{r_n} \right\}^{-\frac{(1-\alpha)}{\alpha}} + \xi \right] - \bar{H}_s \left(\frac{P_s T_s}{P_n T_n} \right)^{\frac{1}{\alpha}}. \tag{6.26}$$

Note that if ξ, r_s, r_n are constant, H_n^Y is also constant. Human capital employed in the R&D sector of North is given by

$$H_n^A = \bar{H}_n - H_n^Y. \tag{6.27}$$

Since each intermediate good industry of South sells exactly the same quantity of output to South (x_s^s is same for all i), and each Northern firm sells exactly the same quantity of output to South (x_s^n is same for all i), the total output of the final goods sector is given by

$$Y_s = T_s (H_s^Y)^{\alpha} [A_s (x_s^s(i))^{1-\alpha} + A_n (x_s^n(i))^{1-\alpha}]$$

In South, H_s^Y is fixed at $\bar{H}_s^Y$. The wage of the skilled labour employed in the final goods production sector of South is given by

$$w_H^s = \alpha P_s T_s (H_s^Y)^{\alpha-1} [A_s (x_s^s(i))^{1-\alpha} + A_n (x_s^n(i))^{1-\alpha}]. \tag{6.28}$$

Using Eqs. (6.13), (6.14), (6.17), (6.18) and (6.25), we have

$$\frac{w_H^s}{w_H^n} = \left(\frac{P_s T_s}{P_n T_n} \right)^{\frac{1}{\alpha}},$$

where $w_H^n = w_Y^n = w_A^n$. So, in this model, the ratio of wage of skilled labour in North and South depends on the price of final goods and technology in both countries. Note that even if this ratio is equal to one, there will be trade since the basis of trade is not the difference in skilled wage. The difference in price of intermediate goods results from the assumption of difference in market structure of intermediate goods in North and South. In North, the producer has monopoly power over each variety of intermediate goods, and in South, each variety of intermediate goods market is perfectly competitive. So, the price charged by South for each unit of intermediate goods is lower compared to that of North. Moreover, South does not have the technical knowhow to produce the intermediate goods that North produces.

6.3.4 *Optimization Problem of Household*

The optimization problem of a Northern household is to maximize

$$\int_0^{\infty} \frac{(C_n)^{1-\sigma} - 1}{(1-\sigma)} e^{-\rho t} dt$$

subject to the asset accumulation function of North given by the equation

$$\dot{B}_n = r_n K_n + w_n H_n - P_n C_n,$$

where B_n is the net asset of a Northern individual. C_n is the control variable, and K_n is the state variable. The rate of growth of consumption is given by

$$\frac{\dot{C}_n}{C_n} = \frac{(r_n - \rho)}{\sigma}. \tag{6.29}$$

Similarly, the optimization problem of a Southern household is to maximize

$$\int_0^{\infty} \frac{(C_s)^{1-\sigma} - 1}{(1-\sigma)} e^{-\rho t} dt$$

subject to the asset accumulation function of South, which is given by the equation

$$\dot{B}_s = r_s K_s + w_s H_s - P_s C_s,$$

where B_s is the net asset of a Southern individual, C_s is the control variable, and K_s is the state variable. The rate of growth of consumption is given by

$$\frac{\dot{C}_s}{C_s} = \frac{(r_s - \rho)}{\sigma}. \tag{6.30}$$

6.4 Balanced Growth Equilibrium

A balanced growth equilibrium is defined as an equilibrium, where $Y_s, Y_n, K_s, K_n, A_s, A_n, A$ grow at constant exponential rate, and ξ, r_n, r_s are constant. Let the constant growth rate of A be g. From Eq. (6.5), A grows at a constant rate, which implies that H_n^A is constant, which again implies that H_n^Y is constant. H_n^Y is not constant unless ξ is constant. The growth rate of ξ is given by $\frac{\dot{\xi}}{\xi} = \frac{g}{\xi} - m - g$. In balanced growth equilibrium, the value of ξ is given by

$$\xi = \frac{g}{(m+g)}. \tag{6.31}$$

The constant value of ξ implies that A, A_s, A_n grow at same constant rate g. Now, using Eqs. (6.3), (6.4), (6.13), (6.14), (6.17) and (6.18) we have

$$\frac{K_s}{A_s} = \left\{\frac{r_s}{(1-\alpha)}\right\}^{-\frac{1}{\alpha}} \left[\frac{H_s^Y}{(P_sT_s)^{-\frac{1}{\alpha}}} + \frac{H_n^Y}{(P_nT_n)^{-\frac{1}{\alpha}}}\right]$$

and

$$\frac{K_n}{A_n} = \left\{\frac{r_n}{(1-\alpha)^2}\right\}^{-\frac{1}{\alpha}} \left[\frac{H_s^Y}{(P_sT_s)^{-\frac{1}{\alpha}}} + \frac{H_n^Y}{(P_nT_n)^{-\frac{1}{\alpha}}}\right].$$

Since r_s, r_n, H_s^Y, H_n^Y are constants, $\frac{K_s}{A_s}$ and $\frac{K_n}{A_n}$ are also constants. It implies that K_s, K_n, A_s, A_n grow at same constant rate g. As the trade is balanced using Eqs. (6.18), (6.19), (6.15), (6.13) and (6.9), we have

$$\begin{aligned}&\left[\left(\frac{r_n}{(1-\alpha)r_s}\right)^{1-\frac{1}{\alpha}}\left(\frac{P_sT_s}{P_nT_n}\right)^{\frac{1}{\alpha}}\frac{\xi}{(1-\xi)}+1\right]\bar{H}_s \\ &= \left[(1-\xi)\left\{\frac{(1-\alpha)r_s}{r_n}\right\}^{-\frac{(1-\alpha)}{\alpha}} + \xi\right]\frac{(r_n+m)}{(1-\alpha)\delta_n}.\end{aligned} \tag{6.32}$$

From the above Eq. (6.32), the ratio of final goods in both countries is obtained.

Using Eqs. (6.10) and (6.14), $\frac{Y_s}{A}$ is given by

$$\frac{Y_s}{A} = T_s\bar{H}_s^Y\left\{(1-\alpha)P_sT_s\right\}^{\frac{(1-\alpha)}{\alpha}}\left[(1-\xi)(r_s)^{-\frac{(1-\alpha)}{\alpha}} + \xi(r_n)^{-\frac{(1-\alpha)}{\alpha}}(1-\alpha)^{\frac{(1-\alpha)}{\alpha}}\right]. \tag{6.33}$$

Using Eqs. (6.11) and (6.15), $\frac{Y_n}{A}$ is given by

$$\frac{Y_n}{A} = T_n \bar{H}_n^Y \left\{(1-\alpha)P_n T_n\right\}^{\frac{(1-\alpha)}{\alpha}} \left[(1-\xi)(r_s)^{-\frac{(1-\alpha)}{\alpha}} + \xi(r_n)^{-\frac{(1-\alpha)}{\alpha}}(1-\alpha)^{\frac{(1-\alpha)}{\alpha}}\right]. \tag{6.34}$$

Note that if ξ, r_s, r_n are constant, $\frac{Y_s}{A}$ and $\frac{Y_n}{A}$ are also constant.

From Eqs. (6.33), (6.34), (6.31), $\frac{Y_s}{A_s}$ and $\frac{Y_n}{A_n}$ are constant. Hence, along a balanced growth path, $Y_s, Y_n, K_s, K_n, A_s, A_n, A$ grow at the same constant growth rate g.

So from Eqs. (6.29) and (6.30), we have

$$g_d = \frac{r_n - \rho}{\sigma} = \frac{r_s - \rho}{\sigma}. \tag{6.35}$$

Hence, in steady-state equilibrium, $r_n = r_s = r(let)$.

Note that, along the balanced growth path, although the marginal cost of capital is the same in North and South, the prices of intermediate goods in both countries are different. This is due to the fact that South cannot produce all the intermediate goods that North produces as South does not have that technical knowhow. On the other hand, once the technology transfer takes place, North cannot produce the imitated intermediate goods that South produces at a much cheaper rate (since $\frac{r}{(1-\alpha)} > r$).

Using Eqs. (6.5), (6.26) and (6.27), we have

$$g = \frac{\dot{A}}{A} = \delta_n[\bar{H}_n - H_n^Y].$$

Hence, we have

$$g_s = \delta_n\left[\bar{H}_n + \bar{H}_s\left(\frac{P_s T_s}{P_n T_n}\right)^{\frac{1}{\alpha}}\right] - \frac{(r_n + m)}{(1-\alpha)\delta_n}[(1-\xi)(1-\alpha)^{1-\frac{1}{\alpha}} + \xi]. \tag{6.36}$$

Equation (6.35) represents the demand-side growth rate, and Eq. (6.36) represents the supply-side growth rate. In equilibrium, $g_d = g_s$. Combining Eqs. (6.31), (6.27), (6.35) and (6.36), we have

$$\begin{aligned} &g^3(1-\alpha+\sigma) + g^2\{(1-\alpha)(m-\delta_n\bar{H}_n) \\ &+ (m+\rho)\} + g[\delta_n m(1-\alpha)\{\bar{H}_s(1-\alpha)^{1-\frac{1}{\alpha}} - \bar{H}_n\} \\ &- \sigma m^2(1-\alpha)^{2(1-\frac{1}{\alpha})}] + m^2(1-\alpha)^{2-\frac{1}{\alpha}}\{\delta_n\bar{H}_s - (m+\rho)(1-\alpha)^{-\frac{1}{\alpha}}\} = 0. \end{aligned} \tag{6.37}$$

Hence, we get

$$ag^3 + bg^2 + cg + d = 0, \tag{6.38}$$

where

$$a = (1 - \alpha + \sigma)$$

$$b = \{(1-\alpha)(m - \delta_n \bar{H}_n) + (m+\rho)\}$$

$$c = [\delta_n m(1-\alpha)\{\bar{H}_s(1-\alpha)^{1-\frac{1}{\alpha}} - \bar{H}_n\} - \sigma m^2 (1-\alpha)^{2(1-\frac{1}{\alpha})}]$$

$$d = m^2(1-\alpha)^{2-\frac{1}{\alpha}}\{\delta_n \bar{H}_s - (m+\rho)(1-\alpha)^{-\frac{1}{\alpha}}\}.$$

Clearly, a is always positive. Regarding sign of b, c and d, the following six cases may emerge:

Case (i) When $\bar{H}_s < \min\{\bar{H}_n(1-\alpha)^{\frac{1}{\alpha}-1}, \frac{(m+\rho)}{\delta_n}(1-\alpha)^{-\frac{1}{\alpha}}\}$, c is negative, d is negative. No matter what be the sign of b in this case, a unique positive steady-state balanced growth rate exists.

Case (ii) When $\bar{H}_n < \frac{(2-\alpha)m+\rho}{(1-\alpha)\delta_n}$ and $\frac{(m+\rho)}{\delta_n}(1-\alpha)^{-\frac{1}{\alpha}} > \bar{H}_s > (1-\alpha)^{\frac{1}{\alpha}-1}(\bar{H}_n + \frac{\sigma m}{\delta_n}(1-\alpha)^{1-\frac{2}{\alpha}})$, b is positive, c is positive, d is negative. In this case, a unique positive steady-state balanced growth rate exists.

Case (iii) When $\frac{(m+\rho)}{\delta_n}(1-\alpha)^{-\frac{1}{\alpha}} < \bar{H}_s < \bar{H}_n(1-\alpha)^{\frac{1}{\alpha}-1}$, c is negative, d is positive. No matter what be the sign of b in this case, two positive solutions of steady-state balanced growth rate exist.

Case (iv) When $\bar{H}_n > \frac{(2-\alpha)m+\rho}{(1-\alpha)\delta_n}$ and $\frac{(m+\rho)}{\delta_n}(1-\alpha)^{-\frac{1}{\alpha}} > \bar{H}_s > (1-\alpha)^{\frac{1}{\alpha}-1}(\bar{H}_n + \frac{\sigma m}{\delta_n}(1-\alpha)^{1-\frac{2}{\alpha}})$, b is negative, c is positive, d is negative. In this case, either three or one positive real steady-state solutions of balanced growth rate exists. If one positive real solution exists, then the other two roots are imaginary.

Case (v) When $\bar{H}_n > \frac{(2-\alpha)m+\rho}{(1-\alpha)\delta_n}$, b is negative,

$\bar{H}_s > \max\{\frac{(m+\rho)}{\delta_n}(1-\alpha)^{-\frac{1}{\alpha}}, (1-\alpha)^{\frac{1}{\alpha}-1}(\bar{H}_n + \frac{\sigma m}{\delta_n}(1-\alpha)^{1-\frac{2}{\alpha}})\}$, c is positive, d is positive. In this case, two positive and one negative steady-state solutions of balanced growth rate exist.

Case (vi) When

$$\frac{(2-\alpha)m+\rho}{(1-\alpha)\delta_n} > \bar{H}_n > \bar{H}_s > \min\{\frac{(m+\rho)}{\delta_n}(1-\alpha)^{-\frac{1}{\alpha}}, (1-\alpha)^{\frac{1}{\alpha}-1}(\bar{H}_n + \frac{\sigma m}{\delta_n}(1-\alpha)^{1-\frac{2}{\alpha}})\},$$

b is positive, c is positive, d is positive. No positive steady-state solution of balanced growth rate exists.

So, a unique solution of steady-state growth rate exists only under case (i) and case (ii). In other cases, multiple equilibria may arise. If aggregate human capital stock of South is sufficiently small, a unique growth rate exists.

Proposition 1 At least one positive balanced growth rate exists. Under case (i) and case (ii), a unique growth rate exists, otherwise multiple steady-state growth equilibria may exist.

6.5 Numerical Results

6.5.1 Numerical Example of Steady-State Balanced Growth Rate

i. When $\alpha = 0.5, \sigma = 0.5, m = 0.5, \delta = 1, \bar{H}_n = 6, \bar{H}_s = 2, \rho = 0.05$ yields growth rate 2.593, and other two growth rates are complex conjugates.
ii. When $\alpha = 0.5, \sigma = 0.01, m = 0.5, \delta = 0.5, \bar{H}_n = 3, \bar{H}_s = 2.5, \rho = 0.05$ yields growth rate 0.557, and other two growth rates are complex conjugates.
iii. When $\alpha = 0.5, \sigma = 0.5, m = 0.1, \delta = 1, \bar{H}_n = 6, \bar{H}_s = 2, \rho = 0.05$ yields two positive growth rates $0.0528, 2.84051$ and one negative growth rate.
iv. When $\alpha = 0.5, \sigma = 0.1, m = 0.4, \delta = 0.5, \bar{H}_n = 3, \bar{H}_s = 2.9, \rho = 0.03$ yields growth rate 0.2, and other two growth rates are complex conjugates.
v. When $\alpha = 0.5, \sigma = 0.1, m = 0.1, \delta = 0.5, \bar{H}_n = 10, \bar{H}_s = 7, \rho = 0.03$ yields two positive growth rates $0.138865, 3.821396$ and one negative growth rate.
vi. For every possible numerical specifications we found that $\frac{(2-\alpha)m+\rho}{(1-\alpha)\delta_n} < \frac{(m+\rho)}{\delta_n}(1-\alpha)^{-\frac{1}{\alpha}}$. If this requirement is satisfied, $\bar{H}_s > \bar{H}_n$. That contradicts our definition of North and South, that is positive b and positive d cannot occur simultaneously. Hence, we could not find any example of non-existence of growth rates.

6.5.2 Effect of Change in IPRs on Growth Rate

In this section, we study the effect of IPRs on growth rate numerically. Following Helpman (1993), we capture the change in IPRs by change in m. Strengthening IPRs implies lowering the value of m. We investigate the effect of change in m on growth rate. We found that in case 2 and case 4, where a unique growth rate exists, there is a positive relationship between m and g. In case 1, with increase in m, initially the growth rate reduces a bit, but afterwards it shows steady increase. In case 3 and case 5, we got two positive-balanced growth rates. In both cases, the higher one of the growth rates declines with response to the increase in m. In case 3, the lower one of the growth rates shows an inverted-U-shaped relationship in response to the increase in m, and in case 5, it shows a steady increase in response to the increase in m (Figs. 6.1, 6.2, 6.3, 6.4, 6.5, 6.6 and 6.7).

Case1:

α=0.5	σ=0.5	δ=1	H_n=6	H_s=2	ρ=0.05

m	g
0.5	2.593
0.6	2.59151
0.7	2.61431
0.8	2.658983
0.9	2.72238
1	2.801289
2	4
3	5.43

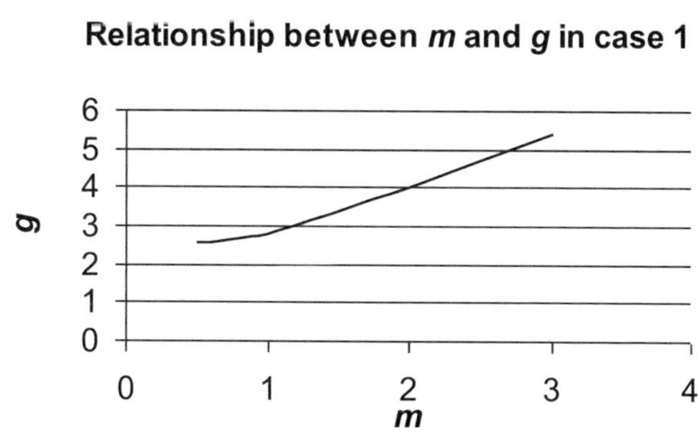

Fig. 6.1 Relationship between m and g in case 1

Case2:

α=0.5	σ=0.01	δ=0.5	H_n=3	H_s=2.5	ρ=0.05

m	*g*
3	4.009
2.4	3.19
2.3	3.056
2.2	2.91
2.1	2.783529
2	2.6471
1.9	2.5106
1.4	1.91877
1	1.2761
0.5	0.557227

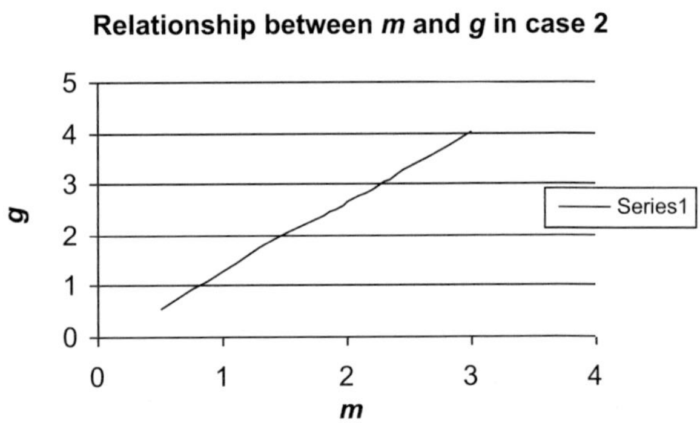

Fig. 6.2 Relationship between *m* and *g* in case 2

Case3:

α=0.5	σ=0.5	δ=1	H_n=6	H_s=2	ρ=0.05

m	*g1*	*g2*
0.1	0.0528	2.84051
0.2	0.081672	2.7466
0.3	0.08013	2.672072
0.4	0.03945	2.620133

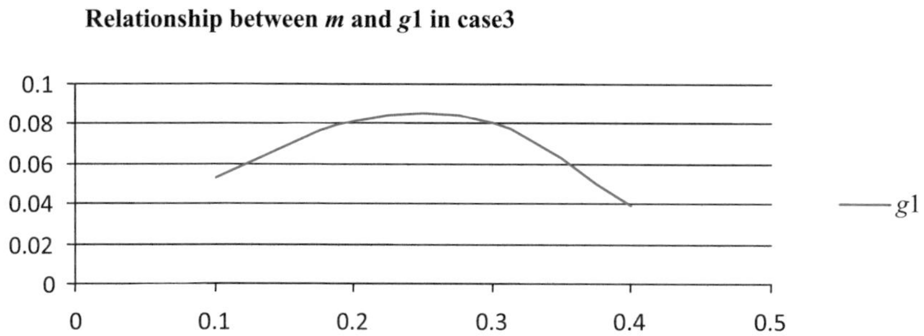

Fig. 6.3 Relationship between *m* and *g*1 in case 3

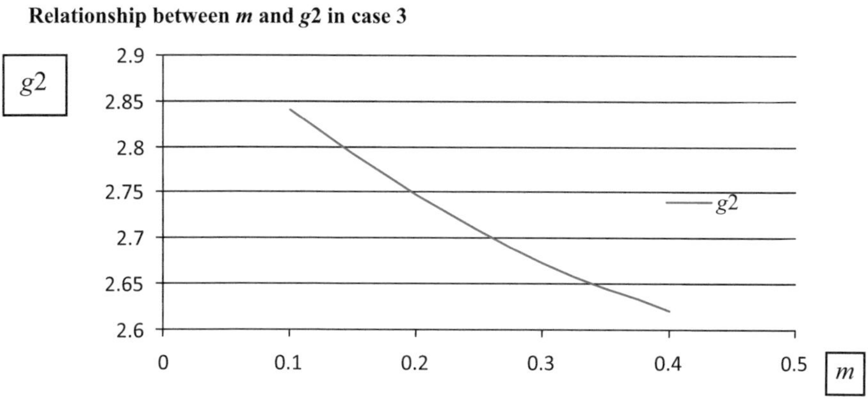

Fig. 6.4 Relationship between *m* and *g*2 in case 3

Case 4:

α=0.5	σ=0.1	δ=0.5	H_n=3	H_s=2.9	ρ=0.03

m	*g*
0.4	0.2
0.41	0.2292
0.42	0.25712
0.43	0.283775
0.44	0.308955
0.45	0.333278
0.46	0.356295

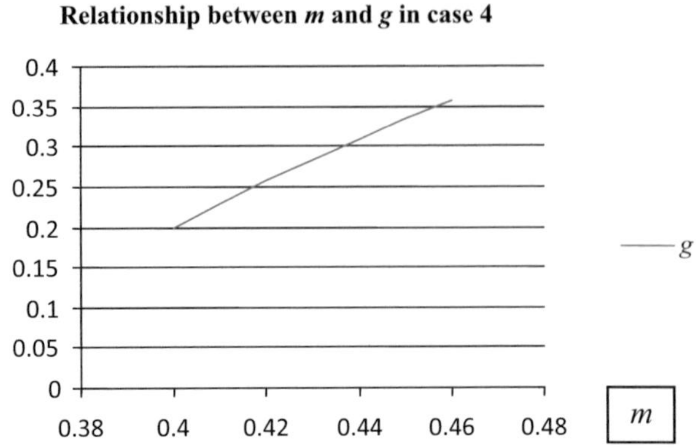

Fig. 6.5 Relationship between m and g in case 4

Case 5:

α=0.5	σ=0.1	δ=0.5	H_n=10	H_s=7	ρ=0.03

m	$g1$	$g2$
0.1	0.138865	3.821396
0.2	0.27747	3.51551
0.3	0.415679	3.197047
0.4	0.55318	2.86317
0.5	0.689295	2.50974
0.6	0.822061	2.130359
0.7	0.942783	1.716568
0.8	0.951024	1.318734

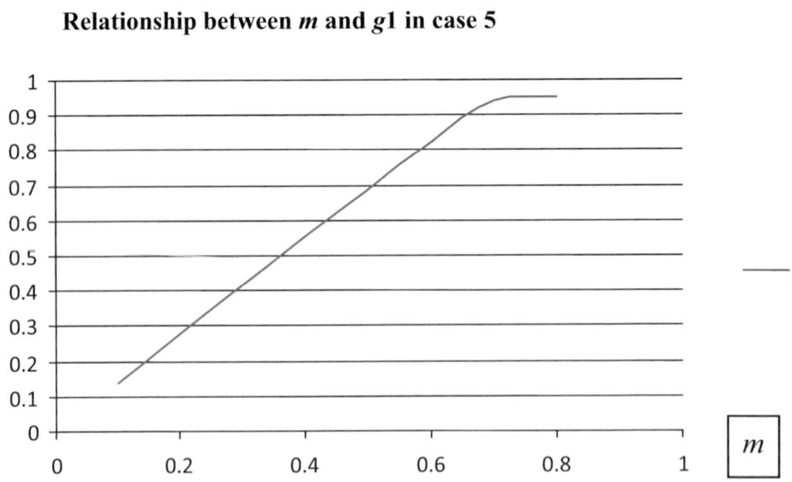

Fig. 6.6 Relationship between m and $g1$ in case 5

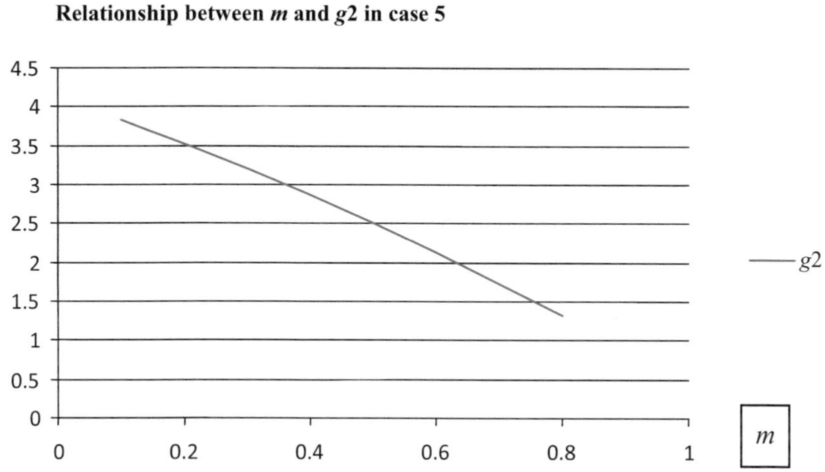

Fig. 6.7 Relationship between *m* and *g*2 in case 5

In Grossman and Helpman (1991b) and Helpman (1993), in the long run, the rate of growth of technology (rate of innovation) is decreased in response to tighter IPRs (lower *m*). So, in their models there is a positive relationship between *g* and *m*. In our model, we have a positive relationship between *g* and *m* in case 2 and case 4 when $\bar{H}_n$ and $\bar{H}_s$ are neither too high nor too low and are quite close. This result is close to the findings of Falvey et al. (2004), who found that IPRs protection and growth are negatively related for middle-income countries.

Note that in case 1 and case 3, except for *m,* all other parameters are the same. If we keep on increasing *m* initially, we get case 3 and then case 1. If we combine Figs. 6.1 and 6.4, we will get a U-shaped curve. So, for parameter specification of case 1 and case 3, the lower one of the growth rates shows an inverted-U-shaped relationship with increase in *m,* while the higher one of the growth rates shows a U-shaped relationship with increase in *m*.

In the Helpman (1993) model, increase in technology transfer (imitation) raises the cost of capital because an increase in the rate of imitation raises the risk of market displacement for the typical Northern firm. Hence, innovation is discouraged. On the other hand, as technology transfer rises, the steady-state share of products manufactured in North is smaller, less labour is employed in R&D and more labour is employed in manufacturing, and so sales of each Northern firm for a given total number of products is higher. Hence, profit rate per brand increases, and innovation is encouraged. So, we get a negative relationship between imitation and innovation through the first channel and a positive relationship between imitation and innovation through the second channel. In the Helpman (1993) model, the second effect outweighs the first effect. But in our model, as the intermediate goods are traded, when imitation is increased though the steady-state share of products manufactured in North decreases, sales per brand may not be higher. This is because the intermediate good firm does not require labour employment. It only requires physical capital as input. Moreover, the Northern final good firm also uses intermediate goods produced in South, in our model, innovation may be discouraged even through the second channel. Similarly, when IPRs are strengthened, imitation is decreased, more intermediate goods are produced in North, the Northern firm faces lower risk of being imitated, and there is a possibility of higher export income earned by intermediate good firms of North. So, innovation may be encouraged. This explains the negative relationship between imitation and innovation. For developed countries, this export income is higher, but for low and middle income countries, the possibility of higher export income is not very high, and we get a positive relationship between imitation and innovation.

Proposition 2 Stronger IPRs may result in either higher or lower balanced global growth rate.

Rivera Batiz and Romer (1991) show that when two countries are innovators, growth rate increases if there is free flow of information between the two countries. In that model, strengthening IPRs would result in decrease in growth rate. But in this model, as IPRs are strengthened in case 3 (Fig. 6.4) and case 5 (Fig. 6.7), the Northern R&D firm faces less threat of their ideas being transferred to South. So, they are more encouraged to produce more ideas. This induces the growth rate to be higher as a result of stronger IPRs. However, note that strengthening of IPRs will negatively affect the trade balance of South.

Using a data set of 47 developed and developing countries from 1970 to 1990, Schneider (2005) suggests that IPRs have a stronger impact on domestic innovation for developed countries and might even negatively impact innovation in developing countries. While analysing panel data of 80 countries, Falvey et al. (2004) find that IPRs protection is positively and significantly related to growth for low- and high-income countries but not for middle-income countries. This chapter suggests that one possible reason for their findings may be that low-income countries are engaged in trade of capital-intensive intermediate goods with high-income countries. Gould and Gruben (1996) find that stronger IPRs correspond to higher economic growth rates in a cross-country sample. The results found in this theoretical chapter tally with this empirical result.

6.6 Conclusion

We have constructed a North–South model of product development, where we have assumed that North innovates the variety of intermediate goods, and South imitates it with a time lag. The intermediate goods market in South is perfectly competitive, while that of North is monopolistic. So, South can sell it at a much cheaper price. Hence, once South imitates a product, North no longer produces it. In this model, capital-intensive intermediate goods are traded, but final goods are not traded. This chapter is new to the literature, considering intellectual property protection in a trade model that allows capital good trade rather than trade in consumption goods. We find some interesting results. We show that a unique steady-state balanced growth equilibrium may exist, or there may be multiple steady-state equilibria, and tighter IPRs may lead to both a higher and lower steady-state balanced growth rate depending on the availability of human capital. Helpman (1993) finds this impact to be negative. No North–South trade model based on product cycle theory has investigated the effect of IPRs on growth considering trade in intermediate goods. This chapter fills the gap.

Our results have a very important policy implication. We observe that in case 3 and case 5, the higher one of the two growth rates shows a negative relationship with the strengthening of IPRs. But this happens only if both countries exhibit a high steady-state balanced growth rate. Therefore, for advanced nations, strengthening IPRs results in a higher growth rate, but for low- and middle-income countries, strengthening IPRs results in lower growth rates. This result tallies with the observation made by Schneider (2005). So, strengthening of IPRs can be advocated in developing countries following the recommendations of TRIPS, but at the same time it is important to raise the human capital level of developing countries by improving their health and education sectors so as to obtain a positive balanced global rate of growth.

However, our analysis is subject to some limitations. We do not consider trade in final goods, the possibility of human capital accumulation, cost of imitation, innovation in South, multinationalization of Northern firms, unemployment in labour market, international migration of physical capital and labour and dynamic interaction between policy makers of North and South. We make only a steady-state analysis and do not analyse transitional dynamics of a model. Hence, in this extended model, we do not derive any results regarding the welfare effect of IPRs on two countries. However, the positive effect of the rate of innovation should influence the welfare of two countries positively.

Appendix

Profit of intermediate good firm of North is

$$\pi_x^n = p_n^n x_n^n + p_s^n x_s^n - r_n (x_n^n + x_s^n).$$

Using Eq. (6.15), we have

$$\pi_x^n = \alpha p^n x^n, \tag{6.39}$$

where x^n is given by Eq. (6.2).

From Eq. (6.23), we have

$$P_A^n = \frac{\pi_x^n}{(r^n + m)}. \tag{6.40}$$

From Eq. (6.15) we know that $p_n^n = p_s^n = p^n$. Hence, replacing p^n by p_n^n given by Eq. (6.11) in Eq. (6.39), we have

$$\pi_x^n = \alpha(1-\alpha)P_n T_n (H_n^Y)^{\alpha}(x_n^n)^{-\alpha}(x_n^n + x_s^n). \tag{6.41}$$

Using Eqs. (6.40) and (6.41), we have

$$P_A^n = \frac{1}{(r^n + m)}\alpha(1-\alpha)P_n T_n (H_n^Y)^{\alpha}(x_n^n)^{-\alpha}(x_n^n + x_s^n). \tag{6.42}$$

Using Eqs. (6.20) and (6.42), we have

$$w_A^n = P_A^n \delta_n A = \frac{1}{(r^n + m)}\alpha(1-\alpha)P_n T_n (H_n^Y)^{\alpha}(x_n^n)^{-\alpha}(x_n^n + x_s^n)\delta_n A.$$

Now, using Eqs. (6.13), (6.14) and (6.18), we have

$$\frac{x_n^s}{x_n^n} = \left(\frac{r_s}{r_n}\right)^{-\frac{1}{\alpha}}(1-\alpha)^{-\frac{1}{\alpha}}$$

and

$$\frac{x_s^n}{x_n^n} = \left(\frac{P_s T_s}{P_n T_n}\right)^{\frac{1}{\alpha}}\frac{H_s^Y}{H_n^Y}.$$

Equating w_A^n and w_Y^n given by the Eq. (6.25) and using the expressions of $\frac{x_n^s}{x_n^n}$ and $\frac{x_s^n}{x_n^n}$, we have H_n^Y given by Eq. (6.26).

Acknowledgements I am grateful to the participants of the DEGIT 2011 conference for their valuable comments.

References

Akiyama T, Furukawa Y (2009) Intellectual property rights and appropriability of innovation. Econ Lett 103:138–141

Eicher T, Penalosa CG (2008) Endogenous strength of intellectual property rights: implications for economic development and growth. Eur Econ Rev 52:237–258

Falvey R, Foster N, Greenaway D (2004) Intellectual Property Rights and Economic Growth. Research Chapter 2004/12, Research chapter series, Internationalisation of Economic Policy, The University of Nottingham

Gould DM, Gruben WC (1996) The role of intellectual property rights in economic growth. J Dev Econ 48:323–350
Grossman G, Helpman E (1991a) Quality ladders in the theory of growth. Rev Econ Stud 58:43–61
Grossman G, Helpman E (1991b) Endogenous product cycles. Econ J 101:1229–1241
Helpman E (1993) Innovation, imitation, and intellectual property rights. Econometrica 61(6):1247–1280
Lai E (1998) International intellectual property rights protection and rate of product innovation. J Dev Econ 55(1):133–153
Mondal D, Gupta MR (2008a) Intellectual property rights protection and unemployment in a North South model: a theoretical analysis. Econ Model 25:463–484
Mondal D, Gupta MR (2008b) Innovation, imitation and intellectual property rights: introducing migration in Helpman's model. Jpn World Econ 20:369–394
Rivera Batiz LA, Romer PM (1991) Economic integration and endogenous growth. Q J Econ 106(2):531–555
Romer P (1990) Endogenous technological change. J Polit Econ 98(5):S71–S102
Schneider PH (2005) International trade, economic growth and intellectual property rights: a panel data study of developed and developing countries. J Dev Econ 78:529–547
Ventura J (1997) Growth and interdependence. Q J Econ 112(1):57–84

Chapter 7
Multi-Market Firms and Export Quota: Effects of Withdrawal of the Multi-Fiber Arrangement

Saibal Kar and Mausumi Kar

7.1 Introduction

A firm's decision to operate and sell its output in multiple markets is driven by many factors. For example, transport costs, which sometimes account for 15–20 % of the total cost of production, significantly influence the decision to operate in more than one market. Exposure to randomness in commodity prices could be an even stronger factor, in particular, when coupled with uncertainty about regulatory policies. A comparison of transaction costs in different markets can also sufficiently alter a firm's decision to diversify sales across markets. A well-known result due to Katz and Paroush (1979), however, showed that for firms operating in multiple markets, total output would not be affected even if price is uncertain in several markets, if at least one market displays price certainty. This 'separation' result holds primarily with respect to choice of output and allocation of sales across markets by a typical firm. Dalal and Katz (2003) later showed that when transport costs are introduced in this framework, the separation result continues to hold, such that the certainty of commodity prices in the domestic market determines total output regardless of the price uncertainty and other exogenous parameters in the foreign market. They also discuss conditions when the separation result is violated. We discuss more on this in Sect. 2, in relation to our main findings.

The present chapter deals with the multi-market choice of a competitive firm that faces an export quota and uncertain price in the foreign market and a certain price and a competitive product market domestically. We model the sales allocation of such a firm, first in the presence of a quota and subsequently when the quota is

S. Kar (✉)
Centre for Studies in Social Sciences, Kolkata, India
e-mail: skar1801@yahoo.com

IZA, Bonn, Germany

M. Kar
Women's Christian College, Kolkata, India
e-mail: mausumi2606@yahoo.co.in

S. Banerjee et al. (eds.), *Understanding Development,* India Studies in Business and Economics, DOI 10.1007/978-81-322-2455-6_7

withdrawn. The problem is interesting in the following sense. During the regime of quota restricted export, the firm enjoys a certain market for its output (foreign sales), even though the quota might have been set at an inefficient level. We assume that, even with a quota, the foreign price is uncertain because there is no guarantee that quotas are fulfilled. On the other hand, the domestic price is certain and the firm sells at the level where price equals marginal cost. Subsequently, when the quota is withdrawn the firm might lose its captive market to competition from others—with a possibility that the foreign price falls. The profit maximizing reallocation of sales should then factor in the changes in the erstwhile captive market and readjust the domestic sales with significant price effects. Unless the domestic price becomes random owing to this regime shift in the international market, the firm continues to produce the same total amount as before owing to the 'separation' result discussed above. As a competing explanation, unless the withdrawal of quota has a significant impact on the firm, such that it exports an amount higher than the total output it produced previously, it continues to produce the amount where marginal cost equals price domestically.

Alternatively, in case the firms do not find the export market to remain viable any longer, they should divert sales to the local market with possible change in prices, *ceteris paribus*. In other words, the loss of foreign market may create excess supply of the good in the local market leading to a fall in price. The production and employment implications of such adjustments can be substantial if the industry to which such a firm belongs is of critical importance. Indeed, the textile and apparel industry in India commands such a position by contributing about 4 % of gross domestic product (GDP), 14 % of industrial production, 17 % of export revenue and by employing approximately 25 million workers directly and indirectly (Kar 2012). Furthermore, the various effects of the withdrawal of export quota on Indian manufacturers did not surface instantaneously. Our statistical observations will show that the stronger effects of greater competition showed up negatively on the export performance and concentration of firms only recently.

In what ways the firms and the industry as a whole respond to this regime shift in policy is an empirical question. We provide evidence from a large number of textile and apparel manufacturing firms in India between 1991 and 2013 to show that the firms have readjusted sales significantly in the aftermath of the withdrawal of the well-known quota system under the aegis of the Multi-Fiber Arrangement (MFA). In this context, we also check for the level of concentration of the firms in terms of sales proceeds over this period. The problem discussed in the previous paragraph leads to a brief theoretical model that explains such an impact for the general case of sales decision by multi-market firms when exposed to trade restrictions, more akin to what is popularly known as the voluntary export restraints (VER) in the related literature (see, Harris 1985; Krishna 1988; Yano 1989, etc.).

In a related context, Kar and Kar (2014) study issues in firm-level concentration as well as employment patterns for firms producing and selling textile and apparel. It is based on firm-level longitudinal data for 15 years encompassing the period over which the MFA phased out gradually. Relating trade and labour market outcomes, our firm-level empirical estimates show that the export-oriented firms in India were not affected adversely and that the aggregate wage bill also rose during this period. The firm-level panel was supplemented by a state-level panel between 1998 and 2008 to capture the region-wise aggregated impact of the withdrawal of MFA on the level of labour earnings across regions in India. One of the stark results of this panel (state) fixed effects regression is that the aggregate state-level wage bill falls as the profit level rises for the industry, implying a more intensive use of capital and technology. The results also showed that regional wage disparity has strong relations with regional disparity in firm concentration at the level of the industry as measured by the number of factories, as well as with regional disparity in sales across the states in India.

Earlier et al. (2009) have argued that the entry of China in the World Trade Organization (WTO) and the removal of the MFA will work against the interest of many smaller countries in the South. The scale of production or sheer efficiency of Chinese manufacturers would negatively affect the erstwhile quota-protected market shares of a large number of countries and might lead to a monopoly outcome. However, as long as the monopoly price set by a large exporting country remains below the import competing price in the importing countries, gains from trade via removal of quota at destinations still improve. Using the constant market share (CMS) analysis (see the original formulation in Richardson 1971), Kar and Kar (2011) also showed that the removal of quota led to significant changes in country-wise export shares—countries with more efficient production techniques captured larger shares of the international market in the post-MFA phase. The expected global implications of the withdrawal of the MFA had earlier been studied in Trela and Whalley (1990).

7.1.1 *The Multi-Fiber Arrangement*

The Agreement on Textiles and Clothing (ATC) ensured the dismantling of only quotas on textile and apparel items, while tariff on these items were to stay.[1] The MFA provided a framework under which developed countries imposed quotas on exports of textiles and apparel from developing countries. These quotas were typically applied on a bilateral basis and were product-specific as defined by fiber and function. This allowed discrimination not only against specific fibers and products but also between exporting countries. The exporting countries' governments administered the MFA export quotas, which were allocated to them based on predetermined criteria. This iniquitous system of quotas thus violated all the fundamental principles of the multilateral trading system and discriminated against the poorest countries and those seeking to move up from reliance on primary commodities to manufacturing.

[1] The Uruguay Round of GATT launched at Punta Del Este led to the Agreement on Textiles and Clothing (ATC) in 1995. It is the institutional shape given to the promise to end quotas in an orderly process within 10 years divided into three consecutive phases.

In other words, despite removal of the MFA, international trade in clothing and textile would still not be entirely free, but only 'quota-free'. In addition, in the presence of political equations in an ever more complicated world of multilateral negotiations the extent of compliance with ATC on the part of importing countries remains unclear. This impending reality brings the issue of competitiveness to the fore for all the exporting countries, including India. In fact, the end of the MFA and the removal of global textile quotas on January 1, 2005 have radically changed the global scenario of apparel production and trade (Appelbaum et al. 2005; Gereffi 2004; UNCTAD 2005; USITC 2004; WTO 2004, etc.). There were widespread expectations that without the restrictions of the quota, large, low-wage countries with well-developed export capacities such as China and India would be the prime beneficiaries at the cost of smaller exporting countries. Developing countries from across the world with some share of textile and apparel exports, such as Lesotho in Africa, Bangladesh in Asia and El Salvador in Central-South America that had previously benefited from the protection of the quota will lose out. The loss of market would also be associated with high-wage countries like the USA, Western Europe and the East Asian 'Big Three' (Knappe 2003; USITC 2004; UNCTAD 2005; WTO 2004, etc.). Statistical support is available for the loss of thousands of textile and apparel jobs in the USA and Latin America (Bair and Dussel 2006), the growing consolidation among large global buyers (Gereffi 2004), the withdrawal of Foreign Direct Investment (FDI) from the garment industries in some small countries, such as Mauritius, Lesotho and Madagascar (Gibbon 2008), and significant price deflation experienced by many apparel exporters worldwide.

In such a volatile and uncertain environment, as countries search for ways to compete, the issue of costs, in particular wage costs, has emerged as a central consideration in the debate over export competitiveness in the apparel industry. For example, in India, where labour laws were regarded as relatively 'inflexible' and therefore would render coping with low wage competition difficult, the industry lobby has undoubtedly put up a case for dismantling several labour protections. This, according to the argument, should allow localized small producers to scale up and subsequently compete with countries like Bangladesh, China and Mexico (Hashim 2005; Gherzi Report 2003). However, Tewari (2006) questions the view as to whether the cost-competitiveness, particularly via low wage costs and large scales of operation, is enough to achieve sustained export competitiveness in the textile and apparel industry after the removal of quotas. It reviews the evidence emerging from a growing body of literature on the institutional organization of global trade networks and production chains to argue that in an environment characterized by uncertainty and regulatory flux, and where buyers demand many more attributes in addition to price—such as product variety, quality, customization and timely delivery—global competitiveness in the apparel industry presently requires competency that goes well beyond traditional factors of relative price and low wages. Indeed, under volatile market conditions and shortened product cycles, large scales of operation can add to the cost unless they are embedded within other capabilities that lower the risk and cost of large volumes (i.e. of rigidity). These capabilities include skills, management practices, productive relationships and some promotional activities that allow firms to combine speed and scale with more skilled functions such as designing, maintaining consistency in quality, keeping low inventories, ensuring timely supply and establishing direct ties with most efficient distribution networks. This should arguably offer greater dynamic comparative advantages replacing exclusive dependence on low wages. The development of these capabilities varies not only across nations, but also among firms and regions within nations.

Based on these observations, we offer a brief analytical section on how a multimarket firm allocates sales. We offer some statistical observations on the industry-level performance in Sect. 3 and conclude in Sect. 4.

7.2 The Model

Consider a firm in a competitive market that produces a single product and sells in two markets—domestic *(D)* and foreign *(F)*. The foreign market in connection with the prevalence of MFA as discussed above exercises a quota on how much a country can sell as a whole. The firm under consideration is one among a large mass *(n)* of homogeneous and identical firms in the country and shares the total output as well as the foreign quota equally with others. This is denoted by $\overline{q}_{\mathrm{f}}^{i}$, $i=1 \ldots n$. If the firm's total output is q^{i}, then the domestic sale is given by, $q_{\mathrm{d}}^{i}=q^{i}-\overline{q}_{\mathrm{f}}^{i}$, of which $\overline{q}_{\mathrm{f}}^{i}$ is the amount of the export quota facing the firm.[2] We assume that the foreign price ($\tilde{p}_{\mathrm{f}}$) is a random variable and therefore uncertain, while the domestic price (p_{d}) is certain. Since $\tilde{p}_{\mathrm{f}}$ is a random variable, it should be noted that for a risk-averse firm, the higher the randomness in prices, the lower the dependence on such markets where prices are volatile. The cost function is convex, such that, $C(q)=q^{\alpha}$, where $\alpha>1$ and $C_{q}>0$, $C_{qq}>0$. There is also a fixed cost of setting up the firm, $k>0$. We do not focus on the distributional aspects of the randomness in foreign price (see Dalal and Katz 2004 for additive or multiplicative distributions). Further, the risk-averse firm maximizes the expected utility of profit under two states of nature. First, we will find out the allocation of sales between home and foreign markets and second, we will observe how this allocation changes when the international market for textile and apparel undergoes a regime shift in policy. In fact, we will offer the condition under which the export (as against domestic sale) by the firm under consideration may rise or fall. Finally, we will assume that the firm representing a developing country produces and exports to a rich country, such that, even with changes in international policies there would be no reversals in the direction of trade. It should be pointed out that in related problems with a firm deciding on a distribution of sales between domestic and foreign markets, it has previously been

[2] If the firms are not identical and vary in terms of size, while being part of a competitive market, the export share can be proportional to the size, and the domestic demand facing the firm should also have different intercepts. Presently, it should not alter our results. In future extensions we wish to consider a distribution of firms on a scale of size and/or risk aversion to cultivate potential differences in the choice problem.

shown that depending on the nature of the transport cost function (nonlinear) present in the domestic market, the separation result alluded to in the beginning fails to hold. In particular, introduction of domestic transport cost essentially lowers output, since it shifts the marginal cost curve to the left. It is independent of whether the transport cost exists in the export market or not (Dalal and Katz 2003). The nonlinearity of the transport cost in the domestic market will render the determination of marginal transport cost in the domestic market a function of the sales in that market and consequently, the 'total output' will also depend on foreign parameters. But, the introduction of positive transport costs in both markets may still lead to positive sales in both places if the marginal expected profits in the foreign market exceed the marginal profits in the domestic market. In our case, the withdrawal of quota does not disrupt the separation condition, but makes the foreign profit at the margin a function of the domestic price and its response to foreign sales.

Thus, when the regime of quota under the MFA is in place, the firm maximizes the expected utility of profit with respect to the choice of domestic and foreign sale, of which the upper limit of the foreign sale is exogenously fixed. Since selling below the quota is inefficient, we will assume that the quota is utilized in full. In fact, Bark and de Melo (1989) point out that if approximately 80% of a quota is fulfilled, it is considered to be in full use. The expected utility function of the firm is given by:

$$\max_{q_{\mathrm{d}},\overline{q}_{\mathrm{f}}} E[U(\pi)] = E[U(p_{\mathrm{d}}q_{\mathrm{d}} + \tilde{p}_{\mathrm{f}}\overline{q}_{\mathrm{f}} - q^{\alpha} - k)]. \tag{7.1}$$

Here, we must re-emphasize the result due to Katz and Paroush (1979), which shows that for a firm operating in a multi-market environment, the total quantity produced is determined directly by the equality of marginal cost and price, if the price in at least one market is certain regardless of uncertainties prevailing in other markets. Using this separation theorem, we obtain the first order condition as:

$$\frac{\delta}{\delta q_{\mathrm{d}}} E[U(\pi)] = \frac{\delta\{E[U(p_{\mathrm{d}}q_{\mathrm{d}} + \tilde{p}_{\mathrm{f}}\overline{q}_{\mathrm{f}} - q^{\alpha} - k)]\}}{\delta q_{\mathrm{d}}} = p_{\mathrm{d}} - \alpha q^{\alpha-1} = 0, \tag{7.2}$$

where $q = q_d + q_f$.

Second, since it is inefficient to sell less than the quota,

$$\frac{\delta\{E[U(p_{\mathrm{d}}q_{\mathrm{d}} + \tilde{p}_{\mathrm{f}}\overline{q}_{\mathrm{f}} - q^{\alpha} - k)]\}}{\delta \overline{q}_{\mathrm{f}}} = -\alpha q^{\alpha-1} = 0. \tag{7.3}$$

The second-order conditions (from 2 and 3) offer a negative value for profit maximization.

Thus, from (2),

$$q^{i}* = \left(\frac{p_{\mathrm{d}}}{\alpha}\right)^{\frac{1}{\alpha-1}} = q*. \tag{7.4}$$

The domestic sale of this firm (and all the other identical firms) is given by $q_{\mathrm{d}}^{*} = q^{*} - \overline{q}_{\mathrm{f}}$. In other words, this offers a combination of $(q_{\mathrm{d}}^{*}, \overline{q}_{\mathrm{f}})$ as allocation of sales in the two markets. This presumes that in the quota-administered regime, the firms utilized the full amount of the quota, because not selling the whole amount allocated by exogenous factors would be inefficient.

7.2.1 Withdrawal of Quota

Next, suppose that the quota system under the MFA is withdrawn following a policy change in the WTO. The withdrawal of the quota is expected to lower the international price and redirect sales to the domestic market where the price may fall in the aggregate. Given that the policy change will have price implications for both the destination and the source countries, it evidently calls for looking at the total change. However, we retain the assumption that even if the domestic price falls, the price is still certain, and therefore the total output is determined according to the previous condition where the firm equates domestic price to the marginal cost in order to determine the level of total output. The more pertinent question is however, as to how much the firm now allocates between *D* and *F*, which is to be decided subject to changes in the foreign market price on which one country (and less still, one firm) has little or no influence. In other words, $q_{\mathrm{f}}(\tilde{p}_{\mathrm{f}})$ is the amount that the firm decides to allocate to foreign sales following the optimization exercise. Here, we must look at the total change in the following way. Equation (7.1) is rewritten as,

$$\max_{q_{\mathrm{f}}(\tilde{p}_{\mathrm{f}})} E[U(\pi)] = E[U(p_{\mathrm{d}}q_{\mathrm{d}} + \tilde{p}_{\mathrm{f}}q_{\mathrm{f}}(\tilde{p}_{\mathrm{f}}) - q^{\alpha} - k)]. \tag{7.5}$$

Differentiating totally,

$$E[U'(\pi)\{q_{\mathrm{d}}dp_{\mathrm{d}} + p_{\mathrm{d}}dq_{\mathrm{d}} + q_{\mathrm{f}}(\tilde{p}_{\mathrm{f}})d\tilde{p}_{\mathrm{f}} + \tilde{p}_{\mathrm{f}}dq_{\mathrm{f}}(\tilde{p}_{\mathrm{f}}) - \alpha q^{\alpha-1}dq - dk\}] = 0.$$

Note that $dk = 0$.

Therefore,

$$E[U'(\pi)\{q_{\mathrm{d}}dp_{\mathrm{d}} + p_{\mathrm{d}}dq_{\mathrm{d}} + q_{\mathrm{f}}(\tilde{p}_{\mathrm{f}})d\tilde{p}_{\mathrm{f}} + \tilde{p}_{\mathrm{f}}dq_{\mathrm{f}}(\tilde{p}_{\mathrm{f}}) - \alpha q^{\alpha-1}dq\}] = 0,$$

such that

$$\frac{dE[U(\pi)]}{dq_{\mathrm{f}}(\tilde{p}_{\mathrm{f}})} = E[U'(\pi)\{q_{\mathrm{d}}\frac{dp_{\mathrm{d}}}{dq_{\mathrm{f}}(\tilde{p}_{\mathrm{f}})} + p_{\mathrm{d}}\frac{dq_{\mathrm{d}}}{dq_{\mathrm{f}}(\tilde{p}_{\mathrm{f}})} + q_{\mathrm{f}}(\tilde{p}_{\mathrm{f}})\frac{d\tilde{p}_{\mathrm{f}}}{dq_{\mathrm{f}}(\tilde{p}_{\mathrm{f}})} + \tilde{p}_{\mathrm{f}} - \alpha q^{\alpha-1}\frac{dq}{dq_{\mathrm{f}}(\tilde{p}_{\mathrm{f}})}\}] = 0,$$

where $\frac{dq}{dq_{\mathrm{f}}(\tilde{p}_{\mathrm{f}})} = [\frac{dq_{\mathrm{d}}}{dq_{\mathrm{f}}(\tilde{p}_{\mathrm{f}})} + 1]$.

So, $E[U'(\pi)\{q_{\mathrm{d}} \frac{dp_{\mathrm{d}}}{dq_{\mathrm{f}}(\tilde{p}_{\mathrm{f}})} + p_{\mathrm{d}} \frac{dq_{\mathrm{d}}}{dq_{\mathrm{f}}(\tilde{p}_{\mathrm{f}})} + q_{\mathrm{f}}(\tilde{p}_{\mathrm{f}}) \frac{d\tilde{p}_{\mathrm{f}}}{dq_{\mathrm{f}}(\tilde{p}_{\mathrm{f}})}$

$$+ \tilde{p}_{\mathrm{f}} - \alpha q^{\alpha-1}(\frac{dq_{\mathrm{d}}}{dq_{\mathrm{f}}(\tilde{p}_{\mathrm{f}})} + 1)\}] = 0,$$

or $E[U'(\pi)\{q_{\mathrm{d}} \frac{dp_{\mathrm{d}}}{dq_{\mathrm{f}}(\tilde{p}_{\mathrm{f}})} + (p_{\mathrm{d}} - \alpha q^{\alpha-1}) \frac{dq_{\mathrm{d}}}{dq_{\mathrm{f}}(\tilde{p}_{\mathrm{f}})}$

$$+ \frac{q_{\mathrm{f}}(\tilde{p}_{\mathrm{f}})}{\frac{dq_{\mathrm{f}}(\tilde{p}_{\mathrm{f}})}{d\tilde{p}_{\mathrm{f}}}} + \tilde{p}_{\mathrm{f}} - \alpha q^{\alpha-1}\}] = 0.$$

Rearranging, $E[U'(\pi)\{q_{\mathrm{d}} \frac{dp_{\mathrm{d}}}{dq_{\mathrm{f}}(\tilde{p}_{\mathrm{f}})} + (p_{\mathrm{d}} - \alpha q^{\alpha-1}) \frac{dq_{\mathrm{d}}}{dq_{\mathrm{f}}(\tilde{p}_{\mathrm{f}})}$

$$+ \frac{\tilde{p}_{\mathrm{f}}}{\frac{dq_{\mathrm{f}}(\tilde{p}_{\mathrm{f}})}{d\tilde{p}_{\mathrm{f}}} \frac{\tilde{p}_{\mathrm{f}}}{q_{\mathrm{f}}(\tilde{p}_{\mathrm{f}})}} + \tilde{p}_{\mathrm{f}} - \alpha q^{\alpha-1}\}] = 0.$$

Define $\eta_{q\mathrm{f}} = -\frac{dq_{\mathrm{f}}(\tilde{p}_{\mathrm{f}})}{d\tilde{p}_{\mathrm{f}}} \frac{\tilde{p}_{\mathrm{f}}}{q_{\mathrm{f}}(\tilde{p}_{\mathrm{f}})}$ as the elasticity of demand facing the firm in the foreign market.

Thus,

$$E[U'(\pi)\{q_{\mathrm{d}} \frac{dp_{\mathrm{d}}}{dq_{\mathrm{f}}(\tilde{p}_{\mathrm{f}})} + (p_{\mathrm{d}} - \alpha q^{\alpha-1}) \frac{dq_{\mathrm{d}}}{dq_{\mathrm{f}}(\tilde{p}_{\mathrm{f}})} + (\tilde{p}_{\mathrm{f}}(1 - \frac{1}{\eta_{qf}}) - \alpha q^{\alpha-1})\}] = 0. \quad (7.6)$$

Further, let $E(\tilde{p}_{\mathrm{f}}) = \overline{p}_{\mathrm{f}}$.

Since $Cov(X,Y) = E(XY) - E(X)E(Y)$, we can rewrite (7.6), which is of the $E(XY)$ form, in the following way:

$$Cov[U'(\pi), \tilde{p}_{\mathrm{f}}] + E[U'(\pi)]$$

$$E[q_{\mathrm{d}} \frac{dp_{\mathrm{d}}}{dq_{\mathrm{f}}(\tilde{p}_{\mathrm{f}})} + (p_{\mathrm{d}} - \alpha q^{\alpha-1}) \frac{dq_{\mathrm{d}}}{dq_{\mathrm{f}}(\tilde{p}_{\mathrm{f}})} + (\tilde{p}_{\mathrm{f}}(1 - \frac{1}{\eta_{qf}}) - \alpha q^{\alpha-1})] = 0. \quad (7.7)$$

The first term on the left-hand side (LHS) of (7.7) is negative because the marginal utility of profit of a risk-averse firm will go down if the randomness in price rises. In other words, $Cov[U'(\pi), \tilde{p}_{\mathrm{f}}] < 0$.

Reorganizing (7.7),

$$Cov[U'(\pi), \tilde{p}_{\mathrm{f}}] + [q_{\mathrm{d}} \frac{dp_{\mathrm{d}}}{dq_{\mathrm{f}}(\tilde{p}_{\mathrm{f}})} + (p_{\mathrm{d}} - \alpha q^{\alpha-1}) \frac{dq_{\mathrm{d}}}{dq_{\mathrm{f}}(\tilde{p}_{\mathrm{f}})}$$

$$+ (\overline{p}_{\mathrm{f}}(1 - \frac{1}{\eta_{qf}}) - \alpha q^{\alpha-1})]E[U'(\pi)] = 0,$$

or

$$\bar{p}_{\mathrm{f}}(1-\frac{1}{\eta_{qf}})-\alpha q^{\alpha-1}=-\frac{Cov[U'(\pi),\tilde{p}_{\mathrm{f}}]}{E[U'(\pi)]}-q_{\mathrm{d}}\frac{dp_{\mathrm{d}}}{dq_{\mathrm{f}}(\tilde{p}_{\mathrm{f}})}-(p_{\mathrm{d}}-\alpha q^{\alpha-1})\frac{dq_{\mathrm{d}}}{dq_{\mathrm{f}}(\tilde{p}_{\mathrm{f}})}. \quad (7.8)$$

Since the firm continues to equate domestic price to marginal cost of production in the domestic market, therefore, $(p_{\mathrm{d}}-\alpha q^{\alpha-1})=0$. So, Eq. (7.8) transforms to

$$\bar{p}_{\mathrm{f}}(1-\frac{1}{\eta_{qf}})-\alpha q^{\alpha-1}=-\frac{Cov[U'(\pi),\tilde{p}_{\mathrm{f}}]}{E[U'(\pi)]}-q_{\mathrm{d}}\frac{dp_{\mathrm{d}}}{dq_{\mathrm{f}}(\tilde{p}_{\mathrm{f}})}. \quad (7.9)$$

The term on the LHS is the expected marginal profit from selling in the foreign market. The right-hand side (RHS) includes a positive term, $\frac{dp_{\mathrm{d}}}{dq_{\mathrm{f}}(\tilde{p}_{\mathrm{f}})}>0$, and a negative term, $Cov[U'(\pi),\tilde{p}_{\mathrm{f}}]<0$. The necessary condition for positive marginal profit in the foreign market is: $-\frac{Cov[U'(\pi),\tilde{p}_{\mathrm{f}}]}{E[U'(\pi)]}>q_{\mathrm{d}}\frac{dp_{\mathrm{d}}}{dq_{\mathrm{f}}(\tilde{p}_{\mathrm{f}})}$, and the sufficient condition is that $\frac{dp_{\mathrm{d}}}{dq_{\mathrm{f}}(\tilde{p}_{\mathrm{f}})}=0$. If the foreign quantity choice by the firm does in no way affect the domestic price, it will continue to sell positive amounts in both markets. It should further mean that the export price must ideally exceed the domestic price for positive participation in both markets.[3]

However, if the price volatility goes down significantly in the foreign market, the marginal utility from profit rises there and the weight assigned by the risk-averse firm to the export market rises. It may lead to a positive economic profit at the margin and that the firm may continue to sell in both markets (with sales under competitive conditions in the domestic market). However, this is hardly ensured. Therefore, when we reformulate the above condition (Eq. 7.9, using 7.2), a positive difference may not exist between the foreign price (weighted by the elasticity of demand in the foreign market) and the domestic price, that is,

$$\bar{p}_{\mathrm{f}}(1-\frac{1}{\eta_{qf}})-p_{\mathrm{d}}=-\frac{Cov[U'(\pi),\tilde{p}_{\mathrm{f}}]}{E[U'(\pi)]}-q_{\mathrm{d}}\frac{dp_{\mathrm{d}}}{dq_{\mathrm{f}}(\tilde{p}_{\mathrm{f}})}. \quad (7.10)$$

From (7.10), it is clearly not possible that the firm will sell a positive amount if the export price weighted by the demand elasticity is lower than the domestic price. For a given amount of output, larger sale in the foreign market must raise the domestic price and vice versa. In case of the withdrawal of the quota under MFA, it is possible that the foreign sale goes down for a firm, leading to excess supply in the domestic market and a fall in price. This should allow the price difference to rise, and beyond a critical level, where the firm is indifferent between domestic

[3] Dalal and Katz (2003) show that a positive profit and positive sale in the export market are feasible even if the export price is lower than the domestic price (essentially if the marginal transport cost at home exceeds that for the foreign country).

and foreign sales, it may fall. The converse may also hold, wherein the difference between the two prices is negative (a case where withdrawal of quota allows a large number of firms from an equally large number of countries) to supply in the previously regulated market, crashing the foreign price and raising the domestic price as a consequence. It might then lead to a 'U-shaped' relation as the entry and exit of firms (and countries) respond heavily to price movements.

Equation (7.9) therefore suggests a possibility. Whether the firm continues to sell in both markets depends on whether the expected marginal profit from foreign sales exceeds that from the domestic sales. If $[\overline{p}_{\mathrm{f}}(1-\frac{1}{\eta_{qf}})-\alpha q^{\alpha-1}]>0$, then the firm continues to participate in both markets, since the condition for sale in the domestic market is based on the equality of marginal cost and price. The marginal expected profit in the foreign market exceeds that in the domestic market, allowing the firm to sell in both. But, more generally, $[\overline{p}_{\mathrm{f}}(1-\frac{1}{\eta_{qf}})-p_{\mathrm{d}}]\gtreqless 0$ does not ensure the distinct possibility of multi-market activity by the firm, because the domestic price responds to how much the firm sells in the foreign market based on the expected foreign price. This result would not hold in the event of a quota, where regardless of the price impact, the firm cannot sell more (and for efficiency reason, less) to the export market.

The withdrawal of MFA as an example is particularly revealing in this case. Since the effect of free entry and exit of countries (and firms) might make the international price more volatile or less, it should determine if the first terms on the RHS of (7.9) dominates or the second term. In either case, this at least opens up the possibility of non-monotonic patterns in the export performance by such firms. The firm may either continue to export more if price becomes less volatile or focus more on the domestic market if the price becomes more volatile. It might give rise to U-shaped or inverted U-shaped export performance by the firm as measured over time.

7.3 Evidence from Indian Textile and Apparel Manufacturers

The statistical observation follows from data selected over 15 years between 1991 and 2013. The number of firms producing textile and apparel goes up to 1300, of which the number of purely exporting firms is actually negligible. Figure 7.1 shows that except for the year 2004, the number of firms that only cater to the export market has not gone up above 30. In terms of annual trend, the number of purely exporting firms was fairly small in the early years, reaching up to 30 in 1998, 32 in 2004 and falling steadily since then. In fact, after reaching a peak in 2004, the year when the final phase of the process of dismantling of MFA began globally, the number of firms involved in the business of exports only hovered around 20 till 2011. In recent years, the number has gone down to just five. Table 7.1 offers

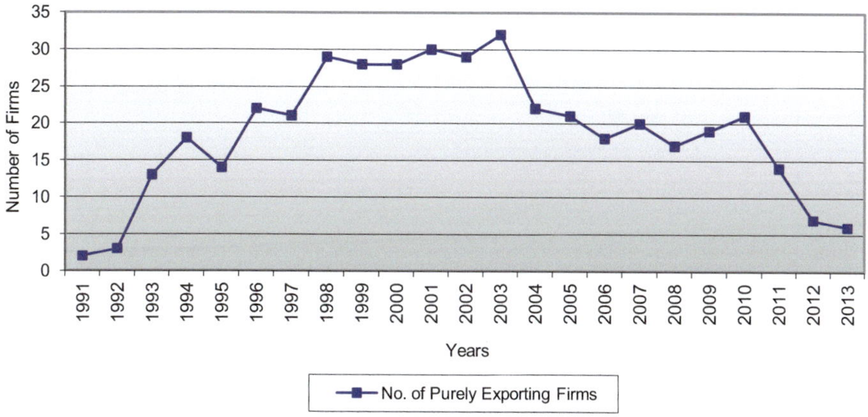

Fig. 7.1 Number of purely exporting firms. (Data source: Centre for Monitoring Indian Economy—Prowess Database)

Table 7.1 Descriptive statistics. (values in million ₹). (Data source: Centre for Monitoring Indian Economy—Prowess Database)

	Mean	Std. dev.	Skewness	Kurtosis	Minimum	Maximum	Num cases
Sales value	2620.65	7546.81	12.0645	237.12	0.02	203,105	5369
Export value	733.203	1945.21	9.4432	160.783	0.1	46,677.4	5456
Dom sale	1868.37	6249.4	12.0741	217.62	0.3	156,427	5456
Export sale	33.91	32.3903	0.726772	2.15836	0.05	126.876	5455

a descriptive statistics regarding the extent of total sales value, the domestic sales component and the revenue from export sales as well as the average percentage of export-to-total sales for approximately 415 firms that operate in both markets. The data accumulated over 13 years offer a large amount of data points, although admittedly, the group of firms is not the same for every year. The export-sale percentage is an average of all firms for a particular year and it shows that the mean of annual averages is approximately 34 %.

The export revenue of the multi-market firms also shows an inverted U-shape analogous to the number of firms exclusively engaged with export. It seems that the analytical conjecture presented above holds in favor of more emphasis on the domestic market for the multi-market firm at the margin. The export as percentage of total sales went up from 20 % in the early 1990s to 40 % in 2003–2004, right before the final phase of the abolition policy took shape. After 2004–2005, the export proceeds as percentage of total sales goes down close to 30 %, and with a slight improvement in 2010–2011, the share remains at 30 % currently.

This is expected to impart certain readjustments at the domestic level, where we measured the concentration of firms according to the total sales reported every year. Since the firms vary in terms of size and sales capacity, it is quite possible that all firms will not be able to cope with the imminent pressure of international price

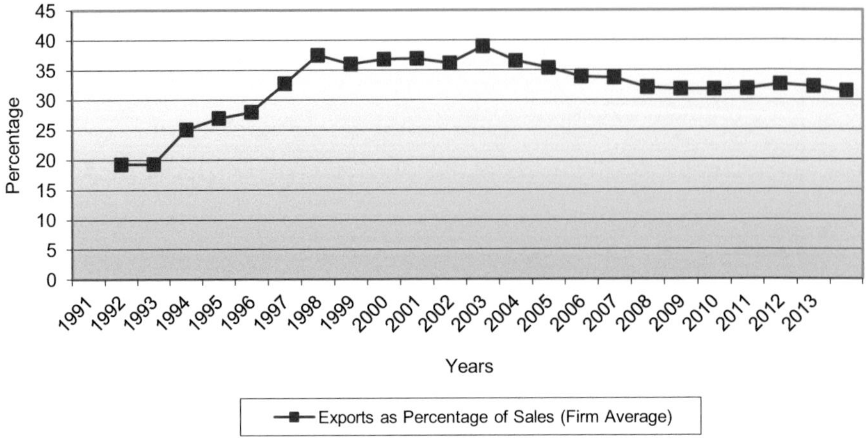

Fig. 7.2 Export performance by Indian textile manufacturing firms. (Data source: Centre for Monitoring Indian Economy—Prowess Database)

meltdown subsequent to the withdrawal of export quota. This might lead to firms either losing business entirely or agglomerating with relatively larger ones in order to remain in business. With the help of the Hirschman–Herfindahl Index (HHI), we showed that over most years the effects were not remarkable (Fig. 7.2).

Figure 7.3 shows that the year-wise concentration of firms as per total sales went down since 1991 and stayed close to 1 % for the entire decade of the 1990s. The concentration index doubled around 2007–2008, but fell subsequently to the lowest level since the beginning of the data used for this analysis. However, from 2010 onwards, the rise has been remarkable and the level of concentration of firms has been close to three times the level in 2010. The price effects in the international market and its implications for the domestic market can be varied and slow at the same

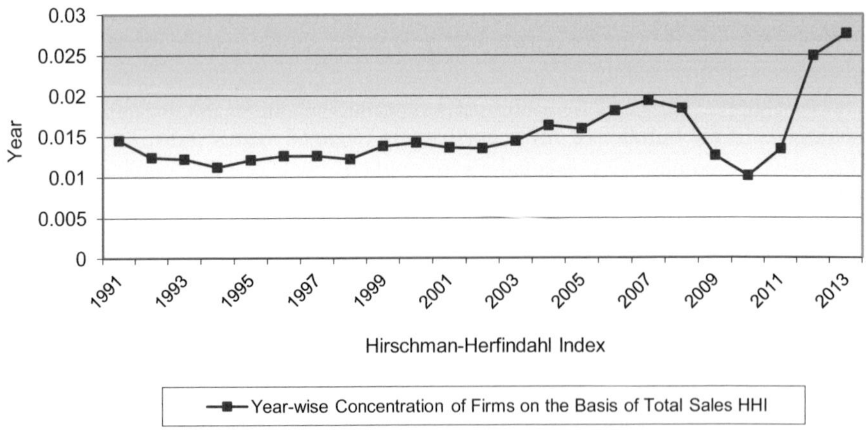

Fig. 7.3 Year-wise concentration of firms on the basis of total sales (HHI). (Data source: Centre for Monitoring Indian Economy—Prowess Database)

time. The higher degree of concentration at the level of the textile and apparel industry is probably suggestive of the fact that the smaller firms are finding it difficult to coexist with the bigger ones after the quota has been completely removed. One pertinent question is: how did the smaller firms compete with the bigger ones even during the regime of quota protection? It is possible that the export quota allowed many firms to focus on the external markets while leaving the internal market to the disposal of small- and medium-sized firms. However, the removal of the quota and the entry of China in the WTO have pushed many such firms to stiff competition from low-cost production from the Chinese industries. This might have influenced the erstwhile exporters and those with substantial interest in the foreign market alongside the domestic market, to depend more on the local sales. The consequent effect on price domestically has made small- and medium-sized firms noncompetitive. Hence, over time, the market share lies with fewer firms compared to that in the previous decades. Note that albeit we did not offer a rigorous empirical exercise to explain the exact degree by which the substitutability between foreign market and domestic market takes place and identify the factors that significantly cause such reallocation, the descriptive analysis still suggests that the reallocation by firms operating in multiple markets can be conditional. In some cases, it is equally feasible that the emphasis on the foreign market goes up despite a price or quantity shock facing the country or the firms.

The effect of MFA phase-out on countries that gained and lost can be largely explained by the competitiveness effect. Much in contradiction to the earlier belief that removal of quota will lead to market expansion for all exporters, several exporting countries and firms therein have witnessed negative impact in the recent times. This holds true for the quinquennial and the annual results for most of the countries including India. On the other hand, that countries like Thailand, Malaysia and Indonesia would suffer more in the face of competition from China and India turns out to be additional outcomes (see Kar and Kar 2011) of the drive towards freeing world trade from noncompetitive barriers.

7.4 Concluding Remarks

This chapter showed that when faced with uncertainty in certain markets vis-à-vis certainty of price in at least one of the markets facing a multi-market firm, the output and allocation decisions depend crucially on the standard comparison of marginal cost and price in the certain market. We used the separation result discussed in the beginning as an important instrument for this chapter, in order to understand the implications of a quantity shock in the uncertain market on the price and sales reallocation in both certain and uncertain markets. To this end, we utilized the withdrawal of quota as a policy shock for the large textile and apparel industry worldwide with huge significance for a host of developing countries. The analytical section suggested that if the change in marginal utility from profit (of a representative firm) owing to the change in the randomness of the foreign price outweighs the potential fall in price in case the firm focuses more on the domestic market, then the firm should continue to export a positive amount. The export share may even exceed the pre-withdrawal level. Conversely, if the withdrawal of quota and larger focus on the domestic market leads to a negative effect on the profit from foreign sales at the margin, then the firm is most likely to withdraw entirely from the foreign market and sell the full amount in the domestic market. Anywhere in between, the level of participation may go up or down over time leading to possible U-shaped curves. We used some statistical observations from the firm-level sales data for a large number of Indian firms dealing with textile and apparel. We did find that both the number of pure exporting firms and the export as a share of the total sales display inverted U-shaped relations between 1991 and 2013. In fact, even though the slow phasing-out of MFA began way back in 1995, the number of pure exporting firms went up in the next 10 years only to plummet to a very low level near the end of the series. It means that while there has been widespread recognition of the fact that India did not fulfill the quota allotted to it even during the regime of protection, the quota still offered substantial protection to firms for exploring the foreign market. The withdrawal of the quota has in turn reduced both participation and sale in such markets. In addition, it may have rendered small- and medium-sized firms unviable in the local market, leading to greater market concentration for this industry.

A host of other issues, including the impact of the textile industry on general growth and welfare levels, should in future help to understand the broader reach of the trade policy dealt with in this chapter. Similarly, it would be interesting to investigate the implications of MFA withdrawal on the labour market in further detail and discuss relevant policy aspects.

Acknowledgments This chapter has benefited from the presentation at the Annual General Conference on Contemporary Issues in Development Economics at Jadavpur University, December 2014 and CTRPFP National Conference at CSSSC held in February 2015. The usual disclaimer applies.

References

Appelbaum RP, Bonacich E, Quan K (2005) The end of apparel quotas: a faster race to the bottom? Center for Global Studies, UC Santa Barbara, October 15–16, 2004. https://escholarship.org/uc/item/40 f8w19g

Bair J. Dussel Peters E (2006) Global commodity chains and endogenous growth: export dynamism and development in Mexico and Honduras. World Development 34(2):203–221

Dalal A, Katz E (2003) The multi-market firm, transportation costs, and the separation of the output and allocation decisions. Oxf Econ Pap 55:644–656

Gereffi G (2004) Industrial adjustment in the North Carolina textile and clothing industry, Presentation at the Global Apparel/Clothing Europe Conference at the University of North Carolina at Chapel Hill, October 15–16, 2004. http://www.unc.edu/depts/europe/conferences/04/global/papers.htm

Gherzi Report (2003) Benchmarking of costs of production of textile products in India vis-à-vis China, Pakistan, Indonesia, Bangladesh and Sri Lanka. Swiss Textile Organization, Geneva

Gibbon P (2008) Governance, entry barriers, upgrading: re-interpretation of some GVC concepts from the experience of African garment exports. Compet Change 12(1):29–48
Harris R (1985) Why voluntary export restraints are 'Voluntary'. Can J Econ 18(4):799–809
Hashim DA (2005) Post-MFA: making the textile and garment industry competitive. Econ Polit Wkly 40:117–127. (January 8)
Kar M (2012) National and global aspects of India's textiles and apparel industry and trade: an overview. South Asian J Macroecon Public Finance 1(1):81–134
Kar M, Kar S (2011) The multi fibre arrangement and South Asia. In: Murshed SM et al (eds) South-South globalisation challenges and opportunities for development. Routledge, UK
Kar M, Kar S (2014) Trade policy and inequality: evidence from post-MFA India and a theoretical model, forthcoming. UNU-WIDER Working Paper Series
Katz E, Paroush J (1979) The effect of forward markets on exporting firms. Econ Lett 4:272–274
Knappe M (2003) Textiles and clothing: what happens after 2005? Int Trade Forum 1(2):16. (International Trade center)
Krishna K (1988) What do voluntary export restraints do? NBER Working Paper No. 2612. NBER, Mass, Cambridge
Marjit S, Kabiraj T, Mukherjee A (2009) Quota as a competitive device. In: Kamigashi T, Zhao L (eds) International trade and economic dynamics: essays in memory of Koji Shimomura. Springer, Berlin
Richardson DJ (1971) Constant market share analysis of export growth. J Int Econ 1:227–239
Tewari M (2006) Adjustments in India's textile and apparel industry: reworking historical legacies in a post-MFA world. Environ Plan A 38(12):2325–2344
Trela I, Whalley J (1990) Global effects of developed country trade restrictions on textiles and apparel. Econ J 100(403):1190–1205
United Nations Commission on Trade and Development (UNCTAD) (2005) TNCs and the removal of textiles and clothing quotas, current studies in FDI and development. UNCTAD, New York
United States International Trade Commission (USITC) (2004) Textiles and apparel: assessment of the competitiveness of certain foreign suppliers to the US market. USITC, Washington D.C. (Report declassified in January 2004)
WTO (2004) Background Statistical Information With Respect to Trade in Textiles and Clothing, Geneva
Yano M (1989) Voluntary export restraints and expectations: an analysis of export quotas in oligopolistic markets. Int Econ Rev 30(4):707–723

Chapter 8
Does Foreign Aid Corrupt? A Theoretical Note

Sugata Marjit and Vivekananda Mukherjee

8.1 Introduction

Foreign aid, traditionally, has been seen as a tool for overcoming the savings gap in developing countries, which resulted in persistent poverty, malnutrition, disease and death. It was supposed to provide the necessary 'big push' to move these countries out of the poverty trap. Most of the aid from developed countries to developing countries flowed in specific directions like improvement of economic and social infrastructure, production and commodity assistance. Maintenance of government/civil society/peace and security also received importance in more recent years. The magnitude of the aid flow is calculated as more than US$ 2.3 trillion (measured in 2006 dollars) over the past 50 years (Easterly and Pfutze 2008). However, the effectiveness of this remains debatable (Sachs 2005; Easterly 2006). It has been argued that the aid flow distorted the natural path of development of the recipient countries to the worse; it turned them inefficient, dependent on rent-seeking and less democratic. In fact, over the past 50 years, the per capita growth rate of the gross domestic product (GDP) in Africa, one of the major recipients of international aid flow, has showed a marked decline (Abuzeid 2009). Djankov et al. (2006) estimate that over a given period of time, a recipient country's democratic quality would deteriorate from average (relative to the average level of democracy of all the aid recipients) to completely absent if the country's aid dependence averaged 1.9 % of GDP over that period. Abuzeid (2009) argues that it had been the same for most of the sub-Saharan countries in Africa. It appears that the foreign aid flow in the past 50 years has defeated its own purpose.

S. Marjit (✉)
Centre for Studies in Social Sciences, Kolkata, India
e-mail: marjit@gmail.com

V. Mukherjee
Department of Economics, Jadavpur University, Kolkata, India
e-mail: mukherjeevivek@hotmail.com

S. Banerjee et al. (eds.), *Understanding Development*, India Studies in Business and Economics, DOI 10.1007/978-81-322-2455-6_8

While the nature of the aid flow in the form of tied aid, food aid and technical assistance, alleged to serve the objective of donor countries more than that of the recipient countries, is widely thought to be one of the major reasons for the failure of foreign aid, the governance failure in the recipient countries is thought to be the other. Burnside and Dollar (2000) find that aid has a positive impact on the growth of developing countries with good monetary, fiscal and trade policies, but has little effect in the presence of poor policies. This calls for selective use of aid policies: more aid for countries with good policies and less aid for the others. But if aid does not reach the poorly governed countries, which are poor due to their poor policies, its purpose is defeated. Also, low-income countries often have more corruption and less democracy (Svensson 2005). So, if aid is targeted to less corrupt and more democratic countries, again, its purpose is defeated. However, Easterly and Pfutze (2008) show with the help of data that in the past 50 years, around 68 % of the aid flow was received by the corrupt countries of the world. The donors who give to the least developed countries end up donating more to the corrupt and less democratic countries, which is not true for the donors donating to the middle/high-income and more democratic countries. So, in spite of its known inefficiency, for various reasons in the past 50 years, foreign aid has not been very selective around the world. Corrupt countries still receive a substantial amount of aid. Against this background, the current chapter constructs a theoretical model to explore the following question: Does foreign aid increase the extent of corruption in the recipient country which is already corrupt?

The usual channels through which foreign aid can increase corruption in the recipient countries are explained in the literature as follows.[1] First, foreign aid may create more inefficient 'white elephant' projects in the recipient country; second, it can be used to increase unproductive employment in the government, making it more inefficient; third, since foreign aid meets the expenditure need of the targeted sector in the recipient country, its revenue can be schemed off for personal consumption by corrupt bureaucrats/politicians; fourth, it increases lobbying as the balance of power tilts towards the executive branch of the government; fifth, the stronger executive power of the government weakens the democracy and therefore also relaxes the checks and balance on the functioning of the government; sixth, if aid is utilized through non-governmental organizations (NGOs), the efficient bureaucrats often leave the government jobs to join NGOs, which may increase corruption in the recipient country.[2] While it is true that foreign aid may weaken democracy in the recipient country as argued above, in a country like India, where democracy is deep rooted, it seems that this effect more or less has remained absent. We show, in this chapter, that given the level of democracy in the recipient country, the effect of foreign aid on corruption may work through a new channel of redistributive politics. In an earlier chapter, Marjit and Mukherjee (2007) use a similar framework to hint towards the existence of a positive correlation between the 'good policies'

[1] See Abuzeid (2009) for a detailed review.

[2] In a recent chapter using African data, Asongu and Mohamed (2013) have shown that the foreign aid channeled through NGOs reduces corruption in the economies.

adopted in utilization of the aid money and the level of corruption in the recipient countries where a government is concerned with maximization of its vote share for its re-election. It ends up demystifying the empirical observation that in the past 50 years, a large portion of foreign aid has flown to corrupt countries: it claims that this set of countries may also be the countries adopting growth-enhancing 'better' policies. They also derive a similar result regarding the relation between foreign aid and corruption as in this chapter. But the framework of the present chapter differs from Marjit and Mukherjee (2007), as unlike the previous chapter, here we assume that the money siphoned off through corruption leaks out of the economy, which is true in a large number of developing countries.[3] So we prove that the result that under certain conditions more foreign aid raises the extent of corruption in a poorer country and promotes honesty in a richer country is robust in this alternative specification too.

In the literature, there had been conflicting claims about the direction in which higher disbursal of aid flow affects the level of corruption of the recipient economy. On the one hand, chapters by Svensson (2000) and Alesina and Weder (2002) claim that more aid corrupts the recipient countries. On the other hand, Tavares (2003) claims that aid promotes honesty of the recipients. The results of our model provide a possible explanation of these conflicting observations. The model also explains the results in chapters by Mosley et al. (1987) and Boone (1995), which had empirically shown that 'in all countries there is no significant correlation between aid and growth'. The results have implications for the fiscal federalism literature, too. It may help us to understand the pattern of corruption and income divergence that emerges among different states in a federal democracy like India, where the state governments receive untied grants from the central government and fight elections at the state level. The results predict that more untied funds transferred to the state governments in the poorer states raise their corruption level, while the opposite happens in the richer states. It also introduces a new channel to explain the income divergence among Indian states.[4]

In the next section of the chapter, we develop the theoretical model and derive the results. In Sect. 3, we conclude the chapter.

8.2 Model and Results

We consider a developing country, which is a democracy with large-scale unemployment and corruption. It receives a monetary grant C from an international agency to spend on creation of infrastructure in sectors like transport, education,

[3] Kar and Freitas (2012) estimate that in the period 2001–2010 the illicit financial outflow from developing countries of the world had been around US$ 859 billion. They found that 61.2% of this outflow had been from Asian countries except the Middle East (five of the ten countries with largest outflow, China, Malaysia, the Philippines, India and Indonesia, are in Asia). The growth of illicit financial outflow, however, was the highest in the Middle East and North Africa region at 26.3% per annum on average, followed by Africa at 23.8% and Asia at 7.8%.

[4] See Dasgupta et al. (2000), Kalra and Sodsriwiboon (2010) for evidence.

health etc. to pursue its long-term development goal. Suppose the recipient country government, which is a democratically elected political party or coalition, is given freedom to choose the allocation of the grant under different heads of expenditure in the project. We assume there are two heads of expenditure. It can spend the money either to procure capital *(I)* or to employ unemployed people in few or unproductive jobs *(M)*. Since the government is corrupt, it keeps aside α fraction of the amount of aid received to distribute among the party members before it decides about the allocation *(I, M)*. We assume this misappropriated money αC leaks out of the system. We draw from the standard public choice and political economy literature to argue that the government, or the ruling party, is partly benevolent and partly selfish.[5] It prefers spending the money both in buying more capital improving the quality of infrastructure and in creating employment that helps its probability of re-election. Since, if not spent in the stipulated period the money goes back to the donor without generating any of these benefits, the recipient country government decides to spend the entire amount left after the leakage $(1-\alpha)C$ on the allocation *(I, M)*, and at the equilibrium the budget constraint is satisfied with equality, that is, $I + M = (1-\alpha)C$.

Redistributive politics in our framework works through employment generation. More employment means more political support and a greater probability of re-election. Note that the redistribution scheme run by the foreign aid money may work parallel to the standard schemes for redistribution available with any sovereign government, such as the land reform program or the tax-transfer mechanisms. Sometimes, the foreign aid relaxes the burden off the government in running other redistribution programs. There are some studies in the literature, such as Pack and Pack (1993) and Swaroop et al. (2000), that point out this possibility. However, in this chapter, we assume that the other programs do not exhaust the possibility of adopting further redistributive policies, and the foreign aid program feeds well into the redistributive politics played by the recipient country government. Even if it substitutes other programs of the government to some extent, all the results of this chapter go through. The government has the choice of spending a lot on capital, that is, choosing a high value of I and to raise the growth rate. But, given the budget constraint the choice of higher I implies lower M, that is, the immediate employment generation potential is being sacrificed. In some situations, this can have serious implications in terms of the re-election possibility of the political party,[6] and it induces the ruling party to practice 'redistributive politics' by choosing a higher value of M. The long-run growth potential of the economy gets sacrificed in the process.

---

[5] Boone (1995) used similar specification of the government's objective function.

[6] The higher value of I may promise employment in the future. However, we assume there is a severe commitment problem on the part of the government, as no one believes in this promise. Typically, the effects of a long-run project unfold themselves gradually in the future with contraction of some of the sectors and expansion of some other sectors. Even if the overall expansionary effect dominates the contractionary effect, the common people suffer from uncertainty about the future in the sense that they cannot see perfectly on which side they will be when the project is implemented. See Fernandez and Rodrik (1991) for similar argument. See Robinson and Torvik (2004) for a treatment of the government's commitment problem.

With such a structure in hand, we propose the following, possibly the simplest, objective function of a risk-neutral government:

$$\max_{\{I,M,\alpha\}} \Omega = \theta I + (1-\theta)[\alpha C + p(I, \alpha C, n)v] \tag{8.1}$$

such that $I + M = (1-\alpha)C$, $I \geq 0, M \geq 0$ and $\alpha \in [0,1]$, where $0 < \theta < 1$, $p_1 > 0$, $p_{11} < 0$, $p_2 < 0$, $p_{22} < 0$, $p_3 > 0$, $p_{33} < 0$, $p_{ij} = 0$ and $i \neq j$. We assume all higher-order derivatives of $p(.)$ are zero. In the first term, I is spent in buying capital. Even if no other benefit is derived from the project, due to the government's social benevolence, it derives a utility from the project. On the other hand, the second term represents its selfish benefits which have two components: the amount αC it takes out of the system through corrupt activities for personal consumption and the expected benefit $p(.)\ v$ it derives through its re-election. In the term $p(.)\ v$, v is a constant utility measure and $p(.)$ is the probability function representing the probability of re-election. The probability of re-election p depends positively on the amount actually spent in buying capital to build the infrastructure, negatively on the amount of leakage from the system through corruption, positively on the amount of employment generated in the short run n. The weight the ruling party attaches to social benevolence is θ and to selfish endeavour is $(1-\theta)$, which reflects the political significance of such outcomes. We use a minimal degree of concavity in $p(.)$ to drive home our point.

Two points should be noted here. First, the political authority is concerned about the expected benefits from re-election, and v is the summary of such benefits in the future. Second, we do not specify the concerns of a median voter simply because the targeted pool of voters is identical.

Since R is the reservation payoff of the people getting employment through the project, the government, in its choice of fund allocation to maximize Ω, must abide by the constraint:

$$\frac{(1-\alpha)C - I}{n} \geq R, \tag{8.2}$$

that is, everyone has to be paid R. Since $\frac{\partial p}{\partial n} > 0$ and $p_{ij} = 0$, constraint (8.2) must be binding.

Therefore,

$$n = \frac{(1-\alpha)C - I}{R}. \tag{8.3}$$

Note that n is pushed to a level which is consistent with the typical labourer earning only the reservation payoff. One could make a provision for a payoff slightly greater than R and employment of fewer people. Hence, an additional trade-off can be introduced. We think that is unnecessary for the basic result we wish to highlight.

Note that as the employment intensity of I is zero, increasing I will always have negative net employment effect given that C as employment will be diverted away from the project.

As we describe the government's choice problem above using Eq. (8.3), the optimization exercise of the government in Eq. 8.1 can be rewritten as:

$$\max_{\{I,\alpha\}} \Omega = \theta I + (1-\theta)\left[\alpha C + p\left(I, \alpha C, \frac{(1-\alpha)C - I}{R}\right)v\right] \tag{8.4}$$

such that $0 \leq I \leq (1-\alpha)C$ and $\alpha \in [0,1]$.

Suppose, the interior solution to the problem (I^*, α^*) exists such that $0 < I < (1-\alpha)C$, $\alpha^* \hat{I}(0,1)$. The first-order condition for optimization implies at (I^*, α^*) the following equations hold:

$$\frac{\theta}{1-\theta} + p_1 v = \frac{p_3 v}{R}, \tag{8.5}$$

$$1 + p_2 v = \frac{p_3 v}{R}. \tag{8.6}$$

We assume that Eqs. 8.5 and 8.6 yield permissible values of I and α. Second-order conditions are satisfied with p_{11}, p_{22} and p_{33} being negative. We are interested in $\frac{d\alpha}{dC}$. Given Eqs. 8.5–8.6,

$$\frac{d\alpha}{dC} = \frac{\frac{1}{R^2}[(1-\alpha)p_{11}p_{33} - \alpha p_{11}p_{22}R^2 - \alpha p_{22}p_{33}]}{\Delta}. \tag{8.7}$$

Suppose, $f(R) = \frac{1}{R^2}[(1-\alpha)p_{11}p_{33} - \alpha\, p_{11}p_{22}R^2 - \alpha\, p_{22}p_{33}]$. Since $\Delta > 0$ by second-order condition, if $f(R) > 0$, from Eq. 8.7 it follows that $\frac{d\alpha}{dC} > 0$. Similarly, if $f(R) < 0, \frac{d\alpha}{dC} < 0$ and if $f(R) = 0, \frac{d\alpha}{dC} = 0$.

Observe, since the derivatives of $p(.)$ with order more than 2 are assumed to be zero, it can be derived:

$$f'(R) = -\frac{d\alpha}{dR}[p_{22}p_{33} + p_{11}p_{33} + p_{11}p_{22}R^2] - 2\alpha p_{11}p_{22}R. \tag{8.8}$$

From (8.5) and (8.6), it also follows:

$$\frac{d\alpha}{dR} = \frac{-\frac{1}{R^2}(p_3 + p_{33}n)p_{11}}{\Delta}. \tag{8.9}$$

We define $\varepsilon_n = -\frac{\partial p_3}{\partial n}\frac{n}{p_3}$ and assume $\varepsilon_n < 1$, that is, p_3 must not be 'too responsive' to changes in *n*. This in turn implies $p_3 + p_{33}n > 0$. Now, from Eq. 8.9 since $\Delta > 0$ by second-order condition, it follows $\frac{d\alpha}{dR} > 0$. Therefore, from Eq. 8.8 clearly $f'(R) < 0$. Again, since $\frac{d\alpha}{dR} > 0$ for all values of $R \geq 0$ (i.e. for lower values of *R*, the ruling party has higher incentive to allocate more of the foreign aid money for the purpose of redistributive politics and to allocate less for corruption and vice versa), we can reasonably assume the implication of this is as $R \to 0$, $\alpha \approx 0$ and as $R \to \alpha$, $\alpha \approx 1$. This in turn implies as $R \to 0$, $f(R) \approx p_{11}p_{33} > 0$ and as $R \to \alpha$, $f(R) \approx (-\alpha)$. Therefore, since $f(R)$ is continuous over $R \geq 0$, there exists a value of $R^* > 0$ such that $f(R) = 0$. It follows from the fact that $f'(R) < 0$, if $R < R^*$, $f(R) > 0$ and $\frac{d\alpha}{dC} > 0$; if $R > R^*$, $f(R) < 0$ and $\frac{d\alpha}{dC} < 0$. We note this result as the next proposition of the model as:

Proposition If $\varepsilon_n < 1$, in poorer countries with $R < R^*$, the aid increases corruption. In richer countries with $R > R^*$, it promotes honesty.

Proof: See the discussion above. (QED)

The intuition behind the proposition is as follows. As more aid is disbursed, on the choice of the higher value of *α*, both the marginal cost from redistributive politics and marginal benefit from increased corruption fall in a country, but in poorer countries the marginal cost falls at a higher rate than the marginal benefit. Therefore, the poorer countries choose a higher value of *α*. However, this leads to a higher choice of *I* too, which in turn suggests lowering the choice of *α*. Since the first effect dominates the second, as more aid is disbursed, the poorer countries end up choosing a higher value of *α*. In the richer countries, as more aid is disbursed, on the choice of the higher value of *α*, both the marginal cost from redistributive politics and marginal benefit from increased corruption fall, but the marginal benefit falls at a higher rate than the marginal cost. Therefore, the richer countries choose a lower value of *α*. This leads to a lower choice of *I*, which in turn reinforces the choice of a lower value of *α*.

This result is a new contribution to the existing literature on foreign aid. It attempts to resolve the ambiguity in the literature which arises from the opposite claims made by Svensson (2000) and Alesina and Weder (2002) on the one hand, and Tavares (2003) on the other. We claim that if $\varepsilon_n < 1$, the result of Svensson and Alesina and Weder that aid promotes corruption holds only for the relatively poorer recipients, whereas the result of Tavares that aid promotes honesty holds only for the relatively richer recipients.

It can also be easily observed that this model is able to explain the empirical findings of chapters by Mosley et al. (1987) and Boone (1995), which had empirically shown 'in all countries there is no significant correlation between aid and growth'. Using Eqs. (8.5) and (8.6), it can be derived:

$$\frac{dI}{dR} = \frac{-\frac{1}{R^2}(p_3 + p_{33}n)Cp_{22}}{\Delta}. \tag{8.10}$$

If $\varepsilon_n < 1,\ p_3 + p_{33}n > 0$. Since from second-order condition $\Delta > 0$, it follows from Eq. 8.10 that $\frac{dI}{dR} > 0$. This implies that in poorer countries the concern for winning elections forces the government in power to allocate more for employing people than for buying capital. Therefore, aid does not promote growth in poorer countries. In the richer countries however, the force of redistributive politics is much weaker. But, as we have already argued $\frac{d\alpha}{dR} > 0$, due to corruption in these countries, no amount of money is left to be allocated in the growth-inducing projects (remember from Eq. 8.4 it must be $I \leq ((1-a)C)$. Therefore, aid fails to induce growth.

8.3 Conclusions

This chapter attempts to provide an explanation for the ambiguity that we observe in the empirical literature on the question of whether aid promotes corruption in the recipient countries. It assumes that (i) foreign aid does not weaken the democracy prevailing in the recipient country and (ii) the proceeds of corruption leak out of the economy and develop a framework which models the recipient country government's choice under the pressure of redistributive politics. It claims that under certain conditions the result of Svensson (2000) and Alesina and Weder (2002) that aid promotes corruption holds only for relatively poorer recipients, whereas the result of Tavares (2003) that the aid promotes honesty holds only for relatively richer recipients. It proves the robustness of similar results derived by Marjit and Mukherjee (2007), which assumed that the proceeds of corruption are spent within the economy itself. The framework can also explain why aid fails to induce growth either in the poorer or richer countries as claimed in chapters by Mosley et al. (1987) and Boone (1995). Though the present model is written in the context of foreign aid, the intuitions developed in it can be applied to understand the pattern of corruption and income divergence that emerges among different states in a federal democracy like India, where the state governments receive untied grants from the central government and fight elections at the state level. The results interpreted in this context predict that more untied funds transferred to state governments in poorer states raise its corruption level, while the opposite happens in richer states. It also introduces a new channel for explaining income divergence among Indian states in the past 50 years.

References

Abuzeid F (2009) Foreign aid and "Big Push" theory: lessons from sub-Saharan Africa. Stanf J Int Relat 11(7):16–23

Alesina A, Weder B (2002) Do corrupt governments receive less foreign aid? Am Econ Rev 92(4):1126–1137

Asongu SA, Mohamed J (2013) On the channels of foreign aid to corruption. Econ Bull 33(3):2191–2201

Boone P (1995) Politics and effectiveness of foreign aid. Centre for Economic Performance, Discussion Chapter No. 272, London School of Economics and Political Science, London

Burnside C, Dollar D (2000) Aid, policies and growth. Am Econ Rev 90:847–868

Dasgupta D, Maiti P, Mukherjee R, Sarkar S, Chakrabarti S (2000) Growth and interstate disparities in India. Econ Polit Wkly 35:2413–2422

Djankov S, Montalvo JG, Reynal-Querol M (2006) The curse of aid. World Bank, Washington DC.

Easterly W (2006) The white man's burden: how the West's effort to aid the rest have done so much ill and so little good. Penguin, New York

Easterly W, Pfutze T (2008) Where does the money go?: best and worst practices of foreign aid. Global Economy and Development Working Chapter No. 21, Brookings Institution, Washington DC

Fernandez R, Rodrik D (1991) Resistance to reform: status quo bias in the individual specific uncertainty. Am Econ Rev 81:1146–1155

Kalra S, Sodsriwiboon P (2010) Growth convergence and spillovers among Indian states: what matters and what does not? IMF Working Chapter WP/10/96

Kar D, Freitas S (2012) Illicit financial flows from developing countries 2001–2010. Global Financial Integrity: Washington. http://iff.gfintegrity.org/iff2012/2012report.html

Marjit S, Mukherjee V (2007) Poverty, utilization of foreign aid and corruption: the role of redistributive politics. In: Lahiri S (ed) Theory and practice of foreign aid, Vol 1. Elsevier, Amsterdam 17–29

Mosley P, Hudson J, Horrell S (1987) Aid, the public sector and the market in less developed countries. Econ J 97:616–641

Pack H, Pack JR (1993) The foreign aid and the question of fungibility. Rev Econ Stat 75(2):258–265

Robinson J, Torvik R (2004) White elephants. J Public Econ 89:197–200

Sachs J (2005) End of poverty: economic possibilities of our time. Penguin, New York

Svensson J (2000) Foreign aid and rent-seeking. J Int Econ 51:437–461

Svensson J (2005) Eight questions about corruption. J Econ Perspect 19(3):19–42

Swaroop V, Jha S, Rajkumar AS (2000) Fiscal effects of foreign aid in a federal system of governance: the case of India. J Public Econ 77:307–330

Tavares J (2003) Does foreign aid corrupt? Econ Lett 79:99–106

Part III
Issues in Public Economics

Chapter 9
Public–Private Partnerships and Governance

Indrani Roy Chowdhury and Prabal Roy Chowdhury

9.1 Introduction

Public–private partnerships (PPPs), where the government and the private sector work together on projects, typically projects of public interest, seem to be in fashion at the moment. One Indian success story in this respect is the Indira Gandhi International Airport in New Delhi. In a partnership between the government of India and the GMR group (one of the top five airport developers), terminal 3 (T3) was built in an impressive 37 months. It is the only airport in India with three runways, one being India's longest at 4430 m. The T3 also boasts 168 checkout counters, 92 walkalators, 31 escalators, 78 aerobridges and 12 baggage reclaim belts, handling 20.6 million domestic, and 9.3 million international passengers in the financial year (FY) 2011. Further, it was rated the world's fourth best airport for *airport service quality (ASQ)* in the 15–25 million passenger category in the FY 2011. Other examples of successful PPPs include the Rajiv Gandhi International Airport in Hyderabad.

By all accounts, PPPs seem to be critical for India's development plans in the coming years. The twelfth Five Year Plan (2012–2017) targets an infrastructure requirement of ₹ 40,992 billion, which is *twice* the ₹ 20,542 billion under the eleventh Five Year Plan. Further, under the twelfth plan, 50% of the projected amount is supposed to come from the private sector, as against 36% under the eleventh plan. Given the projected increase in infrastructural investment, as well as the dependence on the private sector, PPPs would appear inevitable in many cases (the FICCI, Ernst & Young 2012). However, the opinion regarding their usefulness seems divided. While Manmohan Singh, our ex-Prime Minister, said that "PPP projects

I. R. Chowdhury (✉)
Department of Economics, Jamia Millia Islamia, New Delhi 110025, India
e-mail: indranirc1@gmail.com

P. R. Chowdhury
Economic and Planning Unit, Indian Statistical Institute,
Delhi Centre, New Delhi 110016, India

S. Banerjee et al. (eds.), *Understanding Development*, India Studies in Business and Economics, DOI 10.1007/978-81-322-2455-6_9

.... will not only enable us to leverage our limited public resources, but also improve efficiency of service delivery", The New Zealand Treasury was much more circumspect "There is little reliable empirical evidence about the costs and benefits of PPPs" (2009).

Given the importance of PPPs, it is of interest to examine what affects the formation of PPPs. In particular, we focus on the issue of governance. The modern trend towards PPPs seem to have been incubated by the developed world (in particular the UK), where governance levels can be expected to be better vis-à-vis the less developed countries (LDCs), before it became a global phenomenon. In this chapter, we examine if there is any fundamental reason why countries with stronger governance levels are more likely to opt for PPPs. Further, given their widespread global adoption, a subsidiary concern is whether there are any adverse implications in case they are adopted in LDCs.

In a bid to address this issue, we begin by discussing the institutional structure of PPPs, as well as how they fare globally, so as to provide a context for our analysis. We then develop a simple analytical framework which summarises the consensus in the literature regarding the raison d'etre of PPPs. Then we take off from this to develop a simple formal model based on risk sharing that is capable of analysing this issue. We show that PPPs are more likely to form in case the governance is strong. Otherwise, PPPs are unlikely to form, and will be susceptible to contract renegotiation in case they do form.

In the next section, we discuss the institutional structure of PPPs, before discussing the global PPP experiences. This is followed by Sect. 9.3, where we develop a simple analytical framework for PPPs where we provide a non formal discussion of the pros and cons of PPPs. In the next two sections, we build a formal model where we examine if PPPs are more likely under weak, or strong governments. We discuss a few robustness issues in Sect. 9.7, before we finally conclude in Sect. 9.8.

9.2 PPPs: Institutional Organization and Global Scope

In this section, we provide a context to our theoretical framework. To that end, we first discuss the institutional structures of PPPs, and then discuss the global scope of PPPs.

9.2.1 Institutional Organization of PPPs

A PPP is a government service which is built, and sometimes operated and funded through a partnership of the government and one or more private sector companies—sometimes referred to as P3, or P^3 as well. We shall take the viewpoint that a PPP is a contract in which the private party assumes substantial financial, technical and operational risks. Depending on the extent of risk sharing, there are many different institutional mechanisms for implementing such contracts.[1]

Two of the more prevalent contractual modes are the build-operate-transfer (BOT) and the design-build-finance-operate (DBFO). Under a BOT contract, typically the contractor takes responsibility for building the asset, as well as operating and managing it for the duration of the contract. Investment in capital assets is also undertaken by the contractor, but the financial risk is borne by the government. Upon expiry of contract, the asset is transferred to the public authority. Under a DBFO contract, the contractor is in charge of all phases of the operation, including finance. Many other variations exist of course, for example build-lease-transfer (BLT).

Turning to the financing of the private partner, in some types of PPP, the cost of using the service is borne exclusively by the users of the service, which goes to the private firms. In other types, the cost of providing the service is borne wholly, or in part, by the government. The private partner may also be provided with existing assets, for example land. Further, in projects that create public goods like in infrastructure, the government may provide a capital subsidy in the form of a one-time grant. In some other cases, the government may provide revenue subsidies, including tax breaks, or guaranteed annual revenues for a fixed time period (Yescombe 2007).

9.2.2 Global Scope of PPPs

Pressure for PPPs arose from the increasing level of public debt during the macroeconomic stagflation of the 1970s and 1980s following the OPEC oil crisis, which made an increase in government expenditure, even for infrastructural investments, problematic. Consequently, governments sought to encourage PPPs in infrastructure, whereby the private sector could carry some of the financial burden. However, initially this was done on the basis of accounting fallacies arising from the fact that public accounts did not distinguish between recurrent and capital expenditures. The later, more sophisticated arguments were in terms of risk allocation, efficiency and funding (to be discussed in the following sections).

9.2.3 The UK

In 1992, the Conservative government of John Major in the UK introduced the *Public Finance Initiative (PFI),* aimed at encouraging PPPs so as to reduce public

[1] Sometimes a private sector consortium forms a "*special purpose vehicle*" (SPV) for the contracted period. The consortium is usually made up of a building contractor, a maintenance company and bank lender(s). In cases where the government has invested in the project, it is typically (but not always) allotted an equity share in the SPV. It is the SPV that signs the contract with the government and with subcontractors to build the facility and then maintain it.

sector borrowing. As of December 2006, 794 PFI projects have been signed, involving 55 billion £in capital value. The Labour government of Tony Blair, elected in 1997, expanded the PFI initiative but sought to shift the emphasis to the achievement of "value for money", mainly through an appropriate allocation of risk.

The UK government has taken several other steps to ensure the success of PPPs, for example setting up Partnerships UK (PUK) and the Treasury Taskforce. Further, it empowered the National Audit Office (NAO) to independently oversee PPPs.

The evidence seem to suggest that PPPs have achieved a measure of success in the UK. The British NAO estimates 65% of contracts delivered within time and within agreed budget (Nao 2007).[2]

9.2.3.1 Case Study: The London Tube

Not all PPPs were successful though, a case in point being the PPP tasked with upgrading the London tube. In 1993, this project was awarded to two different infra-firms, Tubelines and Metronet, after 19 months of contract negotiations. Tubelines were awarded the Jubilee, the Northern and the Picadilly lines, while Metronet got (a) the Bakerloo, Central and Victoria and (b) the District, Circle, Hammersmith and City lines. The negotiations were extremely complex, with the work being phased over 30 years. Tubelines and Metronet were to do the upgradation, while the London Underground Limited (LUL) was to provide the final services. In fact, the complexity of the contract meant that advisory services themselves cost 109 million £. Further, the delay in project allocation meant that the LUL had to provide substantial compensations to the various bidders, including the losers.

Broadly, the contract specified two aspects: risk allocation among the parties and the payment mechanism. As to risk allocation, the demand risk was borne by LUL as they did the final service provision. The cost overrun risks were however shared, as the amount of cost overruns to be borne by the private companies were capped. This reduced the incentives for checking overruns, as is clear from the Metronet experience. Metronet's incentive for checking costs overruns was not very strong, as Metronet's shareholders were also suppliers of the consortium, so that any higher costs would translate into revenue for them! In fact, Metronet had cost overruns four times that of expected costs. However, Tubelines, which did not have such an interlinked structure, incurred no cost overruns. Finally, financing risk was also shared. While financing was provided privately by the Infracos, the public sector borne substantial risks via a debt guarantee entitling lenders to recoup 95% of their invested funds in case of early contract termination.

[2] As anecdotal evidence, consider the A55 Llandegai to Holyhead Trunk Road project, designed, built and financed by UK Highways A55, a consortium of Carillion Laing and Hyder. This was the first trunk road in Wales under PFI linking Dublin and Ireland with Wales and England and the major markets in Europe. This project was delivered 6 months ahead of time despite wet winters and fuel crisis.

Turning to the payment mechanism, it involved basic Infrastructure Service Charge (ISC), combined with bonuses and deductions. Performance was measured in terms of journey time capability (JTC), that is the time needed for a train to complete a journey. Ambience and general conditions of trains were measured by consumer surveys.

Metronet ran into significant problems, however. By April 2005, Metronet had only started work on 13 out of 32 scheduled stations, and was also 12 months behind on the refurbishment of 78 district lines.[3] Moreover, it received only 121 million £ out of the 551 million needed to cover its cost overruns. Metronet went into administration between July 2007 and May 2008, after which it was bought by two Transport for London (TFL) subsidiaries. The remaining one third of the PPP, being run by Tubelines, was taken back into public control in May 2010 after seven and a half years for a purchase price of 310 million £. While Tubelines did not have overspend problems, there were delays.

Other European countries have also invested in PPPs, especially Ireland, Portugal, Greece, the Netherlands and Spain. However, the numbers have gone down with the recession accompanying the global financial crisis. Thus in 2012, the value of PPP transactions reaching a close in the European market was 35% lower than in 2011.

9.2.4 Australia

PPPs have been prevalent in non-European countries as well. For brevity, we just consider Australia and India. Examples of Australian PPPs include the Airport Link, the Cross City Tunnel and the Sydney Harbour Tunnel, all in Sydney, the Southern Cross Station redevelopment in Melbourne, and the Robina hospital in Queensland. The Sydney Harbor Tunnel facilitated traffic between North Sydney and Sydney's central business district. Developed using a BOT framework, with the Sydney Harbor Tunnel Company Pvt. Ltd. as the preferred private partner, the development of this tunnel led to significant decongestion of traffic.

9.2.5 The Indian Experience

In India, some PPPs could be found as early as the nineteenth century, for example the Great Indian Peninsular Railway Company (1853) and the Bombay Tramway Company (1874). As elsewhere however, in India, PPPs really took off around the 1990s. Between 1991 and 2006, there were 86 PPP projects, worth ₹ 340 billion. The subsequent period, between 2006 and 2011, saw a spectacular growth in the

[3] In the first years, deductions amounted to 32 million, and bonuses were only about 12 million. Despite the delays, Metronet had significant profits at higher than the market average rate, suggesting the penalties were not too large.

number of PPPs from 450 projects in November 2009 (worth ₹ 2242 billion), to 758 PPP projects (worth ₹ 3833 billion in July 2011).[4]

Considering the sector-wise distribution by values in July 2011, roads constituted 53.4%, urban development 20.1 %, ports 8%, tourism 6.6%, and airports 0.7 % of all PPPs.

Distribution across states was also skewed, with five states accounting for 58.3% of the total value of PPPs. These include Andhra Pradesh, Maharashtra, Karnataka, Gujarat and UP, with these states focusing on roads, ports and airports.[5] A few things appear to be common to all these states, namely a proactive state setting up a regulatory structure for PPPs,[6] and state support. This support may take various forms, for example direct financial support in the form of viability gap funding (VGF), exemption from sales tax, stamp duty and seigniorage fees, government-owned land at concessional lease charges, providing linkage infrastructure and administrative support to get clearance, arrangement for rehabilitation and supply of power, water, and land requirements.

9.3 A Simple Analytical Framework for PPPs

We then provide a simple analytical framework aimed at understanding the forces that may help or hinder the formation of PPPs. In the next section, we shall use this framework to set up a formal model where we can pose our central question, namely what effect does good governance have on the formation of PPPs?

The fundamental question can be divided into two sub-questions: (a) Why cannot a fully private company, or the government/government department complete the same project? (b) Even if one involves a private firm, why bundle several activities? Why not follow a traditional procurement route, where the different aspects of a project are handled by different private firms?

There are two conceptually distinct answers to the first question. The first answer jumps out as soon as one observes the sectors where PPPs are most commonly used, namely in infrastructure sectors like transportation, health, water production and distribution, waste disposal, sanitation, etc. All of these sectors have one element in common, namely externality. This immediately implies that a private firm, which cannot extract any revenue of these externalities, will have less of a stake in such

[4] The PPP database from the Department of External Affairs, Ministry of Finance.

[5] In Andhra Pradesh prominent projects include the HITEC City, Hyderabad, RGI Airport and the Krishnapatnam Port. Projects in the pipeline include Hyderabad metro rail project, bridge across Godavari at Rajahmundry, Machilipatnam port, etc. The RGI airport, Hyderabad, partnered with the GMR group, handled 5.8 mn. domestic and 1.9 mn. international passengers in the financial year 2011. It boasts of the second longest runway in India, 146 check-in counters and 46 immigration counters. It was rated the world's best airport for Airport Service Quality (ASQ) in the 5–15 million passenger capacity in the financial year 2011.

[6] In Andhra Pradesh, for example, we have the AP Infrastructure Development Enabling Act, 2001. The act lays down guidelines for developers, specifies the various types of PPPs, and the type of state support applicable.

projects, vis-à-vis the government. The other side of the coin is that the government, whose main job is governance, naturally may not have many of the design, construction or operation skills required to take up such activities. Thus, a PPP may provide synergies in that government participation ensures that the project is carried to fruition, whereas private participation ensures that efficiency is obtained.

The other answer, in turn, follows from an observation of the risk profiles of the projects. Most projects following the PPP route are large ones, involving severe demand, cost, political and exchange rate shocks, among others. In India, for example, large projects contributed a significant fraction of the total PPP value, with projects worth more than ₹ 500 crore constituting 77.9%, projects between ₹ 251 and 500 crore constituting 14.4%, projects between 100 and 250 crore constituting 5.2% and projects worth less than 100 crore constituting about 2.5% of the total value of PPPs. These projects often involve long gestation periods and complex technological problems, which contribute to the riskiness of these projects. Thus, a complementary rational for PPPs arises from risk sharing between the government and private firms. In reality, of course, typically these reasons operate in tandem (Iossa and Martimort 2015; Iossa et al. 2013).

We next turn to the second issue, as to why bundle various activities. Suppose the provision of the service consists of two components: (a) designing/building the infrastructure and (b) the operation of the infrastructure. In such a scenario, why does not the government use traditional procurement whereby the government buys design/infrastructure from a given private firm, and then selects an operator?

One answer lies in a positive synergy between the two activities. Suppose the quality of building/infrastructure lowers the total cost of providing the service. For example, cement concrete roads may reduce maintenance and operation costs vis-à-vis asphalt/bitumen roads. In case the builder opts for the higher quality, it is beneficial for the firm operating the service and providing the service. Consequently, it is beneficial for the government also, as the government can now afford to pay less to the operating firm (Maskin and Tirole 2008).

In such a scenario, under a procurement contract the builder does not care about the operator's cost. Thus, quality will be under-provided which is bad for the economy on two counts: (a) quality of services is low and (b) the operator will require a larger compensation. Whereas under a PPP contract, the builder and the operator are the same entity, thus the benefit to the operator from lower operating costs is internalized, so that quality is supplied at the efficient level. Thus, the government can provide lower transfers to the operator. This provides a rationale for bundling both activities under a PPP. This argument is of course context specific. If, for example, the best developer is not the best operator, then bundling may lead to loss of efficiency.

9.3.1 *Problems with PPPs*

We discuss some potential problems with PPPs that qualify the preceding arguments in favour of PPPs.

To begin with the preceding argument assumes that the government is utilitarian. Consequently, some of these arguments are challenged if the government is corrupt. For example, PPPs open up the scope of pork-barrel politics based on ideology, social or political ties, or simply incentive to pander. Levin and Tadelis (2007) document that local political institutions have a profound impact on such choices in the USA. In France also, it seems efficiency considerations are often secondary to the government's determination to provide private benefits to some groups, with delayed costs. Further, the fact that PPPs typically involve longer procurement periods and tend to be complex, so that there are few consortiums capable of undertaking them (four per project on the average in the UK), increases the chances of collusion at the bidding phase.

Another implicit assumption was that the government could commit to the PPP contracts. However, in many countries, this assumption may be questionable. In the Latin American Countries (LAC), for example, it is common for a new administration to decide not to honour tariff increases granted by previous administrations. Examples include the Limeira water concession in Brazil, which was denied a tariff adjustment allowed by a contract signed by a previous administration.[7]

As the theoretical argument predicts, the evidence regarding the performance of PPPs appears to be mixed. A report commissioned by the Treasury Taskforce estimated a savings of 17% on PPPs in the UK, as compared to public procurements. NAO (2003, 2007) reported that innovative designs helped reduce the level of staffing and thus led to an overall cost reduction of 30% in the UK. However, Blanck-Brude et al. (2009) studied a sample of road projects in all EU-15 countries plus Norway. They found that ex ante construction costs are 20% higher for PPP roads.

9.4 A Formal Framework

We develop a formal model consisting of two agents, the government (denoted *G*) and a private firm (denoted *P*), who can potentially form a public–private partnership, denoted PPP. There is a single public project which might be taken up by either *G* or *P*, or even the PPP, in case it forms. In order to abstract from strategic interactions in project allocation (which is not our focus), we shall assume that the government first decides whether it wants to do the project itself, or more precisely, wants it done by a governmental department. In case it decides otherwise, it can

[7] There are also cases where legislation was passed to nullify contractual clauses. The Buenos Aires water concession indexed local-currency denominated tariffs to the US dollar to protect the contractor against currency risk. However, after a devaluation of the local currency, Congress passed an economic emergence law that nullified these guarantees (Lobina and Hall 2003; Gausch et al. 2008). Brench et al. (2005), say a major obstacle to the PPP policy in Hungary was the frequent change in political attitudes towards PPPs and user tolls.

either leave it to the private sector, which then decides whether to do the project at all or not, or alternatively try and form a PPP to implement the project.

This project yields a benefit of X to those sections of the population directly affected by it, and an indirect benefit of P to the rest of the economy, where $X, P > 0$. The direct benefit, X, can be extracted from the population by the project authority in the form of usage fees, etc. if it so desires. The indirect benefit, however, is in the nature of an externality and cannot be extracted. Alternatively, the indirect benefit P might be interpreted as the reputational returns that accrues to the government in case the project is completed (irrespective of who implements the project).

The project is brought to fruition in two stages: build and operate. Both the stages can be handled by all the agents: the private firm, the government, and the PPP. For simplicity, we assume that the cost of each stage is the same for all three agents and for both stages, though it depends on the state of the world. The cost is c in case the state of the world is bad, which happens with probability p, $0 < p < 1$.Otherwise, the costs are lower and, for ease of exposition, normalized to zero. We shall focus on the case of interest where $X < 2c$.

Remark 1 One can allow for more general project costs, where these depend on both the identity of the operator, as well as whether it involves build or operate. In fact, as discussed earlier, one justification of PPPs hinges on the fact that the private firm may be more efficient in certain aspects of the project. However, since this aspect, an important one, is not our focus, we keep the exposition simple.

The timeline is as follows. First, the government decides on project allocation, that is whether it is done by the government, the private firm, or the PPP. In the next stage, the agents get to see the realization of the project costs before they decide whether to invest or not. In certain cases, to be precise if governance is weak, there may be contract renegotiation following the realisation of project costs.

9.5 The Analysis

We analyze this game using backwards induction. We shall focus on the case where project allocation is done by the government based on the criterion of social welfare. However, the government department which may be charged with running the project, has a narrower objective, of maximising its own utility (to be specified shortly).

For ease of exposition, we assume that irrespective of the institutional organization of the project, the whole of the monetised value of the consumers' surplus is extracted and accrues to the the organization implementing the project. While this is a serious assumption, especially if the project is run by either the government department, or the PPP, we feel that the analysis should qualitatively go through in a more realistic scenario.

9.5.1 Government Department Does the Project

The utility of the government *department* running the project, when it has a direct payoff of, say g, and an externality/reputational payoff of P, is given by

$$G(P, g) = P + u(g), \tag{9.1}$$

where $u(0) = 0, u'(.) > 0, u''(.) < 0$. Thus, the utility from the private benefit is concave in g, which shall play an important part in the analysis.

We shall maintain the following assumption all through:

A1. $P + u(X - 2c) > 0 > X - 2c$.

Note that the utility of the government department, in case the state of the world is bad, is $P + u(X - 2c)$ in case the department goes through with the project. Given *A1*, this exceeds the utility to the government department from not investing in the project, which is zero (since $u(0) = 0$). Thus, the investment will be made even in the bad state of the world, and *ipso facto*, in the good state as well. Thus, the expected utility of the government department is

$$P + pu(X - 2c) + (1 - p)u(X). \tag{9.2}$$

9.5.2 Private Firm Does the Project

The utility of the private firm running the project, when it has a direct payoff of, say f, is given by

$$F(f) = u(f). \tag{9.3}$$

It is straightforward to extend the analysis to the case where $F(g)$ is an increasing, concave function of f, though different from $u(f)$.

Given *A1*, note that $X < 2c$, so that the private firm will not pursue the project in the event that costs are high (since it makes a loss if it does so). Thus, the utility of the private firm is given by

$$(1 - p)u(X). \tag{9.4}$$

We then consider the social welfare under these two institutions. In the present framework, welfare is the sum of utility for the government department and the private firm. Thus, the welfare under government operation

$$W^G = P + pu(X - 2c) + (1 - p)u(X), \tag{9.5}$$

and that under private operation

$$W^F = (1 - p)[P + u(X)]. \tag{9.6}$$

9.6 Public–Private Partnerships

Under a PPP, the two participants agree to bear the responsibilities of investing in one of the stages. For concreteness, suppose the private firm invests in building the project, whereas the government department takes care of the operational stage. Further, for simplicity, assume that the private firm and the government department each obtains half the surplus, that is $X/2$, in case the project is implemented. This is for ease of exposition alone (see Sect. 9.7 for a discussion).

We shall consider two scenarios, the first where governance structure is strong, and the second, where governance structure is weak.

9.6.1 Strong Governance

We define a strong governance structure as one where the government can enforce contracts in both states of the world. Note that, this is of some importance since there is a conflict of interest between the two partners in case the state of the world is bad. Given *A1*, the government department would like to invest even in this state, whereas the private firm would prefer not to do so.

Under strong governance, in the first stage the government department offers a take-it-or-leave-it contract that involves investing even in the bad state. As long the private firm makes nonnegative expected profits, it is going to accept such a contract. Moreover, given strong governance, this contract will be implemented as well.

Under this contract the government department has a utility of $P + pu(X/2 - c) + (1-p)u(X/2)$ and the private firm has a utility of $pu(X/2 - c) + (1-p)u(X/2)$, where, in order for the contract to be acceptable to the private firm, we assume that $pu(X/2 - c) + (1-p)u(X/2) > 0$. Thus, aggregate welfare is given by

$$W_{SG}^{PPP} = P + 2pu(X/2 - c) + 2(1-p)u(X/2). \tag{9.7}$$

We then solve the whole game, showing that optimally the PPP is going to form. Straightforward calculations yield:

Proposition 1 *Welfare under PPP exceeds that under either government, or private ownership.*

Proof From a comparison of (9.5) and (9.7), note that a sufficient condition for W_{SG}^{PPP} to exceed W^P, is that $2u(z/2) > u(z)$ for all *Z*. This is true since $u(.)$ is concave. Finally, note from (5) and (6) that $W^G > W^P$.

Intuitively, the welfare gains under PPP vis-à-vis government operation follow from risk sharing between the government and the private firm. There is an additional welfare gain from PPP formation vis-à-vis private operation, since under a PPP the project will necessarily be implemented even if costs are high.

9.6.2 Weak Governance

We then turn to the issue of interest, the outcome under weak governance. We shall formalise weak governance as the inability to impose the contract when the state of the world is bad. In that case, we assume that there is renegotiation and the private firm obtains c, rather than $X/2$ (recall that $c > X/2$), which allows it to breakeven even in the bad state.[8] Thus, the utility of the government department in the bad state is $P + u(X - 2c)$.

Thus, the expected utility of the government department is $P + pu(X - 2c) + (1 - p)u(X/2)$ and that of the private firm is $(1 - p)u(X/2)$. Thus, aggregate welfare equals

$$W_{WG}^{PPP} = P + pu(X - 2c) + 2(1 - p)u(X/2). \tag{9.8}$$

We next turn to comparing the welfare in this case with that under strong governance. Straightforward calculations yield

Proposition 2 *Welfare under PPP is lower under weak governance compared to that under strong governance, though still higher than that under government ownership.*

Proof Comparing (9.7) and (9.8), a sufficient condition is that $2u(X/2 - c > u(X - 2c)$, which again follows as $u(.)$ is concave.

9.6.3 Empirical Implications

In order to derive sharp empirical predictions, let us assume that PPP formation involves an additional fixed cost of Z. One can interpret Z as capturing additional transactions costs not captured in the baseline model. Then we have the following testable hypothesis:

Proposition 3 Let $Z > 0$.

1. *If* $W_{GG}^{PPP} - Z > W^G > W_{WG}^{PPP} - Z$, *then there is PPP formation under strong governance, but not under weak governance. Under weak governance the government does the project itself.*
2. *In case* $W_{GG}^{PPP} - Z, W_{WG}^{PPP} - Z > W^G$, *there is PPP formation irrespective of whether governance is weak, or strong. Further, contract renegotiation occurs iff governance is weak.*

Proposition 3 follows straightway from Propositions 1 and 2 earlier, and yields the following testable hypothesis:

[8] Cost overruns? In UK with traditional procurements, in 73 % of central government projects, the price to the public sector exceeded budgets, by 2–14 %. With PFI about 22 % of PPPs exceeded estimates (NAO). In case of Metronet, the private tube operator for London Underground, cost overruns led to bankruptcy.

Number of PPPs is greater under strong governance. Further renegotiation is more prevalent under weak governance.

9.7 Robustness Considerations

We then consider the consequences of relaxing some of the assumptions.

9.7.1 Generalized Sharing Rule Under a PPP

Suppose that under a PPP, the private firm obtains $(1-\alpha)X$ and the government obtains αX, where $0<\alpha<1$ is different from $1/2$. Note that under (i) an appropriately modified version of A1 and (ii) $pu(X(1-\alpha)-c)+(1-p)u(X(1-\alpha)>0$ (so as to ensure that the private firm accepts the contract under a PPP with a strong government), it is straightforward to check that given risk aversion all the propositions still go through.

9.7.2 Generalized Utility Function of the Government

Suppose the utility of the government $G(P,g)=u(P+g)$, instead of $P+u(g)$ as in the text. Again, the results go through qualitatively, as they are essentially driven by the fact that the government and private firms are risk averse, rather than the specific functional forms adopted here.

9.7.3 What if the PPP Just Covers Its Costs

We have assumed that even under government ownership, or under a PPP, the whole of the surplus of the consumers are taken away by the project organization. Again, one can relax this. Perhaps one reasonable formulation is that only an amount of $2c$, enough to ensure project sustainability, is taken away under government ownership, or under a PPP. While the results are less obvious in this case, preliminary analysis suggests that the results go through qualitatively in this case as well.

9.8 Conclusion

Given the volume of infrastructural investment required, PPPs seem essential for India's development. We begin by providing a brief survey of PPPs globally, including in India. We then provide a simple analytical framework as to why PPPs may or may not form. We argue that the case in favour of PPPs is based in terms of externality, synergy and risk aversion. The case for bundling is, in turn, based on positive externalities between the various components, whereas the case against bundling can be based on the possibility of the government being corrupt, the government's inability to commit to a contract, etc. All of these mean that there is no one-size-fits-all formula.

We then examine the effect of governance level on whether a PPP forms or not, an issue that has not yet been addressed in the literature. We show that PPPs are more likely to form in case the governance is strong. Otherwise, PPPs are unlikely to form and will be susceptible to contract renegotiation in case they do form.

One policy implication seems to be that building good governance structures is critical for the analysis. This is interesting since recall that, in the Indian context, it appears that the five largest states in terms of PPPs all had invested in developing good governance structures.

References

Blanc-Brude F, Goldsmith H, Valila T (2009) A comparison of construction contract prices for traditionally procured roads and public private partnerships. Rev Ind Organ 35(1–2):19–40. (Special issue edited by by Stephane Saussier, Carine Staropoli and Anne Yvrande-Billon)

Brench A, Beckers T, Heinrich M, von Hirschhausen C (2005) Public-private partnerships in New EU member countries of central and Eastern Europe. Eur Invest Bank 10(2):82–112

FICCI, Ernst & Young (2012) Accelerating public-private partnerships in India. FICCI, New Delhi

Guasch JL, Laffont JJ, Straub S (2008) Renegotiation of concession contracts in Latin America: evidence from the water and transport sectors. Int J Ind Organ 26:421–442. (Special Issue on PPPs)

Iossa E, Martimort D (2015) The simple micro-economics of public-private partnerships, forthcoming. J Public Econ Theory

Iossa E, Spagnolo G, Vellez M (2013) The risks and tricks in public private partnerships, IEFE Working Paper 64, December 2013

Levin J, Tadelis S (2007) Contracting for government services: theory and evidence from U.S. Cities, NBER Working Papers 13350, National Bureau of Economic Research, Inc.

Lobina E, Hall D (2003) Problems with private water concessions: a review of experience, London: PSIRU, available at www.psiru.org/reports/2003-06-W-over.doc

Maskin E, Tirole J (2008) Public-private partnerships and government spending limits. Int J Ind Organ 26:412–420. (Special Issue on PPPs)

NAO, National Audit Office (2003) PFI construction performance. National Audit Office, HC371, London

NAO, National Audit Office (2007) Improving the PFI tendering process. National Audit Office, HC149, London

Yescombe E R (2007) Public private partnerships: principles of policy and finance. Elsevier, London

Chapter 10
Principles of Allocating Development Grant at the Sub-National Level in India: A Suggested Methodology

Sushil Kumar Haldar and Ajitava Raychaudhuri

10.1 Background

Egalitarian distribution of resources among different regions in a country and perfect equality is impossible, and there are many reasons why it may not even be a feasible objective. However, in a federal setup, it is argued that inequality must be kept within tolerable limits. Following Kuznets (1955), we can argue that an increase in inequality in a country during a period of growth is unavoidable and it may even be tolerated if it is accompanied by sufficiently rapid improvement in the living standards of the poor. But, an increase in inequality with little or no improvement in the living standards of the poor may cause regional imbalance and social unrest. Static measures of inequality do not capture the phenomenon of equality of opportunity which needs special attention. Any given level of inequality of outcomes is much more socially acceptable if it results from a system which provides greater equality of opportunity. Distributional concerns have traditionally been viewed as ensuring an adequate flow of benefits to the poor and the most marginalized. Strategy of inclusive growth covers various areas; however, here we have mentioned some important areas of intervention which our central government has been trying to address in different plans:

(a) Reduction of regional imbalance across states in respect of physical, financial, education and health infrastructure. It is believed that physical (and financial infrastructure) directly affects the production activities by facilitating input use and augmenting market activities. On the other hand, social infrastructure comprising health and education indirectly affects the earning capabilities of the mass in the long run.

S. K. Haldar (✉) · A. Raychaudhuri
Department of Economics, Jadavpur University, Kolkata 700032, India
e-mail: sushil.haldar@gmail.com

A. Raychaudhuri
e-mail: ajitava1@gmail.com

S. Banerjee et al. (eds.), *Understanding Development*, India Studies in Business and Economics, DOI 10.1007/978-81-322-2455-6_10

(b) Eradication of mass human deprivation, reduction of poverty and to give equal access to opportunity especially in elementary education and health to all.
(c) Empowerment of the marginalized groups like Scheduled Caste (SC), Scheduled Tribes (ST) and Other Backward Communities (OBC). Historically, the communities like SC, ST and OBC are backward compared to others; as a result different programmes have already been launched by the central as well as different state governments in order to improve the socioeconomic conditions of these categories of the population.
(d) Ensure justice, equal opportunity and peoples' participation in social, economic and political spheres of life.
(e) Reduction of gender disparity and gender empowerment. Women and men share many aspects of living together, collaborate with each other in complex ways and yet end up in most of the cases with different rewards and deprivations. The procedure used for inequality correction in the Gender Development Index involves estimating inequality-corrected achievements in terms of different focus variables and then putting them together in one aggregate measure of inequality-adjusted performance.
(f) Almost all the states have been experiencing gender disparity in respect of literacy rate, mean years of schooling, work force participation rate and life expectancy after rescaling because there is indeed strong evidence that the maximum potential life expectancy for women is greater than that for men—given similar care, including health care and nutritional opportunities. Women's higher potential life expectancy is anticipated in demographic projections as well.
(g) Our national plans since independence, especially the 11th plan, have given priority to eliminating regional imbalance. Poverty imposes an oppressive weight on India, especially in the rural areas where almost three out of four Indians and about 75 % of the Indian poor live. Although poverty has been reduced during the past four decades, it still remains painfully high. It is noted that the record in this dimension of inclusiveness is not so encouraging. The percentage of the population below the official poverty line has been falling but even as that happens, the numbers below the poverty line remain large. According to the latest official estimates of poverty based on the Tendulkar Committee poverty line, as many as 29.8 % of the population, that is, 350 million people were below the poverty line in 2009–2010 (Planning Commission, Govt. of India 2013). Similarly, we are far from achieving the target of the Millennium Development Goals (MDGs) in respect of different indicators of education, health and poverty and gender equality. The 2010 United Nations Summit on the MDGs concluded with the adoption of a global action plan to achieve the eight anti-poverty goals by their 2015 target date and the announcement of major new commitments for women's and children's health and other initiatives against poverty, hunger and disease. The outcome document of the 3-day summit sets out a concrete action agenda for achieving the goals by 2015. The Global Strategy for Women's and Children's Health initiated by the United Nations has the potential of saving the lives of more than 16 million women and children, preventing 33 million unwanted pregnancies, protecting 120 million children

from pneumonia and 88 million children from stunting due to malnutrition, advancing the control of deadly diseases such as malaria and HIV/AIDS, and ensuring access for women and children to quality health facilities and skilled health workers (United Nations 2011–2012).

10.1.1 Regional Inequality in India over Time

Against the backdrop of its high gross domestic product (GDP), the poverty rate in India has declined from 54.9% in 1972–1973 to 29.8% in 2009–2010. In the wake of structural adjustment programme in 1991, Indian policy makers initiated a process of wide ranging economic reforms to shift towards a more market friendly trade and industrial policy regime. The economic reform process has been steady but gradual because of a need for wide consultation and broad consensus necessary in a democratic society. The process of consultation and debate has contributed to non-reversal of policies even under different political parties that have formed the government after the reforms. Whether and to what extent India has achieved the stated objective of inclusive growth and faster poverty removal during the post-reform period has been a matter of intense debate. With such developments, India needs to be taken for an interesting case study to examine the emerging issues in social sector development, poverty reduction and fertility control at the state level.

India is going to enjoy the benefit of demographic dividend roughly after 2025 (Population Reference Bureau 2009). Achievement of this demographic gift requires declining fertility of the nation in favour of the share of working age population (Bloom and Williamson 1998). However, having only the absolute number of the working age cohort cannot ensure to generate sufficient employment and income if the quality of the future human resource remains poor. Recent employment figures of India also suggest that absorption of Indian youth is not as high as one would expect due to poor employability of the work force, which is severely affected by the poor health and educational status of the working population (Chandrasekhar et al. 2006). Quality of the working population can be improved through effective human capital formation, which is possible through investment in social sector. On the other hand, poverty in India is highly associated with fertility (Birdsall et al. 2001). Children from the large family with inadequate income attain less schooling and work as child labour, which also undermines the process of effective human capital formation and hampers the economic growth. In this regard, investment in human capital is important to strengthen the capability of the population, which results in the reduction of poverty and fertility (Birdsall et al. 2001). But in India, the overall scenario is quite different and rather alarming. India spends a very small proportion of its gross national product on health and education expenditure. Many similarly placed countries, whose per capita incomes are well below India's average, spend higher in social sector development compared to India. In 1960–1961, the education and healthcare expenditures, as a percentage of GDP, were 1.69 and 0.37, respectively; in 2010–2011, public expenditure on education is a little over 3% of the

Table 10.1 Inequality of selected socioeconomic variables in different time points across 16 major states of India. (Drawn from Bhattacharya and Haldar (2013))

Time	HCR	PCSDP	PCSSE	IMR	TFR	FLR
1972–1973	0.027	0.121	0.057	0.0421	0.017	0.132
1977–1978	0.041	0.156	0.053	0.041	0.020	0.121
1983	0.068	0.138	0.046	0.043	0.021	0.100
1987–1988	0.062	0.144	0.046	0.042	0.025	0.078
1992–1993	0.053	0.187	0.057	0.044	0.036	0.055
1999–2000	0.155	0.189	0.072	0.047	0.043	0.025
2004–2005	0.109	0.206	0.071	0.050	0.048	0.016
2009–2010	0.095	0.2165	0.072	0.054	0.045	0.011

Inequality is measured using generalized entropy measure using $\alpha=2$ because it gives equal weights of the distribution

HCR head count ratio, *PCSDP* per capita state domestic product, *PCSSE* per capita social sector expenditure, *IMR* infant mortality rate, *TFR* total fertility rate, *FLR* female literacy rate

GDP, but the total investment on public health remains dismally low, around 1 % of the GDP. In a country like India, where a considerable share of population depends largely on public provision of health and education, public investment is not only crucial but also expected to be high in this respect. However, in reality, the situation is very poor.

Is regional inequality aggravating across the major states in respect of key socioeconomic development parameters over time? The trend of inequality over time in respect of key socioeconomic development parameters is shown in the following Table 10.1.

A rising trend of inequalities is found in respect of per capita state domestic product (PCSDP), poverty measured by head count ratio (HCR), per capita social sector expenditure (PCSSE), infant mortality rate (IMR) and total fertility rate (TFR; Bhattacharya and Haldar 2013). This means that the states are not converging in respect of those selected variables. What is noticeable is that instead of getting inclusivity in respect of regional development, we are facing just the opposite phenomena. The inequality in female literacy rate (FLR) shows a declining trend. Since FLR has some asymptotic upper bound (100 %), we have obtained such results (Fig. 10.1).

Malnourishment of children is the outcome of poverty, illiteracy, ill health of mother and low standard of living of the household (Deaton 2003; Wagstaff and Doorslaer 2000; UN 2011, 2012). There exists wide spread incidence of malnourishment in respect of stunting, wasting and underweight children under the age of 3 years (as given in Appendix A; data are drawn from National Family Health Survey (NFHS) 1, 2 and 3) across 15 major states at three time points (1992–1993, 1998–1999, 2005–2006). It is observed that chronic malnutrition was more or less the same during 1992–1993 to 1998–1999 at the aggregate level, but it declined during 1998–1999 to 2005–2006. The inequality of malnutrition across states is found to be high and it is not diminishing, rather it increases which means that the performance of the states in combating malnutrition does differ to a large extent. The incidence of child malnutrition is found mostly in the Bihar, Madhya Pradesh, Rajasthan and Uttar Pradesh (BIMARU) states. Since children are assumed to be the future assets and will

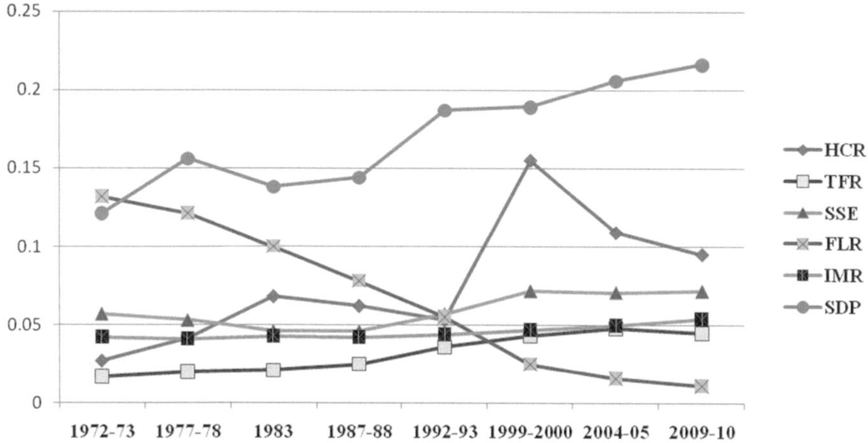

Fig. 10.1 Trend of inequality of selected socioeconomic development parameters across major states over 1972–2009. *HCR* head count ratio, *TFR* total fertility rate, *SSE* social sector expenditure, *FLR* female literacy rate, *IMR* infant mortality rate, *SDP* state domestic product. (Source: Drawn from Table 10.1)

constitute the nation's human capital in the long run, our future demographic dividend may be uncertain since only effective human capital with sound health can generate economic benefits from demographic dividend.

Therefore, the increasing trend of inequality in respect of economic as well as development parameters across states has been a major concern of our policy planner.

10.2 Allocation of Development Grants: A Brief Review of Literature

Numerous debatable questions have already been emerged at the international level in respect of allocating development grants by the donors like World Bank, Organisation for Economic Co-operation and Development (OECD) countries, European Union, United Nations Children's Fund (UNICEF), Asian and African Development Banks. A list of questions is put here before formulating our principle of development grant.

What share of a total amount of aid should be allocated to the different developing countries?

What are the indicators of underdevelopment to be taken into account? How is the initial allocation to be determined? How are the weights to be determined in allocating grants? Is the allocation based on normative approach, positive approach or a combination of both? What characteristics are to be examined in performance-based allocation? Is there any uniform rule followed by all donors as listed above while development grants are disbursed to the poor countries? Does aid necessarily promote growth and help achieving MDGs at a faster rate? How are the structural constraints of poor countries measured and its value to be included while allocating development grants?

Answers of all the above-cited questions remain unsolved, and the corresponding literature in this regard is sparse. However, some notable works are done by Anderson (2008); Collier and Dollar (2001, 2002); Guillaumont and Guillaumont (2007), McGillivray (2004, 2006). The rule of allocation as suggested by them is not beyond criticisms. A detailed review of literature is done by Guillaumont (2008, 2011). Most of the literature has given emphasis on some selected indicators with differential weights—these are per capita income, population size, multidimensional human poverty index (HPI) as suggested by the United Nations Development Programme (UNDP) and some structural constraints emerged from geo-climatic conditions capturing economic vulnerability. The principle of aid allocation does follow certain principles.[1] Regarding allocation of development grants among the states by a particular country in a federal set up faces more or less identical problems. For example, an expert committee on decentralized planning for areas not covered under parts IX and IXA of the Constitution was set up by the Ministry of Panchayat Raj in September 2006, and the committee has identified that about half of the total number of districts in India (about 250 districts) are backward, based on a certain criterion as set by the expert group. This Backward Region Grant Fund (BRGF) aims to reduce regional imbalance in India by filling up critical gaps in local infrastructure and local needs, strengthening capabilities and facilitating participatory planning. BRGF has fixed criteria towards allocating grants.[2] In the recent past, an expert committee under the chairmanship of Raghuram Rajan has formulated an allocation rule of fund and it was submitted to the Ministry of Finance, Govt. of India (2013). Allocation of development grant among the states as suggested by the expert committee is based on (1) actual needs measured by underdevelopment index (which is derived from the outcomes of development parameters) weighted by population and area shares of respective states, (2) performance of the states and (3) a fixed share of the total development grant. A detailed note is given in Appendix B.

[1] Following Guilllaumont (2008), any formula of aid allocation should rely on three principles:1. Effectiveness: Aid should be allocated in such a way that it can contribute effectively to the attainment of its goals, here supposed to be the MDGs.
2. Equity: Aid should be allocated in an equitable manner, depending on what is meant by equity, here supposed to be equalizing the opportunities.
3. Transparency: The main rules of allocation should be clear and available to anybody since they reflect the policy of the international community.

[2] It consists of two funding windows: These are (1) a capability building fund of ₹ 250 crores per annum and (2) a substantially untied grant of ₹ 3500 crore for 2006–2007 (outlay during 11th plan period). Capability building fund is to be used primarily to capacity building in planning, implementation, monitoring, evaluation, improving accountability and transparency. Allocation of untied grants by panchayats and urban local bodies is to be guided by transparent norms so that critical gaps of integrated development are properly addressed. The untied grant is to be distributed among the districts concerned as follows: (a) Every district will receive a fixed amount of ₹ 1 crore per annum, (b) 50 % of the balance amount of the scheme will be allocated on the basis of the population of the district in the total population of all backward districts and (c) the remaining 50 % will be distributed on the basis of the share of the area of the district of the total areas of all the backward districts.

Devolution of fund adopted by the Finance Commission is more realistic compared to earlier BRGF rule of allocation, however it is criticized in many grounds like arbitrary selection of development parameters, differential weights assigned to different components of allocation of fund. The present chapter tries to formulate a principle of allocation of development grants so that it corrects arbitrary selection of the variables and their corresponding weights.

10.3 Basic Framework of the Model

Living standard or the quality of life has been a multidimensional concept comprising level of income, educational attainment and health status of the population of a country. Thus, the backwardness of a particular state should not be measured only by taking HCR, rather allocation of fund should be based on capability shortfalls from human development perspectives. Capability shortfalls may be due to lack of necessary infrastructure. Devolution of fund as introduced by Finance Commission takes into account backwardness index (viz. underdevelopment index) which is based on range equalization method or relative distance methodology. In calculating backwardness index, Finance Commission incorporates both the outcomes (of underdevelopment) as well as input or process variables in the model. This is no doubt an important limitation. It is true that achievement index and deprivation index are reciprocal to each other but it is not one-to-one correspondence. Cross-country study reveals that a country with higher human development index (HDI) does not necessarily manifest lower HPI—this is because HPI does not take into account income and it is absolutely based on the specific country without taking into account any comparison with other countries and there is a difference of methodology for calculating HDI and HPI (Anand and Sen 1997). The most frequent issues related to multidimensional poverty are the choices of dimensions, weighting and aggregation of the indicators (Alkire 2007; Krishnaji 1997; Pillai 2004; Roy and Haldar 2010). Principal component analysis (PCA) technique if applied in multidimensional HPI can correct some problems, and it is assumed to be better for judging the extent of deprivations in achievement. The same can be applied in assessing the deficit of multidimensional public infrastructure stock index of a particular state.

Before going into a brief description about the above methodology, we consider the following dimensions (category/group) and the corresponding indicators (factors/variables) based on basic dimensions of human deprivation. In the same way, in order to estimate the deprivation of the infrastructural stock index (ISI), we categorize the infrastructure as follows (Tables 10.2 and 10.3):

We assume that the human development outcome of a particular state is determined by both demand and supply side factors. Here the infrastructure of different types is considered as supply side factors. At first, we estimate the human deprivation index following the basic principle as suggested by Anand and Sen (1997) and introduced by UNDP in 1997 in the Human Development Report.

Table 10.2 Dimensions of human deprivation and the corresponding indicators

Dimension (category) of human deprivation outcome	Indicators (variables)
Access to resource deprivation (D_1)	Head-count ratio (X_{1A}), proportion of landless workers (X_{1B}), proportion of unemployment (X_{1C}), reciprocal of per capita NSDP (X_{1D}), proportion of households living in kutcha houses (X_{1E}), proportion of household having no safe drinking water facility (X_{1F}), proportion of household having no electricity connection (X_{1G})
Knowledge deprivation (D_2)	Proportion of illiteracy (X_{2A}), proportion of non-enrolled children in class V (X_{2B}), proportion of dropout in class VIII (X_{2C})
Health deprivation (D_3)	Proportion of persons who die before attaining age 40 (X_{3A}), IMR (X_{3B}), CMR (X_{3C}), proportion of children suffering from malnutrition (X_{3D}), proportion of mothers suffering from anaemia (X_{3E}), proportion of non-institutional delivery (X_{3F})
Social exclusion[a] and gender discrimination (D_4)	Proportion of SC/ST population (X_{4A}), excess female child loss between 0–6 age group (assuming equal share of male and female, X_{4B}), gender gap in literacy rate (X_{4C}), gender gap in work force participation rate (X_{4D})

[a] Social exclusion is not a human development outcome, but historically SC/ST populations are backward and a more fragile community; this is why it is incorporated in measuring the vulnerability index. Gender discrimination is the outcome variable which is socially generated

Table 10.3 Categories of infrastructural deprivation and the corresponding indicators

Lack of infrastructure in different categories	Indicators
Deprivation of physical and financial infrastructure (I_1)	Proportion of area not connected by road (Y_{1A}), proportion of area having no rail connectivity (Y_{1B}), proportion of non-irrigated area to total area (Y_{1C}), proportion of household having no bank account viz. financial exclusion (Y_{1D}), proportion of villages having no banks (Y_{1E})
Deprivation of educational infrastructure (I_2)	Proportion of village having no primary school (Y_{2A}), proportion of villages having no high school (Y_{2B}), proportion of blocks having no industrial training institute viz. ITI (Y_{2C}), proportion of blocks having no degree colleges (Y_{2D}), proportion of blocs having no polytechnical college (Y_{2E}), inverse of teachers per school at primary and secondary level (Y_{2F})
Deprivation of health infrastructure (I_3)	Gap[a] of sub-centre (SC) (Y_{3A}), gap of primary health centre (PHC. Y_{3B}), gap of community health centre (CHC, Y_{3C}), inverse of medical bed per 10,000 population (Y_{3D}), inverse of doctors per 10,000 population (Y_{3E}), proportion of villages having no health workers (Y_{3F})

Here all the positive indicators of infrastructure are transformed into negative viz. deprivation

[a] Gap of health infrastructure is calculated on the basis of standard norm of 1983 health policy in India. For example, per 6000, 30,000 and 120,000 of the population, there should be one SC, PHC and CHC, respectively, for plain area; following this principle, one can easily calculate required number of SC, PHC and CHC from state's population size. Thus, the gap is the difference between actual number and required number

$$D_j(\alpha) = [\omega_1(\text{PCD}_1)_j^{\alpha} + \omega_2(\text{PCD}_2)_j^{\alpha} + \omega_3(\text{PCD}_3)_j^{\alpha} + \omega_4(\text{PCD}_4)_j^{\alpha}]^{\frac{1}{\alpha}}, \quad (10.1)$$

where $D_j(\alpha)$ is the multidimensional human deprivation index of state j, α is the order of the average, ω_i ($i=1, 2,\ldots, 4$) is the weights attached to the first principal component (PC) i ($i=1,\ldots,4$) and PCD_1 is the first PC extracted from the set of indicators as listed under the categories of access to resource deprivation. Mathematically, it is defined as:

$$\text{PCD}_1 = a_{11}X_{1A} + a_{12}X_{1B} + a_{13}X_{1C} + a_{14}X_{1D} + a_{15}X_{1E} + a_{16}X_{IF} + a_{17}X_{1G}, \quad (10.2)$$

where $a1_j$ stands for factor loadings of the j-th factor in the first PC. For example, a_{11} is the factor loading of the first deprivation indicator (viz. $X1_A$) in first PC which is nothing but the correlation coefficient between PCD_1 and $X1_A$. The square of a_{11} represents the proportion of variance of $X1_{A'}$, captured by first PC viz. PCD_1. Following Pet et al. (2003) and Johnson and Wichern (2006), it can be easily proved that the sum of the squares of factor loadings is equal to the eigenvalue:

$$\sum_{j=1}^{7} a_{1j}^2 = \omega_1. \quad (10.3)$$

Here ω_1 stands for eigenvalue of the first deprivation PC, PCD_1. We consider eigenvalues as weights of the deprivation component, viz. PCD_1. In the same way, PCD_2, PCD_3 and PCD_4 are the first PCs of deprivations in respect of knowledge, health and social exclusion and gender discrimination, respectively. Therefore, we can define PCD_2, PCD_3 and PCD_4 as follows:

$$\text{PCD}_2 = b_{11}X_{2A} + b_{12}X_{2B} + b_{13}X_{2C}, \quad (10.4)$$

where

$$\sum_{j=1}^{3} b_{1j}^2 = \omega_2, \quad (10.5)$$

$$\text{PCD}_3 = c_{11}X_{3A} + c_{12}X_{3B} + c_{13}X_{3C} + c_{14}X_{3D} + c_{15}X_{3E} + c_{16}X_{3F}, \quad (10.6)$$

where

$$\sum_{j=1}^{6} c_{1j}^2 = \omega_3, \quad (10.7)$$

$$\text{PCD}_4 = d_{11}X_{4A} + d_{12}X_{4B} + d_{13}X_{4C} + d_{14}X_{4D}, \quad (10.8)$$

where

$$\sum_{j=1}^{4} d_{1j}^2 = \omega_4. \quad (10.9)$$

In order to avoid complexity, we consider only the first PC of each dimension of deprivation. It is quite reasonable since the first PC captures the maximum possible proportion of variability of the data. The indicators used in Eqs. (10.2), (10.4), (10.6), (10.8), (10.11), (10.13) and (10.15) have already been defined earlier in Table 10.2. Similarly, we define the deprivation of the ISI, $I_j(\alpha)$, as:

$$I_j(\alpha) = [\lambda_1(\mathrm{PCI}_1)_j{}^{\alpha} + \lambda_2(\mathrm{PCI}_2)_j{}^{\alpha} + \lambda_3(\mathrm{PCI}_3)_j{}^{\alpha}]^{\frac{1}{\alpha}}, \tag{10.10}$$

where $I_j(\alpha)$ stands for the composite infrastructural deprivation index of state j. λ_1, λ_2 and λ_3 are the weights (viz. eigenvalues) attached to PCI1, PCI2 and PCI3, respectively. PCs of infrastructural deprivations with respect to physical and financial, education and health are as follows:

PCI_1 is the first PC of deprivation of physical and financial infrastructure, PCI_2 is the first PC of deprivation of education infrastructure and PCI_3 is the first PC of health infrastructure deprivation. Therefore, symbolically we can write:

$$\mathrm{PCI}_1 = e_{11}Y_{1A} + e_{12}Y_{1B} + e_{13}Y_{1C} + e_{14}Y_{1D} + e_{15}Y_{1E} + e_{16}Y_{IF}, \tag{10.11}$$

$$\sum_{j=1}^{6} e_{1j}^2 = \lambda_1, \tag{10.12}$$

$$\mathrm{PCI}_2 = f_{11}Y_{2A} + f_{12}Y_{2B} + f_{13}Y_{2C} + f_{14}Y_{2D} + f_{15}Y_{2E} + f_{16}Y_{2F}, \tag{10.13}$$

$$\sum_{j=1}^{6} f_{1j}^2 = \lambda_2, \tag{10.14}$$

$$\mathrm{PCI}_3 = g_{11}Y_{3A} + g_{12}Y_{3B} + g_{13}Y_{3C} + g_{14}Y_{3D} + g_{15}Y_{3E} + g_{16}Y_{3F}, \tag{10.15}$$

$$\sum_{j=1}^{6} g_{1j}^2 = \lambda_3. \tag{10.16}$$

For a given α (it is generally taken as 3 by UNDP), one can calculate the human deprivation outcome of a particular state, j, using Eq. (10.1). In the same way, we can determine the infrastructural deprivation index using Eq. (10.10). Therefore, we can estimate the share of the deprivation of state j in respect of two outcomes:

$$\mathrm{SB}_j = \left(\frac{D_j(\alpha)}{\sum_j D_j(\alpha)}\right) + \left(\frac{I_j(\alpha)}{\sum_j I_j(\alpha)}\right), \tag{10.17}$$

where SB_j is the share of backwardness of state j. The first and the second term of the right hand side of Eq. (10.17) represent the share of multidimensional human deprivation and the infrastructural stock deprivation index, respectively, of state j.

Now, devolution of fund based on Eq. (10.17) may be biased because states vary to a large extent in respect of population size. Here, we are ignoring the geographical areas because many areas are there which are inhospitable to human living like hills, desert and forest. Therefore, SB_j is weighted by population proportion.

So, $n_j \cdot SBj$ is the share of fund of state j to be disbursed based on backwardness, where $n_j = \frac{P_j}{\sum_{j=1} P_j}$ and P_j is the population size of state j. This should be the criteria for initial disbursement of fund. Now, in order to combat misuse of funds by the states and to make efficiency of allocation of funds, there should be some incentives, so that states performing better in reducing backwardness get rewarded and states that are underperformed get penalized. Given that poor administration or weak governance in a recipient state can fritter away allocated resources to the detriment of the population, there should be some recognition for effective governance and the efficiency of resource use. Therefore, at the second time, we introduce the following incentive scheme along with the existing deprivation index:

For the allocation of fund at the second time, state j will receive:

$$\rho n_j \cdot SB_j^* + (1-\rho) \cdot n_j \cdot SR_j, \tag{10.18}$$

where SB^*_j stands for the share of backwardness of state j at time t_2, $SR_j = \frac{R_j}{\sum_{j=1} R_j}$.

SR_j stands for the share of reduction of deprivation of state j during t_1 and t_2, where t_1 is the initial period when state j gets fund without any incentive, whereas t_2 is the time when the second disbursement is to be made. $\rho(0<\rho<1)$ stands for the distribution parameter for the policy target which is to be determined by the central planning authority. The determination of ρ is essentially a normative issue which must take into account the need for growth along with welfare. This issue is not dealt with here and requires more elaborate discussion. R_j is the reduction of deprivation of state j during t_1 and t_2. Once the state j gets fund based on Eq. (10.17) weighted by its population share, it can allocate funds at sub-state level where each district is to be taken into account as a unit of disbursement. State j also can disburse fund in different heads based on weights of deprivation parameters as given in Eqs. (10.3), (10.5), (10.7), (10.9), (10.12), (10.14) and (10.16). Therefore, the principle, as suggested above, can be applied at the disaggregate level.

There are many advantages of the PCA technique towards construction of the multidimensional deprivation index of capability shortfalls and infrastructural backwardness index.

It is not restricted to incorporating limited number of indicators (variables). One can include many intercorrelated indicators (variables) falling under specific dimensions. The weights of the indicators (variables) in each dimension (group) are determined endogenously. It is more scientific because it does not consider arbitrary weights of the indicators as well as dimensions. The weights of the indicators (variables) as well as the dimension may be used towards policy formulation and intervention. Fund allocation based on this principle is more cost-effective. Apparently, this approach seems to be difficult to understand, but many scientific software can easily estimate the weights. The problem of overlapping and aggregation in the deprivation index can well be handled through PCA.

10.4 Concluding Remarks

The principle suggested here is simple, scientific and rational in determining the initial quantum of funds to be allocated to a state. The application of PCA in determining the weights of the indicators and dimensions is not arbitrary, rather weights are endogenously determined through the data matrix. Once the amount of fund to be allocated to state *j* is determined, the PCA will help again to determine a district-specific allocation rule to different components of backwardness. In the same way, the rule can well be applied at the sub-district level, where each block can be considered as a unit of analysis. This rule of allocation is consistent with a decentralized planning process, and such an innovative rule tries to capture equity, efficiency and social justice.

Appendix-A

Table 10.A Prevalence of chronic undernutrition of children in 15 major states in India in 1992–1993, 1998–1999 and 2005–2006. (Source: Based on NFHS 1, 2 and 3. Chronic undernutrition includes any form of malnutrition (H/A= stunting, W/H= wasting, W/A= underweight). All values of Z scores are less than −2. H= height, A= age, W= weight. All are measured in percentages of children less than 3 years.)

Major states	1992–1993	1998–1999	2005–2006
Andhra Pradesh	40.8	47.1	38.3
Assam	56.5	53.7	41.4
Bihar	60.3	57.6	49.5
Gujarat	50.1	51.8	49.1
Haryana	50.5	55.4	43.2
Karnataka	47.5	42	42.3
Kerala	32.8	27.8	26.5
Madhya Pradesh	60	56.4	48
Maharashtra	47	47	43.9
Orissa	50.8	49.1	43.9
Punjab	45.2	45.2	34.6
Rajasthan	45.5	59	40.1
Tamil Nadu	40.8	35	31.1
Uttar Pradesh	60	60.3	51.9
West Bengal	56.7	50.1	41.8
Mean	49.63	49.16	41.7
Coeff. of variation	0.162	0.183	0.166

Appendix-B

The methodology developed by the expert committee appointed by the Finance Commission (2013) first allocates funds across states based on needs in line with recommendations of the previous committees. Need is based upon simple index (using relative distance methodology) of underdevelopment comprising ten parameters such as (i) monthly per capita consumption expenditure, (ii) education, (iii) health, (iv) household amenities, (v) poverty, (vi) female literacy rate, (vii) percent of SC/ST population, (viii) urbanization, (ix) financial inclusion and (x) connectivity. The committee proposes allocations based on index with allocations increasing more than linearly to the most underdeveloped states. In order to allocate more to underdevelopment, it was recommended to assign 80 % weight to the share of population and 20 % to the share of area.

An incentive scheme known as performance of the states is also introduced. States experiencing reducing underdevelopment over time are to be rewarded more compared to the states whose performance is bad. Given that poor administration or weak governance in a recipient state can fritter away allocated resources to the detriment of the population, there should be some recognition for effective governance and the efficiency of resource use.

References

Alkire S (2007) Choosing dimensions: the capability approach and the multidimensional poverty, Working Paper 88, Chronic Poverty Research Centre, August

Anand S, Sen AK (1997) Concepts of human development and poverty: a multidimension perspective, Background Papers for Human Development Report

Anderson E (2008) Practices and implications of aid allocation. Background study for the 2008 Development Cooperation Forum, UN Economic and Social Council (ECOSOC) (mimeo)

Bhattacharya G, Haldar SK (2013) Does spending on human capital reduce fertility and poverty in India? A panel data study. Asia Pac Soc Sci Rev 13(2):1–23

Birdsall N, Kelley AC, Sinding SW (eds) (2001) Population matters: demographic change, economic growth and poverty in the developing world. Oxford: Oxford University Press

Bloom DE, Jeffrey DS (1998) Geography, demography and economic growth in Africa. Brook Pap Econ Act 2:207–295

Chandrasekhar CP, Ghosh J, Roy Chowdhury A (2006) The 'demographic dividend' and young India's economic future. Econ Polit Wkly 41(49):5055–5064

Collier P, Dollar D (2001) Can the world cut poverty in half? How policy reform and effective aid can meet international development goals. World Dev 29(11):1787–1802

Collier P, Dollar D (2002) Aid, allocation and poverty reduction. Eur Econ Rev 46(8):1475–1500

Deaton A (2003) Health, inequality, and economic development. J Econ Lit XLI:113–158

Guillaumont P (2008) Adapting aid allocation criteria to development goals: an essay for the 2008 Development Cooperation Forum, United Nations Economic and Social Council. www.un.org

Guillaumont P (2011) Making Development Financing in LDCs More Conducive to Development, Working Paper/P18 (Eng). Retrieved from unohrlls.org

Guillaumont P, Guillaumont SJ (2007) Big push versus absorptive capacity: how to reconcile the two approaches? UNU-WIDER Discussion Paper, n°2007/05, October 23

Johnson RA, Wichern DW (2006) Applied multivariate statistical analysis. Pearson Education, New Delhi

Krishnaji N (1997) Human poverty index: a critique. Econ Polit Wkly 32(35):2202–2205

Kuznets S (1955) Economic growth income inequality. Am Econ Rev 45(1):1–28

McGillivray M (2004) Descriptive and prescriptive analyses of aid allocation: approaches, issues, and consequences. Int Rev Econ Finance 13:275–292

McGillivray M (2006) Aid allocation and fragile states. WIDER Discussion Paper, 2006/1

Ministry of Finance, Govt. of India (2013) Report of the Committee for Evolving a Composite Development Index of States, September, 2013. New Delhi

Pet MA, Laçkey NR, Sullivan JJ (2003) Making sense of factor analysis. Sage Publications, Inc., Thousand Oaks

Pillai VN (2004) CES Function, Generalized Meanand Human Poverty Index: exploring Some Links. Centre for Development Studies, Working Paper No. 360

Planning Commission (2013) Govt. of India 2013, New Delhi

Population Reference Bureau (2009) 2009 World population data sheet. Washington DC

Roy K, Haldar SK (2010) Measuring poverty and socio-economic deprivation inequalities in India at sub-national level. Asia-Pac Soc Sci Rev 10(1):59–84

United Nations. Millennium Development Goals Report (2011, 2012) http://www.un.org/millenniumgoals/11_MDG%20Report_EN.pdf

Wagstaff A, van Doorslaer E (2000) Income inequality and health: what does the literature tell us? Ann Rev Public Health 21:543–67. Accessed 22 Nov 2014

Chapter 11
Fiscal Rule and Social Sector Spending: A Study of North-East India

Vikas Dixit

11.1 Introduction

The public finances of state governments since the mid-1980s had undergone a drastic turnaround. While they had generally been in revenue surplus, they started ending with revenue deficits. Thus, they started financing their current expenditures out of borrowings. This necessitated the imposition of certain restrictions on their fiscal management through Central Finance Commissions, which take care of non-plan current expenditure and its financing. Second generation reforms also could not help in improving fiscal health. Rather, the Central Pay Commission awards helped in their further deterioration.

Consequently, to improve their fiscal health and to get advantage of fiscal incentives as recommended by the Twelfth Finance Commission (TFC), the states initiated a rule-based fiscal consolidation process by enacting fiscal responsibility legislations (FRLs). The consolidated fiscal position of states has since then improved significantly (even faster than that of the centre) (Table 11.1). It may be seen from this table that the fiscal responsibility and budget management (FRBM) target of gross fiscal deficit of less than or equal to 3% of GDP was achieved at the centre in 2007–2008. This was the only year in which the centre's gross fiscal deficit was less than 3% of GDP. It could never eliminate its revenue deficit. On the contrary, measures undertaken by the central government, incentives announced by the Finance Commission and of course the states' own efforts led them to improve their fiscal health and achieve FRL targets more quickly and easily.

Table 11.1 shows that the consolidated gross fiscal deficit of all the states was reduced to less than 3% of GDP in 2005–2006 and surplus on revenue account was observed in 2006–2007 (before the terminal year for achieving the FRL targets). Here it may be mentioned that the TFC recommended a uniform fiscal reform path for all the states. However, the impact of fiscal adjustment may be different for

V. Dixit (✉)
Department of Economics, Jadavpur University, Kolkata 700032, India
e-mail: vikas_alig@rediffmail.com

S. Banerjee et al. (eds.), *Understanding Development*, India Studies in Business and Economics, DOI 10.1007/978-81-322-2455-6_11

Table 11.1 Consolidated fiscal position of central and state governments (percent of GDP). (Source: Computed/compiled from 1. Handbook of Statistics on Indian Economy 2012–2013, Reserve Bank of India; 2. Economic Survey, 2012–2013, Ministry of Finance, Government of India and 3. Handbook of Statistics on Central Government Debt, Ministry of Finance, Government of India.)

Year	RD of states	FD of states	TL of states	RD of centre	FD of centre	TL of centre
2003–2004	2.23	4.24	31.78	3.5	4.3	61.58
2004–2005	1.20	3.32	31.27	2.4	3.9	61.87
2005–2006	0.18	2.43	31.07	2.5	4.0	61.72
2006–2007	−0.57	1.80	28.90	1.9	3.3	59.71
2007–2008	−0.86	1.51	26.63	1.1	2.5	57.68
2008–2009	−0.22	2.39	26.11	4.5	6.0	56.54
2009–2010	0.47	2.91	25.45	5.2	6.5	55.10
2010–2011	−0.03	2.07	23.46	3.2	4.8	51.20
2011–2012	−0.06	2.31	22.32	4.3	5.7	50.95
2012–2013	−0.42	2.14	22.23	3.5	5.1	50.29

RD revenue deficit, *FD* fiscal deficit, *TL* total liabilities The negative (−) sign indicates surplus in the deficit indicator

different groups of states depending upon their level of development, initial financial conditions, capacity to raise revenue, etc. In particular, if the burden of adjustment has been heavier on the low-income states as compared to the other states, and if the adjustment has been more through controlling expenditures than revenue raising, then there are possible serious implications on public supply of services that need to be brought out.

Although a statewise analysis of fiscal adjustments under fiscal consolidation is not attempted here, the consolidated trends for all states presented in Table 11.2 seem to suggest that from 2003–2004 to 2007–2008, compression of revenue expenditure accounted for about 59.4% of the correction of revenue account and of the 40.6% contribution of the increase in revenue receipts, a major share came from devolution from the centre.

Thus, the own revenue base of the states expanded only by a limited extent during the period, with nontax revenue accounting for the major share.

Table 11.2 Correction in revenue account of the state governments (Per cent of GDP). (Source: Misra B (2012).

Component (1)	2003–2004 (2)	2007–2008 (3)	Correction (4=3−2) (4)	Contribution (5)
RD	2.30	−0.86	−3.16	100
RR	11.22	12.51	1.29	40.61
OR	6.94	7.29	0.35	11.08
OTR	5.59	5.75	0.15	4.89
ONTR	1.35	1.55	0.20	6.19
CT	4.28	5.21	0.93	29.53
SCT	2.44	3.04	0.60	19.00
Gr	1.85	2.18	0.33	10.52
RE	13.53	11.65	−1.88	59.41

RD revenue deficit, *RR* revenue receipts, *OR* own revenues, *OTR* own tax revenue, *ONTR* own nontax revenue, *CT* current transfers, *SCT* share in Central taxes, *Gr* grants, *RE* revenue expenditure

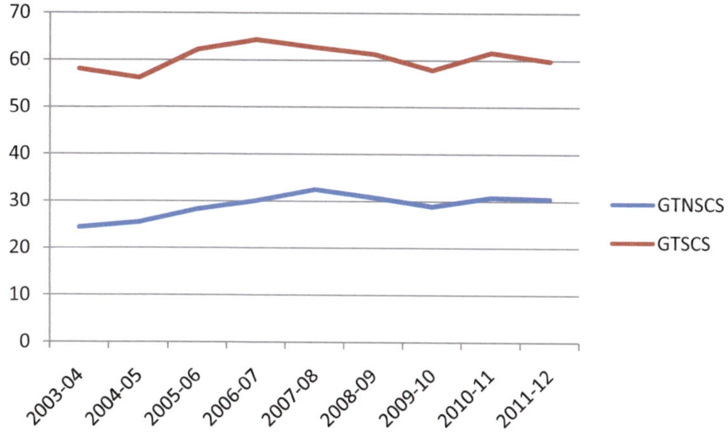

Fig. 11.1 Gross transfers as per cent of aggregate disbursements for NSCS and SCS. *GTNSCS* ratio of gross transfers to aggregate disbursements of non-special category states, *GTSCS* ratio of gross transfers to aggregate disbursements for special category states. (Source: Studies on State Budgets (various issues), Reserve Bank of India).

The increased central devolution is attributable to the buoyant central taxes, while the decline in revenue expenditure is mainly on account of the decline in expenditures on economic and social services and interest burden (Chakraborty and Bhusana 2013, Chakraborty 2005). Thus, the process of fiscal consolidation was revenue-led with a larger role played by the central government transfers. However, the extent to which states have benefitted from these transfers varied across states (Simone and Topalova 2009). Furthermore, in spite of equalisation grants from the Finance Commissions, there is increased dependence of less developed states on fiscal transfers from the centre for financing their priority sectors.

Plotted in Fig. 11.1 are the ratios of gross transfers to aggregate disbursements for special category states (SCS) and non-special category states (NSCS).

This figure shows that in most of the years, over 60% of aggregate disbursements of SCS are financed through central transfers. For NSCS too, the continuous increase in the ratio may be observed from 2003–2004 to 2007–2008. Here, SCS deserve special attention. These states are less developed mainly due to their economic characteristics and geographical features. None of these states has been able to generate adequate funds to meet the budgetary requirements and, thus to a great extent, depends on the flow of financial resources from the central government under the provision of SCS in which out of the total central assistance to states, 90% accounts for grants and the remaining 10% are loans.

A study was conducted by Srivastava and Rao (2009) for the Thirteenth Finance Commission which showed that the per capita transfers to the SCS were several times higher than per capita transfers to the general category states. Furthermore, the shares of transfers in revenue receipts and revenue expenditure were also quite high for SCS.

The high dependence of SCS on fiscal transfers not only reduces their fiscal autonomy but also makes their fiscal position vulnerable to economic slowdown, as that in 2008–2009 and 2009–2010. Moreover, the inherent weaknesses in the Indian system of fiscal transfers make it difficult for less developed states (such as SCS) to devolve their responsibility of delivering universal and quality social services, especially education and health effectively. Transfers are often fragmented, made in an ad hoc fashion and often lacking a normative basis for allocation. This exacerbates inequality among regions and ultimately results in poor outcomes.

The background set out in this section forms the motivation for the present chapter. It would be interesting to examine how northeastern (NE) states (as part of SCS) managed their social sector spending under a rule-based fiscal consolidation era given their own constraints. The period considered for this study is from 2000–2001 to 2011–2012 (including years before and after the enactment of fiscal rules by NE states).

This chapter is organised into five sections. Having set out the background and motivation for the present chapter in Sect. 11.1, Sect. 11.2 presents a brief review of the most relevant studies on the subject. Section 11.3 attempts to trace the broad trends in social sector expenditure of NE states in aggregate terms as well as by its components of social services, rural development and food storage and warehousing. An econometric exercise is carried out in Sect. 11.4 to analyse empirically the impact (if any) of the fiscal rule era on per capita social sector spending of NE states. Finally, Sect. 11.5 concludes the work.

11.2 Review of Literature[1]

The experiences on the fiscal consolidation process in the 1990s have another noteworthy feature, which was the introduction of a sound fiscal framework supported by institutional reforms. Recognising the difficulties associated with discretionary fiscal policies, several advanced countries enacted FRLs during the 1990s as permanent institutional devices aiming to promote fiscal discipline in a credible, predictable and transparent manner. New Zealand was at the forefront of these reforms, adopting FRL in 1994 followed by Australia, the UK and the European Union. In emerging market economies, adoption of fiscal responsibility has been more recent and limited mainly to Latin America (Argentina, Brazil, Chile and Peru) and Asia (India, Indonesia, Pakistan and Sri Lanka).

In practice, fiscal rules have been adopted for a wide variety of reasons such as: (a) to ensure macroeconomic stability, as in post-war Japan; (b) to enhance the credibility of the government's fiscal policy and aid in deficit elimination, as in some Canadian provinces; (c) to ensure long-term sustainability of fiscal policy, especially in light of population ageing, as in New Zealand; or (d) to minimise negative externalities within a federation or international arrangement, as in the European Economic and Monetary Union (EMU). In the emerging countries, the immediate motivation has been to reverse the building of public debt, to restore fiscal sustainability and more generally, to enhance the credibility of macroeconomic management. Present fiscal policy rules are fairly diverse in both design and implementation. While Anglo-Saxon countries (Australia, New Zealand, the UK) emphasise procedural rules aiming to enhance transparency, accountability

[1] This section is drawn upon Misra (2012) and Chakraborty and Bhusana (2013).

and fiscal management, continental Europe (EMU Stability and Growth Pact) and emerging market economies (Argentina, Brazil, Columbia, India, Pakistan, Peru and Sri Lanka) rely far more on a set of numerical reference values (targets, limits) on performance indicators. There are four main types of numerical fiscal rules: deficit rules (e.g. balanced budget), debt rules (e.g. debt ceilings), borrowing rules (e.g. prohibition of central bank financing) and expenditure rules (e.g. ceilings on some types of public expenditure or public expenditure growth).

It has been documented that countries with fiscal rules achieved better results. Fiscal rules with embedded expenditure targets tended to be associated with larger and longer fiscal adjustments and higher success rates. Furthermore, adoption of a spending rule on top of a budget balance rule helped in the achievement and maintenance of a primary balance that was sufficient to stabilise the debt-to-GDP ratio (OECD 2007). Since, in most countries FRLs have not been around for more than few years, evidence on their effectiveness is still preliminary. Still, there seems to be broad agreement that the quality of fiscal institutions does matter for fiscal performance. In this sense, an FRL holds the potential to improve fiscal management, if supported by strong political management to fiscal prudence and sufficiently developed fiscal institutional framework. A well-designed FRL may help contain fiscal deficits and expenditure biases, address issues of time inconsistency, help reduce borrowing costs and output variability and enhance transparency and accountability.

So far as the empirical literature is concerned, both cross-country studies as well as country-specific studies analysing the effectiveness of fiscal rules exist. The major cross-country studies attempted in this regard are by Gali and Perotti (2003), Ballabriga and Martinez-Mongay (2003) and Marneffe et al. (2010) for the European Union; Viren (2002) for OECD countries; and Tapsoba (2012) for 74 developing countries. By and large, these studies found that fiscal rules have been quite successful in serving their purpose. To address country-specific issues, Alesina and Bayoumi (1996), Milesi-Ferretti (1996), Poterba (1997) and Auerbach (2008) for the US; Millar (1997) for Canada; Claeys (2008) for Sweden; and Dupont and Kwarteng (2012) for the UK have examined the impact of fiscal rule on fiscal balance. The findings of these studies are mixed.

The literature on the impact of fiscal rules on the fiscal policies of the emerging economies has been scanty. Most of the studies on the subject for India are limited in their scope and do not cover the impact and/or outcome analysis of fiscal rules on the states' fiscal performance. Close to this issue was an attempt by Rao and Chakraborty (2006) who examined the impact of fiscal reforms (initiated by multilateral lending institutions) on the fiscal balance of the selected states. Another study by Simone and Topalova (2009) presents an assessment of the fiscal performance of the centre and states under fiscal rules, identifies major factors which contributed to the fiscal consolidation process at both levels of government and also proposes some reform measures to improve fiscal rule framework in India. Sucharita and Sethi (2011) have analysed the fiscal performance of the centre and states under fiscal discipline, but examined empirically the impact of the FRBM Act on fiscal deficit of the centre only, thereby neglecting the states. Only recently, a study by Chakraborty and Bhusana (2013) examined the impact of fiscal rule on fiscal balance and on the path of fiscal adjustment, particularly the development spending of Indian states. They concluded that the states followed a path of expenditure compression to achieve fiscal targets. Furthermore, they found that the disparity (as measured by coefficient of variation) in per capita development spending has increased across Indian states over the years, mainly due to an increase in disparity in per capita own revenue and a reduced disparity in central government transfers. However, their study, like most of the other works, is confined to the analysis of major states of India, thereby ignoring the SCS, particularly the NE region of India. The inclusion of the special category states in general, and NE states in particular, in any subnational fiscal analysis for India is important, because these states are faced with several economic and social challenges including financial constraints, poor infrastructure and unfriendly attitude of the neighbouring states. Being an integral part of India, the path of fiscal adjustment under fiscal rule followed by these states will have an impact not only on their own economies but also on the economies of other states as well as on the centre.

11.3 Trend Analysis of NE States' Total and Social Sector Expenditures

As stated earlier, the entire period of this study is chosen so as to include years before and after the enactment of FRLs by the NE states. Since some NE states enacted FRLs in the year 2005–2006, while others did it in 2006–2007, we divided the entire study period 2000–2001 to 2011–2012 into two subperiods, namely, the pre-FRL period (2000–2001 to 2004–2005) and the post-FRL period (2005–2006 to 2011–2012). The trend analysis which follows in this section is based on this division.

Table 11.3 gives the trends in aggregate total and social sector expenditures of NE states. It may be seen from this table that total expenditure as ratio to gross state domestic product (GSDP) is quite high for most of the NE states and exhibited an increasing trend on average from the pre-FRL period to the post-FRL period. Most of the NE states spent a higher proportion of their state's GSDP for the social sectors. Sikkim spent as much as 25.57% of its GSDP for the social sectors, while Assam spent almost 8% during the period 2000–2001 to 2004–2005. Notwithstanding the high proportion, four out of eight NE states, viz., Meghalaya, Mizoram, Sikkim and Tripura have revealed a declining trend in terms of expenditure–GSDP ratios for the social sectors from the pre-FRL period to the post-FRL period. It may further be noted that in case of Sikkim, the difference between the ratios to GSDP of total expenditure and that of social sectors is quite high for all three periods, namely, 2000–2001 to 2004–2005, 2005–2006 to 2011–2012 and 2000–2001 to 2011–2012. Sikkim is last of the NE states to enact FRL in 2010.

Table 11.3 further reveals that fiscal priority to social sectors, defined as the ratio of social sector expenditure to total expenditure, on average, has witnessed a decline from the pre-FRL period to the post-FRL period for four out of eight NE states, namely, Meghalaya, Mizoram, Nagaland and Tripura. During the entire study period, that is from 2000 to 2001 to 2011–2012, the fiscal priority for the social sectors, on an average, was as high as to lie in the interval 35–40% for four NE states, viz., Assam, Meghalaya, Mizoram and Tripura. Arunachal Pradesh and Manipur could maintain their fiscal priority for the social sectors between 30% and 35%, while Nagaland and Sikkim managed it between 25% and 30% for the same period.

Table 11.3 Statewise trends in aggregate total and social sector expenditures of the northeastern region (in per cent). (Source: Handbook of statistics on State Government Finances 2010 and State Finances: a study of budgets (various issues), Reserve Bank of India.)

	Arunachal Pradesh	Assam	Manipur	Meghalaya	Mizoram	Nagaland	Sikkim	Tripura
	TE/GSDP							
2000–2001 to 2004–2005 (Avg)	59.64	22.45	50.54	30.02	65.92	42.52	122.84	35
2005–2006 to 2011–2012 (Avg)	66.63	22.46	58.71	30.22	66.68	44.34	80.89	32.73
2000–2001 to 2011–2012 (Avg)	63.72	22.45	55.30	30.15	66.36	43.58	98.37	33.67
	SSE/GSDP							
2000–2001 to 2004–2005 (Avg)	17.79	8	14.42	11.33	25.12	12.18	25.57	13.45
2005–2006 to 2011–2012 (Avg)	20.56	8.56	18.47	11.07	24.85	12.34	21.40	12.24
2000–2001 to 2011–2012 (Avg)	19.40	8.33	16.78	11.18	24.96	12.27	23.14	12.75
	SSE/TE							
2000–2001 to 2004–2005 (Avg)	29.94	35.88	28.81	37.78	38.22	28.60	21.95	38.40
2005–2006 to 2011–2012 (Avg)	30.83	38.18	31.57	36.72	37.36	27.88	27.85	37.46
2000–2001 to 2011–2012 (Avg)	30.46	37.22	30.42	37.16	37.72	28.18	25.40	37.85
	PCSSE (₹)							
2000–2001 to 2004–2005 (Avg)	4589.35 (13.93)	1415.33 (5.29)	2899.26 (10.20)	2763.63 (1.48)	6665.97 (2.84)	3061.80 (−1.07)	6963.42 (10.06)	3139.60 (1.02)
2005–2006 to 2011–2012 (Avg)	7733.64 (6.45)	1898.77 (8.31)	4849.60 (7.35)	3909.87 (10.38)	9861.25 (9.10)	4500.84 (5.83)	10,675.27 (8.32)	4274.93 (10.38)
2000–2001 to 2011–2012 (Avg)	6423.52 (9)	1697.33 (5.56)	4036.95 (8.75)	3432.27 (6.24)	8529.88 (6.85)	3,901.24 (5.82)	9,128.67 (7.69)	3,801.87 (5.69)

TE total expenditure, *SSE* social sector expenditure, *GSDP* gross state domestic product, *PCSSE* per capita social sector expenditure at (2004–2005 prices deflated using GSDP deflator for each state), *Avg* average over the period

Figures in parentheses indicate the annual average growth rate in PCSSE over respective periods

Among NE states, the real per capita social sector expenditure (RPCSSE) varied from an average of ₹ 9128.67 for Sikkim to an average of ₹ 1697.34 for Assam during the entire study period 2000–2001 to 2011–2012. But large variations could not be observed among their annual average growth rates over the same period. Although in absolute terms, RPCSSE showed an increase on average for all NE states from the pre-FRL period to the post-FRL period; however, in terms of annual average growth rate, it reflected varying trends for different states between the two subperiods under analysis. For example, between 2000–2001 to 2004–2005 and 2005–2006 to 2011–2012, the annual average growth rate of RPCSSE fell from 13.94 to 6.46% for Arunachal Pradesh, from 10.20 to 7.35% for Manipur and from 10.06 to 8.32% for Sikkim. On contrary, opposite trends may be observed for five NE states, whose annual average growth rates of RPCSSE rose over the same two subperiods. Apart from Assam, which recorded a slight increase in its annual average growth rate of RPCSSE, the other four NE states, namely, Meghalaya, Mizoram, Nagaland and Tripura have witnessed a quite sharp increase in their annual average growth rates of RPCSSE.

In terms of the composition of social sector expenditure (SSE), during 2000–2001 to 2004–2005 (pre-FRL period), five NE states, viz., Arunachal Pradesh, Manipur, Meghalaya, Mizoram and Tripura spent over 80% of their SSE on revenue account, ranging from 80.17% by Mizoram to 88.98% by Arunachal Pradesh.[2] Assam topped the list of all NE states in this respect with more than 97% of its social sector spending incurred on revenue account. The remaining two states, Nagaland and Sikkim also spent a sizeable portion (about 3/4th) of their total expenditure for the social sectors on revenue account.

These trends are quite alarming for the simple reason that only a small proportion of aggregate SSE is accounted for by capital expenditure comprising of capital outlay and loans and advances by state governments, that is actually available for investment in social infrastructure of NE states. During 2005–2006 to 2011–2012 (post-FRL period), some improvement is observed in case of Arunachal Pradesh, Assam, Manipur and Tripura. These states reflected a fall in the average share of their SSE on revenue account, whereas the corresponding average share of SSE on capital account (capital outlay and loans and advances) registered an increase. It may further be noted that in two out of these four states, viz., Assam and Tripura, increase in capital expenditure for the social sectors is attributable only to the increase in direct SSE in the form of capital outlay, while indirect SSE in the form of loans and advances fell. Other NE states, namely, Meghalaya, Mizoram, Nagaland and Sikkim showed no sign of improvement in their composition of social sector expenditure. Rather, their average share of SSE on revenue account rose further in the post-FRL period. This happened mainly either due to a marginal increase in one component combined with a sharp decline in the other component or a fall in both components of capital expenditure.

The trends discussed so far in this section present an aggregate picture, for it is not clear from these trends as to what extent the social sector spending at the state level is financed through central government transfers. This assumes significance in light

---

[2] The discussion in this, and subsequent paragraphs of this section is based on the tables compiled from *Handbook of Statistics on State Government Finances 2010* and *State Finances: a Study of Budgets* (various issues) of the Reserve Bank of India. These tables are not produced in this paper to conserve the space, however, the same are available from the author upon request.

of the trends given in Appendix Table 11.1 which shows that the per capita transfers from the centre during the Ninth to Twelfth Finance Commissions for special category states were several times higher than those for non-special category states. Furthermore, the percentage shares of transfers in revenue receipts and in revenue expenditure for special category states were also significantly high as may be seen from Appendix Table 11.2 and Appendix Table 11.3 respectively. One may observe from Appendix Table 11.3 that the extent of dependence on transfers for financing revenue expenditures has increased rather than declined for almost all special category states. It is found that the share of transfers in revenue expenditure has been more than 100% for some states in some years, indicating that a part of the transfers in the form of plan grants meant for capital expenditure is consumed to meet the current requirements. It seems from these trends that SCS actually would find it difficult to finance social and physical infrastructure under the rule-based fiscal consolidation era if they are not given adequate support from the centre.

Being limited in its scope, this chapter does not look further in detail into the bifurcation of the financing of social sector spending at the state level; however, we present in Table 11.4 the financing pattern of per capita public expenditure on health (a major item of SSE) in NE states.

There is no denying of the commendable efforts of NE states to raise their budgetary expenditure on health, but their dependence on central government transfers for health is still quite large, indicating the need for restructuring of the fiscal transfer framework and incentives for higher expenditure for social services. In what follows, we will conduct an econometric exercise to identify some factors which might have helped (or did not help) NE states to manage their social sector spending in an era of rule based fiscal consolidation.

Table 11.4 Per capita public expenditure on health in northeastern states of India (At current prices) (₹). (Source: compiled from Choudhury and Amar Nath (2012).)

	Arunachal Pradesh	Assam	Manipur	Meghalaya	Mizoram	Nagaland	Sikkim	Tripura
Per capita total public expenditure on health in NE states								
2006–2007	1453	320	482	601	1279	1073	1143	600
2007–2008	1405	465	881	738	1646	1161	1476	670
2008–2009	1824	514	838	765	2137	1100	2247	762
2009–2010	2046	715	987	1119	2756	1256	2498	955
Per capita public expenditure on health in NE states (incurred by NE state governments)								
2006–2007	931	183	340	446	666	634	933	440
2007–2008	810	191	526	570	802	758	1148	475
2008–2009	1325	274	519	579	1493	714	1344	534
2009–2010	1486	462	696	813	2093	834	1899	707
Per capita public expenditure on health in NE states (incurred by central government)								
2006–2007	521	137	142	155	613	439	210	160
2007–2008	594	275	355	168	844	403	328	195
2008–2009	500	240	319	186	644	386	903	228
2009–2010	560	253	290	306	663	422	600	248

Total expenditure is the sum of expenditures by the central and state governments at the state level. Central government expenditure at the state level includes expenditure both through the treasury and off-budget root. State level expenditure indicates budgetary expenditure of states, net of grants received from the central government

11.4 Empirical Estimation: Results and Discussion

In this section, we try to estimate the impact of some factors (commonly cited in the literature) on social sector spending of NE states during the fiscal rule regime using standard econometric procedures. The estimation is attempted taking eight NE states over the period 2000–2001 to 2011–2012. Guided by our interest, we consider per capita[3] social sector expenditure (pSSE) as the dependent variable. The set of explanatory variables includes per capita income growth (rpGSDP) and per capita income (pGSDP) to represent business cycle and initial economic conditions respectively[4]; per capita gross devolution and transfer of resources from the centre (pIGT) as a proxy of not only the volume of intergovernmental transfers but also to capture such time-specific factors as increased revenues at the centre and implementation of Finance Commissions' recommendations; per capita own revenues of states (pOR); real effective interest rate (REIR)[5] for considering interest burden and a dummy variable (D89) to capture the effect of expansionary fiscal measures undertaken by states in 2008–2009 and 2009–2010. Another dummy variable (FR) is used to indicate whether a state is following a rule based fiscal consolidation era or not.

All data relating to fiscal variables have been collected from the Handbook of Statistics on State Government Finances 2010 and Studies on State Budgets (various issues) both published by the Reserve Bank of India. Data on gross state domestic product (at current as well as at 2004–2005 prices) are gathered from the website of the Ministry of Statistics and Programme Implementation, Government of India (http://www.mospi.gov.in), while statewise population data are projected data obtained from the Census of India website (http://www.censusindia.gov.in).

Limited by the small number of observations used in the present study, we estimate a one-way (instead of a two-way) fixed effect model accounting for time-invariant heterogeneity in fiscal conditions across NE states such as the adoption of VAT and other fiscal measures undertaken by individual states, political affiliation of a state with the centre, etc. The basic specification serving the purpose of this study is

$$\begin{aligned}\log\left(pSSE\right)_{\mathrm{it}} = \mathrm{a}_0 + \mathrm{a}_1\log\left(pGSDP\right)_{\mathrm{it}} + \mathrm{a}_2 FR_{\mathrm{it}} + \mathrm{a}_3\log\left({}_{\mathrm{p}}\mathrm{OR}\right)_{\mathrm{it}} \\ + \mathrm{a}_4\log\left(\mathrm{pIGT}\right)_{\mathrm{it}} + \mathrm{a}_5 REIR_{\mathbf{it}} + \mathrm{a}_6 D89 + \mu_{\mathrm{i}} + \varepsilon_{\mathbf{it}}\end{aligned} \quad (11.1)$$

Here, subscript i and t denote state and time period respectively. All other variables used in this regression have the same meaning as defined above. M_i is used to capture state-specific unobserved characteristics invariant of time and ε_{it} is the

[3] All variables (dependent and independent) considered in per capita terms are at 2004–2005 prices deflated using implicit GSDP deflator.

[4] For an evidence of cyclicality of expenditure across selected Indian states, see Reserve Bank of India (2014).

[5] Real effective interest rate is calculated by subtracting expected inflation rate from nominal interest rate. Nominal interest rate is obtained by dividing the interest payments in year t by the outstanding liability in year t−1 and multiplied the result by 100. The expected rate of inflation is estimated as the 2-year moving average of the inflation rate based on implicit GSDP deflator.

Table 11.5 Unit root test: summary results. (Source: Author's calculations)

	LLC t-stat	Breitung t-stat	IPS W-stat	ADF Fisher Chi-square stat	PP Fisher Chi-square stat
Variable (in level)					
Log(pSSE)	−5.42*	0.85	−2.26**	29.61**	59.23*
Log(pGSDP)	−5.23*	−0.52	−2.18**	31.37**	31.27**
rpGSDP	−7.57*	−1.84**	−5.32*	53.82*	84.52*
REIR	−7.52*	−1.17	−3.24*	37.57*	27.75**
Log(pIGT)	−2.09**	−1.16	−1.82**	26.09***	44.46*

Unit root tests used in this table are Levin, Lin and Chu (LLC) (2002), Breitung (2000), Im, Pesaran and Shin (IPS) (2003) and Fisher-type tests using ADF and PP tests (Maddala and Wu (1999) and Choi (2001)). The first two tests assume a common unit root process, while other three tests assume individual unit root process

* $p<0.01$, ** $p>0.01$ but <0.05 and *** $p>0.05$ but <0.10

Probabilities for Fisher tests are computed using an asymptotic Chi-square distribution. All other tests assume asymptotic normality

Automatic lag length selected based on Schwarz Information Criteria (SIC) and Newey-West automatic bandwidth selection and Bartlett kernel

These tests are conducted assuming individual effects and individual linear trend

stochastic disturbance term. It may be noted that Eq. (11.1) is re-estimated replacing per capita income (log(pGSDP)) with per capita income growth (rpGSDP) so as to visualise clearly the effects of the two variables in question on per capita social sector expenditure.

All variables under analysis, but the binary ones, have been tested for stationarity using different panel unit root tests (assuming common unit root process and individual unit root process). The summary results of these tests are reported in Table 11.5. It may be seen from this table that majority of the unit root tests fail to accept the null hypothesis of a unit root in level for each of the five variables. We will thus use all variables in their level to estimate our regression. Given the cross-sectional and time series nature of our data, we estimate a feasible GLS specification correcting for both cross-section heteroskedasticity and contemporaneous correlation.[6] The estimation results are given in Table 11.6.

Table 11.6 shows that per capita income has a positive and significant impact on per capita social sector expenditure, whereas the effect of per capita income growth on it is negligible and statistically insignificant. The negative and significant coefficients of FR indicate that the path of 'spending cuts' has been followed by NE states to meet the FRBM targets. However, the negative impact of FR seems to have been partially offset by increased intergovernmental transfers due to higher revenues at the centre and the award of the finance commissions. The coefficients of per capita devolution and transfers exhibit a positive and strongly significant effect on per capita social sector expenditure. The coefficient of own revenues is found insignificant in both regressions. These results along with the trends discussed in Section II seem to suggest that NE states, by and large, have been able to manage their resources,

[6] For detail of estimation methods, see Baltagi (2005), Baltagi and Chang (1994) and Wooldridge (2002).

Table 11.6 Results of panel regression estimation. (Source: Author's estimation)

	(1)	(2)
Log(pGSDP)	0.30*	–
rpGSDP	–	0.000851
FR	−0.05*	−0.05*
Log(pIGT)	0.55*	0.72*
Log(pOR)	0.26	0.35
REIR	−0.00811*	−0.01412*
D89	0.04*	0.04*
a_0	0.32*	1.89*
State effect	Yes	Yes
R-squared	0.99	0.99
Adjusted R-squared	0.99	0.99
DW statistic	2.00	2.00
F-statistic	5420.28*	1873.66*

Column (1) contains results of regression estimated with per capita income alongwith other independent variables and column (2) represents results of regression estimated with per capita income growth alongwith other independent variables

*$p<0.01$

Regressions estimated through FGLS Cross-section SUR; Cross-section SUR (PCSE) standard errors and covariance (no d.f. correction)

including transfers, quite appropriately for their social sector. Although negligible in its magnitude, the negative and significant impact of real effective interest rate on per capita social sector expenditure explains the indirect channel of funding the desired schemes. The fall in interest rate reduces the burden of interest payments for states, thereby cutting down their fiscal imbalances and thus, relaxing more resources for desired areas such as social sector. A progressive decline in interest rate since mid-2000 is one of the factors responsible for making states comfortable in achieving their FRBM debt and deficits targets (Reserve Bank of India 2013).

Though quite different in terms of sample of states considered, all of our empirical results discussed above are in line with the findings of Chakraborty and Bhusana (2013). We have also introduced a dummy variable in our regression to capture the effect of the Sixth Pay Commission award and fiscal stimulus measures taken by states during 2008–2009 and 2009–2010. This variable comes out to be positive and statistically significant, but we cannot find any logical explanation for its positive sign.

11.5 Concluding Remarks

The trend analysis combined with empirical estimation in this chapter leads us to conclude that even in the rule based fiscal regime, NE states could manage to allocate relatively higher funds for social sectors. It should, however, be emphasised here that NE states should reprioritise their social sector expenditure so as to increase investment in social infrastructure. More effort is to be made by these states to raise their budgetary allocations for the social sector thereby reducing their dependence on central transfers. The results of our empirical estimation suggest that the imposition of fiscal rule led NE states to cut their social sector expenditure to meet the FRBM targets. However, the cut in spending has been partially offset by increased central devolution and transfers. The fact that a decline in interest rate allows the government's resources to be diverted to the desired areas such as social sector schemes has also been empirically established in this chapter.

Appendix

Appendix Table 11.1 Per capita finance commission transfers to states (₹). (Source: compiled from Srivastava and Rao (2009).

	1990–1995 (Avg.)	1995–2000 (Avg.)	2000–2005 (Avg.)	2005–2008 (Avg.)
General category states	231.8	386.3	622.0	1119.4
Andhra Pradesh	241.4	454.8	629.6	1100.7
Bihar	284.2	433.1	867.4	1398.8
Chhattisgarh	NA	NA	605.6	1277.7
Goa	870.5	838.6	878.0	1854.3
Gujarat	164.6	327.3	432.4	793.4
Haryana	151.8	245.6	267.4	601.1
Jharkhand	NA	NA	687.9	1283.3
Karnataka	202.0	385.8	612.0	954.4
Kerala	236.4	423.2	626.8	1147.2
Madhya Pradesh	224.1	386.4	713.3	1160.3
Maharashtra	176.7	255.0	299.6	592.0
Orissa	328.1	480.9	855.1	1579.7
Punjab	191.9	288.6	303.1	620.7
Rajasthan	272.5	407.7	683.5	1208.1
Tamil Nadu	249.4	403.3	538.1	1024.9
Uttar Pradesh	233.8	412.9	700.2	1369.5
West Bengal	216.2	366.2	725.0	1193.1
Special category states	714.0	1135.7	1567.5	2891.7
Arunachal Pradesh	1901.7	2890.6	3193.6	5978.8
Assam	336.9	579.4	758.9	1388.9
Himachal Pradesh	715.6	1389.1	2039.4	4383.2
Jammu and Kashmir	980.4	1381.1	2860.2	3797.8
Manipur	1180.9	1742.4	2391.2	5047.5
Meghalaya	910.1	1555.2	1668.8	1772.2
Mizoram	2885.3	3684.8	4000.4	9017.2
Nagaland	2014.6	2681.5	4009.8	6295.4
Sikkim	1012.5	1863.4	4000.0	5347.0
Tripura	1045.5	1582.3	2171.5	4527.4
Uttarakhand	NA	NA	490.9	2565.0
Total	945.83	1522.01	2189.42	4011.05

NA data not available

Appendix Table 11.2 Total transfers from the centre as percentage of revenue receipts: special category states. (Source: Same as for Appendix Table 11.1)

Year	Arunachal Pradesh	Assam	Himachal Pradesh	Jammu and Kashmir	Manipur	Meghalaya	Mizoram	Nagaland	Sikkim	Tripura	Uttara-khand
1990–1991	87.86	60.73	72.70	80.79	89.69	84.50	70.49	89.39	76.17	91.05	NA
1991–1992	88.04	67.96	73.06	84.36	91.99	83.86	91.67	90.79	78.07	91.72	NA
1992–1993	88.42	62.57	72.59	79.30	92.26	85.47	91.51	91.32	79.68	90.88	NA
1993–1994	83.75	71.01	74.31	86.40	91.96	84.76	92.86	93.33	81.39	90.31	NA
1994–1995	85.77	67.63	66.92	85.95	87.53	82.10	92.75	86.19	36.68	90.63	NA
1995–1996	88.23	69.25	73.84	86.74	89.39	80.53	91.77	92.97	31.21	90.77	NA
1996–1997	90.91	71.76	71.94	83.61	90.92	82.91	92.05	91.72	26.48	90.17	NA
1997–1998	92.29	70.80	67.83	84.32	91.16	85.16	92.56	92.06	26.33	90.16	NA
1998–1999	91.79	68.17	66.37	NA	93.06	83.21	93.83	92.25	27.16	89.83	NA
1999–2000	92.07	65.51	54.88	82.64	92.28	80.20	94.53	91.94	28.96	87.63	NA
2000–2001	91.21	65.59	70.27	82.29	91.31	81.87	93.38	92.95	58.86	86.56	61.22
2001–2002	90.07	64.81	70.02	78.65	93.14	79.52	92.63	93.26	33.12	86.28	61.33
2002–2003	61.88	61.32	70.95	79.06	90.84	81.56	92.11	92.44	31.68	85.02	56.61
2003–2004	89.62	61.16	67.94	79.08	91.65	78.08	93.30	94.51	51.89	82.04	55.65
2004–2005	85.37	61.93	59.81	NA	91.34	77.93	92.33	91.51	41.37	83.84	51.24
2005–2006	85.72	61.05	66.66	NA	92.88	77.18	89.41	91.08	42.10	88.11	56.03
2006–2007	88.38	67.65	65.47	NA	90.77	82.04	90.83	92.59	51.36	86.66	56.47
2007–2008	89.04	66.23	62.30	NA	90.09	84.20	91.42	92.64	44.74	86.90	59.75
Averages											
1990–1995	86.77	65.98	71.92	83.36	90.69	84.14	87.86	90.21	70.40	90.92	NA
1995–2000	91.06	69.10	66.97	84.33	91.36	82.40	92.95	92.19	28.03	89.71	NA
2000–2005	83.63	62.96	67.80	79.77	91.66	79.79	92.75	92.93	43.39	84.75	57.21
2005–2008	87.71	64.98	64.81	NA	91.25	81.14	90.55	92.10	46.07	87.22	57.42

NA data not available

Appendix Table 11.3 Total transfers from the centre as percentage of revenue expenditure: special category states. (Source: Same as for Appendix Table 11.1)

Year	Arunachal Pradesh	Assam	Himachal Pradesh	Jammu and Kashmir	Manipur	Meghalaya	Mizoram	Nagaland	Sikkim	Tripura	Uttara-khand
1990–1991	121.92	56.19	65.05	86.13	115.55	95.97	106.82	88.29	94.82	90.74	NA
1991–1992	136.48	76.49	73.79	97.00	109.85	91.98	114.21	91.95	91.84	94.33	NA
1992–1993	130.80	66.71	66.70	73.77	111.31	89.26	103.07	89.08	92.79	99.85	NA
1993–1994	114.73	81.20	80.56	111.84	121.56	87.91	111.46	86.86	96.91	90.28	NA
1994–1995	118.33	61.23	54.15	108.92	101.95	95.28	107.73	75.34	38.06	95.20	NA
1995–1996	131.10	65.38	68.01	92.22	99.92	94.89	101.89	85.92	33.34	108.16	NA
1996–1997	122.12	77.47	66.75	81.76	103.75	98.16	99.01	92.65	27.40	102.27	NA
1997–1998	116.20	75.83	54.55	91.66	98.62	86.61	100.93	91.06	27.20	92.00	NA
1998–1999	113.56	69.56	46.02	NA	105.82	84.97	99.82	91.07	26.16	96.92	NA
1999–2000	114.38	54.25	53.35	89.74	68.75	81.57	100.80	89.12	29.00	86.27	NA
2000–2001	96.43	57.63	48.91	106.12	84.35	85.86	75.71	92.92	66.52	81.77	61.93
2001–2002	92.52	56.47	56.86	93.79	81.92	77.21	71.25	96.15	35.97	88.87	59.17
2002–2003	66.49	58.57	50.49	93.82	85.25	87.28	83.20	85.84	35.01	81.52	49.56
2003–2004	101.49	56.20	48.40	94.11	88.91	83.14	99.33	123.02	58.93	86.26	45.94
2004–2005	84.93	60.16	47.85	NA	96.40	75.48	99.45	99.92	45.43	98.98	41.57
2005–2006	95.06	69.80	67.61	NA	111.63	80.52	93.11	100.21	46.79	111.41	55.29
2006–2007	107.23	65.09	64.97	NA	122.63	95.21	99.64	108.70	63.08	104.69	59.59
2007–2008	95.72	69.93	60.24	NA	105.53	99.90	99.82	115.49	51.96	105.28	66.74
Averages											
1990–1995	124.45	68.36	68.05	95.53	112.05	92.08	108.66	86.30	82.89	94.08	NA
1995–2000	119.47	68.50	57.74	88.85	95.37	89.24	100.49	89.96	28.62	97.13	NA
2000–2005	88.37	57.81	50.50	96.96	87.37	81.79	85.79	99.57	48.37	87.48	51.64
2005–2008	99.34	68.27	64.27	NA	113.26	91.88	97.52	108.14	53.94	107.13	60.54

NA data not available.

References

Alesina A, Bayoumi T (1996) The costs and benefits of fiscal rules: evidence from U.S. states. NBER Working Paper No 5614

Auerbach A (2008) Federal budget rules: the US experience. NBER Working Paper No 14288

Ballabriga F, Martinez-Mongay C (2003) Has EMU shifted monetary and fiscal policies?. In: Buti M (ed) Monetary and fiscal policies in EMU: interactions and coordination. Cambridge University Press, Cambridge

Baltagi BH (2005) Econometric analysis of panel data, 3rd edn. Wiley, West Sussex

Baltagi BH, Chang Y (1994) Incomplete panels: a comparative study of alternative estimators for the unbalanced one-way error component regression model. J Econom 62(2):67–89

Breitung J (2000) The local power of some unit root tests for panel data. In: Baltagi B (ed) Advances in econometrics, vol 15 (Nonstationary Panels, Panel Cointegration, and Dynamic Panels). JAI Press, Amsterdam, pp 161–178

Chakraborty P (2005) Debt swap in low interest rate regime: unequal gains and future worries. Econ Polit Wkly 40(40):4357–4362

Chakraborty P, Bhusana B (2013) Fiscal reforms, fiscal rule and development spending: how Indian states have performed? NIPFP Working Paper No 2013–122, National Institute of Public Finance and Policy, New Delhi

Choi I (2001) Unit root tests for panel data. J Int Money Finance 20(2):249–272

Choudhury M, Amar Nath H K (2012) An estimate of public expenditure on health in India. http://www.nipfp.org.in/media/medialibrary/2013/08/health_estimates_report.pdf. Accessed 25 Nov 2014

Claeys P (2008) Rules, and their effects on fiscal policy in Sweden. Swed Econ Policy Rev 15:7–47

Dupont J, Kwarteng K (2012) Binding the hands of government—a credible fiscal rule for the UK. IEA Current Controversies Paper No 36

Galí J, Perotti R (2003) Fiscal policy and monetary integration in Europe. Econ Policy 18(37):533–572

Im KS, Pesaran MH, Shin Y (2003) Testing for unit roots in heterogeneous panels. J Econom 115(1):53–74

Levin A, Lin CF, Chu C (2002) Unit root tests in panel data: asymptotic and finite-sample properties. J Econom 108(1):1–24

Maddala GS, Wu S (1999) A comparative study of unit root tests with panel data and a new simple test. Oxf Bull Econ Stat 61(1):631–652

Marneffe W, Aarle B, Wielen W, Vereeck L (2010) The impact of fiscal rules on public finances: theory and empirical evidence for the Euro area. CESifo Working Paper No 3303

Milesi-Ferretti, G (1996) Fiscal rules and the budget process. IMF Working Paper No 96/60

Millar J (1997) The effects of budget rules on fiscal performance and macroeconomic stabilization. Bank of Canada Working Paper No 97–15

Misra B (2012) Fiscal consolidation and macroeconomy: India's experience with rule-based fiscal policy and post-crisis challenges. In: Franco D (ed) Rules and Institutions for sound fiscal policy after the crisis. Public finance workshop papers presented at the Bancad'Italia workshop held in Perugia, 31 March-2 April, 2011, vol 11. Bancad'Italia Printing Office, Rome. pp 75–106

Organisation for Economic Cooperation and Development (2007) OECD Economic Outlook.No. 81, June

Poterba J (1997) Do budget rules work? In: Auerbach A (ed) Fiscal policy: lessons from economic research. MIT Press, Cambridge

Rao M Govinda, Chakraborty P (2006) Multilateral adjustment lending to states in India: hastening fiscal correction or softening the budget constraints? J Int Trade Econ Dev 15(3):335–358

Reserve Bank of India (2013) State finances: a study of budgets of 2012–2013. Reserve Bank of India, Mumbai (Chapter VI)

Reserve Bank of India (2014) State finances: a study of budgets of 2013–2014. Reserve Bank of India (Chapter VI)
Simone AS, Topalova P (2009) India's experience with fiscal rules: an evaluation and the way forward. IMF Working Paper No. 09/175, Asia and Pacific Department, International Monetary Fund, Washington, DC
Srivastava D K, Rao C B (2009) Review of trendsiin fiscal transfers in India. Study prepared for the thirteenth finance commission, July
Sucharita S, Sethi N (2011) Fiscal discipline in India. Rom J Fiscal Policy 2(1):1–23
Tapsoba R (2012) Do national numerical fiscal rules really shape fiscal behaviours in developing countries? A treatment effect evaluation. Econ Model 19(4):1356–1369
Viren M (2002) Do the OECD countries follow the same fiscal policy rule?. In: Buti M, et al. (eds) The behaviour of fiscal authorities, stabilisation, growth and institutions. Palgrave Press, London
Wooldridge JM (2002) Econometric analysis of cross section and panel data. MIT Press, Cambridge

Part IV
Social Sector and Poverty Alleviation

Chapter 12
An Analysis on the Impact of Employment Generation Policies on Rural Women in West Bengal, India

Tanmoyee Banerjee (Chaterjee)

12.1 Introduction

Rural women who play a crucial role in socioeconomic and nutritional developments of households are constrained in various ways that deny them equitable access to opportunities, resources, assets and services.[1] Their lack of education training and access to resources hampers them from enjoying benefits of income-generating activities. The problem of unemployment is widespread among rural women in India as well as in other countries. The report of employment and unemployment survey 2009–2010 showed that the overall unemployment rate for women was 146 per thousand people in labour force, and it was even higher 148 per thousand people in labour force in rural areas. [2]The report of employment and unemployment survey 2011–2012 showed some improvement. It was found that the overall unemployment rate for women was 69 per thousand people in labour force, and in rural areas it was 56 per thousand people in labour force [3]. According to the report of employment and unemployment survey 2012–2013, the overall unemployment rate for women was 72 per thousand people in labour force and that of 58 per thousand people in labour force in rural areas.[4] Given this scenario, based on a primary survey this chapter

[1] http://www.un.org/womenwatch/feature/ruralwomen/facts-figures.html. Accessed on 2.8.14.

[2] Source: Report of employment and unemployment survey 2009–2010, Government of India, Ministry of labour and Employment, Labour Bureau. Chandigarh. 2010, Statement 4.1. pp. 33. The data was based on usual principal status (UPS).

[3] Source: Report of employment and unemployment survey 2011–2012, Vol. 1 Government of India, Ministry of labour and Employment, Labour Bureau. Chandigarh., Table 4.6. pp. 41. The data was based on UPS.

[4] Source: Report of employment and unemployment survey 2012–2013., Vol 1 Government of India, Ministry of labour and Employment, Labour Bureau. Chandigarh., Table 4.6. pp. 38. The data was based on UPS.

T. Banerjee (Chaterjee) (✉)
Department of Economics, 188 Raja S.C Mullick Road, Jadavpur University,
Kolkata 700032, India
e-mail: tanmoyee@hotmail.com

S. Banerjee et al. (eds.), *Understanding Development,* India Studies in Business and Economics, DOI 10.1007/978-81-322-2455-6_12

tries to gauge the impact of various policies on employment status of rural women in case of West Bengal, India. The study considers the impact of two such policies undertaken by the Indian government to control the problem of unemployment. One is MGNREGA[5] which was initiated in 2005 and other is SGSY[6] which was initiated from 1st April 1999.

The MGNREGA is an ambitious programme undertaken by the Government of India (GoI) to guarantee employment for rural population at least for 100 days in a year in unskilled manual work. Narayanan and Das (2014) observed three key features of the MGNREGA. First, the act prescribes that at least a third of all workers be women. Second, the act also provides for equal wages for men and women. Third, since the entitlement to at least a 100 days of work is at the household level, the allocation of the work within the household is left to the household members allowing space for the participation of women. Various other studies like those of Khera and Nayak (2009), Drèze and Oldiges (2011), Dutta et al. (2012), Dasgupta and Sudarshan (2011), Dreze and Khera (2011), Liu and Barrett (2012) and Carswell and De Neve (2013) have observed different aspects of this policy, its impact on rural wage and tried to evaluate the performance of this policy across different states of India. On the whole, it was observed that in some states it had worked successfully and had an impact on the livelihood of women but in some cases it was not that successful. Studies by Dey and Bedi (2010), Ghosh (2011) and Das (2012a) showed that the programme was not that successful in different parts of West Bengal. Given these observations, one objective of the present study is to find the impact of MGNREGA programme on the employment status and other outcome variables of surveyed sample of women from North 24 Parganas, West Bengal.

The SGSY was a self-help group-based micro-credit programme that aimed at extending income-generating self-employment activities among poor women in rural areas through financial inclusion. Various impact evaluation studies of micro-credit programmes by Khandker (2003, 2005), McKernan (2002), Swain and Floro (2007), Tedeschi (2008), Banerjee (2009) and Imai et al. (2010) identified different positive impact of micro-credit programmes joining on households in terms of reduced poverty, improved consumption level, improved rate of asset creation of the families and empowerment of women. A primary survey from six states in India (NCAER 2008) by Parida and Sinha (2010) showed that all female groups have performed most efficiently compared to male self-help groups (SHGs). Swain and

---

[5] "Mahatma Gandhi National Rural Employment Guarantee Act", and abbreviated to MGNREGA, is an Indian labour law and social security measure that aims to guarantee the "right to work" and ensure livelihood security in rural areas by providing at least 100 days of guaranteed wage employment in a financial year to every household whose adult members volunteer to do unskilled manual work. http://nrega.nic.in/netnrega/home.aspx. Accessed on 7.10.14

[6] Swarnjaynti Gram Swarojgar Yojana (SGSY) that was initiated in 1999 was a credit-based self-employment programme of Ministry of Rural Development, Government of India for poverty alleviation. It aims at providing assistance to the below poverty level (BPL) rural poor for establishing micro-enterprises through bank credit and government subsidy to acquire an income-generating asset. Source: http://rural.nic.in/FAQ_SGSY.pdf. It also covered all aspects of self employments such as training, credit, technology, infrastructure and marketing and thus enabling the rural poor to take decisions on all issues concerning poverty eradication. Accessed on 7.10.14

Adel Varghese (2009) showed that for Indian SHG members, training by NGOs positively affects asset creation but the type of SHG linkage per se has no effect.

The present study is based on a primary survey carried out in 2009–2010 on female members of households from different areas of North 24 Parganas, West Bengal, India. The survey included women who had participated SHGs under SGSY programme and job card holders under MGNREGA as well as some females who are not within the purview of these two programmes. The chosen SHG members were from SGSY groups that were created prior to 2004–2005. Based on this primary survey, the chapter tries to find the impact of these policy measures on household income, different household expenditures and employment status of rural women using propensity score matching approach. In the impact evaluation study, one needs to find out two groups of individuals that are, at baseline and on average, identical in terms of observed and unobserved characteristics. However, while assigning the treatment to different groups, there may not be any prior randomization. Thus, the group that has received a treatment may be totally different from the group that did not receive the treatment not only in their treatment status but also in other characteristics that affect both participation and the outcome variables. Under this situation, the method of propensity score matching is applied to reduce the bias in the observational studies. Following D'Agostino (2007), the propensity score for an individual can be considered as the probability of being treated conditionally on (or only based on) the individual's covariate values. Intuitively, the propensity score is a measure of the likelihood that a person would have been treated on the basis of only his or her covariate scores. If a treated person and a potential control unit have the same propensity score, then the difference between the treatment and control outcomes is an unbiased estimator of the treatment effect. As Heinrich et al. (2010) has pointed out matching methods find a non-treated unit that is "similar" to a participating unit, allowing an estimate of the intervention's impact as the difference between a participant and the matched comparison case. Averaging across all participants, the method provides an estimate of the mean program impact for the participants.

Rest of the chapter is divided as follows: Sect. 12.2 describes the survey design, Sect. 12.3 presents the result of empirical analysis and Sect. 12.4 concludes the chapter.

12.2 The Survey and Descriptive Analysis

The survey was conducted in the district of North 24 Parganas, West Bengal, during October 2009–March 2010. The survey area includes four rural subdivisions (Bongaon, Barasat, Barackpur and Basirhat) of North 24 Parganas; six blocks[7] namely Bongaon, Barasat I, Barackpur I, Basirhat I, Hasnabad and Hingalgang

[7] One block from each of the subdivisions is selected randomly and rest of the two is selected from the rest of all blocks by simple random sampling method.

Table 12.1 Description of the sample. (Source: Primary survey)

	Having job card under MGNREGA		
Joined SGSY programme			
	No	Yes	Total
No	119	59	178
Yes	107	160	267
Total	226	219	445
	Cramér's $V = 0.2624$ p value$=0.000$		

were randomly selected. From each block one *gram panchayat* area was randomly selected. The total sample size was 445 of which 226 females were job card holders and 276 were SHG members under SGSY programme. In this set, there were 160 females who participated in both programmes and 119 individuals who did not participate in any of these programmes. Thus, our sample set gives a representation of members who are under the purview of SGSY programme and/or MGNREGA as well as none.

Table 12.1 gives a description of the sample and also shows that the sample association between participation in both programmes is small as shown by Cramer's V taking a value of just 0.26.

The survey collected socioeconomic demographic information like religion, age, sex, education, social category (SC/ST), number of family members and dependents, occupation category, husband's occupation category, average family income, savings, female's income, family wealth level, level of agricultural land holding, family consumption expenditure, food expenditure, medical expenditure, number of school drop out in the family, the training received by female and the loan use pattern and other loan-related information. Productive training had been received by those who had joined SHGs under SGSY programme and it was observed that in the sample, only 78 females received such training.

The objective of this present study is to find out the impact of different employment-generating policies on the employment status, family income and family consumption expenditure, family monthly savings, family monthly food expenditure and family monthly health expenditure of rural women. The rural women were asked whether they were involved in income-generating activities for the last 1 year prior to survey to judge their employment status. The women who have earned a positive income per month on an average by giving labour in the reference period are considered to be employed. It was found that women are involved as wage earners in agrarian and nonagricultural activities and other self-employment activities like basket making, bidi binding, sewing, handicraft work, vegetable growing, small-scale selling of fish, flowers, etc. and animal husbandry (like poultry farming, cattle breeding, etc.).

Table 12.2 presents the employment status of the sample. It shows that only 38 % of the surveyed women were employed. The percentage of employment is least (only 21 %) for women who have not participated in any programme. The overall percentage of employment is 45 % for SHG members under the SGSY programme

Table 12.2 Employment status of surveyed women. (Source: Primary survey; percentages are with respect to row total)

		Employment status		Total
		No	Yes	
Did not participate in any programme		94(79 %)	25(21 %)	119
Participated SGSY	Only in SGSY	69(64 %)	38(36 %)	107
	Participated in SGSY and hold job card	79(49 %)	81(51 %)	160
	Total	148(55 %)	119(45 %)	267
Have job card under MGNREGA	Only job card holders	34(58 %)	25(42 %)	59
	Participated in SGSY and hold job card	79(49 %)	81(51 %)	160
	Total	113(52 %)	106(48 %)	219
Total sample		276(62 %)	169(38 %)	445

(and it is only 36 % for those who are only SHG members). Among the job card holders, the overall rate of employment is 48 %, and it is 42 % for those who are job card holders but not SHG members. The rural women with job cards as well as SHG-membership had 50.6 % percentage of employment.

Next, the study compares the family income and family consumption and other expenditures for different groups. Before comparing means and medians, outliers were identified using multivariate outlier detection technique. After eliminating outliers, there are 440 samples.

Table 12.3 shows an interesting result. The average annual family income is highest for the group where females are only SHG members, and it is lowest for the group where females have joined SHGs as well as hold job cards. The same result is observed when we consider average monthly family consumption expenditure. Results of Table 12.4 are also in the same direction as the group of women who participated only in SGSY had higher food expenditure and savings per month for

Table 12.3 Comparison of average annual family income and monthly family consumption expenditures across various groups

	Annual family income (in ₹)			Monthly family consumption expenditure (in ₹)			*N*
	Mean	Median	S. D.	Mean	Median	S. D.	
Did not participate in any programme	32720.00	30000.00	13535.977	2509.13	2200.00	996.44	115
Only in SGSY	36836.60	36000.00	15193.669	2813.62	2500.00	941.11	106
Only job card holders	31701.69	30000.00	11634.913	2586.44	2500.00	957.81	59
Participated in SGSY and hold job card	27095.25	24900.00	9409.0105	2088.41	2000.00	620.28	160
Total	31529.82	30000.00	12926.141	2439.86	2200.00	901.73	440

*Calculated on the basis of data from primary survey

Table 12.4 Comparison of average monthly family food, savings and health expenditures across various groups

	Family food expenditure per month			Family savings per month			Family health expenditure per month		
	Mean	Median	S. D.	Mean	Median	S. D.	Mean	Median	S. D.
Did not participate in any programme	1306.09	1000.00	702.23	250.78	0.00	507.14	268.17	200.00	283.49
Only in SGSY	2032.26	1800.00	808.47	256.79	30.00	568.12	211.13	200.00	296.86
Only job card holders	1725.09	1500.00	733.69	11.53	0.00	68.80	360.17	300.00	385.94
Participated in SGSY and hold job card	1240.38	1037.50	470.74	140.44	25.00	278.02	195.50	200.00	119.49
Total	1513.32	1300.00	738.39	180.02	25.00	423.94	240.34	200.00	264.33

*Calculated on the basis of data from primary survey

the family compared to other groups. However, family health-related expenditure is highest for job card holders. Further, it was noted that yearly family income, monthly family consumption expenditures and other expenditures are not following normal distribution. Thus, the author applied the test for equality of medians instead of analysis of variance (ANOVA). The Chi square statistic for equality of medians across groups for annual family income is 24.83 with p value 0.000 and that of monthly family consumption expenditure is 37.8 with p value 0.00. Again, same results are obtained for family monthly food, savings and health expenditure. Thus, the medians are significantly different across various groups for yearly family income and monthly family consumption saving and food expenditures are highest for females who are only SHG members. SGSY programme aims at capacity creation of rural women through financial inclusion and timely delivery of micro-credit for productive purposes. In many cases, it has been observed that credits received by the women are not directly used by them, but by other male family members for productive purposes. This has caused improvement in family income and family consumption savings and other expenditures though the women remained unemployed. To explore further, Sect. 12.3 will compare impacts of various policy measures using propensity scoring method, which will eliminate the possibility of sample bias.

12.3 Impact of Various Policies on Women Employment Status, Family Income and Family Consumption Expenditure

This section tries to find the impact of SGSY and MGNREGA on women employment status, family income, family monthly consumption expenditure, savings, food expenditure and health expenditure of the sample. Family monthly health expenditure is the average spending of the family on health-related matters of the members as reported by the interviewees.

In this section, first the propensity scores for the sample are determined by estimating logistic regressions that estimate the probability of self-help group joining under SGSY and the probability of the joining of MGNREGA programme using various socioeconomic and demographic variables of the surveyed women. The variables included in the logistic regressions are as follows: religion, natural log of number of family members, education level dummy and natural log of age. These variables are described in Table A1 in Appendix I. In this respect, the author must mention that the studies by Bardhan et al. (2008), Bardhan and Mookherjee (2011) showed the existence of political clientelism in West Bengal. Even so, the present study did not include any variables related to political environment or political support of samples because of the following reasons: the political environment or their political support can have an effect on the probability of joining a programme like SGSY or MGNREGA as well as on the outcome variables. In case of SGSY, political support of the group members or local political environment is one important factor in nurturing the groups. If the groups are properly nurtured (like training of group members, supply of resources or sales or advertising of the products of groups), the performance of members also improves, and it affects the outcome variables. On the other hand, Das (2013) observed that households, which joined MGNREGA and are well connected to the political parties or who support the local ruling political party in power, have significantly higher chances of getting work compared to those who are not connected. Further, the study found that politically well-connected households and ruling party supporters are associated with significantly higher number of days of work. Given this evidence, the present study did not include variables related to political environment or political support of samples in the analysis. The analysis will omit samples that are both job card holders as well as SGSY members[8]. The psmatch 2 module in STATA is used to estimate propensity score and conduct the Gaussian kernel matching with bandwidth 0.05 with common support option. The author has also checked the balancing property of covariates used to measure propensity scores for treated and control group.[9]

Table 12.5 summarizes the results of logistic regression used for measuring propensity scores corresponding to SHG joining. Here, treatment group includes women who only participated in the SGSY programme and the control group consists of women who were not under the purview of any programme.

Table 12.5 shows that religion dummy and log of the number of family members positively affect the probability of group joining; that is, Hindu women were more likely to join the SHGs under SGSY programme against the reference category of Muslims. Second, women from large families are more likely to join the SHGs. Third, age of the member is negatively affecting the probability of joining SHGs and finally, women with more than primary education are less probable to join SHGs. In Tables 12.6 and 12.7, the results are reported to show the impact of SHG joining under SGSY in terms of estimated average treatment on the treated (ATT) along with bootstrapped standard errors for total yearly family income, total monthly consumption expenditure and employment status and family monthly sav-

[8] The descriptions of variables are given in the appendix.

[9] The results of covariates balancing are available with the author.

Table 12.5 Logistic equation to determine the group joining probability

Group dummy	Coeficient	Standard error	*z*	*P*>*z*
Religion dummy	5.035632	1.058676	4.76	0*
ln age	−2.84912	0.818266	−3.48	0*
ln family member	3.462057	0.885468	3.91	0*
Education dummy	−1.50919	0.406371	−3.71	0*
Constant	4.629332	3.159703	1.47	0.143
N=221	Pseudo R2=0.3908		Log likelihood=−93.202647	

*Significant at 1 % LS

Table 12.6 Impact of SGSY on annual family income, monthly family consumption expenditure and employment status

Variable	Annual family income		Family consumption expenditure per month		Employment status of the interviewed sample	
Sample	Unmatched	ATT (on common support)	Unmatched	ATT (on common support)	Unmatched	ATT (on common support)
Treated	36836.6	37556.13	2813.62	2961.19	0.36	0.50
Controls	32720	34379.6	2509.13	2770.94	0.21	0.32
Difference	4116.604	3176.532	304.49	190.26	0.15	0.18
Bootstrap standard error		2391.06		224.36		0.104
z		1.33		0.85		1.74
P>*z*		0.18		0.40		0.08*

*Significant at 10 % LS

ings, family monthly food expenditure and family monthly health expenditure of the women interviewee.

Next, the results reported in Tables 12.6 and 12.7 are discussed. Table 12.6 shows that the estimated ATT measuring the impact of group participation on family income level, family consumption expenditure are all positive, but based on bootstrapped standard errors the study observed that none of them are significant. These results hold true if other matching algorithm like one-to-one nearest neighborhood matching with caliper level 0.01 and radius matching with caliper level 0.01 are used. Thus, based on these results the study can conclude that SGSY programme did not contribute towards significant increase in family income level and family monthly consumption expenditure. Table 12.7 shows that SGSY participation had a significant positive impact at 1 % level of significance (LS) on the monthly food expenditure of the family. Thus, in families where women participated in SHGs created under SGSY experienced an increase in the family food expenditure. This result implies that rural women who got employment and access to micro-credit under this programme contributed significantly to increase the family food expenditure. Secondly, it was observed that estimated ATT for family monthly savings is positive for treatment group but insignificant. SGSY programme tried to inculcate a habit of saving among the rural women as group participants have to save a constant

Table 12.7 Impact of SGSY on monthly food expenditure, monthly family saving and monthly health expenditure

Variable	Family food expenditure per month		Family savings per month		Family health expenditure per month	
Sample	Unmatched	ATT (on common support)	Unmatched	ATT (on common support)	Unmatched	ATT (on common support)
Treated	2032.26	2209.68	256.79	199.03	211.13	231.45
Controls	1306.09	1663.63	250.78	112.10	268.17	359.63
Difference	726.18	546.04	6.01	86.93	−57.04	−128.18
Bootstrap standard error		156.70		90.58		74.66
z		3.48		0.96		−1.72
P>z		0.00*		0.34		0.09

*significant at 1% LS

amount per month towards group-corpus. But the result shows that this saving habit of women did not have any significant impact on the family monthly savings. Finally, we observed that the programme did not have any impact on monthly health expenditure.

Further, in Table 12.6 the estimated ATT for employment status of those women who joined the programme compared to the control group is positive and significant at 10% LS. It indicates the treated sample has a 18% higher probability of being employed vis-à-vis the control group which is significant at 10% LS. However, this may not be due to SHG joining per se but unobserved characteristics that account for group-membership (and/or its impact). Sensitivity analysis explores the vulnerability of this impact estimate to selection on unobservable. Table 12.8 reports the result of sensitivity analysis using "mhbounds" module in STATA, (Becker and Caliendo 2007) to check the robustness of this matching estimate to the unobservable using a number Γ(gamma)≥ 1 where Γ is the ratio of the odds that the treated have this unobserved characteristic to the odds that the controls have it; a low odds ratio (approximately one) indicates that it is not unlikely that such an unobserved variable exists. The number Γ captures the degree of association, of an unobserved characteristic with the treatment and outcome, required for it (the unobserved characteristic) to explain the observed impact. (Rosenbaum (2002)). Basically, sensitivity analysis calculates the minimum Γ at which the estimated impact of SHG joining under SGSY on the outcome variable employment status is no longer statistically significant.

Table 12.8 shows that at $\Gamma = 1$, that is with no heterogeneity (unobservable) in the data, the Mantel–Haensze test statistic is significant. A positive selection bias occurs when an individual who is under the treatment group has a higher probability of being employed even without the treatment given that they have the same set of explanatory variables as the individuals in the comparison group and this can be observed by the significance level of Q_mh+statistic. It is found that the statistics is significant at 5% for $\Gamma \leq 2$ and at 10% up to $\Gamma = 2.20$. The sensitivity

Table 12.8 Sensitivity analysis—Mantel–Haenszel bounds for employment status under SGSY

Gamma	Q_mh+	Q_mh−	p_mh+	p_mh−
1.00	3.81	3.81	0.00	0.00
1.10	3.53	4.13	0.00	0.00
1.20	3.26	4.41	0.00	0.00
1.30	3.01	4.67	0.00	0.00
1.40	2.78	4.91	0.00	0.00
1.50	2.57	5.14	0.01	0.00
1.60	2.38	5.36	0.01	0.00
1.70	2.20	5.57	0.01	0.00
1.80	2.03	5.76	0.02	0.00
1.90	1.86	5.95	0.03	0.00
2.00	1.71	6.14	0.04	0.00
2.10	1.57	6.31	0.06	0.00
2.20	1.43	6.48	0.08	0.00
2.30	1.30	6.64	0.10	0.00
2.40	1.17	6.80	0.12	0.00
2.50	1.05	6.95	0.15	0.00

Gamma odds of differential assignment due to unobserved factors
Q_mh+ Mantel–Haenszel statistic (assumption: overestimation of treatment effect)
Q_mh− Mantel–Haenszel statistic (assumption: underestimation of treatment effect)
p_mh+ significance level (assumption: overestimation of treatment effect)
p_mh− significance level (assumption: underestimation of treatment effect)

analysis suggests that the impact on employment status is robust and is insensitive to unobserved factors even for a high value of $\Gamma \leq 2.20$. Thus, the average treatment effect on employment status for group participation is significant and insensitive to unobservable even with a high value for $\Gamma = 2.20$ (DiPrete and Gangl 2004; Duvendack and Palmer-Jones 2012). Thus, this subsection shows that even if SGSY has an insignificant positive impact on family income and family consumption expenditure of women under the purview of the programme, but has a positive significant impact on the employment status of the women.

Next the study tries to gauge the impact of MGNREGA programme on different outcome variables. In this case also, first the study measures the propensity score of the surveyed sample by estimating a logistic regression to determine the probability of joining MGNREGA programme using religion, natural log of number of family member, education level dummy and natural log of age as explanatory variables. Table 12.9 depicts the result.[10]

Table 12.9 shows that religion dummy positively affects the probability of joining MGNREGA programme that is Hindu women are more likely to hold a job card vis-à-vis Muslim women. This result is in line with the findings of Table 12.5, which shows that Muslim women are also less likely to take part in SGSY pro-

[10] In this case also treatment group consists of women who have joined MGNREGA and hold job cards and the control group includes women who are not under purview of any programme. Further, women who were group members as well as job card holders not included in the analysis.

Table 12.9 Logistic regression to determine the probability of joining MGNREGA (captured by probability of holding a job card)

Group dummy	Coefficient	Standard error	*z*	*P*>*z*
Religion dummy	3.181836	1.099626	2.89	0.004*
ln age	0.091227	0.986812	0.09	0.926
ln family member	4.230992	0.890386	4.75	0*
Education dummy	−0.28514	0.391325	−0.73	0.466
Constant	−7.76127	3.839778	−2.02	0.043
N=174	Pseudo R2=0.1927		Log likelihood=−89.95	

*Significant at 1 % LS

Table 12.10 Impact of MGNREGA on annual family income, monthly family consumption expenditure and employment status

Variable	Annual family income		Family consumption expenditure per month		Employment status of the interviewed sample	
Sample	Unmatched	ATT (on common support)	Unmatched	ATT (on common support)	Unmatched	ATT(on common support)
Treated	31701.69	32214.81	2586.44	2625.93	0.42	0.44
Controls	32720.00	39628.75	2509.13	3197.30	0.21	0.31
Difference	−1018.31	−7413.93	77.31	−571.38	0.22	0.13
Bootstrap standard. error		3015.70		237.72		0.10
Z		−2.46		−2.40		1.38
P>*z*		0.01		0.02		0.16

gramme. Both findings point to the fact that Muslim women are still out of reach of various employment generation programmes undertaken by the GoI. The other variable that is significant is the natural log of number of family members. This result was observed in Table 12.5 also. Thus, in large families women are more likely to join employment generation programme. Tables 12.10 and 12.11 show the estimated ATT measuring the impact of group participation on employment status, family income level and different family expenditures.

Table 12.10 clearly shows that participation in the MGNREGA programme did not improve annual family income and or monthly consumption expenditure of the interviewed women. In this case also psmatch 2 module in STATA is used to estimate propensity score and perform the Gaussian kernel matching with bandwidth 0.05 with common support option. In case of employment status, the study observes a positive impact but it is insignificant. This result is not robust and may be attributable to the existence of unobservable as the sensitivity analysis shows that this impact on employment status becomes insignificant for $\Gamma > 1.55$.[11] Table 12.11 shows

[11] Results of the sensitivity analysis are with the author.

Table 12.11 Impact of MGNREGA on monthly food expenditure, monthly family saving and monthly health expenditure

Variable	Family food expenditure per month		Family savings per month		Family health expenditure per month	
Sample	Unmatched	ATT (on common support)	Unmatched	ATT (on common support)	Unmatched	ATT (on common support)
Treated	1725.08	1748.15	11.53	12.59	360.17	358.33
Controls	1306.09	1852.80	250.78	230.42	268.17	455.26
Difference	419.00	−104.65	−239.26	−217.83	92.00	−96.93
Bootstrap standard error		177.8676		79.55		87.66
Z		−0.59		−2.74		−1.11
P>z		0.556		0.01		0.27

that the MGNREGA participation did not have any impact on monthly family food expenditure, savings and health expenditure.

The comparison of the results presented in Tables 12.6, 12.7, and 12.10, 12.11 brings out some interesting facts. It shows that group participation under SGSY has a positive impact on family food expenditure and employment status of the surveyed women, though its impact on annual family income and monthly family consumption expenditure and family savings is insignificant. On the other hand, MGNREGA, aims at guaranteeing 100 days of wage employment in unskilled manual work to aspiring adult members of household who did not have any significant impact on employment status of the surveyed women as well as on their annual family income and monthly consumption, savings and other expenditure. Reason may be as follows: SGSY aimed at supplying micro-credit to rural women for a productive purpose to make them self-sufficient. The survey observed that group members received productive training like poultry farming, animal husbandry, handicraft works and others to start their own projects.[12] Though the survey observed that in some cases the loans received by the women are used by the family members or for consumption purpose, but at least a small fraction went in the right direction. The result showing a positive impact on employment status and family food expenditure of women indicates towards this fact. On the other hand, MGNREGA is an employment guarantee programme that offers employment in nonskilled jobs. It was observed that many women who hold job card did not actually get employment. Various authors have cited different reasons for this phenomenon. Das (2012b) observed in a field survey that villagers in northern parts of West Bengal have not been able to get the full benefits of the scheme. They proposed that one possible reason of the poor performance of this programme is that people were often not aware of the basic guidelines regarding wage structures and other legal entitlements. This has

[12] It was observed that out of 106 group members who are included in propensity scoring analysis, 33 members received productive training and among them 12 members were employed at the time of survey.

led to corruption and reduced the efficacy of the programme. Das (2013) considered that women participation is low because of low level of awareness about the process and entitlements of the programme, lack of child care facility, work site facility and illegal presence of contractors.

12.4 Conclusion

Based on a primary survey on selected blocks from 24 Parganas (North), West Bengal, India, this chapter tries to find the performance of two employment generation policies namely, SGSY and MGNREGA on the employment status, annual family income and monthly average consumption, savings, food and health expenditures of the surveyed women. The descriptive analysis showed that measures of central tendency for family income, consumption savings and food expenditures are significantly higher for SGSY participants than the other categories. The econometric analysis also showed some interesting results. First, it has been observed that the probability of joining SGSY programme and MGNREGA is low for Muslim women than the Hindu women. This indicates towards inefficiencies and failure of employment policies to include Muslim women who are still unable to enjoy the benefits of these policies. Second, in large families women are more likely to join employment generation programmes. This may be due to two reasons. In large families women receive help from other family members in household chores or for child care. So they have a better chance to join employment generation programmes. Alternatively, women from large families join employment generation programme as these families need more income to cover expenditures. Results of propensity score matching (Gaussian kernel matching with 0.05 bandwidth under common support option) show that SGSY participants have significantly higher monthly food expenditure and higher rate of employment compared to non-participants in any employment policy; that is, SGSY participation had a positive significant impact on employment generation of surveyed rural women. This in turn increased the family food expenditure also. However, this policy showed an insignificant positive impact on annual family income, monthly consumption expenditure and savings. Alternatively, MGNREGA failed to register any significant impact on the employment status, annual family income and monthly consumption and other expenditures of surveyed rural women. This result is in concurrence with the findings of other studies like Dey and Bedi (2010), Ghosh (2011) and Das (2012a). These studies also showed that in different parts of West Bengal MGNREGA did not have much success in generation of employment. Thus, our result brings out an interesting policy implication. It simply shows that the employment status of rural women cannot be improved by an employment guarantee programme like MGNREGA, which provides wage employment in unskilled works. This programme did not provide any training to women to make them self-sufficient. In this respect, SGSY was ahead of this programme. SGSY, which was a self-help group-based micro-credit programme actually tried to generate gainful self-employment for rural women through productive training and financial inclusion. It had its drawbacks, but it realized that in a patriarchal rural society like India where women had to devote hours to household chores and child care, involving women in self-employment projects, which they can run from their houses is a much better option than wage employment in unskilled public works. Furthermore, supply of micro-credit not only helped these women to start their own project but also helped families to become financially included. Thus, future employment policies for rural women must try to make women self-sufficient through training and capacity creation so that they can have equal access to productive assets and infrastructure and become truly empowered (Table. A1).

Appendix I

Table A1 Description of the variables

		N	
Dependent variable:	Group dummy = 1	106	
	Group dummy = 0	115	
Independent variables	Religion dummy = 1 if Hindu	51	
	Religion dummy = 0 if Muslim	170	
	Education dummy = 1 for above primary education	93	
	Education dummy = 0 for below primary education	128	
	Party at gram panchayat during 2004–2008		
	Gram panchayat party-dummy = 1 if gram panchayat was under control of left-front	62	
	Gram panchayat party-dummy = 0 if gram panchayat was under control of left-front	159	
	Log of age of the sample (ln age)	mean	3.571834
		s.d	0.244534
		median	3.583519
	Log of total family member(ln family member)	mean	1.544201
		s.d	0.217202
		median	1.609438

Acknowledgements The author acknowledges the financial support provided by University Grants Commission, India for undertaking the primary household survey.

References

Banerjee (Chatterjee) T (2009) Economic impact of self-help groups—A case study. J Rural Dev 20(4):451–467

Bardhan P, Mitra S, Mookherjee D, Sarkar A (2008) Political participation, clientelism and targeting of local government programs: analysis of survey results from Rural West Bengal, India. Discussion paper, ERU/2008-03. http://www.isical.ac.in/~eru/erudp/2008-03.pdf. Accessed 09 May 2012

Bardhan P, Mookherjee D (2011) Political clientelism and capture: theory and evidence from West Bengal. http://emlab.berkeley.edu/users/webfac/bardhan/papers/clientcapmay2011.pdf. Accessed 09 May 2012

Becker SO, Caliendo M (2007) Sensitivity analysis for average treatment effects. STATA J 7(1):71–83

Carswell G, Neve G De (2013) Women at the crossroads implementation of employment guarantee scheme in Rural Tamil Nadu. Econ Polit Wkly xlviii(52):82–93

D'Agostino Ralph B Jr (2007) Propensity scores in cardiovascular research. Circulation doi:10.1161/CIRCULATIONAHA.105.594952

Das SK (2013) A brief scanning on performance of Mahatma Gandhi National Rural Employment Guarantee Act in Assam, India. Am J Rural Dev 1(3):49–61. doi:10.12691/ajrd-1-3-3

Das U (2012a) Accuracy of targeting and implications of rationing in Mahatma Gandhi National Rural Employment Guarantee Scheme: evidence from West Bengal, India. http://ssrn.com/abstract=2157089 or http://dx.doi.org/10.2139/ssrn.2157089. Accessed 07 Oct 2014

Das U (2012b) Awareness about Mahatma Gandhi National Rural Employment Guarantee Act: some evidence from the northern parts of West Bengal, India. Econ Bull 32(1):528–537

Das U (2013) Does political connections and affiliation affect allocation of benefits in the Rural Employment Guarantee Scheme: evidence from West Bengal India. http://ssrn.com/abstract=2262533 or http://dx.doi.org/10.2139/ssrn.2262533. Accessed 07 Oct 2014

Dasgupta S, Sudarshan RM (2011) Issues in labour market inequality and women's participation in India's National Rural Employment Guarantee Programme, Policy Integration, Department International Labour Office Geneva, Working Paper 98. http://www.ilo.org/wcmsp5/groups/public/---dgreports/---integration/documents/publication/wcms_153042.pdf. Accessed 07 Oct 2014

Dey S, Bedi AS (2010) The National Rural Employment Guarantee Scheme in Birbhum. Econ Polit Wkly 45(41):19–25

DiPrete TA, Gangl M (2004) Assessing bias in the estimation of causal effects: Rosenbaum bounds on matching estimators and instrumental variables estimation with imperfect instruments. Sociol Methodol 34(1):271–310

Dreze J, Khera R (2011). The battle for employment guarantee. In Khera R (ed) The battle for employment guarantee. Oxford University Press, New Delhi

Drèze J, Oldiges C (2011) NREGA: the official picture. In Khera R (ed) The battle for employment guarantee. Oxford University Press, New Delhi, pp 21–39

Dutta P, Murgai R, Ravallion M, Walle D van de (2012) Does India's Employment Guarantee Scheme guarantee employment. Econ Polit Wkly XLVII(16):55–64

Duvendack M, Palmer-Jones R (2012) The microfinance of reproduction and the reproduction of microfinance: understanding the connections between microfinance, empowerment, contraception and fertility in Bangladesh in the 1990s. Working paper 40, DEV working paper series, The School of International Development, University of East Anglia, UK. https://www.uea.ac.uk/documents/6347571/6504346/paper-40/789deb18-9a59-4538-85d0-d4dcb5622874. Accessed 07 Oct 2014

Ghosh J (2011) Impact of NREGA on wage rates, food security and rural urban migration in West Bengal. Study no. 169. Agro-Economic Research Centre Visva-Bharati Santiniketan. http://www.visvabharati.ac.in/InstitutionsCentresSchools/Contents/AERC-DETAIL/Final-Report-169.pdf. Accessed 07 Oct 2014

Heinrich C, Maffioli A, Vázquez G (2010) A primer for applying propensity-score matching impact-evaluation guidelines. Technical Notes No. IDB-TN-161. Office of Strategic Planning and Development Effectiveness, Inter-American Development Bank. http://idbdocs.iadb.org/wsdocs/getdocument.aspx?docnum=35320229. Accessed 03 Aug 2013

Imai SK, Thankom A, Annim SK (2010) Microfinance and household poverty reduction: new evidence from India. World Dev 38(12):1760–1774. doi:10.1016/j.worlddev.2010.04.006

Khandker S (2003) Micro-finance and poverty evidence using panel data from Bangladesh. Policy research working paper 2945, World Bank, Research Development Group

Khandker S (2005) Microfinance and poverty: Evidence using panel data from Bangladesh. World Bank Econ Rev 19(2):263–286

Khera R, Nayak N (2009) Woman workers and perceptions of the NREGA. Econ Polit Wkly 44(43):49–57

Liu Y, Barrett CB (2012) Heterogeneous pro-poor targeting in India's Mahatma Gandhi National Rural Employment Guarantee Scheme. IFPRI Discussion paper 01218. http://ssrn.com/abstract=2198460 or http://dx.doi.org/10.2139/ssrn.2198460. Accessed 09 Oct 2014

McKernan Signe-Mary (2002) The impact of microcredit programs on self-employment profits: do noncredit program aspects matter? Review Econ Stat 84(1):93–115

Narayanan S, Das U (2014) Employment guarantee for women in india evidence on participation and rationing in the MGNREGA from the National Sample Survey. http://www.igidr.ac.in/pdf/publication/WP-2014-017.pdf. Accessed 07 Oct 2014

Parida CP, Sinha A (2010) Performance and sustainability of self-help groups in India: a gender perspective. Asian Dev Rev 27(1):80–103

Rosenbaum PR (2002) Observational studies. Springer, New York

Swain Bali R, Floro M (2007) Effect of microfinance on vulnerability, poverty and risk in low income households. Working Paper 2007:31, Department of Economics, Uppsala University

Swain Bali R, Varghese A (2009) Does self-help group participation lead to asset creation? World Dev 37(10):1674–1682

Tedeschi G (2008) Overcoming selection bias in microcredit impact assessments: a case study in Peru. J Dev Stud 44(4):504–518

Chapter 13
Poverty in West Bengal: A Review of Recent Performance and Programmes

Siddhartha Mitra

13.1 Introduction

The objective of this chapter is to review the performance of West Bengal in regard to poverty alleviation from the 1970s to the beginning of this century. The review is done in a comparative perspective, that is, Bengal is compared to other major states in India in regard to poverty incidence and alleviation, and districts within West Bengal are compared to each other in regard to incidence of poverty. Finally, the performance of West Bengal in a recent poverty alleviation programme—that which is run under the Mahatma Gandhi National Rural Employment Guarantee Act (MNREGA)—is compared to other recent states as well as analysed in regard to the differential performance of districts.

13.2 Poverty Alleviation and Incidence in West Bengal: A Comparison with Other Major States

13.2.1 Poverty Incidence and Alleviation in West Bengal and Other Major States: 1973–1974 to 2009–2010

Estimates for 1973–1974, 1977–1978, 1983 and 1987–1988 are comparable as these estimates use the same rural and urban poverty line baskets formulated on

The author is grateful for funding and research assistance to the Centre for West Bengal Economy, Department of Economics, Jadavpur University, Kolkata, under the University Grant Commission's UPE-II (Universities with Potential for Excellence) scheme.

S. Mitra (✉)
Department of Economics, Jadavpur University,
700032 Kolkata, India
e-mail: mitsid@yahoo.com

S. Banerjee et al. (eds.), *Understanding Development*, India Studies in Business and Economics, DOI 10.1007/978-81-322-2455-6_13

the basis of 1973–1974 National Sample Survey (NSS) consumer expenditure data after making allowance for differences in prices across states and time periods. The estimates for 1993–1994, 2004–2005 and 2009–2010 are also mutually comparable as these are all based on a poverty line basket formulated on the basis of 2004–2005 NSS data. However, poverty estimates for years preceding 1993–1994 are not comparable with those for years following it because of the use of different poverty line baskets in arriving at these respective estimates (Table 13.1).

In 1973–1974 the poverty incidence in West Bengal was as high as 63.43 % (in other words, 63.43 % of the population exhibited personal consumption expenditure that was below the poverty line). This was distinctly higher than the All India incidence of 54.9 %. Only one state—Orissa—exhibited a higher incidence of poverty (66.18 %). The next 4 years—from 1973–1974 to 1977–1978—did not see any dramatic poverty alleviation either in West Bengal or India as a whole. While in India poverty dropped marginally to 51.3 %, in West Bengal poverty declined to 60.52 %—the magnitude of poverty decline in India was 3.6 percentage points at the rate of 0.9 percentage points per annum, and in Bengal it was a comparable 2.88 percentage points at a rate of 0.72 percentage points per annum. Orissa (70.07), Madhya Pradesh (61.78) and Bihar (61.55) exhibited higher incidence of poverty than West Bengal in 1977–1978. Thus, among the major 15 states of India, Bengal was the fourth poorest state (by 'poorest' state we mean the state with the highest incidence of poverty; similarly the fourth poorest state would mean the state with the fourth highest incidence of poverty) in 1977–1978 as opposed to being ranked the second poorest state in 1973–1974.

Table 13.1 Poverty incidence in India and large states. (Source: Rangarajan et al. (2014); Bandyopadhyay (2010))

	Old methodology				Tendulkar methodology		
	1973–1974	1977–1978	1983	1987–1988	1993–1994	2004–2005	2009–2010
State							
Andhra Pradesh	48.86	39.31	28.91	25.86	44.6	29.6	21.1
Assam	51.21	57.15	40.47	36.21	51.8	34.4	37.9
Bihar	61.91	61.55	62.22	52.13	60.5	54.4	53.5
Gujarat	48.15	41.23	32.79	31.54	37.8	31.6	23
Haryana	35.36	29.55	21.37	16.64	35.9	24.1	20.1
Karnataka	54.47	48.78	38.24	37.53	49.5	33.3	23.6
Kerala	59.79	52.22	40.42	31.79	31.3	19.6	12
Madhya Pradesh	61.78	61.78	49.78	43.07	44.6	48.6	36.7
Maharashtra	53.24	55.88	43.44	40.41	47.9	38.2	24.5
Orissa	66.18	70.07	65.29	55.58	59.1	57.2	37
Punjab	28.15	19.27	16.18	13.2	22.4	20.9	15.9
Rajasthan	46.14	37.42	34.46	35.15	38.3	34.4	24.8
Tamil Nadu	54.94	54.79	51.66	43.39	44.6	29.4	17.1
Uttar Pradesh	57.07	49.05	47.07	41.46	48.4	40.9	37.7
West Bengal	63.43	60.52	54.85	44.72	39.4	34.2	26.7
India	*54.9*	*51.3*	*44.5*	*38.9*	*45.3*	*37.2*	*29.8*

From 1977–1978 to 1983, there was a substantial decline in poverty in West Bengal to 54.85 %. The magnitude of this decline was 5.67 percentage points at a rate of 0.945 percentage points per annum. In comparison, the incidence of poverty for the whole of India registered a decline of 6.8 percentage points at a rate of 1.13 percentage points per annum to reach 44.5 %. Thus, though West Bengal achieved significant poverty alleviation this was not as large as that for the whole of India. In regard to ranking of states on the basis of poverty in 1983, out of the states which were ranked as more poor than West Bengal in 1977–1978 (Madhya Pradesh, Orissa and Bihar), Madhya Pradesh's poverty incidence went below that of West Bengal to reach 49.78 %. Thus, West Bengal was ranked as the third poorest state after Orissa and Bihar, which were, respectively, the poorest and the second poorest states.

From 1983 to 1987–1988, Bengal did much better in terms of poverty alleviation than the whole of India. Poverty in Bengal dropped from 54.85 to 44.72 %—a decline of 10.13 percentage points at a rate of 2.53 percentage points per annum. In comparison, the incidence of poverty in India as a whole dropped less substantially from 44.5 to 38.9 %—a drop of 5.6 percentage points at the rate of 1.4 percentage points per annum. However, despite Bengal's impressive showing in this period the state continued to be ranked as the third poorest major state, with only Orissa and Bihar exhibiting more poverty.

We now shift to the year 1993–1994; as mentioned earlier, the poverty numbers for this year and subsequent ones are not comparable to those for 1987–1988 and earlier years. Therefore, we should not work out the magnitudes of and rates of poverty alleviation for the period 1987–1988 to 1993–1994. Only the rankings for 1993–1994 can be scrutinized and compared to the rankings for previous years. As many as nine states emerge as poorer than West Bengal in 1993–1994—in order of declining incidence of poverty Bihar, Orissa, Assam, Karnataka, Uttar Pradesh, Maharashtra, Andhra Pradesh, Madhya Pradesh and Tamil Nadu. Thus, over the period 1987–1988 to 1993–1994 Bengal transformed itself from being ranked the third poorest out of 15 major states to the sixth least poor (tenth poorest) state.

Over the period of 1993–1994 to 2004–2005, West Bengal continued to undergo significant poverty alleviation—poverty declined by 5.2 percentage points at a rate of 0.47 percentage points per annum from 39.4 to 34.2 %. However, the rate of poverty alleviation was much slower than that for the whole of India—from 1993–1994 to 2004–2005 the incidence of poverty in India declined from 45.3 to 37.2 %. This implied a decline of 8.1 percentage points at a rate of 0.74 percentage points per annum. In terms of ranking Karnataka, Andhra Pradesh and Tamil Nadu which were ranked as 'more poor' in 1993–1994 now became 'less poor' than West Bengal while exactly the opposite was true for Rajasthan. As a result Bengal was ranked as the eighth least poor (as well as the eighth poorest) state.

From 2004–2005 to 2009–2010, poverty in West Bengal declined from 34.2 to 26.7 %. This was an impressive decline of 7.5 percentage points at the rate of 1.5 percentage points per annum. For India as a whole, poverty declined by 7.4 percentage points from 37.2 to 29.8 % at a rate which was very similar to that of Bengal at 1.48 percentage points per annum. In terms of rankings, the state slipped a bit

Table 13.2 Rankings of major states in terms of poverty incidence

	1973–1974	1977–1978	1983	1987–1988	1993–1994	2004–2005	2009–2010
Andhra Pradesh	11	12	13	13	9	11	11
Assam	10	5	8	9	3	6	2
Bihar	3	3	2	2	1	2	1
Gujarat	12	11	12	12	12	10	10
Haryana	14	14	14	14	13	13	12
Karnataka	8	10	10	8	4	9	9
Kerala	5	8	9		14	15	15
Madhya Pradesh	4	2	5	5	8	3	5
Maharashtra	9	6	7	7	6	5	8
Orissa	1	1	1	1	2	1	4
Punjab	15	15	15	15	15	14	14
Rajasthan	13	13	11	10	11	7	7
Tamil Nadu	7	7	4	4	7	12	13
Uttar Pradesh	6	9	6	6	5	4	3
West Bengal	2	4	3	3	10	8	6

A ranking of 1 is given to the state with the highest incidence of poverty; higher numbers are assigned as ranks for lower incidence of poverty

in 2009–2010—only five states (as opposed to seven states in 2004–2005) were ranked as more poor than it, namely in descending order of poverty Bihar, Assam, Uttar Pradesh, Orissa and Madhya Pradesh.

Table 13.2 gives the rankings of various states in different years in terms of poverty incidence. Overall, Bengal progresses in terms of its rankings in regard to incidence of poverty—from being a state which had the second highest incidence of poverty among the 15 major states in 1973–1974 to being ranked the sixth highest in regard to the same aspect in 2009–2010. Eight states saw deterioration in rankings in the mentioned period—Bihar (3 to 1), Assam (10 to 2), Uttar Pradesh (6 to 3), Rajasthan (13 to 7), Maharashtra (9 to 8), Gujarat (12 to 10), Haryana (14 to 12) and Punjab (15 to 14)—while Andhra Pradesh did not see any change in rankings. Five states other than Bengal saw an improvement in rankings—Orissa (1 to 4), Madhya Pradesh (4 to 5), Karnataka (8 to 9), Tamil Nadu (7 to 13) and Kerala (5 to 15). Only two of the states—Tamil Nadu and Kerala—saw a bigger improvement in rankings than West Bengal during the relevant period.

Table 13.3 presents the rates of poverty alleviation in the periods 1973–1974 to 1987–1988 and 1993–1994 to 2009–2010 for West Bengal and other major states as well as India as a whole. It is seen that in the first period West Bengal at 1.336 percentage points per annum witnessed faster poverty alleviation than India as a whole at 1.143 percentage points per annum. During this period only three states exhibited faster poverty alleviation than West Bengal—Kerala (2 percentage points per annum), Andhra Pradesh (1.643) and Haryana (1.337). However, during the second of the mentioned periods Bengal at 0.794 percentage points per annum was way below the national average of 0.969 percentage points per annum. Ten states

Table 13.3 Poverty alleviation rates in major states

	1973–1974 to 1987–1988		1993–1994 to 2009–2010	
State	Rate of poverty alleviation[a]	Rank	Rate of poverty alleviation	Rank
Andhra Pradesh	1.643	2	1.469	3
Assam	1.071	9	0.869	9
Bihar	0.699	15	0.438	14
Gujarat	1.186	7	0.925	8
Haryana	1.337	3	0.988	7
Karnataka	1.210	6	1.619	2
Kerala	2.000	1	1.206	6
Madhya Pradesh	1.336	4	0.494	13
Maharashtra	0.916	11	1.463	4
Orissa	0.757	14	1.381	5
Punjab	1.068	10	0.406	15
Rajasthan	0.785	13	0.844	10
Tamil Nadu	0.825	12	1.719	1
Uttar Pradesh	1.115	8	0.669	12
West Bengal	1.336	4	0.794	11
India	*1.143*		*0.969*	

[a]Calculated as percentage points per annum

which alleviated poverty at a higher rate were Tamil Nadu (1.719 percentage points per annum), Karnataka (1.619), Andhra Pradesh (1.469), Maharashtra (1.463), Orissa (1.381), Kerala (1.206), Haryana (0.988), Gujarat (0.925), Assam (0.869) and Rajasthan (0.844). The four states which had a worse performance than West Bengal were Uttar Pradesh (0.669 percentage points per annum), Madhya Pradesh (0.494), Bihar (0.438) and Punjab (0.406).

One significant observation which emerges is that the pre-liberalization period (1973–1974 to 1987–1988) saw a higher rate of poverty alleviation in West Bengal than the post-liberalization period (1993–1994 to 2009–2010)—1.336 percentage points per annum in the first period as opposed to 0.794 in the second period. West Bengal was not an aberration in this regard. Nine other states exhibited the same tendency—Andhra Pradesh with poverty alleviation at the rate of 1.643 percentage points per annum in the first period as opposed to 1.469 percentage points in the second period; Assam (1.071 vs. 0.869); Bihar (0.699 vs. 0.438); Gujarat (1.186 vs. 0.925); Haryana (1.337 vs. 0.988); Kerala (2 vs. 1.206); Madhya Pradesh (1.336 vs. 0.494); Punjab (1.068 vs. 0.406) and Uttar Pradesh (1.115 vs. 0.669). However, the difference in the rates of poverty alleviation corresponding to the two periods is large in the case of West Bengal (0.542 percentage points per annum) and is surpassed only by Kerala (0.794), Madhya Pradesh (0.842) and Punjab (0.662). It deserves note here that there were five states which experienced faster poverty alleviation in the post-liberalization phase than in the pre-liberalization phase—Tamil Nadu was the frontrunner among these states and averaged 1.719 percentage points per annum in the second period (1993–1994 to 2009–2010) as opposed to 0.825 percentage points in the first period (1973–1974 to 1987–1988); others were Karnataka (1.619

Table 13.4 Rural and urban incidence of poverty and urban bias in poverty in 2009–2010. (Source: Rangarajan et al. (2014))

	Poverty			Ranks[a]		
	Rural	Urban	Urban bias in poverty	Rural poverty	Urban poverty	Urban bias in poverty
Andhra Pradesh	22.8	17.7	5.1	11	13	12
Assam	39.9	26.1	13.8	3	3	3
Bihar	55.3	39.4	15.9	1	1	2
Gujarat	26.7	17.9	8.8	8	12	6
Haryana	18.6	23	−4.4	13	5	15
Karnataka	26.1	19.6	6.5	10	9	11
Kerala	12	12.1	−0.1	15	15	13
Madhya Pradesh	42	22.9	19.1	2	6	1
Maharashtra	29.5	18.3	11.2	6	10	5
Orissa	39.2	25.9	13.3	5	4	4
Punjab	14.6	18.1	−3.5	14	11	14
Rajasthan	26.4	19.9	6.5	9	8	11
Tamil Nadu	21.2	12.8	8.4	12	14	7
Uttar Pradesh	39.4	31.7	7.7	4	2	8
West Bengal	28.8	22	6.8	7	7	9

[a]A lower level of poverty or urban bias implies a higher rank

vs. 1.210), Orissa (1.381 vs. 0.757), Maharashtra (1.463 vs. 0.916), and Rajasthan (0.844 vs. 0.785). Significantly three of these states—Maharashtra, Karnataka and Rajasthan—had attained a poverty level lower than that attained by West Bengal at the end of the first phase. Thus, their higher post-liberalization rates of poverty alleviation can in no way be attributed to a higher level of poverty at the end of the first phase leaving room for rapid poverty alleviation in the second phase.

As a last exercise, we work out the urban bias in poverty (rural poverty rate less urban poverty) in various states of India for the year 2009–2010 after noting how states compare in terms of rural and urban poverty (refer to Table 13.4). We note that Bengal is seventh highest out of 15 states in terms of both rural and urban poverty, that is, there are eight states each doing better than Bengal in terms of rural and urban poverty (i.e. exhibiting respectively lower rural and urban poverty). The states doing better on the rural front are Kerala, Punjab, Haryana, Tamil Nadu, Andhra Pradesh, Karnataka, Rajasthan and Gujarat. The states doing better on the urban front are Kerala, Tamil Nadu, Andhra Pradesh, Gujarat, Punjab, Maharashtra, Karnataka and Rajasthan. Thus, as many as seven states (Kerala, Punjab, Tamil Nadu, Andhra Pradesh, Karnataka, Rajasthan and Gujarat) do better than Bengal in terms of both rural and urban poverty. The six states performing worse than West Bengal on the rural front are Bihar, Madhya Pradesh, Assam, Uttar Pradesh, Orissa and Maharashtra. The first five of these states (the sixth being Haryana) also do worse than West Bengal on the urban front.

In regard to urban bias in poverty (alleviation), a lower number (which is calculated as the algebraic difference between rural and urban poverty) denotes lower bias. With an urban bias of 6.8 percentage points the rank that Bengal gets is 9—there are as many as eight states with a higher urban bias than Bengal. The states with a higher urban bias are Madhya Pradesh (19.1 percentage points), Bihar (15.9), Assam (13.8), Orissa (13.3), Maharashtra (11.2), Gujarat (8.8), Tamil Nadu (8.4) and Uttar Pradesh (7.7). The six states that show lower urban bias are Haryana (−4.4 percentage points), Punjab (−3.5), Kerala (−0.1), Andhra Pradesh (5.1), Karnataka (6.5) and Rajasthan (6.5).

13.2.2 Poverty Incidence in the Districts of West Bengal

Gupta and Chaudhuri (2009) use the 61st round of National Sample Survey (for 2004–2005) to work out district level estimates of poverty. What worked to their advantage was the sampling scheme used in this round of the NSS survey—districts were taken as strata and their rural and urban parts as sub strata. The poverty estimates were computed using the state-specific poverty lines as released by the Planning Commission in March 2007—for West Bengal this is ₹ 382.82 for rural areas and ₹ 449.32 for urban areas. This yields a head count ratio for West Bengal of 28.4 % in rural areas and 13.5 % in urban areas. Note the difference of this estimate with that worked out using the Tendulkar Methodology (one which involved poverty lines of ₹ 572.51 in urban areas and ₹ 445.38 in rural areas): The incidence of poverty in rural and urban areas according to the Tendulkar methodology was 38.2 % and 24.4 %, respectively (Table 13.5).[1]

If we look at the poverty figures for districts of West Bengal (as worked out by Gupta and Chaudhuri), the district with the lowest incidence of urban poverty is Kolkata (2.3 %). Kolkata is followed in order of increasing incidence of urban poverty by Medinipur (7.4 %), Barddhaman (7.55), North 24 Parganas (9.1), Howrah (9.53), Darjeeling (9.6), Dakshin Dinajpur (9.8) and Maldah (9.9). There are thus as many as eight districts with an incidence of urban poverty of less than 10 % (low urban poverty districts). On the other hand, there are as many as 5 districts with an incidence of urban poverty exceeding 20 % (high-urban-poverty districts): Puruliya (36.9 %) followed by Uttar Dinajpur (31), Birbhum (30.9), Bankura (28.3) and Cooch Behar (22.4). There are 5 other districts with moderate incidence of urban poverty (between 10 and 20 %): South 24 Parganas (10.2 %), Murshidabad (12.33), Hooghly (14.2), Nadia (16.5) and Jalpaiguri (18.5).

If one looks at regions, then the **Southeast** is characterized by low to moderate incidence of urban poverty—Kolkata has the lowest incidence (2.3 %) while Nadia has the highest (16.5). The **Southwest** with the exception of Medinipur (7.4 %) exhibits very high-urban-poverty levels with Puruliya at 36.9 %, Bankura at 28.3 % and Birbhum at 30.9 %. In the northern zone, the districts of Darjeeling, Dakshin Dinajpur and Maldah exhibit low levels of urban poverty at 9.6, 9.8 and 9.9 %, respectively; Jalpaiguri exhibits moderate level of poverty at 18.5 % and Cooch Be-

[1] These were adopted as official estimates using the Planning Commission.

Table 13.5 Poverty in the districts of West Bengal

	Rural	Urban
Southwest		
Bankura	28.5	28.3
Birbhum	39.2	30.9
Medinipur	21.8	7.4
Puruliya	31.2	36.9
Southeast		
Barddhaman	20.3	7.55
Howrah	21.6	9.53
Kolkata		2.3
Nadia	18.3	16.5
Murshidabad	55.9	12.33
Hooghly	21.1	14.2
North 24 Parganas	20.6	9.1
South 24 Parganas	18.5	10.2
North		
Cooch Behar	11.2	22.4
Darjeeling	14.7	9.6
Dakshin Dinajpur	48.9	9.8
Jalpaiguri	29	18.5
Maldah	46	9.9
Uttar Dinajpur	49	31

har and Uttar Dinajpur exhibit high levels of urban poverty at 22.4 and 31 %, respectively. Thus, the intensity of urban poverty varies across the districts of this zone.

While looking at rural poverty, we keep in mind the general tendency for rural poverty to exceed urban poverty—West Bengal is no exception with the incidence of poverty at the state level being 28.4 % for rural areas and 13.5 % for urban areas (according to Gupta and Chaudhuri 2009). Keeping this in mind, we consider, in our district level analysis, rural poverty below 20 % to be low, between 20 and 30 % to be moderate and above 30 % to be high. As far as the **Southeast** is concerned, Murshidabad is the outlier with a rural poverty of 55.9 %; the other districts exhibit low to moderate poverty—the highest is exhibited by Howrah (21.6 %) and the lowest by Nadia (18.3). The **Southwest** exhibits moderate to high rural poverty—the incidence of poverty ranges from 21.8 % (Medinipur) to 39.2 % (Birbhum). In regard to the North, the incidence of rural poverty ranges from low to moderate to high: Darjeeling and Cooch Behar exhibit low rural poverty at 14.7 and 11.2 %; in Jalpaiguri rural poverty is moderate at 29 % and finally in Dakshin Dinajpur, Maldah and Uttar Dinajpur rural poverty is high at 48.9, 46 and 49 %. Among all districts, Murshidabad (55.9 %) has the highest incidence of rural poverty followed by Uttar Dinajpur (49), Dakshin Dinajpur (48.9), Maldah (46) and Birbhum (39.2). The first of these districts belong to the southeastern zone, the next three to the northern zone and the last to the southwestern zone. The district with the lowest incidence of rural poverty (note that Kolkata is excluded from the analysis of rural poverty as only ur-

Table 13.6 Incidence of urban and rural poverty by region

Constituent districts	Incidence of urban poverty	Incidence of rural poverty	
Southeast	Barddhaman, Howrah, Kolkata, Nadia, Hooghly, North 24 Parganas, South 24 Parganas, Murshidabad	Low to moderate	Low to moderate with Murshidabad the only outlier exhibiting very high rural poverty
Southwest	Bankura, Medinipur, Puruliya, Birbhum	High (Medinipur is the exception)	Moderate to high
North	Cooch Behar, Darjeeling, Dakshin Dinajpur, Jalpaiguri, Uttar Dinajpur, Maldah	Varies: low in large areas but there are pockets of both moderate and high poverty	All three levels of poverty—low, moderate and high—are to be found in different districts

Table 13.7 Urban bias in poverty among districts in West Bengal

	Urban bias in poverty (percentage points)	Rank for urban bias
Bankura	0.2	3
Barddhaman	12.75	12
Birbhum	8.3	8
Cooch Behar	−11.2	1
Dakshin Dinajpur	39.1	16
Darjeeling	5.1	5
Hooghly	6.9	6
Howrah	12.07	11
Jalpaiguri	10.5	9
Maldah	36.1	15
Medinipur	14.4	13
Murshidabad	43.57	17
Nadia	1.8	4
North 24 Parganas	11.5	10
Puruliya	−5.7	2
South 24 Parganas	8.3	7
Uttar Dinajpur	18	14

ban population resides in that district) is Cooch Behar (11.2 %) followed by Darjeeling (14.7), Nadia (18.3), South 24 Parganas (18.5) and Barddhaman (20.3)—these districts either belong to the **North** or **Southeast**.

From Table 13.6, it can be observed that the performances in regard to urban and rural poverty are well correlated. In regard to urban bias in poverty (see Table 13.7), the lowest bias is exhibited by Cooch Behar (− 11.2 percentage points) followed by Puruliya (5.7) and Bankura (0.2). While the first district belongs to the North, the other two belong to the **Southwest**. The highest bias among all districts is exhibited by Murshidabad (43.57) followed by Dakshin Dinajpur (39.1) and Maldah (36.1). All three districts belong to the **central** region.

13.3 The Implementation of MNREGA in West Bengal: A Comparative Analysis

The MNREGA guarantees 100 days of unskilled employment to any rural adult who seeks it. It alleviates poverty in at least three ways: First, it provides employment at a respectable wage; second, by doing so it forces others using unskilled labour to match the MNREGA wage; third, since the labour employed by the MNREGA is used to create assets (sources of irrigation, rural roads, etc.), it is indirectly the cause of production and employment born out of these assets. We now go on to analyse the impact MNREGA has had in West Bengal and compare it with the impact felt in other major states. A good measure of impact would be the percentage of rural households provided employment through MNREGA (Table 13.8).

We see that West Bengal does reasonably well in terms of percentage of rural households employed through MNREGA without being at the top. In terms of this variable, it is ranked sixth, seventh, sixth and fifth in the years 2008–2009, 2009–2010, 2011–2012 and 2012–2013. During the first 3 years, the mentioned percentage for West Bengal is around 24–25 % (one out of every four rural households gets employed through MNREGA) with the leader (Rajasthan for the first 2 years and Tamil Nadu for the last of these 3 years), respectively, at 63.97 %, 59.25 % and 72.82 %. In the last of these 4 years, the mentioned percentage for West Bengal jumps to 37.43 % (more than one out of every three rural household gets employed through MNREGA), while the leader, Tamil Nadu, is at 86.21 %.

Let us now look at the performance of various districts of West Bengal in regard to registration of population, creation of employment and works completed (Table 13.9).

In regard to registration, a higher figure for percentage of population registered gives rise to a higher rank (thus, if a household has a rank equal to 1, this implies that it has the lowest percentage of population registered under MNREGA). While one would expect the districts with high rural poverty to have a high rank, this is often not the case: Murshidabad with the highest rural poverty has a rank equal to 6, 4, 4 and 4 among 17 districts in the years 2009–2010, 2010–2011, 2011–2012 and 2012–2013, respectively; Maldah with fourth highest poverty of 46 % has ranks of 5, 3, 3 and 3, respectively; Uttar Dinajpur with the second highest poverty of 49 % has ranks of 9, 6, 6 and 5, respectively. On the other hand, we find districts with low or moderate rural poverty often performing better in regard to 'percentage of population' registered: Cooch Behar with the lowest rural poverty at 11.2 % has ranks of 15 each in all the mentioned 4 years; Jalpaiguri with a moderate rural poverty of 29 % has the highest possible rank of 17 in all the years; Nadia with the third lowest rural poverty at 18.3 % has ranks of 11, 10, 11 and 10 in the mentioned years. Thus, to summarize, there is a tendency for some districts with high rural poverty to register relatively low proportions of rural population under MNREGA and some districts with low rural poverty to register high proportions of rural population under MNREGA. This is reflected in the magnitude and sign of Pearson's correlation coefficients between the 'rural poverty rank' and the rank for 'percentage of population

Table 13.8 Households directly benefitted by MNREGA. (Source: Computed on the basis of data given in nrega.nic.in)

	Percentage of rural households provided employment				Rank			
	2008–2009	2009–2010	2011–2012	2012–2013	2008–2009	2009–2010	2011–2012	2012–2013
Andhra Pradesh	50.87	49.68	36.93	46.87	3	2	4	3
Assam	36.08	31.57	16.41	16.30	5	5	8	8
Bihar	21.66	0.00	3.91	7.76	7	15	15	13
Gujarat	12.51	18.65	9.29	8.30	11	8	11	12
Haryana	5.03	3.35	6.09	6.32	14	14	13	14
Karnataka	12.10	27.98	10.18	9.88	12	6	10	11
Kerala	18.66	16.56	37.87	48.53	8	9	3	2
Madhya Pradesh	51.28	47.07	25.45	22.72	2	3	5	6
Maharashtra	7.51	4.39	6.56	10.01	13	13	12	10
Orissa	17.54	11.39	15.14	18.66	9	11	9	7
Punjab	4.31	5.02	5.42	4.88	15	12	14	15
Rajasthan	63.97	59.25	39.00	37.72	1	1	2	4
Tamil Nadu	45.57	44.52	72.82	86.21	4	4	1	1
Uttar Pradesh	14.45	13.41	19.28	13.78	10	10	7	9
West Bengal	24.68	24.72	24.22	37.43	6	7	6	5

Table 13.9 Percentage of rural population registered under MNREGA. (Source: Computed on the basis of data given in nrega.nic.in)

	Percentage of rural population registered			Rank				
	2009–2010	2010–2011	2011–2012	2012–2013	2009–2010	2010–2011	2011–2012	2012–2013
Bankura	40.02	42.00	41.55	42.15	10	11	10	11
Barddhaman	43.44	45.77	45.47	46.53	13	13	13	15
Birbhum	45.08	46.16	45.69	45.92	14	14	14	14
Cooch Behar	46.51	46.75	46.21	45.90	15	15	15	13
Dakshin Dinajpur	41.97	42.84	42.44	43.43	12	12	12	12
Darjeeling	34.15	38.32	38.19	39.98	8	9	9	9
Hooghly	33.70	36.35	36.32	37.63	7	7	7	7
Howrah	20.37	21.40	21.78	22.91	2	1	1	1
Jalpaiguri	72.57	77.32	80.90	85.42	17	17	17	17
Maldah	33.49	33.81	33.40	33.51	5	3	3	3
Medinipur	19.90	37.62	37.17	37.68	1	8	8	8
Murshidabad	33.61	34.49	34.13	34.60	6	4	4	4
Nadia	40.92	41.78	41.66	42.12	11	10	11	10
North 24 Parganas	33.37	35.33	35.16	35.72	4	5	5	6
Puruliya	48.52	49.11	48.56	48.77	16	16	16	16
South 24 Parganas	26.94	27.95	27.84	28.58	3	2	2	2
Uttar Dinajpur	36.45	36.24	35.50	35.05	9	6	6	5

registered'. From an intuitive point of view, we would expect the high-rural-poverty districts (those with high ranks) to have higher proportions of population registered. Thus, we would expect the Karl Pearson's coefficient of rank correlation to be large and positive. However, this coefficient turns out to be 0.047, −0.12192, −0.07843 and −0.06618 in the four mentioned years (Table 13.10).

We now look at the number of works completed under MNREGA in various districts. The data are for 2012–2013. Note that a higher incidence of rural poverty corresponds to a higher 'rural poverty rank' and a higher number of works completed per 1000 corresponds to a higher rank for 'works completed per 1000'. Again, intuitively one would expect higher MNREGA activity in the high-rural-poverty districts, and therefore Karl Pearson's rank coefficient of correlation to be large and positive. But we find that the opposite is the case—the coefficient turns out to be −0.174. If we eyeball the data, we find why this is the case: North 24 Parganas, which has by far the largest number of works per 1000 at 8.956, only has a moderate incidence of poverty at 20.6% (it is the sixth lowest among 17 districts); similarly, Medinipur with a poverty rank of 9 (at a moderate 21.8%) ranks 14 in regard to works completed per 1000 at 2.562; on the other hand, Murshidabad with the highest incidence of rural poverty (and therefore a rank of 17) ranks only 5 in terms of works completed; similar is the case for Uttar Dinajpur and Maldah (ranked 16 and 14 in terms of rural poverty), which are ranked as the lowest and the second lowest in terms of works completed per 1000.

13.4 Conclusion

The position of West Bengal in terms of incidence of poverty has improved relative to other states since the 1970s. It also exhibits very little urban bias in regard to incidence of poverty as the gap between urban and rural poverty is low compared to many other states. A worrying fact, however, is that the pace of poverty alleviation in the post-liberalization period has slackened compared to that in the pre-liberalization period.

The districts of West Bengal exhibit varying poverty incidence: The districts in the southeastern zone exhibit low to moderate rural as well as urban poverty; those in the southwestern zone exhibit moderate to high poverty, while the poverty in the northern districts shows large variations from low to moderate to high.

In regard to performance of poverty alleviation programmes, we focus on the MNREGA—West Bengal does very well in terms of percentage of rural households provided employment and ranks among the top 5–7 major states in this regard. However, the relative performance of districts leaves a lot to be desired: It is observed that the high-poverty districts often exhibit lower impact of the programme (in terms of percentage of rural population registered and works completed per 1000 persons), when these districts should exhibit higher impact.

Table 13.10 Works completed and rural poverty: a comparison. (Source: Computed on the basis of data given in nrega.nic.in)

	Rural poverty in 2004–2005	Rural poverty rank	Works completed per 1000 population in 2012–2013	Rank in terms of works completed per 1000
Bankura	28.5	10	1.680	11
Barddhaman	20.3	5	1.598	10
Birbhum	39.2	13	4.757	16
Cooch Behar	11.2	1	1.100	7
Dakshin Dinajpur	48.9	15	0.717	3
Darjeeling	14.7	2	1.083	6
Hooghly	21.1	7	1.997	12
Howrah	21.6	8	1.118	8
Jalpaiguri	29	11	3.316	15
Maldah	46	14	0.686	2
Medinipur	21.8	9	2.562	14
Murshidabad	55.9	17	0.875	5
Nadia	18.3	3	0.729	4
North 24 Parganas	20.6	6	8.956	17
Puruliya	31.2	12	2.067	13
South 24 Parganas	18.5	4	1.429	9
Uttar Dinajpur	49	16	0.456	1

References

Bandyopadhyay KR (2010) Poverty in India: a chronological review on measurement and identification. Asian Institute of Transport Development. http://mpra.ub.uni-muenchen.de/25691/. Accessed June 2013

Gupta N, Chaudhuri S (2009) Levels of living and poverty patterns: a district wise analysis for India. Econ Polit Wkly XLIV(9):94–110

Rangarajan C, Mahendra Dev S, Sundaram K, Vyas M, Datta KL (2014) Report of the expert group to review the methodology for measurement of poverty. Planning Commission, Government of India

nrega.nic. in The Mahatma Gandhi National Rural Employment Guarantee Act 2005, Ministry of Rural Development, Government of India. Accessed June 2013

Chapter 14
The Impact of MGNREGS on Rural Households: Evidence from a Quasi-experiment

Amit Kundu and Sanjib Talukdar

14.1 Introduction

The history of public works programmes (PWPs) or Welfare through Workfare has been old for centuries in India. Dreze and Sen (1991) in 'Hunger and Public Action' had talked about 'Arthashastra' which was written by Chanakya in the fourth century B.C. mentioning about welfare measures in the form of public works during calamitous period. Later, colonial India also witnessed such workfare programmes especially designed as famine relief measures. But the most gigantic programme[1] in the history of India's state-sponsored workfare initiatives is the National Rural Employment Guarantee Scheme (NREGS), which is named after Mahatma Gandhi as Mahatma Gandhi National Rural Employment Guarantee Scheme (MGNREGS).

The Government of India initiated this PWP in 2005, where the basic objective was to provide 100 full man-days of employment to each willing rural household. It was expected that MGNREGS can generate income support for the poor by providing them employment and can raise agricultural productivity as well as profitability in the long run by creating different productive assets related to agriculture. As for example, the Employment Guarantee Programme in Maharashtra had been credited with averting a famine during the draught of 1970–1973 to alleviate poverty. The Rural Public Works Programme in Bangladesh has been commended for its contribution to rural development and increased agricultural productivity through the creation and maintenance of rural infrastructure (Dreze and Sen 1991). Employment

[1] The annual outlay of MGNREGS was 0.31% of the GDP covering 21 million households in 2006–2007, and it immensely increased to 1.29% of the GDP covering 54.95 million households in 2011–2012 (www.nrega.nic.in).

A. Kundu (✉)
Department of Economics, Jadavpur University, Kolkata, 700032, India
e-mail: akundu29@gmail.com

S. Talukdar
Sree Chaitanya Mahavidyalaya, 24 PGNS (N), Habra, India
e-mail: reach4gb@gmail.com

S. Banerjee et al. (eds.), *Understanding Development,* India Studies in Business and Economics, DOI 10.1007/978-81-322-2455-6_14

generation through MGNREGS emphasized its role as income insurance in the presence of seasonality in agricultural labour market (Basu 2011). In this context, the MGNREGS can be thought of as a policy to boost rural income and stabilize agricultural production. Johnson (2009) found that MGNREGS allowed households to mitigate the effects of weather-induced income shocks. Although he was unable to precisely identify the relationship between changes in income and participation in MGNREGS, he showed that the relationship is strong enough to be practically significant. Jha et al. (2008) using pooled household level data for the Indian states of Rajasthan and Andhra Pradesh found that the size of landholdings is a negative predictor of participation in this employment programme. In state-level analysis, this pattern survives in Rajasthan but reverses in Andhra Pradesh, where there is a positive relationship. They also found evidence of complementarities between MGNREGS and the Public Distribution System (PDS). Dasgupta (2011) examines the role of this public policy in buffering the negative effects of early childhood exposure to rainfall shocks on long-term health outcomes. The study finds that while the policy does not help correct long-term past health deficiencies, it is useful in buffering recent drought shocks, which vary by policy-relevant subgroups.

On the contrary, McCord and Farrington (2008) are of the opinion that the types of impact achieved by both long- and short-term PWPs, such as MGNREGS are often limited to smoothing income or consumption during the period of employment, and given the additional costs associated with PWP implementation, PWP may not be as cost-effective as other measures seeking these types of limited impact. Dutta et al. (2012) found that although the scheme is reaching the rural poor and backward classes and is attracting poor women into the workforce, yet there is considerable unmet demand for work on the scheme in all states, and more so in the poorest ones, where the scheme is needed most. Liu and Barrett (2013) using the 2009–2010 National Sample Survey data, describe patterns of job-seeking, rationing and participation in MGNREGS. At the national level, it finds that the self-targeting design of it leads to greater rates of self-selection into the programme by poorer and scheduled-tribe (ST) or scheduled-caste (SC) households. However, the administrative rationing of MGNREGS jobs is not pro-poor but exhibits a sort of middle-class bias.

After the lapse of 8 years from the initiation of the scheme, the recently elected central government raised questions about the efficacy of MGNREGS, particularly pertaining to the aspects of targeting and productive asset creation under the scheme. The government is doubtful whether the implementation of MGNREGS has been at its best, especially in respect of the aims and objectives with which the corresponding act was devised. Hence, the government is contemplating to revamp the scheme.

Against this backdrop, we want to investigate the effectiveness of MGNREGS in the agriculturally backward areas to improve the livelihood of rural people. To do so, we carried out a quasi-experimental study, which was conducted in four gram panchayats of two separate blocks in Birbhum district of West Bengal.

14.1.1 Sample Design and Methodology

In West Bengal, out of 19 districts, we have chosen Birbhum district as sample district for our impact evaluation. While the choice of the district was primarily driven by pragmatic concerns, the selection can be justified on several grounds. In 2006, the Ministry of Panchayati Raj named Birbhum one of the country's 250 most backward districts. It is also one of the first-phase districts in West Bengal as regards implementation of MGNREGS, and it is also one of the three most backward and vulnerable districts in West Bengal. The soil type is older alluvial in the east and laterite in the west. The district is climatically varied and is prone to both drought and flood situation. It is primarily an agricultural district with around 75% of the population being dependent on agriculture.

According to Census 2001, the share of workers in total population is 37.4% in Birbhum, which is marginally higher than the state average of 36.8%. Between the two census years (viz., 1991 and 2001) the district has experienced only 4 percentage point increase in work participation rate (from 33.2 to 37.4%). Like in other districts, the work participation rate is very high for men compared to women. While the share of male workers in the total male population is 54%, that of female workers is only 20% (2001 Census). However, the female work participation rate has increased from 13% in 1991 to 20% in 2001. It is important to note that in Birbhum, increasing work participation is associated with the increasing share of marginal workers in total work force.[2] The share of marginal workers in total workers in the district increased from 8% in 1991 to 26% in 2001. The number of workers engaged in agriculture as a percentage of total workers has decreased from 72% in 1991 to 60% in 2001. This corresponds to the overall common perception that more people are now engaged in nonagricultural activities, such as fishing, retail sales, vegetable vending, selling milk, and so on. As all these activities are at the lower end of the spectrum of marketable skills, it remains doubtful if these activities generate enough return for their family's sustenance. The share of agricultural labour in total workers engaged in agriculture (the latter includes both cultivators and agricultural workers—two Census categories) increased over the Census decade (53% in 1991 to 62% in 2001). As a matter of fact, between 1991 and 2001, the absolute number of cultivators in Birbhum came down from 289,155 to 260,955 indicating a 10% decennial fall, while during the same period, the number of agricultural labourers increased from 324,701 to 416,949 indicating a decennial growth rate of 28%.

We now look at the incidence of rural poverty and its connection with the composition of employment across blocks. The below-poverty-line (BPL) household survey carried out in 2006 provides information on the total number of families and BPL families line at a highly disaggregated level (viz., the *Sansad* level). Despite the controversies surrounding the BPL survey and the reliability of the data, the figures can highlight certain important aspects of the spatial distribution of the poor

[2] By census definition, marginal workers are those who do not work for the major part of the year, which could be either due to the lack of opportunities or other reasons.

people if we assume that the alleged upward bias is more or less evenly distributed across blocks. The percentage of BPL families across blocks shows that there are only three blocks where the percentage of BPL households is less than 30 %, whereas there are five blocks where the percentage of BPL households is even more than 50 %.

Birbhum district is historically rich, economically poor, climatically both dry and wet depending on different locations and politically challenging. Since MGNREGS is primarily aimed at poverty alleviation, Birbhum can be regarded as a good platform for citing the impact of MGNREGS.

Birbhum district has 19 blocks, out of which we have randomly chosen two blocks, Rajnagar and Suri-1. Again, from Rajnagar, we have randomly chosen Tantipara and Gangmuri-Joypur gram panchayats, whereas from Suri-1 we have randomly chosen Mallickpur and Nogori gram panchayats. As the prime objective of MGNREGS is to improve the livelihood of the rural people, for proper effectiveness of this public policy, we have to consider the household as a unit.

In any impact evaluation study, we have to investigate how outcomes have changed with the intervention relative to what would have occurred without intervention. But it is difficult to judge the outcome of the same individual with and without intervention because people can only be in one circumstance at a time. Often, treatments that influence outcomes do not just happen naturally; they are implemented precisely to influence outcomes. Different public policies implemented by the government are an example of it. Sometimes, treatments are made on the basis of some noneconomic factors such as political considerations. In this situation, an investigator cannot randomly assign people or two separate units such as treatment group and control group. Therefore, to do a proper impact evaluation, instead of 'control group', we can consider a 'comparison group', and the experiment becomes not a natural experiment but a quasi-experiment. In any quasi-experimental study, two sets of households are required. We have a 'treatment group', a set of households which are affected by policy change and a 'comparison group', a set of households which are not or are partially affected by policy change. Actually, finding a proper counterfactual to treatment is always a challenge. After 8 years of the implementation of the scheme, it is hardly possible to find out nonparticipants of this programme, at least in our study area among the poor households. Hence, a participant–nonparticipant approach will not be applicable; instead, two kinds of households are selected in our experiment according to the number of days they got employment in MGNREGS in the reference period 2012–2013.

Initially, from the official website of MGNREGS we have identified the beneficiary households of the sample gram panchayats which got 60 man-days or more through MGNREGS in the entire reference period, and the households which received 15 or fewer man-days job in those same sample gram panchayats in the entire reference period. All such households were surveyed on the basis of our well-designed questionnaire. The agro-climatic and farming conditions were almost identical in the sample villages, where predominance of monocropping was observed. The sample villages were not particularly prosperous, and the residents in the survey area had limited opportunities for alternative employment.

The survey work was done between June and August 2013. So this quasi-experiment is based on cross-sectional primary data. Different socioeconomic information was collected from the sample households. The focus group discussions (FGDs) were also conducted in all the selected villages with the village community including workers to substantiate the data collected from the individual worker.

Here, we have used the average monthly income (AVMI) of a household as an indicator of its livelihood. The investigation tries to locate whether households getting more than 60 days of work under the scheme are living better in terms of their income as compared with the households getting less than 15 days of work under the same. As there is a clear demarcation of the number of days of work, the households getting 15–60 days of work under MGNREGS have not been considered in our investigation. In this impact evaluation, the households that got more than 60 person-days of work through MGNREGS are considered as 'treatment group', and the households that worked less than 15 man-days through MGNGEGS are considered as 'comparison group'.

The total number of sample households is 286, out of which 180 households belong to the treatment group, and 106 belong to the comparison group. We took special care to ensure that the comparison group closely matched the treatment group by economic, physical and social attributes.

14.2 Description of the Household-Level Data Collected from the Field Survey

MGNREGS is designed to supplement agricultural employment, which implies that it is primarily meant for the monocropping areas. Birbhum is a district dominated by monocropping areas. Our sample solely comprises monocropping villages. Thus, the selection of the district and the sample is expected to fulfil the requirement of the study.

Our sample households are composed of general as well as SC and ST categories. Within the treatment group more than 80 % belong to either SC or ST communities. On the contrary, just above 30 % of the households are from reserved categories among the sample households that belong to the comparison group. This brings out an important feature, namely that participation in MGNREGS is much more rigorous among SC/ST communities vis-à-vis the general ones. Beside this, we observed that less than 25 % of the households in the treatment group possessed BPL cards and a little over 10 % of the households in the comparison group belonged to BPL category.

So far as the distribution of the number of person-days in MGNREGS is concerned, we observed that within the reference period mentioned above, nearly 43 % of the treatment group households received employment between 60 and 80 days. Moreover, within the whole treatment group, 49 households got 100 days of employment. On the other hand, more than 26 % of the households belonging to the comparison group received less than 10 days of employment. The rest 74 % of the

Table 14.1 Distribution of households in terms of female participation in MGNREGS. (Source: Field survey conducted by the authors)

Person-days	Treatment group	Comparison group
Nil	21 (11.67%)	85 (80.19%)
01–15	01 (0.005%)	21 (19.81%)
15–60	151 (83.89%)	–
Above 60	07 (4.43%)	–
Total	180 (100%)	106 (100%)

households of the comparison group received employment between 10 and 15 days in the same reference period.

Low level of awareness regarding the provisions of the MGNREGS Act is rampant among the beneficiaries. We observed that in our sample households, there is lack of awareness about the 33% reservation of job for female workers. Only 2.8% of the male respondents within the treatment group and 1.9% of the male respondents within the comparison group were aware of the provision. But there was absolutely zero awareness among the female respondents of both the groups. However, as the participation of female workers is an important component of the scheme, we tried to look at the person-days generated among the female members of both treatment and comparison group households.

Table 14.1 shows that within the comparison group, female participation is very poor, and all households except only twenty one sample households replied that their female members did not or could not participate in the programme. On the contrary, only 11.67% of the households in the treatment group have nonparticipant female members. Moreover, above 83.89% of the households within the same group have female members who worked for sizable number of days in the reference period. This invokes us to hypothesize that female participation can be regarded as a vital force driving a household to seek for greater number of person-days in MGNREGS as a whole in our study region. A very notable feature observed in the study area was that the female participation in the programme is guided by cultural factors nourished either consciously or subconsciously by different village communities. Moreover, it should be mentioned that female participation is higher in tribal communities.

Among our sample households nearly 33% of the households within the treatment group were land owners (owned and/or leased) and nearly 37% of the households were so within the comparison group. Again, the compatibility among the sample households is further strengthened by the fact that all the surveyed households owning land are marginal farmers.[3] Within the treatment group nearly 18% of the households hold less than 2 bighas of land each, 14% hold 2–5 bighas of land each, and only 1% holds 5–7 bighas of land. Alongside, within the comparison group, nearly 9% own less than 2 bighas of land each, 22% hold 2–5 bighas each, and approximately 6% of the households own 5–7 bighas of land each. Besides

[3] Farmers who own up to 1 ha of land are called marginal farmers.

Table 14.2 Distribution of households in terms of aggregate net farm income

Range of income (₹)	Treatment group	Comparison group
Nil	116 (64.44%)	67 (63.2%)
1000–5000	34 (18.89%)	26 (24.5%)
6001–12,000	14 (7.77%)	13 (12.3%)
12,001–20,000	16 (8.9%)	
Total	180 (100%)	106 (100%)

that, it should be mentioned that most of the marginal farmer households both in the treatment and comparison groups have monocropping land. Besides, it was observed that MGNREGS has benefitted a few households to go for second crop cultivation in the form of horticulture although in small scale after their main crop cultivation and farming is done entirely on the basis of family labour force.

We have calculated net total farm income of the marginal farmer households by first computing their value of total output sold (total output sold × market price). Then, we add the total value of the output kept for self consumption (amount × market price), and thus get the value of total output produced (total revenue). After that, we calculate the total cost of cultivation under different heads (total cost).[4] Finally, after subtracting the total cost from the total revenue, we can get the net total farm income in monetary terms.

Table 14.2 shows that in the case of both treatment group and comparison group, the majority of the households among the marginal farmers earn less than ₹ 5000/year from their output. This implies that they earn marginally above ₹ 400/month from farming, which means they need to supplement their agricultural income for sustenance of livelihood. Within the treatment group, 16 households responded that their net farm income was enhanced as a positive fallout of MGNREGS. MGNREGS has improved their irrigation facilities, which in turn induced them to carry out cultivation of vegetables after the prime crop cultivation. Moreover, in this case they exclusively depend upon family labourers, viz. female labourers and not hired labourers. Hence, it is found that the farmers although a few in numbers in our study area have witnessed the opportunity of asset creation in MGNREGS.

As regards employment in private nonfarm activities within the village, nearly 54% of the households from the treatment group are not engaged in the same, and another 27% of the households are engaged for less than 50 days in the entire year corresponding to the reference period. Again, around 54% of the sample households belonging to the comparison group do not have access to private nonfarm activities, and another 27% have fewer than 50 man-days of work throughout the year. Moreover, in almost all sorts of nonfarm engagement, the wage rate per man-day is ₹ 100. It is observed that more than 80% of the sample households each from the treatment group and the comparison group remain jobless for a significant time

[4] Here, total cost includes cost of seeds, hand tractors/bullocks, different fertilizers at purchase price, pesticides at purchase price, water, hired labour in terms of total wage bill and other costs if any.

Table 14.3 Distribution of private nonfarm activities among the sample households in terms of man-days. (Source: Field survey conducted by the authors)

Number of man-days in private nonfarm activities	Treatment group	Comparison group
Nil	97 (53.89%)	57 (53.77%)
01–50	49 (27.22%)	29 (27.36%)
51–100	26 (14.44%)	13 (12.26%)
Above 100	8 (4.44%)	7 (6.6%)
Total	180 (100%)	106 (100%)

period. Thus, it is imperative that their tenure of joblessness can be reduced in our study area by formulating a comprehensive policy for employment.

Table 14.3 shows that in the study area, there are few opportunities for alternative supplementary employment beyond agriculture, which urgently necessitates for a comprehensive PWP.

A significant characteristic of the region we studied is that there is almost no incidence of distress migration. More than 90% of the households within the treatment group do not migrate in the lean period, and above 95% of the households belonging to the comparison group are nonmigrants. Although the reason behind nonmigration is not explicitly cited by the sample households, yet we apprehend that for these people, the cost of migration might be very high.

Table 14.4 depicts the incidence of migration outside the village among the sample households. Besides the fact that a large section within the treatment group and the comparison group do not migrate, we also observe that 5% of the households from the treatment group and a little over 3% of the households from the comparison group migrate for less than 50 days throughout the whole year.

As mentioned earlier, the chosen study area in Birbhum district is predominantly monocropping in nature. Further, the sample farming households both in the treatment group and the comparison group are mostly marginal farming households. Apart from this, a gigantic portion of the sample households within both groups belongs to agricultural labour class. Moreover, the illustration of Tables 14.3 and 14.4 brings out that a remarkable number of the sample households have little or no access to either private nonfarm activities within the village or migrated jobs available outside their villages, implying very meagre sources of alternative employment opportunities. Thus, the sample households in the study area are not only poor, but their poverty is also accompanied by limited or no employment opportunities in the agriculturally lean period, making them absolutely vulnerable.

Table 14.4 Incidence of daily distress migration among sample households. (Source: Field survey conducted by the authors)

Number of days of daily distress migration	Treatment group	Comparison group
Nil	163 (90.56%)	101 (95.28%)
01–50	09 (5%)	04 (3.77%)
Above 50	08 (4.44%)	01 (0.9%)
Total	180 (100%)	106 (100%)

14.2.1 The Model and its Results

As the outcome variable is observed both for the treatment group and the comparison group, we here apply a two-step treatment effect model developed by Heckman (1976) to determine the impact of the MGNREGS on rural households. We carry out the analysis by using a cross-section data of 286 households collected for the financial year 2012–2013.

The original equation is

$$\text{AVMI}_i = \alpha_0 + \alpha_1\text{TREATDUMMY} + \alpha_2\text{AEM}_i + \mu_i \ldots\ldots \quad (14.1)$$

The selection equation is:

$$\text{TREATDUMMY} = \beta_0 + \beta_1\text{PSPDUMMY}_i + \beta_2\text{FEMP}_i + \beta_3\text{TNONFARM}_i + \beta_4\text{MIGR}_i + \beta_5\text{NERLAND}_i + \varepsilon_i \ldots\ldots \quad (14.2)$$

It is expected that there may be few economic and noneconomic factors due to which in the same geographical area some households had sought employment more than 60 man-days, and some households had sought employment less than 15 man-days in the entire reference period. We can have the possible causes behind it from our selection equation.

This treatment effect method estimates two regressions simultaneously. Equation (14.1) is the prime equation whose parameter estimates are necessary for impact evaluation of MGNREGS. Eq. (14.2) is the selection equation, where explained variable is dummy in nature. Initially we have to estimate Eq. (14.2) through a probit model, which predicts the probability of being in the treatment group from a set of strictly exogenous variables. We can now rewrite Eq. (14.1); in the new equation, we have the original explanatory variables of Eq. (14.1) plus an additional explanatory variable—the inverse Mill's ratio or hazard rate, i.e. $\hat{\lambda}_i$ constructed from the estimated coefficients of the selection Eq. (14.2). The reformed equation of Eq. (14.1) will be:

$$\text{AVMI}_i = \alpha_0 + \alpha_1\text{TREATDUMMY} + \alpha_2\text{AEM}_i + \alpha_3\hat{\lambda}_i + \mu_i \ldots. \quad (14.3)$$

Both μ_i and ε_i are bivariate normal distributions with mean zero and the covariance matrix is expressed as $\begin{bmatrix}\sigma_\mu & \rho \\ \rho & 1\end{bmatrix}$. Here ρ indicates the correlation between the two error terms mentioned in Eqs. (14.3) and (14.2). Now $\hat{\alpha}_3 = \rho\sigma_\mu$. As $\sigma_\mu > 0, \hat{\alpha}_3 > 0 > 0$ iff and only if $\rho > 0$. If it is proved that $\hat{\alpha}_3 \neq 0$, then we can establish that the two-step treatment effect model is appropriate for this quasi-experimental study because at least there exists one factor due to which 'TREATDUMMY' in Eq. (14.3) is endogenous in nature.

14.2.2 Description of the Variables in Eqs. (14.1) and (14.2)

$AVMI_i$ implies 'average monthly income' of the *i*th household. The total annual income of the *i*th household in the entire reference period is the sum total of different nonfarm incomes in the entire reference period including wage income through MGNREGS, earnings as agricultural labourer and, for the marginal farmer households, the net farm income. Dividing that by 12, we get AVMI.

TREATDUMMY is a dummy variable which is endogenous in Eq. (14.1). It takes the value 1 if the household belongs to the treatment group; otherwise 0 for the household belonging to the comparison group.

PSPDUMMY indicates 'panchayat-specific' dummy. The field survey has profoundly shown that getting jobs (and even number of days of jobs) under MGNREGS depends to a large extent on the efficacy of the local panchayat. Along with this, political clientism and affiliation to the household by the ruling party play a vital role as well. As most of the households are not explicit about their political stand, here we took the PSPDUMMY indicating whether they are satisfied with the work of the panchayat or not (1 if yes, 0 if no) to capture the flavour of all the above facts.

FEMP indicates 'female participation' dummy in MGNREGS work. The number of days of work received under MGNREGS must undoubtedly go up if there is female participation. Hence, we take female participation in MGNREGS as a dummy (1 if yes, 0 if no).

$TNFARMDAY_i$ implies the 'total number of man-days' the *i*th household got employment in different private nonfarm sectors in the entire reference period. The study area in the present analysis is monocropping in character reflecting that there will be no contestability between agricultural employment and MGNREGS. Thus, the number of days getting farm employment is not influential in determining the number of days getting MGNREGS job. Instead, the number of days of nonfarm employment within the village can be a determining factor.

MIGRDAY implies 'migration' dummy. The migration dummy reveals whether the household is engaged in jobs outside the village (1 if yes, 0 if no). If the household works outside the village, then this may affect its involvement in MGNREGS as well as the number of man-days securing job under the scheme.

$NERLAND_i$ implies 'net farm income from owned land' of the *i*th sample household in the entire reference year. In our investigation, 64 out of 180 sample households belonging to the treatment group and 39 out of 106 sample households belonging to the comparison group were land owners. It has already been mentioned that the survey area is mainly monocropping area. Still, there is a possibility that members of these landholding farm households will seek less employment through MGNREGS for these farm activities. So, this variable is accommodated in the selection equation.

AEM implies total earning members of the sample household.

The results of Eqs. (14.3) and (14.2) are given in Table 14.5:

Table 14.5 Results of regression

Dependent variable: AVMI (Eq. 14.3)			Dependent variable: TREATDUMMY (Eq. 14.2)		
Variable	Coefficient	SE	Variable	Coefficient	SE
TREATDUMMY	1178.688*	71.9407	PSPDUMMY	3.55*	0.642
AEM	226.21*	44.2004	FEMP	1.707*	0.351
			TNONFARM	−0.018**	0.0084
$\hat{\lambda}_1$	−288.0513*	111.344	MIGR	−0.0164	0.011
Constant	657.673*	111.344	NERLAND	−0.00009	0.00005
			Constant	−0.9856	0.251

SE standard error

* ≥ significant at 1 %; ** ≥ significant at 5 %

14.3 Discussion

The parameter estimate of $\hat{\lambda}_1$ is statistically significant, and the value of its coefficient is significantly different from zero, which establishes the fact that the two-step treatment effect model is here appropriate for our quasi-experiment.

The results from Eq. (14.2) show that the coefficients of both PSPDUMMY and FEMP are positive and their estimates are statistically significant, which implies that both the panchayat-specific factor and female participation are significant in influencing the number of man-days of seeking job under MGNREGS, which corroborates with our field-level experience. Further, the field-level experience tells us that the role of the panchayat is crucial in the overall performance of MGNREGS on village level. Although employment generation under MGNREGS is done on the basis of 'self-selection' mechanism, still it is observed that due to interference of the local panchayat, a willing household may be deprived of seeking desirable man-days of employment through this programme.

Secondly, the estimated coefficients of TNONFARM and MIGR are negative as should be anticipated. But their values are comparatively low, signifying that the effect of these two regressors on the treatment dummy is somewhat dampened. Although total number of days of nonfarm employment may seem to be significant in general perspective, yet so far as the migration factor is concerned, our data and results suggest that at least in our study area, migration did not have a significant impact in determining the number of man-days of seeking MGNREGS job. The regressors influencing the treatment dummy in Eq. (14.2) are in turn guided by both economic as well as noneconomic factors. Except TNONFARM, which depends on the character of local economy, all others are influenced otherwise. For example, PSPDUMMY as discussed earlier is affected by attributes such as political clientism and/or affiliation to the households by the party ruling the panchayat, etc. Similarly, both FEMP and MIGR are governed by the attributes that have some sociocultural dimensions pertaining to the particular village in question.

All the estimated coefficients in Eq. (14.1) are positive and statistically significant at 1 % level. This implies that all of them have a positive and convincing influence on the outcome variable, i.e. AVMI. It is prominent that the value of the coefficient of the treatment dummy is very high if we compare it with the parameter estimates of other regressors. Thus, we observe that the livelihood symbolized by AVMI in our model is better for the rural poor having more number of man-days of work through MGNREGS in our study area.

14.4 Conclusion

This quasi-experimental study aimed to investigate the impact of MGNREGS on the livelihood of rural poor. During this course, the livelihood of the rural poor has been epitomized by AVMI. The study reveals that the rural poor are benefitted from MGNREGS in terms of their income. Further, for a few farming households, MGNREGS helps them to enhance their net farm income, which indicates the exploration of the asset-creating potentiality of this scheme. Hence, assuming status quo, it is prudent to continue MGNREGS effectively to improve the livelihood of the rural people.

References

Basu AK (2013) Impact of rural employment guarantee schemes on seasonal labour market: optimum comensation and worker's welfare. J Econ Inequal 11(1):1–34 (Springer)

Dasgupta S, Sudarshan RM (2011) Issues in labour market inequlity and women's participation in India's National Rural Employment Guarantee Programme. Working Paper No. 98 Policy Integration Department, International Labour Office, Geneva. http://www.ilo.org/wcmsp5/groups/public/—dgreports/—integration/documents/publication/wcms_153042.pdf

Dreze. J, Sen A (1991) Strategies of entitlement protections. In: Hunger and public activities. Oxford University Press, pp 104–121

Dutta P, Murgai R, Ravallion M, van de Walle D (2012) Does India's employment guarantee scheme guarantee employment? Econ Politi Wkly xlviI(16):55–64

Heckman J (1976) The common structure of statistical models of truncation, sample selection, and limited dependent variables and a simple estimator for such models. Ann Econo Social Meas 5(4):475–492

Jha R, Bhattacharyya S, Gaiha R, Shankar S (2008) Capture of anti-poverty programs: an analysis of the National Rural Employment Guarantee Program in India ASARC WP 2008/07. https://cnnd.crawford.anu.edu.au/acde/asarc/pdf/papers/2008/wp2008_07.pdf

Johnson D (2009) Can workfare serve as a substitute for weather insurance? the case of NREGA in Andhra Pradesh. Centre for Micro Finance Working Paper Series No. 32. http://ssrn.com/abstract=1664160

Liu Y, Barrett CB (2013) Heterogeneous pro-poor targeting in the National Rural Employment Guarantee Scheme. Econ Poli Wkly xlviii(10):46–53

McCord A. Farrington J (2008) Digging holes and filling them in again? How far do public works enhance livelihoods? Overseas Development Institute Natural Resource Perspectives 120. www.odi.org/sites/odi.org.uk/files/odi-assets/publications-opinion-files/3435.pdf

Chapter 15
Does Parental Education Have Any Role to Play on Female Child Disadvantage?

Soma Mandal and Arpita Ghose

15.1 Introduction

As opposed to a gender-neutral society, India possesses a masculine sex ratio—a sex ratio that is biased towards male population (940 in 2011, Census of India 2011). The male population outnumbers their female counterparts for a very long period of time. Post-independence data show that sex ratio has dropped from 941 in 1961 to 927 in 1991 (Census of India publications). This fact proves the existence of gender bias in our country as claimed by many researchers (Sen (1989, 1990a, b); Coale (1991); Klasen (1994); Klasen and Wink (2002)). The chapter is basically concerned with discrimination against female children that may generally be manifested in low sex ratio in the age group of 0–6.[1]

The discrimination towards females is observed in daily cares, food and nutrition, regular and curative medical care, education and in every sphere of life. Parents and family members try to shed off an unwanted fetus before it can see the light of the earth using new technology only because it is female. Deliberate killing procedures may also be adopted by the family and friends immediately after birth for those who cannot afford the technological measure. Sheer negligence may also be used as weapon for an unwanted new born so that they fall ill and die in a premature death. The death toll of female children increases for the reason that in many cases they have to do the household work from the very early childhood. The discussions of the above arguments can be found in Pande (2003), Pal (1999), Pitt et al. (1990) and Asfaw et al. (2010).

[1] We have reported data since 1961 as this was the first census to distinguish between child sex ratio and overall sex ratio. (see Hatti et all. (2004), Lives at Risk: Declining Child Sex Ratios in India, Lund Papers in Economic History, number 93. http://www.ekh.lu.se/publ/lup/93.pdf).

S. Mandal (✉) · A. Ghose
Department of Economics, Jadavpur University, Kolkata 700032, India
e-mail: smsomamandal@gmail.com

A. Ghose
e-mail: dhararpita@yahoo.co.in

S. Banerjee et al. (eds.), *Understanding Development*, India Studies in Business and Economics, DOI 10.1007/978-81-322-2455-6_15

One can visualize the effect of all these fatal measures against females in low female–male ratio of many countries including India (Sen 1989, 1990a, b).[2] Sen estimated the number of women having premature death somewhat near 100 million. In India, the female–male ratio is found to be declining from 941 in 1961 to 927 in 1991 (Census of India publications). Even though the female–male ratio shows a rising trend thereafter (933 in 2001 and 940 in 2011), the further complication is expected due to the fact that child female–male ratio is declining steadily over time, from 976 in 1961 to 914 in 2011 (Census of India publications). We have included our data on 0–6 sex ratio since 1961 as this was the first census to distinguish between child sex ratio and overall sex ratio (see Hatti et al. 2004).

The above-mentioned problem is observable in almost all the states of India, but the extent is different. The difference in the extent is attributed to the difference in kinship patterns prevailing in the states (Dyson and Moore 1983; Kishor 1993; Karve 1965).

The perusal of the literature suggests that there are different dimensions of the issues of gender bias. The manifestation of the problem can be felt at different levels: occupation structure, wage rate, employment level inequality, power structure differential at the household level, upbringing of a girl child, etc. The present chapter attempts to look at the issue of female child disadvantage (FCD) visualized through the nutritional attainment of a girl child as compared to a boy child.

The discrimination against females, especially in their childhood, can be termed henceforth as FCD, is therefore a serious concern and needs to be analysed with great importance so that one can estimate the extent of its prevalence, identify the causes behind it and can find out the measure to reduce it.

One important cause of such FCD may be lack of education. Parents as well as relatives of children fail to realize the importance of females due to wrong values adopted from the aged people. Education by giving proper knowledge may change these wrong perceptions. Thus, the measurement of the effect of education especially of parents on the discrimination against female children seems necessary.

15.2 Review of Literature

Many national and international studies tried to explore the effect of education on discrimination against females (Klasen and Wink 2002; Dasgupta 1987; Pal 1999; Bhuiya and Streatfield 1991; Chowdhury 1994; Dasgupta and Bhat 1997). However, both of them differ with respect to the method how they are estimating (i) the decimation against female children and (ii) the education level. Klasen and Wink (2002) estimated discrimination against female children by comparing mortality

[2] Sex ratio may be defined either as male–female ratio or as the female–male ratio. The present chapter uses female–male ratio.

and found that both female and male literacy has the same effect on it. Dasgupta (1987) and Dasgupta and Bhat (1997) found that the mothers' education has a negative effect on the level of disadvantage.

Pal (1999) used separate regression for males and females and found that the mothers' education widens the gap of nutritional status of the male and female child. Bhuiya and Streatfield (1991) measured the gender inequality by the difference between mortality of two sexes and took three groups for education, namely (i) no schooling, (ii) 1–5 years of schooling and (iii) 6 or more years of schooling and found no improvement of gender inequality with education. Chowdhury (1994), on the other hand, measured the gender inequality by the fertility behaviour of women and also found no improvement in gender equality with the enhancement of schooling for Bangladesh data.

All the previous studies measured FCD, either at state level or community level, by using data on immunization as well as nutritional status. Such measure at the household level based on primary survey is still lacking.

The present study contributes significantly to the literature by checking the existence of FCD with the help of the data collected from primary survey and then estimating the effect of parental education on such a disadvantage. The percentage number of households showing bias against the female child is obtained. The anthropometric measure of underweight following the World Health Organization's (WHO) measure is used to obtain FCD.

The format of the chapter is as follows: Section 15.3 represents the data and methodology of estimating FCD, describes the variables which are assumed to influence the behaviour of such disadvantage and also the model used for determination of the significant factors influencing it. The results of the estimation are presented in Sect. 15.4. Section 15.5 concludes the chapter with some policy prescriptions for reducing the possibility of the existence of this disadvantage.

15.3 Data and Methodology

15.3.1 The Data

The primary data are collected from household surveys conducted over the unplanned settlements in and around the Kalyani Township of Chakdaha block in Nadia district of West Bengal, India. The term "household" is used here to mean a husband, a wife and their children even if there may exist other members eating from the same kitchen (constitute family). This is due to the fact that those mothers are taken as our respondent, who have at least one female and one male child of her own (whom she gave birth to) within the age interval of 6 months to 6 years. If two or more sisters or sisters-in-law or some other relatives of the same family fulfill the said criterion, all of them are taken as respondents in the sample. The number of sample is 219 and is not very high due to the above characteristics of the respondents.

The questionnaire has two main parts—the first part is for the general information about the household (such as the parents' age, education, income, etc.) and the family (such as family income, religion, caste, etc.), and the second part is specific for the child of the specific age group, that is, 6 months to 6 years (such as age, height, weight, etc.). The information corresponding to the second part is collected separately for each child.

15.3.2 Measurement of Disadvantage

Existence of FCD in this study is checked by comparing the level of malnutrition among the child of two sexes in the household. Among the available measures of malnutrition, some common measures are stunting (less height than usual for age), wasting (less weight than usual for height) and underweight (less weight than usual for age; Bisika and Mandere 2008). According to Bisika and Mandere (2008), stunting represents chronic malnutrition, wasting represents acute malnutrition, whereas underweight represents both chronic and acute malnutrition. The present chapter uses the measure of underweight for computing the existence of FCD as it is a manifestation of both chronic and acute malnutrition.

Nutritional deficiency is calculated using "WHO child growth standards" and "WHO reference 2007" tables for (i) children aged up to 5 years and (ii) children aged more than 5 and up to 6 years, respectively. "The WHO growth standard identifies breastfed child as the normative model for growth and development standards, depicts normal early childhood growth under optimal environmental conditions and can be used to assess children regardless of ethnicity, socio-economic status and type of feeding."

In WHO's calculation, the median of the reference group is taken as the representative value, and the measure of deficiency is calculated by estimating the Z-score, which is defined as the ratio of the deviation of the observed weight for age from the representative value to the standard deviation of the reference group. Thus,

$$Z\text{-}score = \frac{WA - MeW}{SDW}$$

where

WA = Weight for the said child

MeW = Median for the weight for the reference group of children of the same age and sex (obtained from the WHO tables)

SDW = Standard deviation for the weight of the reference group of children of same age and sex (obtained from the WHO tables)

In this chapter, FCD is measured for every household by comparing nutritional deficiency (measured by Z-score) of the female child and the male child.

Following steps are used to measure the FCD:

Step 1: Z-scores are calculated for all surveyed children.

Step 2: For those households which have more than one boy and (or) girl within the stipulated age, the average value of the Z-scores are computed separately for both girl and boy children.

Step 3: The difference is computed between the average Z-score for boys and the average Z-score for girls for every household.

Step 4: FCD is assumed to exist for the cases where the value of the difference between the average Z-score for the boys and the girls is positive.

More compactly, the existence of FCD can be tested by constructing the binary variable *FCDW* showing the presence of FCD as defined by the relation Eq. (15.1).

$$FCDW = 1, \text{ if } VA > 0 \tag{15.1}$$

$$= 0 \text{ otherwise,}$$

where

$VA = Zm - Zf.$

Zm = Average Z-score for male children

Zf = Average Z-score for female children.

15.3.3 The Determinants of Female Child Disadvantage

The objective of the chapter is to find out the effect of education on the existence of FCD. However, apart from education, FCD is also affected by some other socio-economic variables, and thus one needs to take into account all those variables to a possible extent to get the total effect.

The following variables are taken into account to explain the existence of FCD:

1. **Working status of the respondent, the mother *(W)*:** It may be argued that a working mother has more outside exposure, and hence she may be free from bias against the female child as compared to a nonworking mother. In order to test this hypothesis, a binary variable W is considered which gives the working status of the respondents (the mothers of the children) and is defined as follows:
   $W = 1$, if the mother is working;
   $= 0$, otherwise.
2. **Educational attainment of the respondent, the mother *(ER)*:** It is possible that the more educated the respondent, the more she is free from wrong social values, as a result of which she may not be biased against the female child. To test this hypothesis, an ordered variable *ER*—depicting the educational attainment of the respondents is included. *ER* takes the values from 1 to 7—a higher value will imply a higher educational attainment and is defined as follows:
   $ER = 1$, if the mother is completely illiterate—cannot even read any document or anything on the wall or hoardings

=2, if the mother is able to read and write to some extent (so that the posters and advertisements here and there can change her decision), but has not availed any schooling facility
=3, if the mother obtained primary education
=4, if the mother attained class V–VIII
=5, if the mother attained class IX–X
=6, if the mother attained class XI–XII
=7, otherwise

3. **Educational attainment of the husband of respondent, the father *(EH)*:** By a similar logic, educational attainment of the husband father is likely to affect the existence of FCD. To take this into account, an ordered variable *EH*—depicting the educational attainment of the husbands of the respondents (the father of the children) is included. *EH* takes the values from 1 to 7—a higher value will imply a higher educational attainment; the values are defined similarly as *ER* for the mothers' education.
4. **Religion of the family of the respondent *(RE)*:** It may be possible that the treatment towards females, especially towards the female child, is different for different religions. To take this into account, *RE,* a categorical variable, is included, which gives the religion of the family of the respondent, and is defined as follows:
   RE=1, if the household is Hindu
   =2, if the household is Muslim
   Only these two religions are found in the present sample, and thus no other religion is considered here.
5. **The existence of the custom of dowry *(DO)*:** As the existence of the custom of dowry makes the females liable towards their family, it can enhance the bias against them. To test this hypothesis, a binary variable *DO* is included in the model and is defined as follows:
   DO=1, if there exists the custom of dowry in the household
   =0, otherwise
6. **Social group of the respondent:** It may be possible that for different social groups, the treatment towards females is different. In the present sample there are four types of social groups: scheduled caste, scheduled tribe, other backward community and general. To take into account the effect of social groups on FCD, and to avoid the problem of dummy variable trap, three dummy variables *CASC, CAST, CAOBC* are included, indicating the social groups in which the family of the respondents belongs to, which are defined as below:
   CASC=1, if the respondent belongs to scheduled caste household
   =0, otherwise
   CAST=1, if the respondent belongs to scheduled tribe household
   =0, otherwise
   CAOBC=1, if the respondent belongs to other backward community household
   =0, otherwise

7. **Income of the Family** ***(I)*:** It is a continuous variable—indicating the income of the family of the respondent and is measured at ₹ 1000 unit. This variable is included to test whether differential treatment towards female child is affected by the income level.

15.3.4 The Model Used to Explain the Existence of Female Child Disadvantage

The dependent variable of the model is *FCDW*, which is a binary variable and can take the value either one or zero. Thus, we have some kind of a qualitative response model, where our dependent variable is binary, having categorical in nature. One way, one can estimate the model is by using logit model where the probabilities describing the possible outcomes of a single trial are modelled, as a function of the explanatory (predictor) variables, using a logistic function. Logistic regression measures the relationship between the categorical dependent variable and one or more independent variables, by using probability scores as the predicted values of the dependent variable. In logit analysis the binary variable can be converted into a continuous variable $Y = \log(P/1 - P)$, defined as the log odds ratio, which ranges from $-\infty$ to $+\infty$, P being the probability that any observation belongs to the group having 1 as the value of the dependent variable. The log odds ratio will be a function of the included explanatory variables.

To get the effect of the ith explanatory variable, one needs to calculate the marginal effect, which is defined as $a_i\, P(1-P)$ and represents the effect of a change in explanatory variable on P, where a_i denotes the coefficient of the ith explanatory variable in the regression explaining the outcome value of the binary dependent variable *FCDW.*

15.4 Results

In order to estimate the FCD first we have computed extent of malnutrition for each of the child for each of the sample household. The percentage of children suffering from severe malnutrition is presented in Table 15.1.

In Table 15.1, the first column shows the different age groups, the last entry shows all age group taken together. For any age group the percentage of male children, female children and the total children suffering from severe malnutrition are presented in column 2, 3 and 4, respectively. For any age group percentage figure is computed by taking the ratio between actual male children suffering from severe malnutrition to total male children in that age group. The percentage figures for female and total child are similarly computed. From the table it is obtained that the percentage distribution of severe malnutrition is not same for the girls and boys.

Table 15.1 Percentage distribution of children according to different age and sex group suffering severe malnutrition

Age	Percentage of male children suffering severe malnutrition (%)	Percentage of female children suffering severe malnutrition (%)	Percentage of children suffering severe malnutrition (%)
6–12	40.47619	38.46154	39.50617
13–18	53.84615	57.14286	55.55556
19–24	50	44.44444	47.22222
25–30	39.13043	73.68421	54.7619
31–36	63.63636	46.66667	56.75676
37–42	38.09524	46.15385	41.17647
43–48	50	57.14286	53.84615
49–54	70.58824	46.66667	59.375
55–60	62.5	50	55.88235
61–66	38.88889	59.25926	51.11111
67–72	64.28571	60	61.53846
All	50	52.23214	51.12108

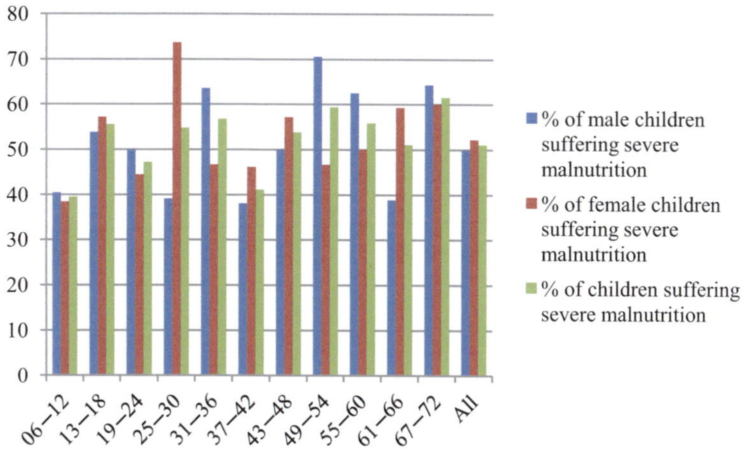

Fig. 15.1 Percentage distribution of children according to different age and sex group suffering severe malnutrition

For male children, the age group that suffer most from the severe malnutrition is the age group of 49–54 (70.59 %). Whereas, 37–42 years is the age group for which the boys suffer least malnutrition (38.10 %). For all the age group taken together, 50 % of the male child is suffering from severe malnutrition. For the girls most suffered group is 25–30 years (73.68 %) and the least suffered group is 6–12 years (38.46 %). For the entire female children the percentage turns out to be 52.23 %. If the children of both sexes are taken together, the percentage figure ranges from a high of 61.54 % for the age group 67–72 to a low of 39.51 % for 6–12 age group.

The percentages of the child suffering from severe malnutrition against age group for male and female children as well the total children (sum of male and female child) are plotted in Fig. 15.1. However, no clear relationship between the age groups and the percentage of children suffering from malnutrition is observed for any group.

Our next step is to measure the extent of FCD, the estimated results on which are summarized in the next subsection.

15.4.1 The Descriptive Statistics and the Percentage of Households Having Gender Bias

Table 15.2 summarizes the results of the descriptive statistics of the present sample as well as the measured percentage of household having bias against the female child.

Among the surveyed respondents maximum (91.78 %) are housewives and only 8.22 % of them are found to be working.

Table 15.2 Descriptive statistics and the percentage of household having the bias

Variables	Values of the variables	Percentage of respondent belonging to the said category (%)	Percentage of respondent belonging to the said category show bias against female child (%)
Working status of the mothers (*W*)	Working (=1)	8.22	50
	Non-Working (=0)	91.78	62.19
Educational attainment of the mothers (*ER*)	Illiterate (=1)	24.20	79.25
	Can only read and write (=2)	10.05	72.73
	Attains primary school (=3)	17.35	76.32
	Studied in class V to class VIII (=4)	28.77	58.73
	Studied in class IX to class X (=5)	9.13	30
	Studied in class XI to class XII (=6)	5.94	15.38
	Studied in college (=7)	4.57	20
Educational attainment of the father (*EH*)	Illiterate (=1)	16.44	77.78
	Can only read and write (=2)	8.68	78.95
	Attains primary school (=3)	18.72 %	70.73
	Studied in class V to class VIII (=4)	34.25	60
	Studied in class IX to class X (=5)	11.87	42.31
	Studied in class XI to class XII (=6)	4.11	33.33
	Studied in college (=7)	5.94	23.08
Religion (*RE*)	Hindu (=1)	90.87	59.30
	Muslim (=2)	9.13	80
Existence of the custom of dowry (*DO*)	Custom of dowry exists (=1)	59.82	76.34
	Custom of dowry does not exist (=0)	40.18	38.64
Whether belongs to the scheduled caste community or not	Belongs to the scheduled caste community (=1)	34.25	58.67
	Does not belong to the scheduled caste community (=0)	65.75	62.50

Table 15.2 (continued)

Variables	Values of the variables	Percentage of respondent belonging to the said category (%)	Percentage of respondent belonging to the said category show bias against female child (%)
Whether belongs to the scheduled tribe community or not	Belongs to the scheduled tribe community (=1)	8.22	44.44
	Does not belong to the scheduled tribe community (=0)	91.78	62.69
Whether belongs to the other backward community or not	Belongs to the other backward community (=1)	6.39	71.43
	Does not belong to the Other Backward Community (=0)	93.61	57.94
Whether belongs to any reserve category or not	Belongs to the any reserve category (=0)	51.14	64.29
	Does not belong to any reserve category (=1)	48.86	60.49

If the educational attainment of the respondents is considered, it can be observed that highest proportion of the respondent belongs to the category 4 (having educational level between class V and class VIII), followed by category 1 (illiterate), category 3 (attains primary school), category 2 (can only read and write), category 5 (having educational level between class IX and class X), category 6 (having educational level between class XI and class XII), and the lowest proportion of respondents belongs to category 7 (studied in college).

On the other hand, highest proportion of the husbands of the respondent belongs to the category 4, followed by category 3, category 1, category 5, category 2, category 7, and the lowest proportion of respondents belongs to category 6, in their educational attainment.

Among the 219 sample households, Hindu household constitutes 90.87 %, whereas the other 9.13 % covered by the Muslim population.

The existence of the custom of dowry is exposed by 59.82 % of the household.

It is found that 34.25 % of surveyed households are from the Scheduled Caste Community, 8.22 % are from the Scheduled Tribe Community, 6.39 % are from the Other Backward Community and remaining 51.14 % are not specific belonging to any of the reserved category.

The percentage of households showing bias against the female child for the entire sample turned out to be 61.19.

Thus, the present sample corroborates the general findings of Sen (1989, 1990a, b); Klasen (1994, 2002); Coale (1991); Dasgupta (1987) and others—supporting the existence of FCD.

A glimpse on the proportion of the household in different category having bias against the female child reveals that:

The existence of bias is evident for 50 %of the working mothers. This proportion for the nonworking mothers turned out to be 62.19 %. As expected, the percentage of bias is found to be higher for the nonworking mothers.

So far as the educational attainment of the biased respondents is concerned, highest proportion of biased respondent belongs to category 1 of the education level (79.25 %), followed by category 3 (76.32 %), category 2 (72.73 %), category 4 (58.73 %), category 5 (30 %), category 7 (20 %), and the lowest proportion of respondents belongs to category 6 of the education level (15.38 %).These results support the view that probability of existence of bias should decrease with the increase in the educational attainment of the respondent.

On the other hand, the data on the educational attainment of the husbands of the respondents reveals the fact that highest proportion of biased household belongs to category 2 of the education level (78.95 %), followed by category 1(77.78 %), category 3(70.73 %), category 4 (60 %), category 5(42.31 %), category 6(33.33 %), and the lowest proportion of respondents belong to category 7 of the education level (23.08 %). Here, also the estimated figure confirms that the level of education of husband has a positive impact on the possibility of reducing the existence of FCD.

The Hindu households are found to be less biased against the female child (59.30 % are found to be biased) than the Muslim households (80 % are found to be biased).

Among the households who themselves confirmed the existence of the custom of dowry, 76.34 % turned out to be biased against the female child. The same figure for the respondents, who denied the existence of dowry, is 38.64 %. Thus, the percentage of respondent showing gender bias is higher for the households for whom there exists the custom of dowry. This finding supports the argument that the existence of the custom of dowry has a positive role to play in determining the bias.

Among different castes, it is observed that the Other Backward Community shows the highest percentage of bias (71.43 %) followed by those households who does not belong to any reserved category (60.49 %) and the Scheduled Caste Community (58.67 %).The bias is least for the Scheduled Tribe households (44.44 %).

The results presented in Sect. 15.2.1 confirm that the percentage of households showing bias vary with the working status of mother, educational attainment of parents, religion of the household, the existence of the custom of dowry in the household and the caste of the household. Thus, an interesting problem will be to consider the joint influence of all these variables for the analysis of the bias. Apart from these, another factor that may affect the existence of FCD is income.

15.4.2 Results on the Determinants of FCDW

The results of these regressions are summarized in the tables below.

The estimated logit regression with all the explanatory variables is presented in Table 15.3. While carrying out the regression it is found that the variables *EH* and *ER* are correlated, the correlation coefficient is statistically significant. As a result two separate regressions are carried out (i) omitting *EH* from the set of explanatory variables (Model 1) and (ii) omitting *ER* from the set of the explanatory variables (Model 2). The Table 15.3 provides the estimated value of the coefficient of the explanatory variables, their marginal effects, the McFadden R-square. The marginal effects of the explanatory variables are given in the first parenthesis.

From the results of estimation of Model 1 and Model 2, it can be found that some of the included variables are statistically not significant. A fresh regression has been performed for each of the model omitting the variables which are not statistically significant. The results of these regressions are summarized in Model 3 and Model 4 and are presented in Table 15.4.

The effect of the education of the respondent can be determined from Model 3 whereas the effect of the education of the husband can be found from Model 4.

It can be observed that for model, the variables *ER* and *DO* are found to be important in determining the existence of FCD. For the second model, the important variables are *EH* and *DO*.

Table 15.3 Results of logit regression taking all the explanatory variables

		Model 1	Model 2
		Coefficient (marginal effect) [z-Statistic]	Coefficient (marginal effect) [z-Statistic]
Explanatory variables	*Constant*	0.209051 (0.02544) [0.242782]	−0.01027 (−0.00156) [−0.01162]
	W	−0.68322 (−0.08314) [−1.25572]	−0.58311 (−0.08851) [−1.10238]
	ER	−0.4638 (−0.05644) [−4.11807]	—
	EH	—	−0.31405 (−0.04767) [−2.57611]
	I	0.0026 (0.000316) [0.064378]	−0.01268 (−0.00192) [−0.30497]
	RE	0.902974 (0.109885) [1.434533]	0.730189 (0.110828) [1.206592]
	DO	1.421105 (0.172938) [4.3476]	1.466282 (0.222553) [4.523182]
	CASC	0.311035 (0.037851) [0.832513]	0.251127 (0.038116) [0.686742]
	CAST	−0.36825 (−0.04481) [−0.64544]	−0.16109 (−0.02445) [−0.26679]
	CAOBC	0.07226 (0.008794) [0.110893]	0.350009 (0.053125) [0.512193]
	McFadden R-squared	0.201748	0.162311

For Model 3, the marginal effect of *ER* is −0.0622. This result shows that 1 % increase in mother's education will reduce the probability of occurrence of a households showing bias against the female child by something around 6 %, and hence highlighting the role of the mother's education in reducing the probability of existence of FCD.

For Model 4, the marginal effect of *EH* is at −0.0732. This result can similarly be interpreted as earlier and shows that fathers' education also has a significant role in reducing the probability of the existence of FCD.

As expected, parents' education has a favourable effect on reducing this bias.

A strong positive association is observed between the existence of dowry and the FCD. The reason behind this is that the existence of the custom of dowry makes the female as liability whereas the males as an asset.

Table 15.4 Results of logit regression showing the significant explanatory variables

Explanatory variables	Model 3	Model 4
	Coefficient (marginal effect) [z-Statistic]	Coefficient (marginal effect) [z-Statistic]
Constant	1.151921 (0.16375) [2.616363]	0.893466 (0.192023) [1.887204]
ER	−0.43798 (−0.06226) [−4.26426]	—
	—	−0.34158 (−0.07341) [−3.2187]
DO	1.378734 (0.195992) [4.381975]	1.422669 (0.305758) [4.635682]
McFadden R-squared	0.1818	0.148819

15.5 Conclusion

The present chapter estimates whether there exist FCD by taking the difference between the average under weight levels of male and female children of stipulated age for each household, using household level data collected directly from the field survey. Average underweight level is estimated by using WHOs criterion. The effect of the education level of the parents on such disadvantage is measured. Both mother's and father's education are found to be significant in determining FCD. The other variable which is found to have significant effect on the occurrence of FCD is the prevalence of dowry system.

It can therefore be concluded that enhancement of the education level of the people (potential parents) and enhancing the opportunity of adult education (existing parents) will definitely be helpful to reduce the probability of occurrence of FCD. Also making the existing law on dowry much more stringent and arrangement of programmes like puppet shows, movies or drama to make people aware of the bad effects of the system of dowry may be helpful. The programmes to make people aware of the values of females and female children are necessary to reduce these fatal practices against females and make the society more prosperous.

Acknowledgments The fund provided for the project by the Centre for Advanced Studies, Department of Economics, Jadavpur University is gratefully acknowledged.

References

Asfaw A, Lamanna F, Klasen S (2010) Gender gap in parents' financing strategy for hospitalization of their children: evidence from India. Health Econ 19(3):265–79

Bhuiya A, Streatfield K (1991) Mothers' education and survival of female children in a rural area of Bangladesh. Popul Studies 45:253–264

Bisika T, Mandere G (2008) Integration of nutrition in the antiretroviral therapy scale up plan for Malawi. Malawi Med J 20(3):93–98

Chowdhury MK (1994) Mother's education and effect of son preference on fertility in MATLAB, Bangladesh. Popul Res Policy Rev 13:257–273

Coale AJ (1991) Excess female mortality and the balance of sexes in the population: an estimate of the number of 'missing females'. Popul Dev Rev 17:517–523

Dasgupta M (1987) Selective discrimination against female children in rural Punjab, India. Popul Dev Rev 13:77–100

Dasgupta M, Mari Bhat PN (1997) Fertility decline and increased manifestation of sex bias in India. Popul Studies 51:307–315

Dyson T, Moore M (1983) On kinship structure, female autonomy and demographic behaviour in India. Popul Dev Rev 9:35–60

Hatti N, Sekhar TV, Larsen M (2004) Lives at risk: declining child sex ratios in India. Lund Pap Econ Hist 93:1–42. http://www.ekh.lu.se/publ/lup/93.pdf; 2004. Accessed 8 April 2011

Jayachandran S, Kuziemko I (2009) Why do mothers breastfeed girls less than boys? Evidence and implications for child health in India. NBER Working Paper No. 15041

Karve I (1965) Kinship organization in India. Asia Publishing House, Bombay

Kishor S (1993) May god give sons to all: gender and child mortality in India. Am Soc Rev 58:247–265

Klasen S (1994) Missing women reconsidered. World Dev 22:1061–1071
Klasen S, Wink C (2002) Missing women: current trends in gender bias inmortality. Fem Econ 28(2):285–312
Pal S (1999) An analysis of childhood malnutrition in rural India: role of gender, income and other household characteristics. World Dev 27:1151–1171
Pande RP (2003) Selective gender differences in childhood nutrition and immunization in rural India: the role of siblings. Demography 40:395–418
Pitt MM, Rosenzweig MR, Hassan MdN (1990) Productivity, health and inequality in the intra-household distribution of food in low-income countries. Am Eco Rev 80:1139–1156
Sen A (1989) Women's survival as a development problem. Bull Am Acad Arts & Sci 43:14–29
Sen A (1990a) Gender and cooperative conflict. In: Tinker I (ed) Persistent inequalities: women and world development. Oxford University Press, New York
Sen A (1990b) More than 100 million women are missing. The New York Review of Books, 20 December, 60–66
http://www.who.int/childgrowth/en/. Accessed 12 Dec 2014
http://www.who.int/growthref/en/. Accessed 12 Dec 2014

Chapter 16
School Attendance and Employment of Youth in India: Convergence Across Caste and Religious Groups?

Tushar K. Nandi

16.1 Introduction

Age structure of India's population is often claimed to give its economy a distinct advantage to reap the demographic dividend. Due to the decrease in birth rates in the past decades, fewer children have been added to the population. Thus, the working age population has grown in size as compared to the number of dependents. Within the working age population, the majority are young (15–30 years old). The age structure, particularly higher share of working age population, is going to persist for a long duration. However, there is a debate on whether this demographic advantage can be translated into a demographic dividend. A general consensus is that demographic dividend crucially depends on the skill formation among the youth and their productive employment.

Though recent economic growth in India has been able to reduce the poverty, there is growing concern that the benefit of growth has not reached every section of the society (World Bank 2011). Social difference in education and employment has been widely studied (Dreze and Kingdon 2001; Dostie and Jayaraman 2006; Asadulla et al. 2009; Mitra and Verick 2013). Often caste has received more attention than religion in this literature. Moreover, education and employment have often been studied separately. For youth, there is a clear trade-off between continuing education and employment. On one hand, education enhances the prospect of higher earnings in future. The cost of continued education includes direct costs as well as foregone earnings. On the other hand, entering labour market at younger age fetches immediate but lower income due to less education and experience. It also negatively affects the future prospect in the labour market if the entry with low human capital has a long-term effect.

This chapter analyses the school attendance and employment of youth in India. Using data from three rounds of the National Sample Survey Office (NSSO)

T. K. Nandi (✉)
CTRPFP, Centre for Studies in Social Sciences (CSSS), Kolkata, India
e-mail: nandi.tushar@gmail.com

S. Banerjee et al. (eds.), *Understanding Development*, India Studies in Business and Economics, DOI 10.1007/978-81-322-2455-6_16

survey, we focus on the difference in school attendance and employment across different castes and religious groups. Historically, caste has played an important role in almost every aspect of life in India. Several studies documented the education and employment difference across castes. Recently, religion has also come to the forefront in the discussion of social inequality. This chapter studies the school attendance and employment of youth in India during the period of rapid economic growth. We examine how education and employment of youth from different castes and religions have evolved in the last decade. In doing so, we compare school attendance and employment of youth across rural–urban and male–female divides. We use both descriptive statistics and an econometric model to study the caste and religion difference in school attendance and employment of youth. We find that the caste and religious difference in school attendance and employment has decreased in the last decade. There is an indication of convergence in the education and employment among urban males. The difference in school attendance declined at a greater pace than the difference in employment. We find that the school attendance patterns across castes and religions are more similar in recent years than they were a decade ago. However, there remain substantial differences in employment of female youth from different castes and religions.

The rest of the chapter is organised as follows. Section 16.2 presents the conceptual framework behind the schooling versus work decision of youth. It also reviews the relevant literature. Section 16.3 reports the descriptive statistics from the three rounds of survey data. Section 16.4 uses an econometric model to estimate the effects of a set of variables including caste and religion on school attendance and employment. Section 16.5 presents the comparison across castes and religions on the basis of predicted probabilities of school attendance and employment of youth. The last section concludes the chapter.

16.2 Conceptual Background

At the age of 15, an individual can choose between two alternatives—to continue education or to enter the labour market.[1] The human capital investment model provides a convenient framework to understand this decision. An individual will invest in further education if the present value of expected benefit is higher than the present value of expected costs (Becker 1964).

In this framework, the caste and religion division in education versus work decision can be thought of as arising from differential cost and return from education. Economic backwardness of lower castes and minority religion affects their ability to invest in schooling in the presence of credit constraints. Discrimination in the labour market also negatively affects human capital investment of disadvantaged groups. However, discrimination can have opposite effects on human capital investment.

[1] As in many countries, the legal age to enter the labour market in India is 15 years, below which work is considered as child labour.

After controlling for family background, high school graduates from ethnic minority groups in the USA and UK are found to be more likely to proceed for post-high school education. One explanation is that the ethnic minority invests more in education in order to counter the possibility of racial discrimination (Rice 1999).

Recently, there has been a growing recognition of network effects on education and employment decisions (Munshi and Rosenzweig 2006; Burns et al. 2010; Nandi 2010). In a context where network plays a key role for labour market outcomes, the education decision is perturbed by the network effect. An individual with network contacts who has low education and less favourable labour market outcomes may decide to invest less in education if his/her prospect of obtaining employment through the network is high. Cross-country evidence suggests that networks are often formed along ethnic lines within a geographic area. Caste- and religion-based networks can be instrumental in observed social difference in education and employment.

Social norms, across castes and religions, have implication for the education and work decision of youth, particularly that of females. Preferences and practices intrinsic to a religion may inhibit household investment in education and skills valued in the labour market. In case of India, Borooah and Iyer (2005) speculate that for Muslims, deficit in education may in part result from a preference for religious education over secular education. The effect of religion-specific preference can be more pronounced for education and employment outcomes of females.

Often education versus work decision of youth is modelled as a binary outcome. Acknowledging that a youth may face a choice between four options—schooling, work, both and nothing—the multinomial model has also been used in a number of studies (Nguyen and Taylor 2003; Rouse 1994). In this chapter, we use a multinomial logit model to estimate the education and work decisions of youth in India.

16.3 Data and Descriptive Statistics

We use data from three rounds of the Employment and Unemployment Survey—55th round (1999–2000), 61st round (2004–2005) and 66th round (2009–2010)—conducted by the NSSO. In each round, the NSSO surveyed a national representative sample of households from all states in India. The information collected pertains to the employment and unemployment situation of household members. Apart from the employment-related information, the survey data set also contains socio-demographic information, including current school attendance and educational attainment of all household members.

We focus on these three rounds as they coincide with the period of rapid economic growth in India. In the National Youth Policy of India (2012), young people are defined as those who are in the age bracket of 16–30 years. In our analysis, we use youth within the age bracket of 15–24 years. Since our analysis focuses on both education and employment of youth, this age group is particularly important as 15 years is the legal lower age limit to be employed and by 24 years the majority of the youth is likely to finish their education. This is also the age bracket within which the school-to-work transition takes place for the majority.

The changes in school attendance and employment of 15–24-year-old individuals are presented in graphs in this section. A table in the Appendix gives exact numbers behind the graphs. The graphs allow comparisons across rural–urban, male–female and different rounds of the survey. Three distinct bars stand for school attendance, employment and idle (doing nothing) status of a young individual. Conceptually, there can be an overlap between schooling and working (doing both). Since this group represents less than 1 % in all rounds of the survey and in all subsamples, the group has been clubbed with the status employed. Hence, the status "employed" stands for both "working and attending school" and "only working".

Figure 16.1 presents the percentage of school attendance and employment of two age groups—15–19 years and 20–24 years. The four panels in the graph correspond to four subsamples—rural male, urban male, rural female and urban female. The difference between the age groups is evident for both males and females. For males, the younger group is more likely to be in school and less likely to be in employment than the older group. However, for females, the younger group is more likely to be in school and less likely to be idle than the older group. The difference is more pronounced in rural areas than in urban areas. Over the years (rounds of survey), the school attendance of both males and females has increased. This increase is much higher in rural areas than in urban areas. However, there is indication that increased schooling is able to reduce labour market engagement of older group males in both rural and urban areas. We also observe that school attendance of older group females caused the percentage being idle to decline in both rural and urban areas. However, the percentage of 20–24-year-old females being idle still stands at an alarming height (more than 60%).

Figure 16.2 presents the school attendance and employment of four castes—Scheduled Tribes (ST), Scheduled Caste (SC), Other Backward Caste (OBC) and General Caste (GEN). We observe a similar pattern of change for males of both rural and urban areas—increase in school attendance and decline in employment, except that school attendance (employment) of GEN males in urban area records a decline (increase) from 1999–2000 to 2004–2005. In rural areas, changes in school attendance of males from ST, SC, OBC and GEN are very similar, except that the percentage attending school among the GEN was much higher than other castes in 1999–2000. Surprisingly, males from ST in urban areas have a higher percentage of schooling than other castes over the years. For females, a similar pattern is found—increase in school attendance and decrease in being idle in both rural and urban areas. Again, school attendance among ST is the highest among all castes in urban areas over the years. Being idle is the majority category among SC, OBC and GEN in all years in rural areas. It remains the majority category for SC and OBC also in urban areas.

The school attendance and employment of different religious groups are presented in Fig. 16.3. For males, the general pattern prevails—increase in school attendance and decrease in employment in both rural and urban areas over the years, except that the school attendance rate declined slightly for male Hindus in urban

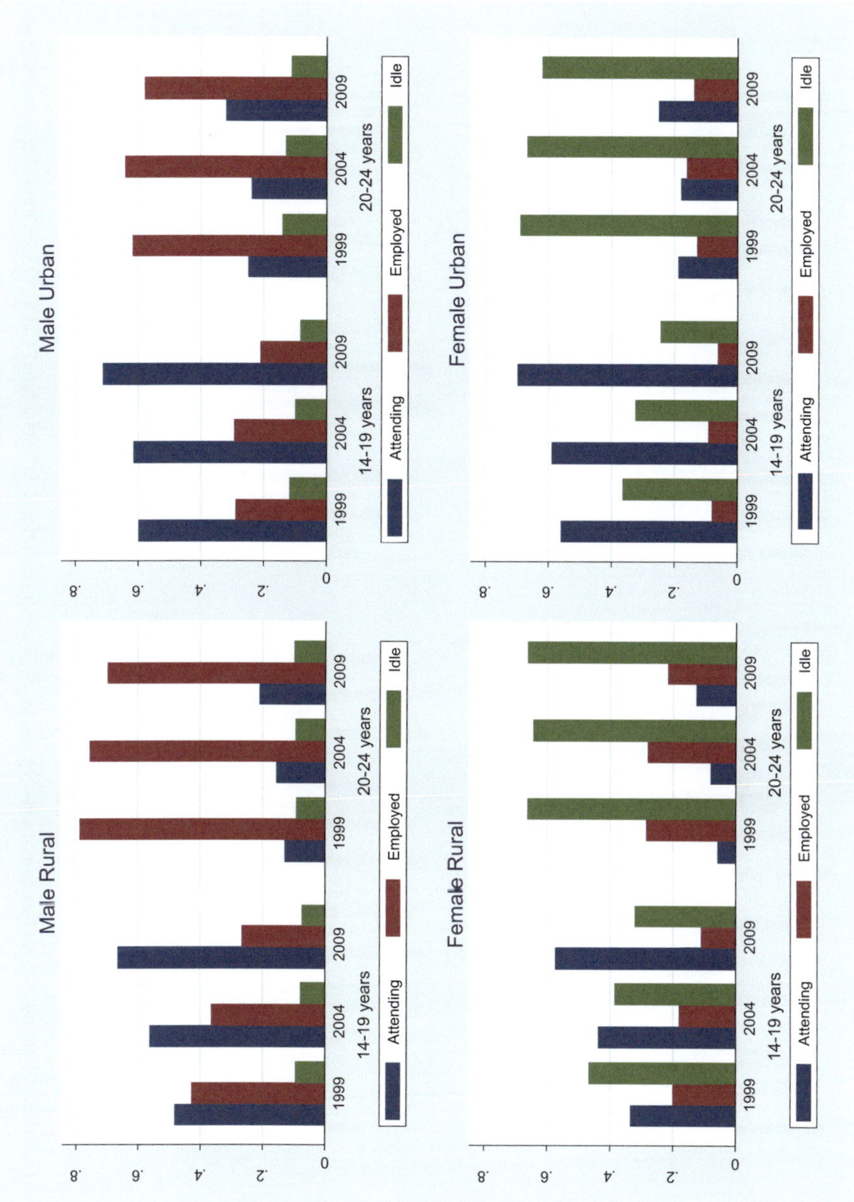

Fig. 16.1 School attendance and employment—by age group

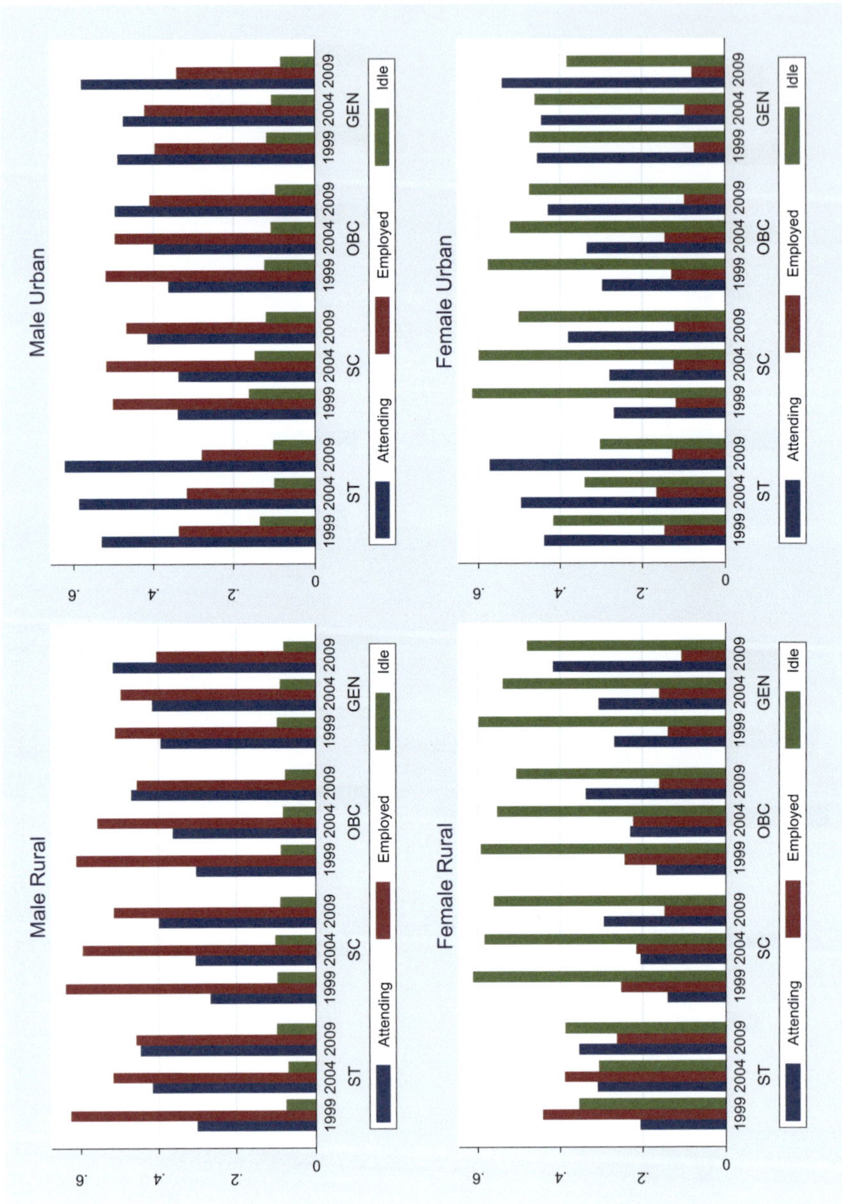

Fig. 16.2 School attendance and employment—by caste. *ST* Scheduled Tribes, *SC* Scheduled Caste, *OBC* Other Backward Caste, *GEN* General Caste

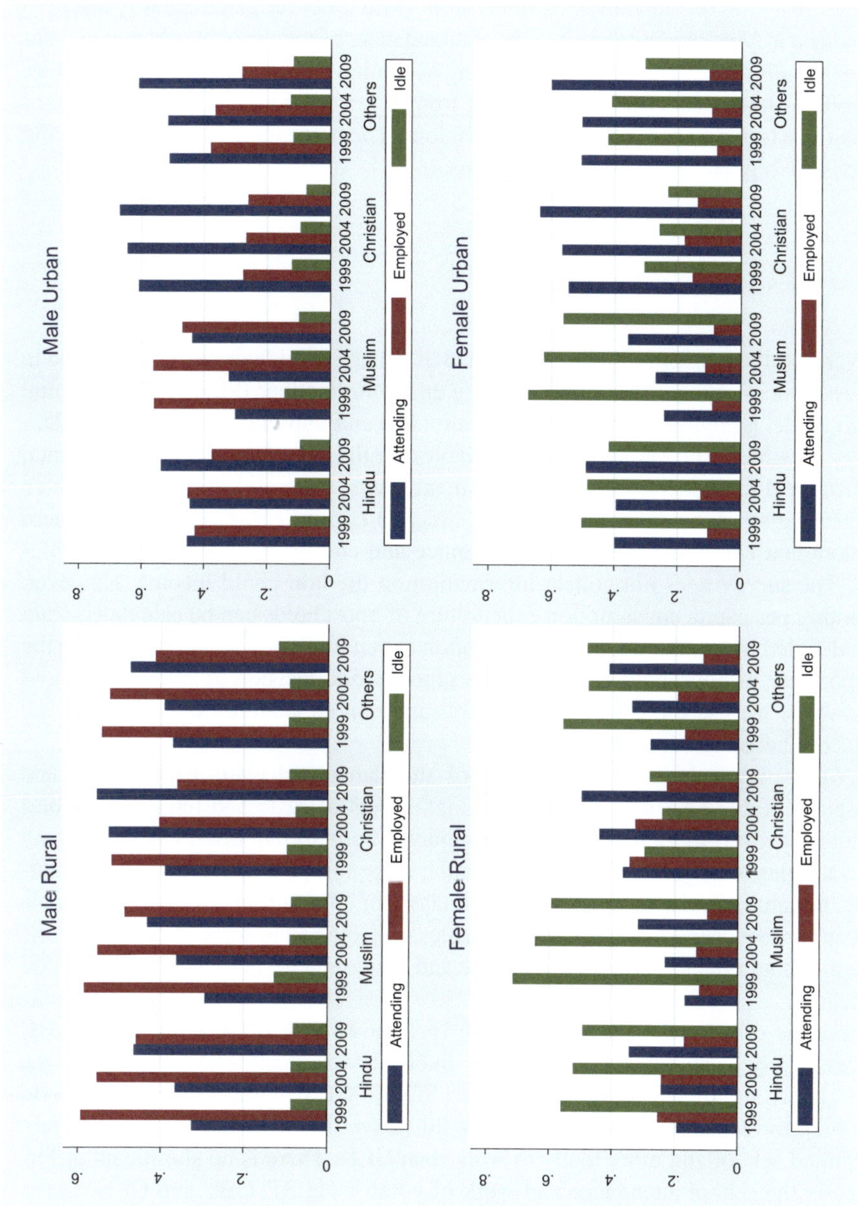

Fig. 16.3 School attendance and employment—by religion

areas in the year 2004–2005. Hindu and Muslim males appear very similar in rural areas. However, Hindu–Muslim difference is evident for urban male individuals. In urban areas, school attendance among Hindus (both male and female) is much higher than that of Muslims. Christians along with other religions are way ahead of Hindus and Muslims in terms of school attendance, particularly in urban areas. For female individuals, we observe increasing schooling in both rural and urban areas. Muslims along with Hindus stand apart from other religions, as the percentage of being idle is higher among the former religions. The percentage of individuals being idle is the highest among female Muslims.

16.4 Estimation Results

Given that the work and school attendance of young individuals can be presented in three groups—attending school, working and doing neither (idle)—a multinomial logit model is estimated incorporating individual and family background as explanatory variables. The model includes variables for the age of the individual, parental educational attainment, father's employment status, caste and religion. State-fixed effect is also included in the model in order to control for the state-level macro factors that can affect the school attendance and employment of young individuals. The survey does not collect information on the household income. However, monthly per capita consumption expenditure of households can be calculated from the detailed information on the consumption expenditure of a household. Given the importance of household income on the school/work decision of young household members, we use monthly per capita consumption expenditure to control for the effect of household income.

We focus on the difference in school attendance and work across castes and religions. Table 16.1 presents the marginal effects of caste and religion variables calculated from the multinomial logit model. The marginal effects of the full set of variables are reported in Table A2 in the Appendix. For each round of the survey, the multinomial logit model is estimated for four subsamples—urban males, urban females, rural males and rural females. For each subsample, the table reports the marginal effect on school attendance and employment, holding idle as the base category.

For the urban male subsample, Table 16.1 shows that in 1999–2000 only OBC is less likely to attend school and more likely to work than GEN. There is also a marginally significant difference between SC and GEN in the probability of work. Turning to the same subsample in 2004–2009, we find that only SC is less likely to attend school and more likely to work than GEN. There is no significant difference in the school attendance and work of youth from ST, OBC and GEN. In the 2009–2010 urban male subsample, none of the caste variables is significant. There is no significant difference in the school attendance and work of youth across castes.

For the rural male subsample, we observe that in 1999–2000 the only significant estimate is the positive effect for OBC on work. For school attendance, there is no

Table 16.1 Marginal effects of castes and religions from the multinomial logit model

1999–00 (55th round)

	Male Urban				Female Urban				Male Rural				Female Rural			
	Education		Work		Education		Work		Education		Work		Education		Work	
	Marginal effect	S. E.	Marginal effect	S. E.	Marginal effect	S. E.	Marginal effect	S. E.	Marginal Effect	S. E.	Marginal Effect	S. E.	Marginal Effect	S. E.	Marginal Effect	S. E.
Caste (ref. General Caste)																
Scheduled Tribe	0.08	0.07	-0.07	0.07	-0.22***	0.08	0.45***	0.12	-0.01	0.05	0.04	0.03	-0.15**	0.08	0.74***	0.05
Scheduled Caste	0.02	0.04	-0.07*	0.04	-0.11**	0.05	0.05	0.09	0.05	0.04	-0.01	0.02	-0.11*	0.06	0.23***	0.05
Other Backward Caste	-0.07***	0.03	0.09***	0.03	-0.17***	0.04	0.20***	0.07	-0.04	0.03	0.04**	0.02	-0.18***	0.05	0.21***	0.04
Religion (ref. Hindu)																
Muslim	-0.14***	0.03	0.11***	0.03	-0.34***	0.04	-0.11	0.08	-0.07*	0.04	0.02	0.03	-0.33***	0.07	-0.11**	0.06
Christian	0.17**	0.08	-0.22***	0.08	0.25***	0.09	0.20	0.14	0.13	0.08	-0.10**	0.05	0.24**	0.11	-0.03	0.09
Other Religion	-0.04	0.06	0.05	0.06	0.09	0.07	-0.07	0.15	-0.05	0.07	0.06	0.04	-0.03	0.10	-0.09	0.09
Log likelihood				-12,198.91				-10,537.54				-16,134.08				-16,702.28
Number of observations				18,690				17,892				27,362				26,041

2004–05 (61st round)

	Male Urban				Female Urban				Male Rural				Female Rural			
	Education		Work		Education		Work		Education		Work		Education		Work	
	Marginal effect	S. E.	Marginal effect	S. E.	Marginal effect	S. E.	Marginal effect	S. E.	Marginal Effect	S. E.	Marginal Effect	S. E.	Marginal Effect	S. E.	Marginal Effect	S. E.
Caste (ref. General Caste)																
Scheduled Tribe	-0.01	0.08	-0.04	0.08	0.00	0.10	0.32**	0.14	0.13***	0.05	-0.05	0.03	0.25***	0.07	0.48***	0.05
Scheduled Caste	0.10**	0.05	-0.15***	0.05	-0.12**	0.05	-0.01	0.09	0.05	0.04	-0.01	0.03	0.00	0.05	0.08*	0.05
Other Backward Caste	-0.01	0.03	0.03	0.03	-0.14***	0.04	0.19***	0.07	-0.03	0.03	0.05**	0.02	-0.05	0.04	0.11***	0.04
Religion (ref. Hindu)																
Muslim	-0.14***	0.04	0.07**	0.04	-0.32***	0.05	-0.15**	0.08	-0.01	0.04	0.03	0.03	-0.20***	0.06	-0.18***	0.06
Christian	0.36***	0.10	-0.39***	0.10	-0.02	0.10	0.24	0.16	0.22***	0.07	-0.12**	0.05	0.22**	0.09	-0.11	0.09
Other Religion	-0.04	0.07	0.00	0.07	0.22***	0.08	-0.23	0.15	-0.09	0.07	0.08	0.05	-0.06	0.09	-0.03	0.09
Log likelihood				-8,905.10				-8,739.41				-15,431.75				-17,090.10
Number of observations				14,630				14,190				27,037				25,529

2009–10 (66th round)

	Male Urban				Female Urban				Male Rural				Female Rural			
	Education		Work		Education		Work		Education		Work		Education		Work	
	Marginal effect	S. E.	Marginal effect	S. E.	Marginal effect	S. E.	Marginal effect	S. E.	Marginal Effect	S. E.	Marginal Effect	S. E.	Marginal Effect	S. E.	Marginal Effect	S. E.
Caste (ref. General Caste)																
Scheduled Tribe	-0.04	0.06	-0.01	0.09	0.03	0.08	0.08	0.16	-0.06	0.04	0.03	0.04	-0.15***	0.06	0.53***	0.07
Scheduled Caste	0.01	0.04	-0.03	0.05	-0.05	0.05	0.10	0.10	-0.05	0.03	0.07**	0.04	-0.10**	0.05	0.20***	0.07
Other Backward Caste	-0.02	0.03	0.02	0.04	-0.12***	0.04	0.06	0.08	0.01	0.03	0.00	0.03	-0.13***	0.04	0.31***	0.06
Religion (ref. Hindu)																
Muslim	-0.02	0.03	0.02	0.05	-0.31***	0.04	-0.20**	0.09	-0.09***	0.04	0.10***	0.04	-0.22***	0.05	-0.14**	0.07
Christian	0.14*	0.08	-0.16	0.12	0.15	0.09	0.01	0.20	-0.05	0.07	0.07	0.07	0.11	0.09	0.22**	0.11
Other Religion	0.04	0.06	-0.14	0.09	0.14**	0.07	0.26*	0.16	0.11*	0.06	-0.12*	0.07	0.03	0.08	-0.44***	0.13
Log likelihood				-8,007.18				-7,662.84				-12,664.13				-13,317.88
Number of observations				14,153				13,289				22,531				20,969

Note: *, ** and *** stand for significance at 10%, 5% and 1% level, respectively.

significant difference between castes. In 2004–2005, SC appears to be less likely to attend school and more likely to work than GEN. The positive significant effect for OBC on work also persists in 2004–2005. In 2009–2010, again, the only significant estimate is the positive effect for SC on work. For school attendance, there is no significant difference across castes.

Now turning to the female youth subsample, we find that in 1999–2000 most of the caste variables are significant. Female individuals from ST, SC and OBC are less likely to attend school and more likely to work than female from GEN in both urban and rural areas. In 2004–2005, for the urban subsample the marginal effect for ST on school attendance is not significant. OBC is still less likely to attend school in urban as well as in rural area. ST is more likely to work in both rural and urban subsamples. Surprisingly, ST is more likely to attend school than GEN in rural areas indicating a lower probability of being idle among ST. In 2009–2010, for the urban subsample the only significant estimate is the negative marginal effect for OBC. Otherwise, there is no significant difference between castes in urban areas. However, all the caste variables are significant in the female rural subsample, indicating GEN is more likely to attend school and less likely to work than all other castes.

The estimates of the variables for different religions show that in 1999–2000 Muslim (Christian) males are less (more) likely to attend school and more (less) likely to work than Hindus in urban areas. The same difference is observed in the 2004–2005 urban male subsample. However, in 2009–2010, there is no significant (at least at 5 %) difference between different religious groups. In the rural male subsample, we find that Christians are less likely to work in 1999–2000. They are more likely to attend school and less likely to work than Hindus in 2004–2005. A significant difference between Hindus and Muslims is not evident in these two rounds. However, Muslims are less likely to attend school and more likely to work than Hindus in 2009–2010.

Turning to the estimates of religion for the female subsample we find that in 1999–2000 Muslims are less likely to attend school and less likely to work than Hindus in both urban and rural areas—indicating higher probability of being idle among Muslim females. The same pattern prevails in 2004–2005 and 2009–2010 subsamples. Christian female individuals are more likely to attend school in both urban and rural areas in 1999–2000. Their school attendance advantage continues only in rural areas in 2004–2009. In 2009–2010, there is no significant difference between Hindu and Christian females in school attendance. Christian females are, however, more likely to work in rural areas.

Marginal effects of other variables are reported in Table A2 in the Appendix. We observe that age is negatively associated with education and positively with work in all subsamples in all rounds. Father's educational attainment is positively associated with education and negatively with work of an individual. A similar pattern is observed for mother's education. However, the effect is not significant for all levels of mother's education in all subsamples of the three rounds of the survey. Fathers being wage earners is consistently associated with higher probability of school attendance and lower probability of working.

To sum up the estimation results, we find that in the urban male subsample the caste difference in school attendance and employment has almost disappeared in recent years. In the urban female subsample the caste difference in school attendance has declined. In any round, there is no significant caste difference in the urban female subsample. The same is observed among rural males—a declining difference across castes in school attendance and employment. However, the caste difference is evident and persistent among rural females both in school attendance and employment. The difference across religions in the urban male subsample is declining both in employment and school attendance. This is not the case among females in urban areas. Religion difference does not seem to reduce in the rural subsample. The difference between religions is substantial among rural females.

16.5 Comparison of Predicted Probabilities

In this section, we compare predicted probabilities of school attendance and work, calculated from the multinomial model. The graphs below allow an age-wise comparison of the probabilities for different castes in urban and rural areas.

Figure 16.4 presents the probability of work from the male sample of the three rounds. Visual inspection of the graph reveals that there is little variation in the probability of school along the caste and urban–rural line in 2009–2010, though the variation is slightly visible in 1999–2000 and 2004–2005. One interesting finding in 2009–2010 is the crossover by ST males in urban areas. They are less likely to attend school than other castes up to the age of 18 years. However, from the age of 20 years, they are more likely to attend school than others. In general, the difference between different castes and in urban–rural areas has reduced over the decade.

Probability of work of the male subsample is presented in Fig. 16.5. Though differences across castes are evident in 1999–2000 and 2004–2005, there seems to be convergence in 2009–2010 at least for the younger age group. The urban–rural difference has also narrowed down over the decade. Urban ST and urban SC in 1999–2000 and 2004–2005 are distinct groups with lower probability of work than others. Their difference with the rest declines in 2009–2010. However, in the higher age group, they are still less likely to work than others.

Predicted probability of school attendance of females for different castes is presented in Fig. 16.6. First thing to notice from the figure is that the urban–rural difference is not substantial. In 1999–2000, the urban GEN has higher probability of school attendance than others up to the age of 19 years. From the age of 20, urban SC has higher probability than others, though the difference between the castes (both urban and rural areas) is very small. Rather a slightly higher variation is observed in 2004–2005. Again, up to the age of 19 years, urban GEN has higher probability of school attendance. In the higher age group, rural SC has the highest probability of school attendance. In 2009–2010, the inter-caste and rural–urban variations are lowest in three rounds of the survey. However, school attendance in rural areas is always slightly less than that in urban areas.

Turning to the probability of work of females from different castes (Fig. 16.7), we observe a considerable variation within a year, but the variation seems to be

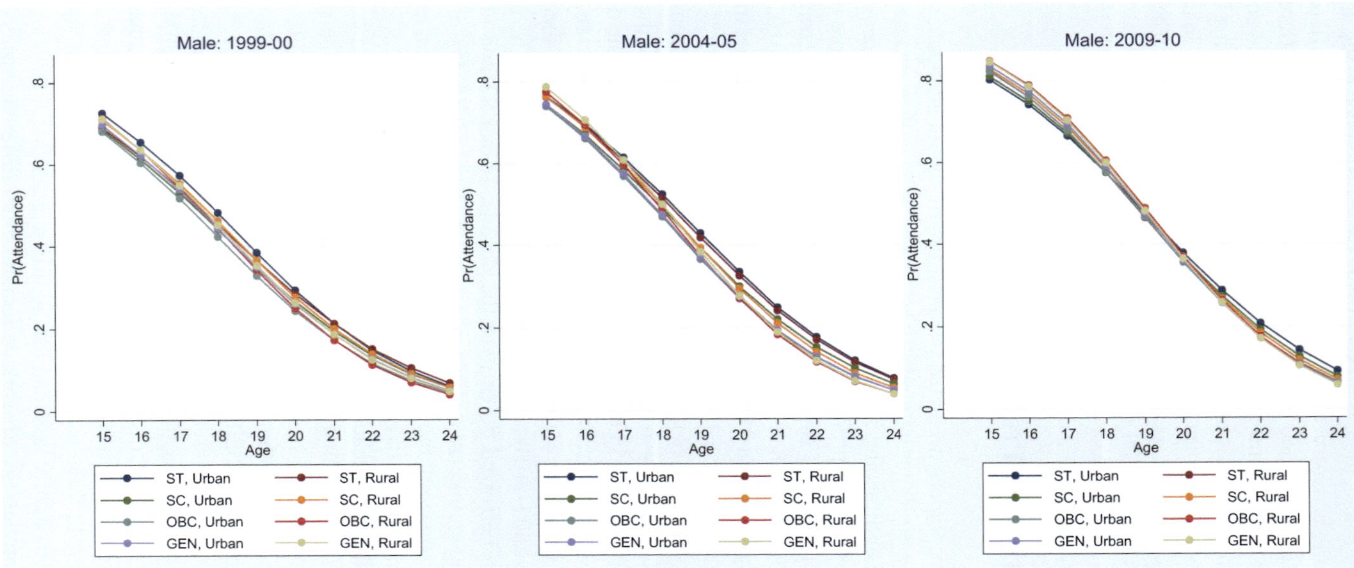

Fig. 16.4 Predicted probability of school attendance of males by caste and rural–urban areas. *ST* Scheduled Tribes, *SC* Scheduled Caste, *OBC* Other Backward Caste, *GEN* General Caste

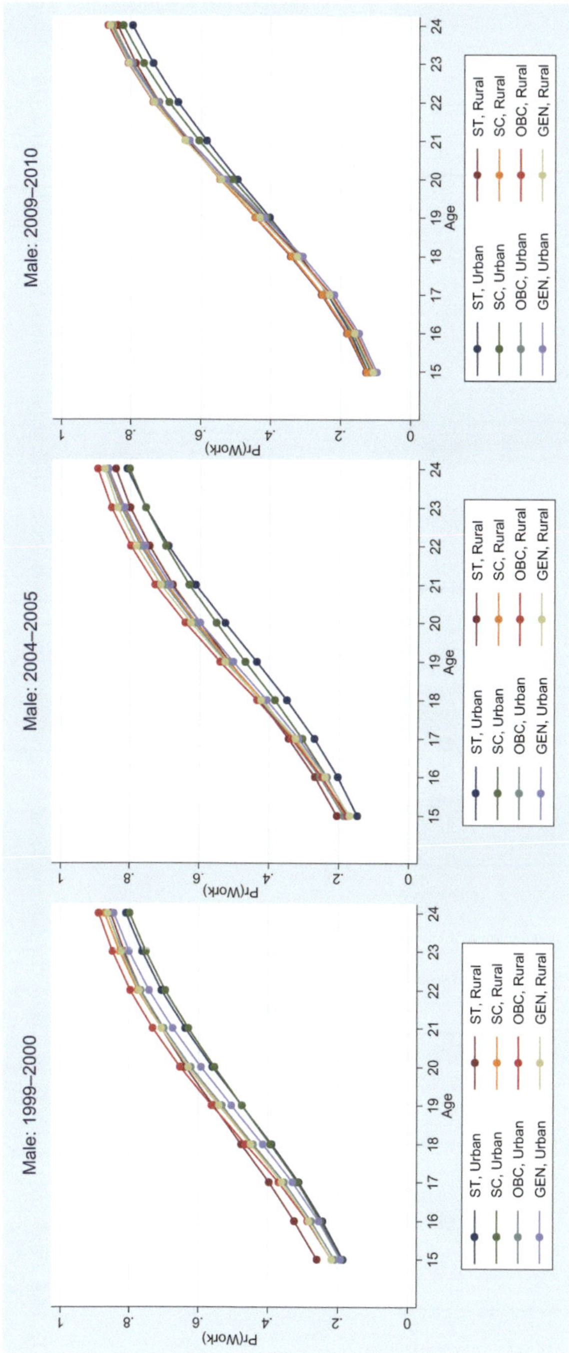

Fig. 16.5 Predicted probability of work of males by caste and urban–rural areas. *ST* Scheduled Tribes, *SC* Scheduled Caste, *OBC* Other Backward Caste, *GEN* General Caste

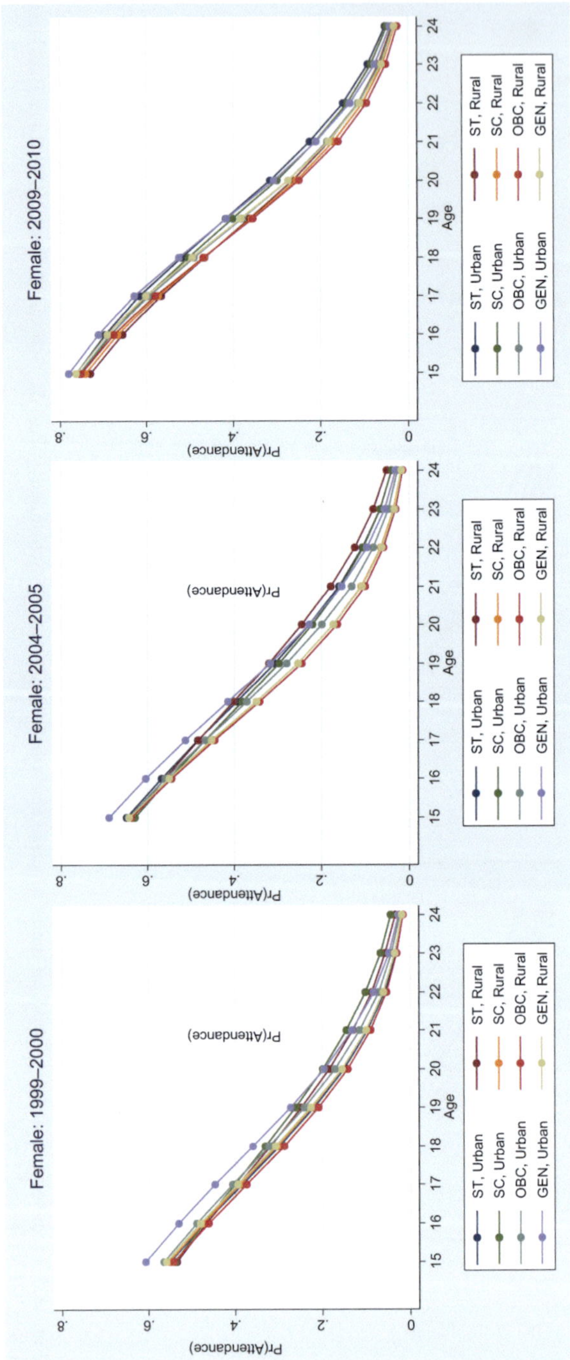

Fig. 16.6 Predicted probability of school attendance of females by caste and rural–urban areas. *ST* Scheduled Tribes, *SC* Scheduled Caste, *OBC* Other Backward Caste, *GEN* General Caste

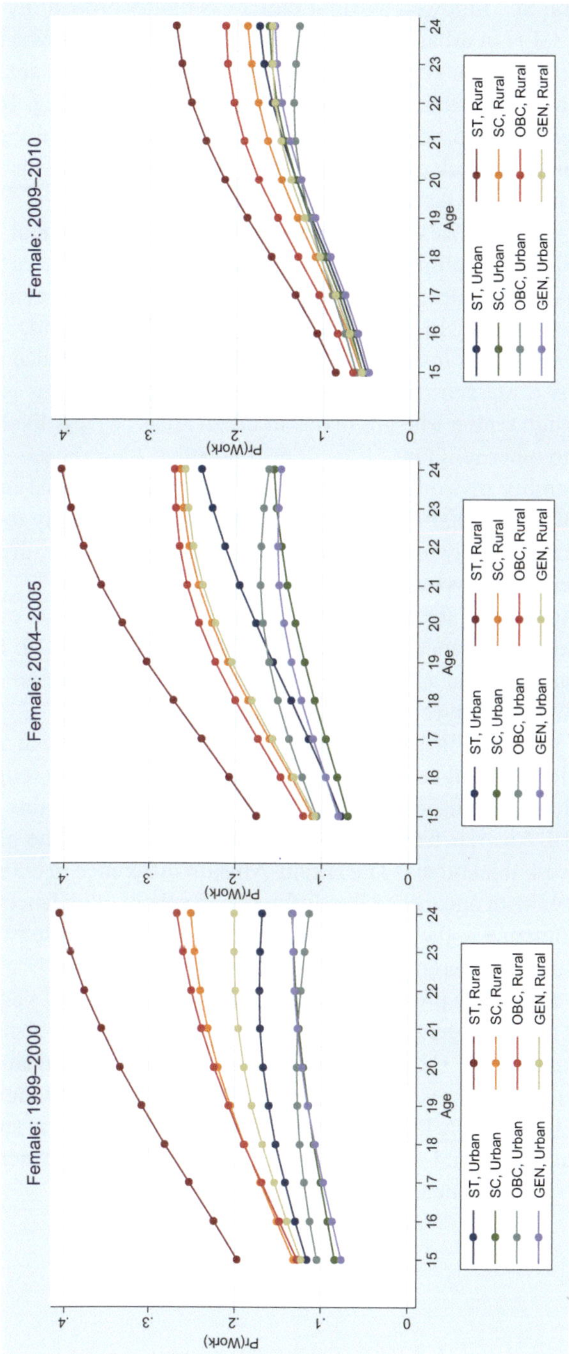

Fig. 16.7 Predicted probability of work of females by caste and rural–urban areas. *ST* Scheduled Tribes, *SC* Scheduled Caste, *OBC* Other Backward Caste, *GEN* General Caste

reducing over the years. Urban–rural difference is substantial in a year, but declining over time. Rural SC, followed by rural OBC, has higher probability of work in all the years. And, GEN in urban area, followed by urban SC, has lower probability of work. We observe that convergence across caste and rural–urban areas has been more in the older age group than in the younger age group. From Fig. 16.6, we observe that for the older group, school attendance has not increased substantially. So, decreasing probability of work over years for this group implies that the probability of being "idle" in this group has increased over time.

Next, we turn to differences in the predicted probability of school attendance and work among different religions. Figure 16.8 presents the predicted probability of work for the male subsample. The difference across religions is evident in both 1999–2000 and 2004–2005. In both rounds, the probability of school attendance of younger Muslim males is lower than other religions. The difference across religions in rural areas is not substantial. The difference across religions is much less in 2009–2010, though young Muslim males in urban areas are less likely to attend school compared to other religions.

Predicted probability of work of the male subsample is presented in Fig. 16.9. In round 1999–2000 and 2004–2005, Christian males are less likely to work than others, as they are more likely to attend school than others. However, the difference across religions becomes less evident in 2009–2010.

In the female subsample the difference across religious groups is evident. The probability of school attendance of females is presented in Fig. 16.10. Muslim females in both urban and rural areas are less likely to attend school than others. The difference seems to persist over the years.

Probability of work of different religious groups is presented in Fig. 16.11. First thing we notice is that there is a considerable difference across religions in all rounds. Though there is indication of decline in difference, it remains substantial even in 2009–2010. Muslim females in urban areas, particularly the older group, are less likely to work than others. The Hindu–Muslim difference in both urban and rural areas increases with age. Since the difference in school attendance is not substantial, higher difference in the probability of being idle across these two religions is the counterpart of the difference in their probability of work.

To sum up, the analysis of predicted probabilities of different castes and religions shows a tendency of convergence. The urban–rural difference has substantially reduced. The male subsample shows a greater pace of convergence than the female subsample. The difference in school attendance across castes and religions is less evident in 2009–2010 than in 1999–2000. However, the difference is still substantial across castes, religions and urban–rural areas as far as the employment of young female individuals is concerned.

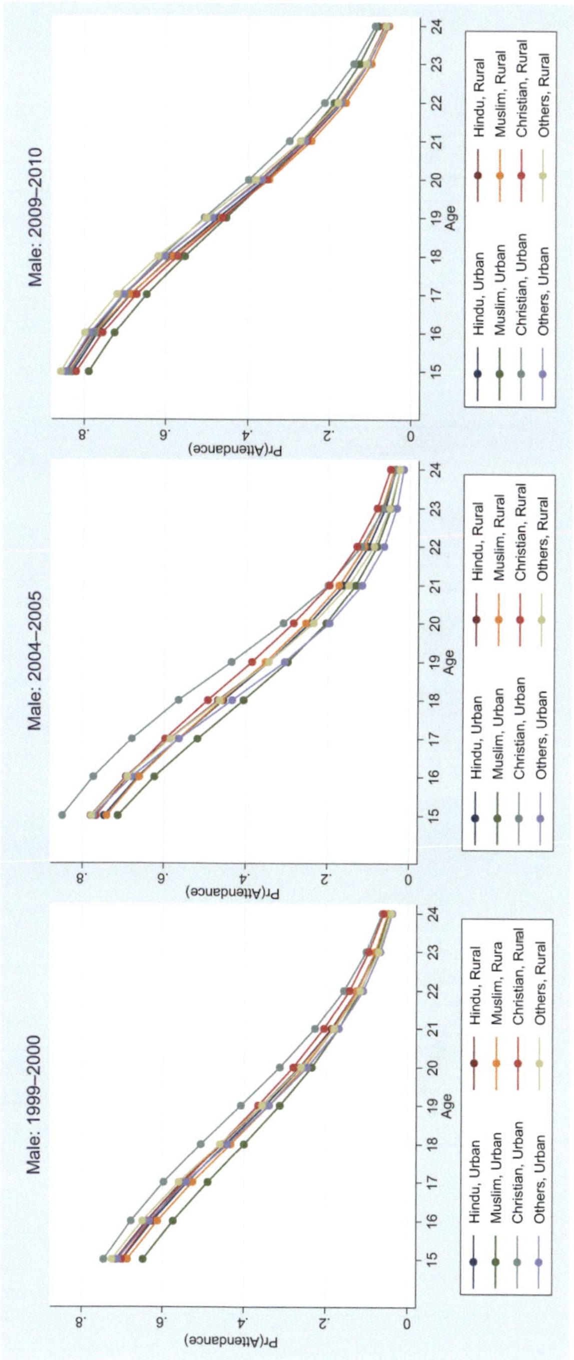

Fig. 16.8 Predicted probability of school attendance of males by religion and rural–urban areas

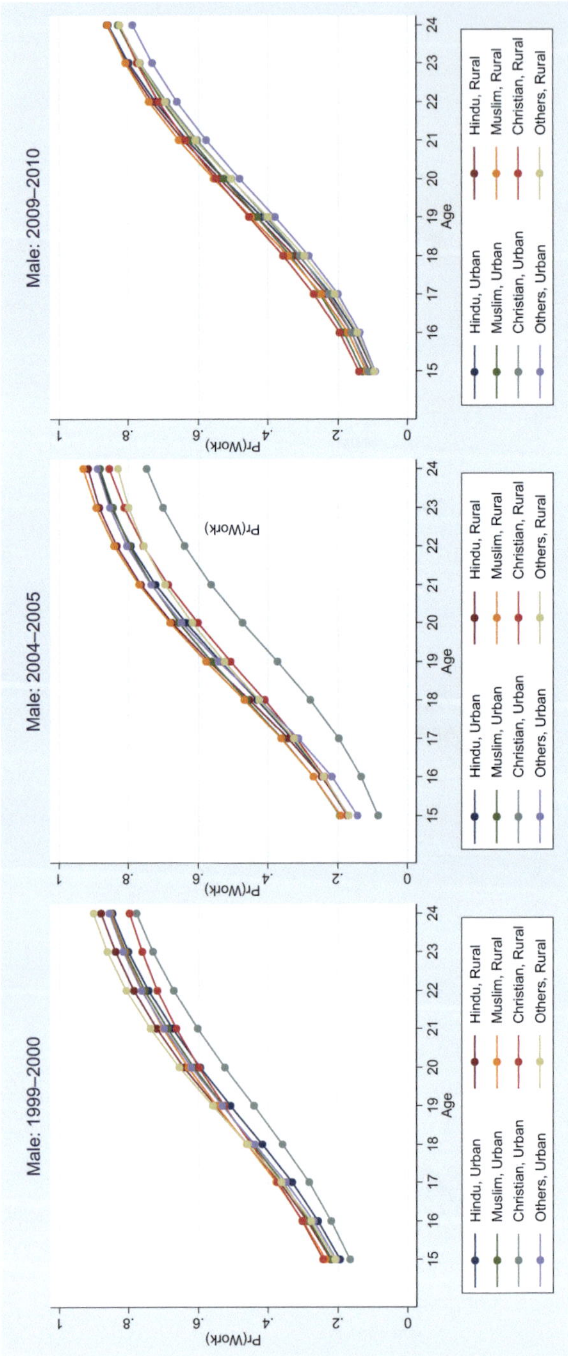

Fig. 16.9 Predicted probability of work of males by religion and rural–urban areas

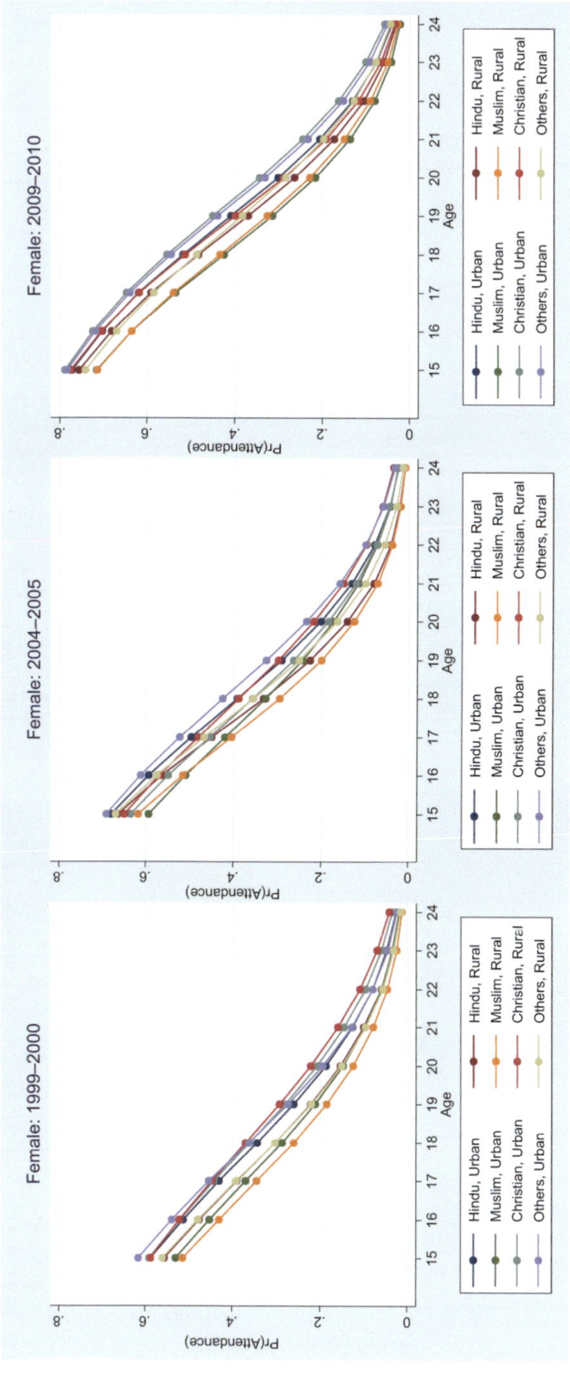

Fig. 16.10 Predicted probability of school attendance of females by religion and rural–urban areas

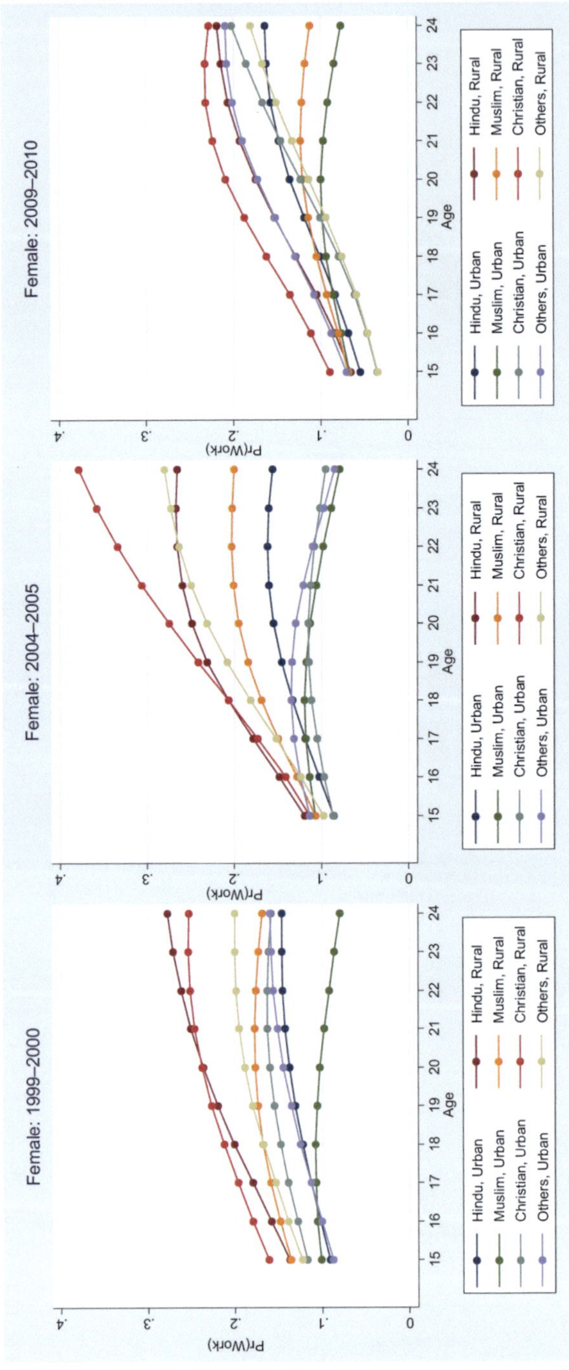

Fig. 16.11 Predicted probability of work of females by religion and rural–urban areas

16.6 Conclusion

In this chapter, we have analysed the school attendance and employment of youth in India. Using data from three rounds of a nationally representative survey, we found indications of convergence across castes and religious groups. Among the urban males, the difference in school attendance and employment across castes has declined over the last decade. In recent years, the difference has almost disappeared. We observed a similar pattern among urban females and rural males. However, the difference seems to persist among the rural females.

For different religious groups, we observed a slightly different pattern of evolution of school attendance and employment. Though the difference in school attendance and employment of youth across religions seems to decline for males in both urban and rural areas, the pace of convergence is higher in school attendance. Females, from different castes, still have varying propensity to attend school. There seems to be less convergence in school attendance. Substantial difference in employment is found between females of different religions, though the difference declined over time.

The findings of this chapter lend partial support to the convergence in school attendance and employment of youth across castes and religions. It is important to note that the present analysis does not account for the quality of education and employment that may be substantially different across castes and religion. Future research should address the issue using further details of schooling and employment of youth in India.

Appendix

Table A1 Descriptive statistics—1999–2000, 2004–2005 and 2009–2010

	1999–2000 (NSS 55th round)											
	Urban						Rural					
	Male			Female			Male			Female		
	Attending	Employed	Idle	Attending	Employed	Idle	Attending	Employed	Idle	Attending	Employed	Idle
All	43.13	44.35	12.52	38.00	10.19	51.81	32.28	58.61	9.11	19.89	23.99	56.12
Age 15–19 years	59.70	28.88	11.42	55.81	7.98	36.21	48.01	42.72	9.27	33.46	19.89	46.65
Age 20–24 years	24.65	61.60	13.75	18.69	12.58	68.73	12.69	78.40	8.91	5.66	28.29	66.05
ST	52.90	33.75	13.35	43.91	14.54	41.55	30.01	62.53	7.46	20.53	44.19	35.28
SC	33.88	50.11	16.01	26.86	11.77	61.37	26.62	63.88	9.50	13.96	25.05	60.99
OBC	36.10	51.80	12.10	29.60	12.86	57.54	30.21	61.15	8.64	16.57	24.29	59.14
Gen	48.80	39.53	11.67	45.48	7.28	47.24	39.33	51.04	9.63	26.71	13.79	59.50
Hindu	45.13	42.73	12.14	39.81	10.12	50.07	32.49	59.08	8.43	19.06	25.17	55.77
Muslim	29.93	55.80	14.27	24.08	8.80	67.12	29.27	58.25	12.48	16.61	11.98	71.41
Christian	60.54	27.54	11.92	54.54	15.10	30.36	38.82	51.62	9.56	36.25	34.36	29.39
Others	50.88	37.67	11.45	50.49	7.46	42.05	36.96	53.92	9.12	27.65	16.88	55.47
Number of observations			33,052			29,324			47,246			44,936

Table A1 (continued)

	2004–2005 (NSS 61st round)											
	Urban						Rural					
	Male			Female			Male			Female		
	Attending	Employed	Idle	Attending	Employed	Idle	Attending	Employed	Idle	Attending	Employed	Idle
All	43.59	45.40	11.01	38.62	12.35	49.03	37.66	53.92	8.42	25.97	22.89	51.14
Age 15–19 years	61.27	29.14	9.59	58.80	8.93	32.27	55.99	36.35	7.66	43.68	17.98	38.34
Age 20–24 years	23.53	63.85	12.62	17.56	15.93	66.51	15.42	75.24	9.34	7.85	27.92	64.23
ST	58.66	31.59	9.75	49.51	16.56	33.93	41.55	51.68	6.77	30.85	38.75	30.40
SC	33.60	51.78	14.62	27.93	12.37	59.70	30.42	59.44	10.14	20.34	21.49	58.17
OBC	39.89	49.64	10.47	33.51	14.48	52.01	36.30	55.66	8.04	22.87	22.09	55.04
Gen	47.45	42.18	10.37	44.41	9.56	46.03	41.58	49.65	8.77	30.52	15.86	53.62
Hindu	44.32	44.87	10.81	39.28	12.35	48.37	36.41	55.20	8.39	24.12	23.94	51.94
Muslim	31.92	55.96	12.12	26.77	11.03	62.20	36.10	55.04	8.86	22.82	12.98	64.20
Christian	64.26	26.61	9.13	56.61	17.77	25.62	52.31	40.23	7.46	43.73	32.51	23.76
Others	51.25	36.39	12.36	50.13	9.10	40.77	39.02	52.02	8.96	33.48	19.06	47.46
Number of observations			21,293			19,199			37,964			36,185

Table A1 (continued)

	2009–2010 (NSS 66th round)											
	Urban						Rural					
	Male			Female			Male			Female		
	Attending	Employed	Idle	Attending	Employed	Idle	Attending	Employed	Idle	Attending	Employed	Idle
All	52.82	37.87	9.31	47.89	9.62	42.49	46.59	45.14	8.27	35.33	16.02	48.65
Age 15–19 years	71.11	20.87	8.02	69.67	5.98	24.35	66.32	26.48	7.20	57.19	10.84	31.97
Age 20–24 years	31.66	57.54	10.80	24.66	13.50	61.84	20.93	69.41	9.66	12.52	21.43	66.05
ST	62.17	27.77	10.06	57.24	12.69	30.07	44.50	45.73	9.77	35.26	26.08	38.66
SC	41.43	46.82	11.75	37.89	12.09	50.02	39.80	51.43	8.77	29.33	14.67	56.00
OBC	49.56	40.89	9.55	42.93	9.74	47.33	46.99	45.40	7.61	33.65	15.92	50.43
Gen	57.84	34.11	8.05	53.98	7.84	38.18	51.64	40.48	7.88	41.64	10.50	47.86
Hindu	53.50	37.28	9.22	48.86	9.56	41.58	46.27	45.82	7.91	34.16	16.81	49.03
Muslim	43.62	46.66	9.72	35.60	8.34	56.06	43.06	48.45	8.49	31.44	9.54	59.02
Christian	66.75	25.80	7.45	63.49	13.58	22.93	55.13	35.86	9.01	49.56	22.53	27.91
Others	60.65	27.77	11.58	60.05	9.85	30.10	47.16	41.12	11.72	40.94	11.06	48.00
Number of observations			18,509			16,385			27,483			25,459

Table A2 Marginal effects from the multinomial logit model of education and work status

1999–2000 (55th round)

	Male Urban						Female Urban					
	Education			Work			Education			Work		
	Marginal effect		S. E.	Marginal effect		S. E.	Marginal effect		S. E.	Marginal effect		S. E.
Age	−0.37	***	0.01	0.36	***	0.01	−0.44	***	0.01	0.23	***	0.01
Father's Education												
Primary	0.00		0.04	0.00		0.04	0.01		0.05	−0.06		0.08
Secondary	0.19	***	0.03	−0.22	***	0.03	0.21	***	0.04	−0.58	***	0.08
Higher Secondary	0.37	***	0.05	−0.39	***	0.06	0.41	***	0.06	−0.68	***	0.13
College or University	0.43	***	0.05	−0.50	***	0.06	0.49	***	0.06	−0.62	***	0.13
Father's Employment												
Self–employed	−0.04		0.03	0.15	***	0.03	−0.04		0.04	−0.08		0.06
Regular wage earner	0.27	***	0.03	−0.39	***	0.03	0.09	**	0.04	−0.29	***	0.07
Mother's Education												
Primary	0.11	***	0.04	−0.11	***	0.04	0.10	**	0.05	−0.31	***	0.09
Secondary	0.18	***	0.03	−0.16	***	0.04	0.20	***	0.04	−0.10		0.09
Higher Secondary	0.14	**	0.06	−0.15	**	0.07	−0.01		0.06	0.01		0.15
College or University	0.31	***	0.07	−0.19	***	0.08	0.27	***	0.07	−0.14		0.17
Caste												
Scheduled Tribe	0.08		0.07	−0.07		0.07	−0.22	***	0.08	0.45	***	0.12
Scheduled Caste	0.02		0.04	−0.07	*	0.04	−0.11	**	0.05	0.05		0.09
Other Backward Caste	−0.07	***	0.03	0.09	***	0.03	−0.17	***	0.04	0.20	***	0.07
Religion												
Muslim	−0.14	***	0.03	0.11	***	0.03	−0.34	***	0.04	−0.11		0.08
Christian	0.17	**	0.08	−0.22	***	0.08	0.25	***	0.09	0.20		0.14
Other Religion	−0.04		0.06	0.05		0.06	0.09		0.07	−0.07		0.15
Log likelihood						−12,198.91						−10,537.54
Number of observations						18,690						17,892

	Male Rural						Female Rural					
	Education			Work			Education			Work		
	Marginal Effect		S. E.	Marginal Effect		S. E.	Marginal Effect		S. E.	Marginal Effect		S. E.
Age	−0.46	***	0.01	0.26	***	0.00	−0.58	***	0.01	0.16	***	0.01
Father's Education												
Primary	−0.08	**	0.04	0.02		0.02	−0.04		0.05	−0.04		0.04
Secondary	0.14	***	0.03	−0.10	***	0.02	0.24	***	0.05	−0.22	***	0.04
Higher Secondary	0.13	**	0.06	−0.08	**	0.04	0.31	***	0.09	−0.33	***	0.10
College or University	0.33	***	0.08	−0.17	***	0.05	0.56	***	0.10	−0.31	***	0.12
Father's Employment												
Self–employed	0.04		0.03	0.02		0.02	−0.03		0.05	−0.05		0.03
Regular wage earner	0.34	***	0.05	−0.24	***	0.03	0.36	***	0.07	−0.32	***	0.06
Mother's Education												
Primary	0.05		0.04	−0.05	**	0.03	0.07		0.06	−0.06		0.05
Secondary	0.30	***	0.05	−0.18	***	0.03	0.26	***	0.06	−0.18	***	0.06
Higher Secondary	0.26	*	0.15	−0.14		0.09	0.16		0.15	0.18		0.18
College or University	0.06		0.22	0.00		0.14	0.05		0.21	0.15		0.29
Caste												
Scheduled Tribe	−0.01		0.05	0.04		0.03	−0.15	**	0.08	0.74	***	0.05
Scheduled Caste	0.05		0.04	−0.01		0.02	−0.11	*	0.06	0.23	***	0.05
Other Backward Caste	−0.04		0.03	0.04	**	0.02	−0.18	***	0.05	0.21	***	0.04
Religion												
Muslim	−0.07	*	0.04	0.02		0.03	−0.33	***	0.07	−0.11	**	0.06
Christian	0.13		0.08	−0.10	**	0.05	0.24	**	0.11	−0.03		0.09
Other Religion	−0.05		0.07	0.06		0.04	−0.03		0.10	−0.09		0.09
Log likelihood						−16,134.08						−16,702.28
Number of observations						27,362						26,041

Table A2 (continued)

2004–05 (61st round)

	Male Urban						Female Urban					
	Education			Work			Education			Work		
	Marginal effect		S. E.	Marginal effect		S. E.	Marginal effect		S. E.	Marginal effect		S. E.
Age	−0.39	***	0.01	0.38	***	0.01	−0.45	***	0.01	0.23	***	0.01
Father's Education												
Primary	0.06		0.04	−0.07	*	0.04	0.13	**	0.05	−0.20	***	0.08
Secondary	0.20	***	0.04	−0.20	***	0.04	0.26	***	0.05	−0.43	***	0.08
Higher Secondary	0.43	***	0.06	−0.47	***	0.06	0.38	***	0.07	−0.53	***	0.13
College or University	0.58	***	0.06	−0.59	***	0.06	0.55	***	0.07	−0.59	***	0.12
Father's Employment												
Self–employed	0.06		0.04	0.00		0.04	0.00		0.04	−0.07		0.06
Regular wage earner	0.34	***	0.04	−0.42	***	0.04	0.11	**	0.05	−0.34	***	0.07
Mother's Education												
Primary	−0.05		0.04	0.07		0.04	0.02		0.05	−0.02		0.08
Secondary	0.06		0.04	−0.07	*	0.04	0.09	*	0.05	−0.07		0.08
Higher Secondary	0.10		0.07	−0.03		0.08	−0.02		0.08	−0.24		0.18
College or University	0.04		0.07	−0.02		0.08	0.12		0.08	0.06		0.15
Caste												
Scheduled Tribe	−0.01		0.08	−0.04		0.08	0.00		0.10	0.32	**	0.14
Scheduled Caste	0.10	**	0.05	−0.15	***	0.05	−0.12	**	0.05	−0.01		0.09
Other Backward Caste	−0.01		0.03	0.03		0.03	−0.14	***	0.04	0.19	***	0.07
Religion												
Muslim	−0.14	***	0.04	0.07	**	0.04	−0.32	***	0.05	−0.15	**	0.08
Christian	0.36	***	0.10	−0.39	***	0.10	−0.02		0.10	0.24		0.16
Other Religion	−0.04		0.07	0.00		0.07	0.22	***	0.08	−0.23		0.15
Log likelihood						−8,905.10						−8,739.41
Number of observations						14,630						14,190

	Male Rural						Female Rural					
	Education			Work			Education			Work		
	Marginal Effect		S. E.	Marginal Effect		S. E.	Marginal Effect		S. E.	Marginal Effect		S. E.
Age	−0.44	***	0.01	0.32	***	0.00	−0.55	***	0.01	0.20	***	0.01
Father's Education												
Primary	0.02		0.03	−0.01		0.02	−0.03		0.05	−0.03		0.04
Secondary	0.09	***	0.03	−0.06	***	0.02	0.05		0.04	−0.14	***	0.04
Higher Secondary	0.38	***	0.06	−0.24	***	0.04	0.32	***	0.07	−0.47	***	0.08
College or University	0.39	***	0.06	−0.25	***	0.05	0.39	***	0.07	−0.42	***	0.09
Father's Employment												
Self–employed	0.02		0.03	0.01		0.02	0.07		0.04	−0.07	**	0.04
Regular wage earner	0.39	***	0.04	−0.31	***	0.03	0.38	***	0.06	−0.32	***	0.05
Mother's Education												
Primary	0.01		0.04	−0.02		0.03	0.01		0.05	−0.18	***	0.05
Secondary	0.09	**	0.04	−0.07	**	0.03	0.20	***	0.05	−0.04		0.05
Higher Secondary	−0.16		0.10	0.11		0.08	−0.02		0.12	0.14		0.14
College or University	−0.01		0.13	−0.02		0.11	−0.08		0.14	0.31	*	0.16
Caste												
Scheduled Tribe	0.13	***	0.05	−0.05		0.03	0.25	***	0.07	0.48	***	0.05
Scheduled Caste	0.05		0.04	−0.01		0.03	0.00		0.05	0.08	*	0.05
Other Backward Caste	−0.03		0.03	0.05	**	0.02	−0.05		0.04	0.11	***	0.04
Religion												
Muslim	−0.01		0.04	0.03		0.03	−0.20	***	0.06	−0.18	***	0.06
Christian	0.22	***	0.07	−0.12	**	0.05	0.22	**	0.09	−0.11		0.09
Other Religion	−0.09		0.07	0.08		0.05	−0.06		0.09	−0.03		0.09
Log likelihood						−15,431.75						−17,090.10
Number of observations						27,037						25,529

Table A2 (continued)

	2009–10 (66th round)																							
	Male Urban						Female Urban						Male Rural						Female Rural					
	Education			Work			Education			Work			Education			Work			Education			Work		
	Marginal effect		S. E.	Marginal effect		S. E.	Marginal effect		S. E.	Marginal effect		S. E.	Marginal Effect		S. E.	Marginal Effect		S. E.	Marginal Effect		S. E.	Marginal Effect		S. E.
Age	−0.35	***	0.01	0.48	***	0.01	−0.41	***	0.01	0.32	***	0.01	−0.41	***	0.01	0.42	***	0.01	−0.49	***	0.01	0.26	***	0.01
Father's Education																								
Primary	0.02		0.04	−0.04		0.06	0.09	*	0.05	−0.57	***	0.11	0.00		0.03	−0.04		0.03	−0.01		0.04	−0.08		0.05
Secondary	0.20	***	0.03	−0.31	***	0.05	0.21	***	0.04	−0.58	***	0.09	0.18	***	0.03	−0.24	***	0.03	0.15	***	0.04	−0.32	***	0.05
Higher Secondary	0.33	***	0.05	−0.48	***	0.07	0.33	***	0.06	−0.94	***	0.15	0.37	***	0.05	−0.44	***	0.06	0.33	***	0.06	−0.42	***	0.11
College or University	0.43	***	0.05	−0.63	***	0.08	0.46	***	0.06	−0.75	***	0.14	0.39	***	0.06	−0.48	***	0.06	0.38	***	0.07	−0.53	***	0.12
Father's Employment																								
Self–employed	0.01		0.03	0.08	**	0.04	0.05		0.04	0.00		0.07	0.01		0.03	0.04		0.03	0.01		0.04	0.00		0.05
Regular wage earner	0.19	***	0.03	−0.33	***	0.05	0.09	**	0.04	−0.32	***	0.09	0.27	***	0.04	−0.32	***	0.04	0.20	***	0.05	−0.17	**	0.07
Mother's Education																								
Primary	0.04		0.04	−0.10	**	0.05	0.13	***	0.05	0.00		0.10	0.03		0.03	−0.02		0.03	0.09	**	0.04	−0.04		0.06
Secondary	0.14	***	0.03	−0.21	***	0.05	0.17	***	0.04	−0.18	*	0.10	0.16	***	0.03	−0.14	***	0.04	0.12	***	0.04	−0.04		0.07
Higher Secondary	0.15	***	0.06	−0.27	***	0.09	−0.01		0.06	−0.03		0.17	0.08		0.09	−0.01		0.10	0.02		0.09	−0.15		0.18
College or University	0.27	***	0.06	−0.32	***	0.10	0.08		0.07	0.19		0.17	0.17		0.13	−0.18		0.15	0.18		0.13	−0.23		0.25
Caste																								
Scheduled Tribe	−0.04		0.06	−0.01		0.09	0.03		0.08	0.08		0.16	−0.06		0.04	0.03		0.04	−0.15	***	0.06	0.53	***	0.07
Scheduled Caste	0.01		0.04	−0.03		0.05	−0.05		0.05	0.10		0.10	−0.05		0.03	0.07	**	0.04	−0.10	**	0.05	0.20	***	0.07
Other Backward Caste	−0.02		0.03	0.02		0.04	−0.12	***	0.04	0.06		0.08	0.01		0.03	0.00		0.03	−0.13	***	0.04	0.31	***	0.06
Religion																								
Muslim	−0.02		0.03	0.02		0.05	−0.31	***	0.04	−0.20	**	0.09	−0.09	***	0.04	0.10	***	0.04	−0.22	***	0.05	−0.14	**	0.07
Christian	0.14	*	0.08	−0.16		0.12	0.15		0.09	0.01		0.20	−0.05		0.07	0.07		0.07	0.11		0.09	0.22	**	0.11
Other Religion	0.04		0.06	−0.14		0.09	0.14	**	0.07	0.26	*	0.16	0.11	*	0.06	−0.12	*	0.07	0.03		0.08	−0.44	***	0.13
Log likelihood						−8,007.18						−7,662.84						−12,664.13						−13,317.88
Number of observations						14,153						13,289						22,531						20,969

Note: *, ** and *** stand for significance at 10%, 5% and 1% level, respectively.

References

Asadullah MN, Kambhampati U, Bóo FL (2009) Social divisions in school participation and attainment in India: 1983–2004. Inter-American Development Bank, Washington
Becker G (1964) Human capital: a theoretical and empirical analysis, with special reference to education. Columbia University Press, New York
Borooah VK, Iyer S (2005) Vidya, Veda, and Varna: the influence of religion and caste on education in rural India. J Dev Stud 41(8):1369–1404
Burns J, Godlonton S, Keswell M (2010) Social networks, employment and worker discouragement: evidence from South Africa. Labour Econ 17(2):336–344
Dostie B, Jayaraman R (2006) Determinants of school enrollments in Indian villages. Econ Dev Cult Chang 54(2):405–421
Dreze J, Kingdon GG (2001) School participation in rural India. Rev Dev Econ 5(1):1–24
Mitra A, Verick S (2013) Youth employment and unemployment: an Indian perspective. ILO Asia-Pacific Working Paper Series
Munshi K, Rosenzweig M (2006) Traditional institutions meet the modern world: caste, gender, and schooling choice in a globalizing economy. Am Econ Rev 96(4):1225–1252
Nandi TK (2010) Social networks and employment in India. Econ Bull 30(4):2769–2778
Nguyen AC, Taylor J (2003) Post-high school choices: new evidence from a multinomial logit model. J Popul Econ 16(2):287–306
Rice P (1999) The impact of local labour markets on investment in further education: evidence from England and Wales youth cohort studies. J Popul Econ 12:287–312
Rouse C (1994) What to do after high school: the two-year versus four-year college enrollment decision. In: Ehrenberg RG (ed) Choices and consequences: contemporary policy issues in education. ILR Press, Ithaca
World Bank (2011) Poverty and social exclusion in India. World Bank, Washington DC

Chapter 17
Adverse Effect of Biomass Fuel Use on Pregnancy Outcome in Rural India

Poulomi Roy, Jayanti Ghosh and Rahuldeb Sarkar

17.1 Introduction

"Clean air is a basic requirement of life," reads the opening statement of the WHO guideline on indoor air quality. It goes on to state that 1.6 million deaths annually across the globe and 3 % of the global disease burden can be attributed to indoor air pollution, most of which is caused by the use of biomass fuel (BMF) for cooking in developing countries. For obvious reasons, women of child-bearing age and their offspring, including the unborn, are exposed heavily to pollution caused by BMF as they dwell most of their time indoors.

The type of fuel used by a family reflects their economic status (e.g., rich use finer fuel such as electricity or biogas, and the poor use cruder BMF). There is a scope to investigate the health effects of the use of BMF. One of the major public health problems in India is low birth weight (LBW) in babies. In almost 30 % of India's institutional deliveries, babies have a weight below 2.5 kg, which is the criterion of LBW defined by WHO.

Review of literature reveals that one of the main reasons behind LBW is the exposure to cooking fuel pollution caused by BMF. Used by 2.4 billion people worldwide, BMF has been shown to be associated with LBW by Boy et al. (2002) and is a well-known health hazard. A meta-analysis by Pope et al. (2010) showed a strong

P. Roy (✉)
Department of Economics, Jadavpur University, Kolkata, India
e-mail: poulomi.roy@gmail.com

J. Ghosh · R. Sarkar
Sushmita Foundation, Kolkata, India
e-mail: jayantighosh@ymail.com

R. Sarkar
Medway Maritime Hospital, Gillingham, Kent, UK
e-mail: rahuldebsarkar@yahoo.com

S. Banerjee et al. (eds.), *Understanding Development,* India Studies in Business and Economics, DOI 10.1007/978-81-322-2455-6_17

association between BMF exposure and LBW. Various studies internationally have pointed to a relation between LBW and BMF used for cooking (Sram et al. 2005, Boy et al. 2002, Wang et al. 1997). Carbon monoxide (CO), in particular, is considered to have the most detrimental effect on intrauterine growth. Burning of BMF, such as wood, dung, fiber residual, etc., leads to the production of CO. When inhaled, it combines with hemoglobin to form CoHb, a stable compound that prevents easy passage of oxygen to fetus (Smith 1987). In developing countries where a large number of households still depend on BMF for cooking, a strong association has been seen. A meta-analysis by Pope et al. shows the connection between BMF exposure and poorer birth outcome. Studies from Pakistan (Siddiqui et al. 2008), Zimbabwe (Mishra et al. 2004), Guatemala (Boy et al. 2002), and India (Tielshch et al. 2009) have also reported about possible association between maternal exposure to BMF and adverse birth outcome. Again, in a Gujarat-based study, Mavalankar et al. (1991) showed that indoor cooking smoke exposure was significantly associated with stillbirths.

The Indian National Family Health Survey (NFHS-3), in 2005–2006, collected data on nearly 230,000 individuals across India on various aspects of maternal and child health along with other socioeconomic parameters. Out of these individuals, nearly 124,000 women were of reproductive age. According to the NFHS-3, 70% of the Indian households use BMF, including charcoal, wood, straw, shrubs, grass, animal dung, agricultural crop. A small number of families use chimneys to vent out the smoke outside the house.

While indoor air pollution due to use of BMF during cooking is an important explanatory variable for the occurrence of LBW, poor maternal health and malnutrition have been shown to be strong predictors of pregnancy outcome.

Thus, the objective of this chapter is to identify (i) the impact of maternal health, nutrition, and fuel use pattern on adverse pregnancy outcome in terms of LBW, and (ii) how this varies by economic status of the family, and what are the probable causes behind this.

The rest of the chapter is organized as follows. Section 17.2 discusses the data sources and methodology, Sect. 17.3 analyzes the results, and Sect. 17.4 provides concluding remarks.

17.2 Data Sources and Methodology

We used micro-level data from the NFHS-3 (2005–2006) coordinated by the International Institute of Population Sciences (IIPS) under the aegis of the Government of India. It is a large-scale multi-round survey carried out with a representative sample of households, which addresses issues such as fertility, mortality, family planning, parental care, HIV-related knowledge, important aspects of nutrition, health, and health-care initiatives with various indicators. The data set mainly confined to married women with a sample size of 124,328 from all over India. The study dealt with various demographic and health aspects of women between 15 and 49 years and was conducted in one of the 18 Indian languages, and produced a high response rate. The NFHS data are highly regarded and widely used for planning purpose in India.

Our study examines the association between women's exposure to BMF and its adverse pregnancy outcomes in terms of childbirth weight in rural India. Although the key dependent variable of the model is binary or dichotomous, we used a logistic regression model. Depending on the objective being addressed for the study, multiple logistic regression was performed to assess the effects of "exposure to biomass fuel" and "chimney use" on the risk of LBW with adjustment for different wealth strata. These models are used to reproduce a relationship between a discrete dependent variable that represents a choice or category, from a set of mutually exclusive choices or categories, and one or more independent variables. The independent variables are presumed to affect the choice or category or the choice maker, and represent priori beliefs about the causal or associative elements important in the choice or classification process. It is basically called the estimation of conditional probability of an event, given a set of explanatory variables. It is a better estimation process than an ordinary least square (OLS) method which is used for estimation of unknown parameters of a linear regression model (where data are modeled using linear function and estimate conditional probability, given explanatory variables). The logit models compared to the OLS method concede the nonlinear relationship between probability of occurrence and predictor variables.

We estimate logistic regression models predicting the probability of being underweight. Here, we first estimate the model predicting the probability of being underweight, while controlling the socioeconomic condition and a number of other individual and household characteristics—this is our baseline empirical regression model. Then, we run the baseline model for the poorer group and the wealthier group. The propensity score method is also applied to find out the impact of BMF on adverse pregnancy outcome.

17.2.1 Dependent Variable

Our dependent variable, LBW child is a dummy variable: 1 if underweight and 0 otherwise.

17.2.2 Independent Variables

The explanatory variables for our economic exercise are mother's age at birth squared, place of residence, regional dummy, mother's education, sanitary latrine facilities, nutritional level of mother, antenatal care (ANC) visits, sex of the child, mother's body mass index (BMI), type of cooking fuel, father's presence during ANC visits, and chimney use by the household. These are directly computed from raw data. The exact definitions of variables used in this analysis are provided in the appendix (Table 17.2).

17.3 Econometric Model

This section empirically investigates our baseline model. The logistic regression model that we estimated is of the following form:

$$\mathrm{Log}[Pi/(1-Pi)] = \beta_0 + \beta_1 X_{1i} + \ldots + \beta_m X_{mi} + U_i \ldots, \quad (17.1)$$

where Log $[Pi/(1-Pi)]$ is the logit of the direct response variable of ith individual, X is the individual predictor variable, β_0 is the constant term or intercept, $\beta_1 \ldots \beta_m$ denote a set of fixed effects associated with m predictor variable (Table 17.1). Pseudo R^2 is a measure of goodness of fit in a logistic model. The ratio suggests the level of improvement over the intercept model of the full model.

Table 17.1 Adverse impact of BMF on LBW by wealth groups

	Odd ratio by household group		
Low birth weight	All ($N=5610$)	Poor ($N=1483$)	Wealthier ($N=4127$)
Mother's age birth	0.9984***	0.9987*	0.9983***
Mother's age birth square	1.0000***	1.0000*	1.0000***
Region north	2.5741***	2.7997***	2.6354***
Region east	1.3800***	1.3039	1.6094***
Region west	2.2238***	2.2367***	2.3531***
Region south	1.2872***	1.5084*	1.2727**
Region central	1.7359***	1.7785**	1.9286***
Mother illiterate	1.2639***	1.0446	1.5302***
Primary educated	1.3108***	1.3569**	1.2319**
Distance of drinking	0.8989	0.8072	1.0310
Wealth index poor	1.1506*	–	–
Hindu dummy	1.2797***	1.3532*	1.2362**
SC dummy	1.0860	1.6531**	1.0406
Sanitary latrine	1.1023	0.9306	1.1751*
Anemia level severe	1.0573	1.1647	1.0192
Type of cooking fuel	1.2024**	0.7617	1.1586*
Mother working	0.8840**	0.8439	0.9067
ANC visit (three or more)	0.9650	0.9258	0.9753
Mother's BMI	0.9612***	0.9340***	0.9687***
Sex of the children	0.7956***	0.8037**	0.7955***
Pseudo R-square	0.0347	0.0257	0.0416
LR chi^2(20)	279.47(0.000)***	52.45(0.001)***	225.06(0.000)***

*** signicant at 1% level of significance, ** significant at 5% level of significance, * significant at 10% level of significance

We report odd ratio estimated through logistic regression. An odd ratio greater than 1 implies exposure associated with higher odds of outcome. Similarly, an odd ratio less than 1 indicates exposure associated with lower odds of outcome. Again, an odd ratio of 1 shows that exposure does not affect the odds of the outcome.

17.4 Data Analysis

Now, we present the result of estimates of our baseline model, which is a simple logistic regression catering the marginal impacts of women health characteristics, education, work status, basic amenity to household, residential area, region, and ethnicity and population factor on adverse pregnancy outcome measured by LBW dummy.

We observe that the risk of LBW is significantly higher in all other regions of India compared with the Northeast region. Again, illiterate mothers as well as those with primary level education (only until 5th standard) are at a higher risk of birthing an LBW child. Thus, literacy reduces the risk of adverse pregnancy outcome. Mother's work status affects the risk of delivering LBW babies only at 10 % level of significance for the overall data. However, the wealth status of the mothers, poor or wealthy, does not significantly affect the adverse pregnancy outcome. Distance from available drinking water measures how much a woman has to travel to fetch water. We used this variable as a proxy of energy expenditure indicator and we found that in all the three cases, it did not have any significant impact on the risk of having LBW child. Similarly, we observed that the presence of no sanitary latrine facility did not increase the risk of LBW in poorer households but the risk of adverse pregnancy outcome is higher among wealthier households. This may be due to the fact that there is not much variation in sanitary latrine facility among the poorer households whereas among the wealthier households there may still be households lacking a sanitary latrine facility. Social class dummies such as Hindu dummy and Scheduled Caste (SC) dummy were researched in our empirical analysis and we found that the risk of delivering LBW baby is significantly higher among the Hindu families across the entire wealth group. On the other hand, backward class dummy indicates that the risk of having LBW child is significantly higher only among the poorer families but no such significant higher risk exists among other wealth classifications. Anemia level of mother did not affect significantly the adverse pregnancy outcome, but it was found that the risk of having LBW babies decreased as mothers BMI increased. BMI is an indicator of mother's current health condition. Controlling the influence of the above-discussed variables, we observed that exposure to BMF use during cooking significantly increased the risk of delivery an LBW child among wealthier group. The risk of adverse pregnancy outcome was found to be not significantly higher among the poorer families.

One of the important differences between the wealthier and poorer rural households in India is that poor people do not have a proper house to stay and usually cook outside their house. Mostly they manage to eat only one meal a day and sometimes not even that. As a result, even though they use traditional BMF, we found it to have no significant impact on LBW. The comparison of these two economic groups reveals that only in relatively wealthy population, BMF use increases the risk of LBW.

17.5 Conclusions

Major factors that contribute to the risk of LBW include mother's poor diet, her current health status, cooking fuel and method used, under chimney or not. The analysis of two different wealth groups—poor and rich—reveals that BMF use affects the occurrence of LBW in the rich group and not the poor group. On the other hand, BMF use affects significantly the incidence of LBW.

One possible explanation of this is that poorer families cook in the open air, since they do not have a closed kitchen in their house. They also cook only once a day, which means they spend little time in kitchen. This probably precludes the adverse effects of BMF smoke. Cooking amount and duration is, however, more homogenous in wealthier families, which thus better reflect the adverse effects of BMF.

Our result suggests that the health of the child is affected by the type of fuel used in rural India. Availability of free good-quality fuel or at subsidized rate to the BMF user group will reduce the probability of delivering LBW babies in rural India.

Disparity in results of two economic classes calls for a detailed analysis of occurrence of LBW and other important variables. This would require primary survey in the rural households in different parts of India.

Appendix

Table 17.2 Variable explanation

ANC visits more than three times = 1	Continuous	More than three visits = 1
		Less than three visits = 0
Sex of the child (male = 1)	Male = 1	Male = 1
	Female = 2	Others = 0
Religious identity of respondent	1 = Hindu	1 = Hindu
	2 = Muslim	
	3 = Christian	
	4 = Sikh	
	5 = Buddhist	
	6 = Jain	
	7 = Jewish	
	8 = Parsi	
	9 = No religion	
	10 = Donyi polo	
	96 = Other	0 = Other
Caste identity	Sc = 1	Sc = 1
	St = 2	Other = 0
	Other = 3	
Wealth index	Poorest = 1	Poorer = 1
	Poorer = 2	Middle = 1
	Middle = 3	Richest = 1
	Richer = 4	Reference: richer
	Richest = 5	
Mother's BMI	Continuous variable	Continuous variable
Sanitary latrine facilities (No. = 1)	10 = FLUSH TOILET	Yes with flush toilet = 0 No (other) = 1
	11 = Flush—to piped sewer system	
	12 = Flush—to septic tank	
	13 = Flush—to pit latrine	
	14 = Flush—to somewhere else	
	15 = Flush—don't know where	
	20 = PIT TOILET LATRINE	
	21 = Pit latrine—ventilated improved pit (VIP)	
	22 = Pit latrine—with slab	
	23 = Pit latrine—without slab/open pit	
	30 = NO FACILITY	
	31 = No facility/uses bush/field	
	41 = Composting toilet	
	44 = Dry toilet	
	96 = OTHER	

Table 17.2 (continued)

Type of cooking fuel (coal, charcoal wood, etc. = 1)	1 = Electricity	Coal and other backward material = 1
	2 = LPG/natural gas	
	4 = Biogas	
	5 = Kerosene	
	6 = Coal, lignite	
	7 = Charcoal	
	8 = Wood	
	9 = Straw/shrubs/grass	
	10 = Agricultural crop	
	11 = Animal dung	
	96 = Other	
Distance of drinking water facility	Calculating as continuous variable, time taken to reach nearest drinking water facility	Up to 30 min = 1
		Other = 0
LBW child	Continuous variable weight taken at birth	Less than 2500 g = 1
		Other = 0

References

Boy E, Bruce N, Delgado H (2002) Birth weight and exposure to kitchen wood smoke during pregnancy in rural Guatemala. Environ Health Perspect 110(1):109–114

Mavalankar DV, Trivedi CR, Gray RH (1991) Levels and risk factors for perinatal mortality in Ahmedabad, India. Bull World Health Organ 69(4):435–442

Mishra V, Dai X, Smith KR, Mika L (2004) Maternal exposure to biomass smoke and reduced birth weight in Zimbabwe. Ann Epidemiol 14(10):740–747

Pope DP, Mishra V, Thompson L, Siddiqui AR, Rehfuess EA, Weber M, Bruce NG (2010) Risk of low birth weight and stillbirth associated with indoor air pollution from solid fuel use in developing countries. Epidemiol Rev 32(1):70–81

Siddiqui AR, Gold EB, Yang X, Lee K, Brown KH, Bhutta ZA (2008) Prenatal exposure to wood fuel smoke and low birth weight. Environ Health Perspect 116(4):543–549

Smith KR (1987) Biofuels, air pollution and health: a global Review, New York, Plenum Publishing Co.

Sram RJ, Binkova B, Dejmek J, Bobak M (2005) Ambient air pollution and pregnancy outcomes: a review of the literature. Environ Health Perspect 113:375–382

Tielsch JM, Katz J, Thulasiraj RD, Coles CL, Sheeladevi S, Yanik EL, Rahmathullah L (2009) Exposure to indoor biomass fuel and tobacco smoke and risk of adverse reproductive outcomes, mortality, respiratory morbidity and growth among newborn infants in south India. Int J Epidemiol 38:1351–1363

Wang X, Ding H, Ryan L, Xu X (1997) Association between air pollution and low birth weight: a community-based study. Environ Health Perspect 105:514–520

MIX
Papier aus verantwortungsvollen Quellen
Paper from responsible sources
FSC® C105338

If you have any concerns about our products,
you can contact us on
ProductSafety@springernature.com

In case Publisher is established outside the EU,
the EU authorized representative is:
Springer Nature Customer Service Center GmbH
Europaplatz 3, 69115 Heidelberg, Germany

Printed by Libri Plureos GmbH
in Hamburg, Germany